# YEATS

## THE MAN AND THE MASKS

### RICHARD ELLMANN

PENGUIN BOOKS

*To Erwin*

PENGUIN BOOKS

Published by the Penguin Group
Penguin Books Ltd, 27 Wrights Lane, London W8 5TZ, England
Penguin Books USA Inc., 375 Hudson Street, New York, New York 10014, USA
Penguin Books Australia Ltd, Ringwood, Victoria, Australia
Penguin Books Canada Ltd, 10 Alcorn Avenue, Toronto, Ontario, Canada M4V 3B2
Penguin Books (NZ) Ltd, 182–190 Wairau Road, Auckland 10, New Zealand

Penguin Books Ltd, Registered Offices: Harmondsworth, Middlesex, England

This edition first published by W. W. Norton & Co. Inc. 1979
Published in Penguin Books 1987
7 9 10 8 6

Printed in England by Clays Ltd, St Ives plc

# CONTENTS

# PREFACE

THIS book is based in part on published materials and in part on some 50,000 pages of unpublished manuscripts of W. B. Yeats which Mrs. Yeats, unbounded in her generosity, permitted me to examine in Dublin. The manuscripts include autobiographical notes, drafts of poems, letters, diaries, and other papers. I am indebted to the Rockefeller Foundation for a Post-War Fellowship in the Humanities which enabled me to spend thirteen months in Ireland and England.

I have had the privilege, too, of talking with many of Yeats's friends, acquaintances, and relations, and among these I must mention my special gratitude to Frank O'Connor for constant help, to Sean O'Faolain for many important suggestions, to Jack B. Yeats and Lily Yeats for their reminiscences, and to the following: Clifford Bax, Professor Thomas Bodkin, Professor C. M. Bowra, Austin Clarke, Sir Sydney Cockerell, C. P. Curran, Edmund Dulac and Mrs. Dulac (Helen Beauclerk), T. S. Eliot, Norman Haire, Edith Shackleton Heald, Joseph Hone, Madame Maud Gonne MacBride, Sir Eric MacLagan, H. M. Magee, W. K. Magee ('John Eglinton'), Ethel Mannin, John Masefield, Mrs. T. Sturge Moore, Professor Gilbert Murray, P. S. O'Hegarty, Lady Elizabeth Pelham, Dr. Edith Sitwell, Sir Osbert Sitwell, John Sparrow, Dr. James Starkey ('Seumas O'Sullivan'), James Stephens, L. A. G. Strong, Mrs. Iseult Stuart, Ninette de Valois, Allan Wade, Ernest Walsh, and the Duchess of Wellington (Dorothy Wellesley). Norman Holmes Pearson, then my commanding officer in the Office of Strategic Services in London, made it possible for me to go for the first time to Dublin in 1945. Peter Allt, Gerard Fay, Ellsworth Mason, and Roger Manvell have also put me under obligation. Diarmuid Russell has kindly permitted me to quote from some unpublished letters of his father.

I wish to thank Dean William C. DeVane of Yale University for his guidance and encouragement when I submitted this book, in another form, as a doctoral dissertation at Yale, where it received the John Addison Porter Prize in 1947; Professor H. O. White of Trinity College, Dublin, for his help on the early chapters which, also in another form, were prepared for a degree there; my brother, Erwin B. Ellmann, for his most generous and most valuable criticism of all the drafts of this book; Charles N. Feidelson, Jr., for aiding me with difficult problems of revision; Andrews Wanning, John V. Kelleher, and Mary Donahue, for reading the manuscript and preserving me from many inaccuracies; Dr. R. J. Hayes, Director of the National Library, and his able and cooperative staff, for facilitating my work in Ireland; and the United Arts Club, where I lived in Dublin, for hospitably admitting me to membership.

R. E.

*Cambridge, Massachusetts*
*April 2, 1948*

## PREFACE TO THE 1979 EDITION

*Yeats: The Man and the Masks* was completed eight years after the poet's death, a time when many of his friends were alive, and above all, his wife. George Yeats has since died, on 23 August 1968, and it seems an appropriate moment to think back on that distinguished woman. I should perhaps explain how we first met. The fortunes of the Second World War had propelled me to England, where I was serving in the Navy with a temporary assignment to the Office of Strategic Services. After V-E Day the neutral Irish government relaxed their restriction on visits by American servicemen, and the moment seemed propitious for me to write to Mrs Yeats, asking if she would see me about a study of her husband which I had begun three years previously. Fortunately I knew nothing of her well-earned reputation for never replying to letters. She answered yes. I then, in September 1945, went to the head of my section of the O.S.S. in London: this was Norman Holmes Pearson, once a fellow graduate student at Yale and later to be a professor there. I requested a week's leave, and he replied, 'Take two.'

At 46 Palmerston Road, Rathmines, the first sight of Mrs Yeats's study, which had been her husband's, was astonishing. There in the bookcases was his working library, often heavily annotated, and in cabinets and file cases were all his manuscripts, arranged with care by his widow. She was very good at turning up at once some early draft of a poem or play or prose work, or a letter Yeats had received or written. When complimented, she said she was just a hen picking up scraps. Among the scraps were all Yeats's letters to Lady Gregory, done up in innumerable small bundles according to year, with ribbons to hold them together. I asked her about Yeats's first meeting with Joyce, and she showed me an unpublished preface to *Ideas of Good and Evil* (1903) in which Yeats described that singular occasion. I evinced a perhaps unexpected interest in

ix

the magical order to which Yeats belonged, the Golden Dawn; she opened a chest and took out his implements and regalia and rituals. Agape at such profusion, I could only say that I would like to return after the War, and she replied, 'I hope you will.' So it came about that I spent the year 1946–7 in Dublin, working with these books and papers.

It was obviously impossible for me to knock every day at her door, but Mrs Yeats was equal to the problem of logistics. She produced an old suitcase and filled it with the manuscripts that I wanted to examine. At the beginning she was anxious about one of them, the unpublished first draft of Yeats's autobiography, and asked me to return it speedily. I felt that I must make a copy of it at once, but found Yeats's handwriting very difficult to decipher. There was nothing for it but to stay up all night, and towards dawn I discovered that during this vigil I had begun to sense his rhythm and to recognize his characteristic turns of phrase, so that I was able to allay her disquiet by returning the manuscript on time.

I can hardly express adequately my gratitude for Mrs Yeats's kindness, which extended not only to the loan of the manuscripts, but sometimes to their interpretation. For example, I once suggested to her that the 'Old Rocky Face' in Yeats's poem, 'The Gyres,' might be the moon, presiding there over the ages of human history. But she remembered that, at the time he composed the poem, her husband had been reading up on the Delphic oracle, and was excited by the image of the oracle speaking through a cleft in the rock. She felt sure that it was the oracle who was being described, and not the moon. No doubt she was right. Another day, I asked her with some embarrassment whether she thought that the outburst of blood, which in several poems Yeats associated with the end of each 28-phase lunar cycle, might not be based on the menstrual cycle. After all, Freud had for a time indulged his friend Fliess in the theory that the basic numbers of the universe were for the same reason 23 and 28. But on this matter Mrs Yeats was firm. 'W. B. knew very little about all that when we married,' she said, 'and in fact until well after that part of A Vision had been settled.' Some thirty years later, I can see that Yeats had in mind a blood-letting like sexual violation rather than the habitual process I had proposed.

I came to know Mrs Yeats well during this year, and to apprehend that, with all her self-effacement, she had played a great role with aplomb. Once I quoted to her a remark in a letter from Yeats's father, written while she was ill with influenza and in danger of death in 1918. J. B. Yeats said that if she died, Willie would fall to pieces. 'I haven't read the letter,' she said, 'and anyway, it wasn't true.' All she would admit was that it was useful for Yeats to have someone so much younger than he with whom he could converse. But he himself wrote, with greater accuracy, 'For how could I forget / The wisdom that you brought, the comfort that you gave?' She provided him with a tranquil house, she understood his poems, and she liked him as a man. She could also offer help. For example, it was she who suggested that the medium in his play, *The Words upon the Window-Pane*, should count the money paid her for the séance—just the realistic scrap that he needed.

She talked to me with candour about 'the marriage,' as—to her amusement—I pedantically found myself calling it, perhaps in unconscious response to her own objectivity about it. She had met Yeats in 1911, when she was eighteen, having been born on 17 October 1892. If he noticed her then, it was simply as 'a girl / Perched in some window of her mother's house.' By that time she had already spurned her mother's wish for her to lead an upper middle-class life of balls and parties, on the grounds that she wished to become an artist. Her artistic career did not get far, but she used her freedom to look into subjects her mother considered un-womanly, such as philosophy and occultism, just as earlier she had read the 'forbidden' novels of George Moore. The interest in occultism was one she shared with Yeats; he encouraged her to join the Golden Dawn in 1914, and at her initiation acted as her Hiereus or sponsor. She quickly passed through the early stages and was initiated into the Inner Order, which he himself had reached only a little time before. Then, with the outbreak of war, she had to shift her interests, and became first a hospital cook—which she enjoyed, and then a nurse, which she liked less.

Yeats was well acquainted with her mother and their friends, but some years passed before he took a stronger interest in her. It was known that one of his reasons for attending seances so diligently at this time had to do with matrimonial plans: he would ask the mediums first the secrets of life after death, and then the likelihood of his marrying his old sweetheart Maud Gonne during his present life. Since Maud Gonne was already married, and had been converted to Catholicism, this question was academic until 1916. Then the Easter Rebellion brought about her widowhood: her husband John MacBride, from whom she had long been separated, was one of those executed. To Yeats MacBride had appeared to be 'a drunken vainglorious lout,' and when he heard that MacBride had refused a blindfold, saying, 'I've been staring down rifle butts all my life,' he remarked that MacBride might better have said that he had been staring down pintpots all his life. His antipathy to MacBride at first made him see the rebellion as all wrong, and he and Maud Gonne had—according to her daughter Iseult—a furious argument on the subject. Then he brought himself to recognize the importance of the blood sacrifice that had been made, and even MacBride's part in it. The poem he wrote, 'Easter 1916,' did not give up his reasons for opposing the rebellion, or his dislike of MacBride, but he now attributed the rebels' 'bewilderment' to 'excess of love,' a malady with which he could thoroughly sympathize, and one appropriate to Easter in any year.

Yeats seems to have felt honourbound to propose marriage to Maud Gonne, though he knew well enough the difficulties that might ensue. As Iseult (Gonne) Stuart remarked to me, 'My mother is not a woman of much discernment, but she had enough to know better than to marry Yeats, to whom she wasn't suited.' It was then that Yeats considered for a time the possibility of marriage to Iseult, whom he had known since childhood, and whose severe beauty he greatly admired. (In the characterology of A Vision, she is one of the denizens of the sixteenth phrase, where beautiful women foregather.) Iseult was quite different from her mother. At that period of her life she was bored by Maud Gonne's politics, though she came to share them; many years later she would harbor a Nazi espionage agent at her house in Glendalough. As a young woman, her interests were literary and artistic. She and Yeats read some French writers such as Péguy together, and she took great interest in what he was composing. In 1916 he remarked to her, as she recalled to me, that he had been rereading Keats and Shelley, and now thought it strange that he had ever seen anything in them. The poem which he wrote to her, entitled 'To a Young Beauty', bids her attend not to these poets but to Landor and Donne. At the age of fifteen, she confided to her diary (as she told me) that she was in love with Yeats, and asked him to marry her, only to be rejected. Now he bethought himself, and said to her that he would take her away from her mother's atmosphere of extremist politics; though he was an old man, he would give her a life among agreeable people. 'You wouldn't say you loved me, would you?' she asked. Being uncertain, he would not. Iseult Stuart told me that she had thought to keep Yeats about as her mother had done, but he became very decisive. They met by arrangement at a Lyons Corner House in London, to discuss the matter. She tried to equivocate, but he said, 'Yes or no?' At this she could only say no. Years afterwards he said to her nostalgically, 'If only you and I had married,' and she caught him up with, 'Why, we wouldn't have stayed together a year.'

At this time Yeats began to think seriously about Georgie Hyde-Lees. She was more intelligent than Maud Gonne or Iseult, and more companionable, with a sense of humour that was lacking in them. If she had not the 'beauty to make a stranger's eye distraught', she was attractive, with bright, searching eyes and a high colour which gave her, as he described her to a friend, a barbaric beauty. She was interested in his subjects; she had the virtue of being in love with him. Yeats had felt for some years that he must marry. An incident in 1914, when a woman with whom he had been having an affair thought she was pregnant, had alarmed him, and though she proved to be mistaken, Lady Gregory advised that marriage would be a good idea. (Dorothy (Shakespear) Pound told Mrs Yeats that at one time Yeats and Lady Gregory had planned to marry, but Mrs Yeats never had the courage to ask him if this were true.) To Lady Gregory the best candidate was Iseult: she liked Iseult's unworldliness, and thought she would be easier to control because of it. But Dorothy Pound's mother, Yeats's friend Olivia Shakespear, preferred Georgie Hyde-Lees, in part because she saw a wildness or strangeness in her. Yeats was open with Miss Hyde-Lees about his previous attachments; he described himself as a Sinbad who after many misadventures had at last found port. Their intimacy blossomed. In August 1917 she gave up her job as a nurse. When he confided to Lady Gregory that he and Georgie (whom he would soon rechristen George) were to be married, he asked if he should bring her to Coole for a visit. Lady Gregory replied, 'I'd rather you didn't come till you were married and nothing could be done about it.'

Under such unpropitious auspices Yeats and Miss Hyde-Lees were married on 17 October 1917. But during the first days following the ceremony, Mrs Yeats saw, as she told me, that her husband was 'blue'. They were staying at the Ashdown Forest Hotel. She knew his situation and understood that he felt he might have done the wrong thing in marrying her rather than Iseult, whose resistance might have weakened in time. Mrs Yeats wondered whether to leave him. Casting about for some means of distraction, she thought of attempting automatic writing. Yeats was familiar with this procedure although it was disapproved of by the Golden Dawn. Her idea was to fake a sentence or two that would allay his anxieties over Iseult and herself, and after the session to own up to what she had done. Accordingly on 21 October, four days after their marriage, she encouraged a pencil to write a sentence which I remember as saying, approximately, 'What you have done is right for both the cat and the hare.' She was confident that he would decipher the cat as her watchful and timid self, and the hare as Iseult—a fleet runner. ('Two Songs of a Fool' offers a similar bestiary.) Yeats was at once captured, and relieved. His misgivings disappeared, and it did not occur to him that his wife might have divined his cause of anxiety without preternatural assistance.

Then a strange thing happened. Her own emotional involvement—her love for this extraordinary husband; and her fears for her marriage—must have made for unusual receptivity, as she told me later, for she suddenly felt her hand grasped and driven irresistibly. The pencil began to write sentences she had never intended or thought, which seemed to come as from another world. As images and ideas took pencilled form, Yeats went beyond his initial relief about his marriage. Here were more potent revelations: he had married into Delphi. To Maud Gonne and her daughter he appeared to be buried in what they always referred to as 'the prosaic marriage'. But nothing could have been less prosaic than what he was experiencing. His excitement entered into a long epithalamion he now wrote, 'The Gift of Harun Al-Rashid'. In it he continued the Arabian imagery initiated by his image of Sinbad, this time casting himself as the court poet Kusta Ben Luka.

Sultan Harun Al-Rashid is exhilarated because with spring he has as usual taken a new bride, and he urges the ageing and celibate Kusta Ben Luka to marry too. Kusta is anything but eager. For him, he says, if not for the sultan, love is not a matter of seasons, and he despairs of finding a lasting love. The sultan—who represents Yeats's more worldly and promiscuous aspect—maintains that an unlasting love is the better, something transitory and animal, because it is man's mockery of the changeless soul. Knowing Kusta's opposite mind, however, he has found for the poet a woman who shares the 'thirst for those old crabbed mysteries,'

> And yet herself can seem youth's very fountain,
> Being all brimmed with life . . .

If that be true, says Kusta, 'I would have found the best that life can give.' He marries her and soon after the marriage she sits bolt upright in bed and speaks of mysteries, not so much in her own person as in the voice of a Djinn.

He is at once delighted yet anxious, as Yeats must have been, for fear that she should suppose he loves her only because of 'that midnight voice'—like the automatic script—and all it reveals. No, he insists,

> The voice has drawn
> A quality of wisdom from her love's
> Particular quality. The signs and shapes;
>
> . . .
>
> All, all those gyres and cubes and midnight things
> Are but a new expression of her body
> Drunk with the bitter sweetness of her youth.

The preternatural drew its power from the natural and affirmed that.

Along with intellectual excitement and emotional involvement there came to Yeats a great serenity of spirit, which lasted until the Irish Civil War broke out five years later. He liked being husband, and he liked being father; they soon had a girl and then a boy. The volume he published in 1919, *The Wild Swans at Coole*, contained a number of poems about his new life and thought, and in 1921 another volume, *Michael Robartes and the Dancer*, formed an elaborate tribute to his wife. The title poem and the one that followed it, 'Solomon and the Witch,' celebrated with urbanity their matrimonial conflation of wisdom and love. Several of the poems following these dealt in one way or another with gleanings from the automatic script. The birth of Anne Yeats was heralded in 'A Poem for My Daughter'. The final poem, 'To Be Carved on a Stone at Thoor Ballylee', proudly associated husband and wife,

> I, the poet William Yeats,
> With old mill boards and sea-green slates,
> And smithy work from the Gort forge,
> Restored this tower for my wife George . . .

Changing her name had been rewarded with this magnificent line.

In the meantime he had an opportunity to demonstrate his freedom from his old life. Maud Gonne had rented her house at 73 Stephen's Green in Dublin to him in 1918. She herself had been forbidden by the British authorities to enter Ireland. But she smuggled herself in, disguised as a beggar woman, and presented herself at Yeats's door asking to be taken in. At this point George

Yeats was extremely ill with influenza. Yeats knew that Maud Gonne's presence in the house was bound to create turmoil, and he refused to admit her. She refused to leave, it being her own house, even when the doctor advised her that her presence might endanger his patient. Yeats became quite fierce until Maud Gonne gave in and decamped. He knew where his true loyalty lay.

He worked passionately to embody in systematic form, for which A *Vision* offered an appropriate title, the fragmentary revelations in the automatic script. He was in hot pursuit of a much more complete symbology than he had achieved in his earlier efforts to compound the poetic and mystical traditions. He asked his wife about the books she had read before their marriage—William James, Hegel's *Philosophy of History*, Croce—and read them himself to see if the automatic writing unconsciously reflected them. Happily it was independent of them:

> Truths without father came, truths that no book
> Of all the uncounted books that I have read,
> Nor thought out of her mind or mine begot,
> Self-born, high-born, and solitary truths,
> Those terrible implacable straight lines
> Drawn through the wandering vegetative dream . . .

The vocabulary of the script included unusual words for grand discourse, such as 'funnel' and 'spiral' (which he altered to gyre) and names of household pets (the Yeatses had a great many) that the communicating voices took over for themselves. He insisted that his wife keep up the automatic writing for two or three hours a day, usually from three to six in the afternoon. It was a great strain for her. She feared as well that it might become simply a new obsession for him, like the obsession with 'spooks' that he had had before his marriage. That one had alienated old friends from coming to his Monday evenings at Woburn Buildings. A reluctant Sybil, she therefore broke off the communication several times, and insisted that he return to writing verse. Yet the verse began to register its effect, too. Not only were there explicitly symbological poems like

'The Phases of the Moon,' but he would scarcely have conceived of 'The Second Coming' as the extinction of rationality, she felt, if it had not been for the automatic script. His daily behaviour was also affected: to place people in their appropriate phases of the moon, as the script required, entailed listening to what they said and watching the way they behaved, and for the purpose he took a much greater interest in the outside world. This interest proved surprisingly congenial to him.

For a time he accepted without qualification the messages that came through the automatic writing. The fact that his wife could answer during sleep by word of mouth, without the need of writing, made him try that method of communication as well, though much less frequently than the other. Some matters did not seem capable of resolution by either method. For example, as Mrs Yeats informed me, he was never sure how much control the daimon had of the self; and while he sometimes thought of the antiself as a spirit, at other times he did not.

That all this revelation must some day come to an end in a book was Yeats's idea from the start. The method of presentation worried him. Mrs Yeats wished him to present the material directly, without introduction, but Yeats's mind was too modulated and subtle for that. After all, he had spent most of his writing life couching in gracious terms conceptions that would otherwise have made his audience recoil. He therefore began within weeks of the start of the automatic script to concoct a transmission myth. This was the elaborate fable in which Giraldus Cambrensis, the historian of England, joined forces with Kusta Ben Luka. (Two characters from the early stories, Michael Robartes and Owen Aherne, were also incorporated.) To Giraldus he attributed—much to the amusement of better Latinists—the *Speculum Angelorum et Hominorum* (for *Hominum*), to Kusta the dance which choreographed the principal symbols of the automatic script. He got his friend Edmund Dulac to carve a woodcut portrait of Giraldus, obviously modelled on Yeats's face, and since this was completed by January 1918, the primary fable must have been constituted in the first two months of his marriage.

The first edition of A Vision did not appear until early 1926. Soon after, Yeats realized that much of it was too close to the original automatic writing, and that further elucidation was necessary. He decided to do a second edition of the book, and this time to tell about the automatic writing. Mrs Yeats was absolutely opposed to this, and they had then, as she told me, the first and only serious quarrel of their marriage. Yeats prevailed, but included his mythical variations as well as his realistic account. The second edition of 1937 made room for many second thoughts and also for many doubts. When Allan Wade asked him if he believed in A Vision, he said evasively—though accurately, 'Oh, I draw from it images for my poetry.' The book hovered between philosophy and fiction, bread and cake.

Yeats heard that Ezra Pound had commented, after the first edition of A Vision was published, that no one should be allowed to read the book before he was forty. The implication was that it would go well with senescence. As Yeats knew, the book contained exactly the sort of abstract schematizing that Pound disliked. In riposte he decided to dedicate the book to his friend, and wrote 'A Packet for Ezra Pound' for the purpose. Willynilly, Pound would be obliged to have his part in the book, for A Vision comprehended all possible opponents of itself within its scheme. Once Yeats had revised the book, he was free to do other work, though a surviving document called 'Seven Propositions' indicates that during his last decade he pushed his speculations about final matters even further. He also did a good deal of reading in philosophy with the hope of confirming and enlarging his theories. Sometimes he joked about mysticism, but as his wife pointed out, one can do that and still be serious about it. My own attitude toward automatic writing, and indeed toward spiritualist phenomena in general, seemed too sceptical to Mrs Yeats. 'Do you not believe in ghosts at all?' she asked me. 'Only in those inside me,' I replied. 'That's the trouble with you,' she said with unexpected severity.

I still know very little about ghosts. But I can see that the metaphysical urge in Yeats was inseparable from his greatness as a poet. Were it removed, there would be few poems left. He regarded as metaphysical certain experiences which others might regard as within merely human compass: moments when memory offers bitterness or sweetness like a taste, or when, for no mere reason, the being becomes radiant. There is a poem in Yeats's series, 'Vacillation', which describes such an experience,

> My fiftieth year had come and gone,
> I sat, a solitary man,
> In a crowded London shop,
> An open book and empty cup
> On the marble table-top.
>
> While on the shop and street I gazed
> My body of a sudden blazed;
> And twenty minutes more or less
> It seemed, so great my happiness,
> That I was blessed and could bless.

Mrs Yeats said that this had actually happened to him, and that, in part because it was his only such experience, he attached great importance to it. He seems however to have had a later one, a country cousin to the first, which he wrote about in 'Stream and Sun at Glendalough',

> What motion of the sun or stream
> Or eyelid shot the gleam
> That pierced my body through?
> What made me live like those that seem
> Self-born, born anew?

Besides these accesses of feeling, there were others (possibly less certain in provenance) in which it seemed that two worlds converged, offering totality of being, insight into the heart of things, foreknowledge of what was to come.

I learned from Mrs Yeats, in fragments of recollection, something of what Yeats was like. One day she spoke about his hands, for example. His palm was very large in relation to the hand's outer surface; the fingers were tapered to very thin, square edges, with

rounded nails. In Sean O'Sullivan's portrait of him at the Abbey
Theatre, Yeats is shown, inaccurately, with pointed nails on round
fingers. She told me how before their marriage he had been investi-
gated by the Inland Revenue, because his reported income was so
small. Until well after 1900 it was only a few hundred pounds a
year. George Russell was invoked as a character witness. The
officials ended up apologizing and explaining that they had not
supposed it possible that someone so much in the newspapers could
be making so little money. She talked of his late preference for blue
shirts, and of how people wrongly assumed that he wore them in
sympathy with the Irish fascist organization, the Blue Shirts, when
in fact blue went well with his white hair. It was true that he had met
with General Eoin O'Duffy, the Blue Shirt leader, but she noticed
that 'they spoke on different lines and neither listened to the other.'
In describing O'Duffy to other friends, Yeats always called him 'the
swashbuckler,' a label derisory enough to indicate the labeller's
unenthusiasm. For, notwithstanding such parleying, Yeats never
ceased to advocate 'the right of every man to see the world in his
own way,' as he wrote to John Quinn in 1905. He was always ready
to denounce authority when this right was impinged upon, and so
could never have accepted an authoritarian regime.

She told me of Yeats's sense of humour. Sometimes this took the
form of prankishness, as when he allowed his wife, on their first
visit together to Coole, to bring their cat along. Lady Gregory's
life was made up of prohibitions; when she was twenty-four she
had given up hunting because she enjoyed it too much. She had
an absolute rule against animals in the house. So Yeats had to wait
until their hostess was asleep to bring the cat in, and to take it out
early in the morning before she woke up. Mrs Yeats asked why he
had not forewarned her, and he replied, 'I wanted to see what she'd
say.' He liked to force his friend George Russell to play croquet with
him, and then spent all his time keeping Russell from getting his
ball beyond the first wicket. Russell's only recourse was to pay his
calls at 9:30 in the morning, a time when Yeats would not impose
recreation. A story of her husband that gave his wife less pleasure
was one he told with Tory irony to Frank O'Connor: it seemed that

Mrs Yeats, who was as far to the left in politics as he was to the right, disliked their next-door neighbours as fascist sympathizers. On a certain day she went out and discovered that one of her democratic hens was missing, and assumed it had been devoured by the neighbours' police dog. She wrote them a letter. A prompt reply came back, 'Dog killed.' She was still reeling from this message when the democratic hen reappeared. She wanted to write to the neighbours, but Yeats said, 'You won't be able to bring back the fascist dog.' On a milder note, Yeats always addressed her in letters as 'My dear Dobbs,' Dobbs being the name of a round man, and she being a bit round herself. But he never used this epithet in conversation.

Mrs Yeats found her husband to be very 'human'. The description he gives of himself in 'Coole Park, 1929',

> There one that ruffled in a manly pose
> For all his timid heart,

was true, as she assured me: he *was* shy. She once remarked to Frank O'Connor, on rescuing him as he came into a party of unfamiliar people, that she had seen him to be shy because he had put his hand through his hair with the same gesture as her husband in the same state. To tide him over such situations, she told me, Yeats evolved a patter. He had to, because, as he complained to her, people looked at him as if her were the zoo. Lady Gregory, he said to his wife, was very sensitive, but had no idea that he was sensitive too.

When his children were born he was perhaps too old to respond intimately to them, though there are accounts of his romping with them when they were very small. He was inclined to be partial to Anne over Michael; and once when he refused to take anyone but Anne on some errand, Michael gazed at his retreating back climbing the stairs and amid sobs asked his mother, 'Who is that man?' But Yeats's later letters indicate he did have pride and affection for them; he describes in one how Michael, 'tall and elegant,' had come in fresh from winning a mathematics prize, and in another how Anne, attired in a new dress, had shown it off to him. In 1937, during the Czechoslovakian takeover, Yeats explained the situation to Michael, then sixteen. When he had finished, the boy suddenly said, 'Well, that's not quite right,' and he proceeded to tell it correctly. Yeats was dumbfounded.

Because Yeats's poetry and life were pervaded by Maud Gonne, I paid a number of visits to that grand vestige of an ancient flame. Madame MacBride, as she was always called (in my ignorance I called her *Mrs* until her friend Ethel Mannin sternly reproved me), was then eighty-two, six feet tall, majestic in her skin and bones. She received me as a young man come to call, and I too regarded it as a courtly visit. I can see more clearly now that she had many mysteries. In the annals of Irish emancipation from British rule, she had a peculiar status. Her family and birthplace were English, yet she claimed Irishness for reasons which, though creditable, remain puzzling. Her passion for her adopted country was in many ways admirable, but it was adulterated by a fanatical quality which led her from the time of the Dreyfus case to antisemitism, and from the time of Hitler to pro-Nazi sympathy. Hitler was to carry out the attack on Britain for which she had always longed. To consecrate her work she would have to have been martyred, like Madame Roland, but she lived on, habited in black, not mourning the executed husband from whom she had been separated after two years of marriage, but an Ireland similarly partitioned. Longevity brought its grandeur. Yeats had conferred upon her an immortality which she had perhaps not earned. Gradually young men, like those who had once adored her for her beauty, came as I did to visit because they adored Yeats's images of her; and she died, rather unwillingly, into his poems, which she had never greatly liked. John Sparrow told me he owned a copy of one of Yeats's books, inscribed to her by the poet, in which the only pages that she had troubled to cut were the ones that contained poems written to her.

Maud Gonne said that all her letters from Yeats had been destroyed during the Irish 'troubles,' though some late ones, at least, lie unimpaired in a Dublin bank vault. She did not agree with

Yeats's version of their relationship, which I largely followed. He thought she had never decisively discouraged him, she thought she had never given him reason for hope. Probably she had forgotten the 'spiritual marriage' that, according to his first autobiographical draft, she had contracted with him. He said in verse,

> Others because you did not keep
> That deep-sworn vow have been friends of mine.

When she wrote to inform him of her marriage to John MacBride, Yeats felt that she had betrayed that vow. He overcame his initial shock and anguish, however. He was too good a poet, and too generous a man, not to understand that beauty has its privileges, including cruelty, and many of his poems, while making clear the injury suffered, are elaborate acts of forgiveness.

I had always assumed that Yeats remained an unrequited lover, an impression fostered in Maud Gonne's writings. But one day in Dublin, reading an occult journal kept by Yeats in 1908, I came across a passage written late in the year while he was staying with Maud Gonne at Colleville, her house in the Norman countryside. There was an obscure reference to her feeling that they could not continue. I asked Mrs Yeats what was meant, and she said, 'I wouldn't have volunteered the information, but since you have found it out for yourself, I can confirm that W. B. and Maud Gonne were lovers at that time.' Subsequently I heard the same thing from a woman whom Yeats loved late in life, Edith Shackleton Heald, to whom he had also confided it. I realized the meaning of the reference in 'A Man Young and Old', where he wrote in one section,

### His Memories

> We should be hidden from their eyes,
> Being but holy shows
> And bodies broken like a thorn
> Whereon the bleak north blows,
> To think of buried Hector
> And that none living knows.

> The women take so little stock
> In what I do or say
> They'd sooner leave their cosseting
> To hear a jackass bray;
> My arms are like the twisted thorn
> And yet there beauty lay;
>
> The first of all the tribe lay there
> And did such pleasure take—
> She who had brought great Hector down
> And put all Troy to wreck—
> That she cried into this ear,
> 'Strike me if I shriek.'

For Yeats, at least, this autumnal flowering of a springtime passion had an importance out of proportion to its brevity. It made him feel he had vindicated his earlier fleshless pursuit of her.

As I try to imagine Maud Gonne's relationship with Yeats from her point of view, I can now comprehend it somewhat better. At the time when she paid her momentous first visit to the Yeats household in 1889, she was already, unbeknownst to him, deeply in love with a Frenchman. A year later, in January 1890, she became the mother of a small boy (not girl) named Georgette. The father was Lucien Millevoye, a newspaper editor and a married man, whose political extremism was a point of affinity with her. Millevoye had ardently supported the political ambitions of General Boulanger, and Maud Gonne carried secret messages about Europe to promote the cause. But in 1889, Boulanger, his oven having cooled, fled from France. Maud Gonne turned to the Irish independence movement. Yeats, instantly enamoured of her, gathered her into his own activities and found some new ones that they could engage in together. Oblivious to Millevoye's existence, he felt that the spiritual marriage to which she had acceded might eventually become material too.

To Maud Gonne's grief, Georgette died, I think late in 1893. She questioned Yeats and his friend George Russell on what might happen to the soul of a dead child, and Russell pronounced that it was often reborn in the same family. Yeats noticed her emotion, and in his unpublished autobiography says he wanted to tell her that what Russell spoke of as a likelihood was only a speculation. It actuated her to descend with Millevoye to the dead child's vault in the hope of there re-conceiving the soul of the lost child in another body. A daughter, Iseult, was in fact evoked. The theatricality is less than the pathos. In many ways, as Yeats knew and said, Maud Gonne had a kind of hapless innocence in her experiences. He speaks in 'A Bronze Head' of murmuring at the thought of her, 'My child, my child!' As for her lover Millevoye, he treated her badly, but she did not break with him until he appeared one day in 1896 to see Iseult, in the company of a more recent mistress.

Iseult was born on 6 August 1894, and for a year or more Maud Gonne occupied herself with her daughter's care and stayed in France. During that time Yeats met Lionel Johnson's cousin, Olivia Shakespear. Mrs Shakespear was a solicitor's wife, unhappy in her marriage. She had already borne a daughter, Dorothy, who was later to marry Ezra Pound. In his unpublished autobiography Yeats always described this charming woman by the *Rob Roy* name of Diana Vernon. I used this pseudonym in this book. Mrs Yeats was sure that Dorothy Pound would not mind her mother's real name being used, but felt that with Ezra Pound in such trouble over his wartime activities, it would not be proper to bother her by asking. The affair with Mrs Shakespear, which was straightforward, was one for which Yeats always remained grateful. She had dis-burdened him, he wrote in the poem 'Friends', of 'youth's dreamy load'. Unfortunately, after a few months Maud Gonne wrote to say she had had a dream about him; Yeats's resultant agitation was patent to Mrs Shakespear, who thereupon broke off their affair. They resumed it later, more casually, and remained good friends for life.

Yeats did not really obtain his sexual freedom until Maud Gonne was married in 1903. Then he took up with a number of women, including the actress Florence Farr and a masseuse named Mabel Dickinson, about whom he had his pregnancy scare. His evident sexual interest caused a falling-out over a woman with his friend John Quinn, the New York lawyer and collector. Quinn accused him of making overtures to Quinn's mistress, Dorothy Coates, while Miss Coates was in Paris. Yeats denied it in Edwardian style: 'If it had been your wife, yes,' he said to Quinn, 'but your mistress—never!' Quinn, unmarried and unamused, did not speak to him again for several years.

In Yeats's later years, and especially after a long period of illnesses culminating in Malta fever, from 1927 to 1928, he felt keenly his regret over his celibate youth. He wrote the poems of sexual reminiscence in the volume, *The Winding Stair*. Then in 1934, feeling his powers diminished, he submitted to a Steinach operation by Norman Haire. The physcial results of this were less dramatic than the imaginative ones. For several years, until the illnesses which were to bring him to his grave developed, Yeats had a 'marvellous' renewal of sexual and poetic fervor, which he had always regarded as allied. I did not feel at liberty in this book to describe Yeats's late love affairs, but he had several towards the end of his life. Mrs Yeats knew how important they were to him, and, conscious of her role as poet's wife, she countenanced more than she discountenanced them. 'After your death,' she once said to him, 'people will write of your love affairs, but I shall say nothing, because I will remember how proud you were.'

She sometimes talked to me about another burden, besides Maud Gonne, which Yeats had brought with him to their marriage. This was his lifelong tension with his father. Yeats considered that his father's influence upon him was incalculable. It had begun in childhood, when J. B. Yeats, suddenly taking note that William could not read, taught him himself, often by physical coercion. The other children, Lily, Lollie, and Jack, were permitted to go their own ways, though J. B. Yeats always took over the young men who came to visit, and the daughters never had a chance to get married. He made Willie his special concern. He knew his son through and through, and could pierce his self-protective armour with a word. The pressure included much physical pushing around, at least until early youth. Jack Yeats, observing one scene of paternal belligerence in the bedroom he shared with his brother, cried out to William, 'Mind, not a word until he apologizes.' J. B. Yeats would rag his son into the night about his marks in high school, or about not going to Trinity College, or about wasting his talent in occult activities, or even about his decision in 1903 to change publishers and go to Fisher Unwin. Their quarrels only ceased when J. B. Yeats went to America in 1908 and remained there until his death in 1922. He and George Yeats, who met in New York in 1920, got along well, and he greatly admired the poems that emerged from his son's marriage. They accorded with his theory of the necessity of grounding art in experience.

J. B. Yeats always insisted that his son's stubbornness was due to his Pollexfen genes—his mother's side, as though such a quality had never been heard of among the Yeatses. Yet no one was ever more stubborn than himself, whether in his resolution to become an artist or in his determination to defuse William's inveterate metaphysical urge. In later life he took more relaxed pleasure in his son's achievement: 'Old Priam was not much in himself, but then Hector was his son,' he would say. What he did for his son was to make available for twentieth-century use ideas that had been prematurely discredited in the 'nineties. One was that poetry and art were forms of truth superior to all others, which J. B. Yeats improved by making clear that they were in no way separated from life. The other was that the individual should not, like Pater, value experience for its own sake, nor should he subordinate experience to moral or religious principle. Rather he should search for what J. B. Yeats called Unity of Being, in which all the qualities of the personality could chime together.

In these theories his son followed him, though with much additional complexity. J. B. Yeats had worried excessively that his son would put occult theory upon everything. He need not have concerned himself. The system which William evolved in A Vision was one that had a sort of anti-system built into it. Ostensibly deterministic, it had many elements of free will. While in favour of totality of being, it recognized that the saint's annihilation of selfhood had a place in the world too. It trembled throughout on the edge which separated a doctrinal account of personality and history from a myth with an uncertain epistemological status. As Mrs Yeats said to me, sometimes he believed it, sometimes he didn't. In one section of it, phase 17, Yeats described people like himself who were always outgrowing their own systems like bursting pods.

The history of Yeats's last years is a sad one, with illness challenging his constant desire to renew himself. Three years before his death, he told his wife that it was harder to live than to die. He revealed, closer to the end, 'I must be buried in Italy, because in Dublin there would be a procession, with Lennox Robinson as chief mourner.' She told me that it would have taken him a hundred years to complete his work. I surmise that he was roughening the edges of the two forces he had always seen at work in the world, the one regarding reality as temporary, provisional, tidal; the other regarding it as hive- or nest-like, tenacious, lasting. 'Let all things pass away,' says a world-conqueror in 'Vacillation', while in A Vision Yeats quotes with approval an impromptu song of Iseult Stuart, 'O Lord, let something remain.' These were related to the two forms of love he had contrasted in 'The Gift of Harun Al-Rashid,' the one mocking the permanence which the other sought. In May 1938 he wrote a quatrain for Edith Shackleton Heald in which he offered, as 'the explanation of it all,' that

From nowhere into nowhere nothing's run.

The same word resounds in two of his last plays: the old man in *Purgatory* says at the end, 'Twice a murderer and all for nothing,' and the last speech of *The Herne's Egg* includes the line, 'All that trouble and nothing to show for it . . .' Yet in another late work, the poem entitled 'The Gyres,' Yeats insisted that out of 'any rich dark nothing' the whole gazebo would be built up once again. He could conceive of nothing as empty and also as pregnant. I think he saw with increasing rawness the clash between the urge to have done with fine distinctions, subtle passions, and differentiated matter, and the urge to keep them at all costs. In his last play, *The Death of*

*Cuchulain*, the final chorus asks,

> Are those things that men adore and loathe
> Their sole reality?

Yeats had begun to evolve a theory beyond *A Vision*, of how the varying panoply of the material world is really the reflection of spirits and their changing relations to each other. This was perhaps one of the explorations he did not live to complete. With a bow to scepticism, and yet a last rebellion against it, he said in one of his final letters, 'Man can embody the truth but he cannot know it.'

Mrs Yeats held views sufficiently at odds with his own to protect him from complacency. Mostly she tried to make possible his last poems. She knew his agitated spirit, knew also that he could be absurd and difficult as well as witty and sympathetic. She knew as well how he could overstate and then have second thoughts, and had helped him save himself from many follies. She had made it possible for him to shape the symbology and ideology of his major poetry. One quality in her husband never ceased to astonish her, and she pointed it out to me as something I had not mentioned. This was his extraordinary sense of the way things would look to people later on. Very possibly he knew that she would be at the centre of his story. If she bore his impress, he also bore hers.

When I had completed this book, of which she did not disapprove, I wrote, after the passage of some years, a biography of Yeats's friend James Joyce. I asked Mrs Yeats if I might dedicate it to her, and she acquiesced. Should I say, 'To Mrs W. B. Yeats,' 'To Mrs George Yeats,' or 'To George Yeats'? I asked her. 'That's for you to decide,' she said. I settled on 'To George Yeats,' to make explicit what I hope I have represented here, her independence, her astuteness, her humour. Marriage to Yeats was as problem-ridden as it was magnificent. She lived through it with self-possession, with generosity, with something like nobility.

R. E.

*New College, Oxford*
*27 June 1978*

## CHAPTER I

# INTRODUCTION

*In after time they will speak much of me
And speak but fantasy.*

YEATS, ' The Gift of Harun Al-Rashid '

WILLIAM BUTLER YEATS, since his death just before the recent war, has come to be ranked by many critics as the dominant poet of our time. It is not easy to assign him a lower place. During a long lifetime, from 1865 to 1939, he was largely responsible for founding a literary movement and for bringing a national theatre into being ; he drew into creative activity Synge and Lady Gregory, strongly influenced a host of other writers, and evolved a new way of writing verse which still attracts young men. By his constant advance and change in subject-matter and style, by his devotion to his craft and his refusal to accept the placidity to which his years entitled him, he lived several lifetimes in one and made his development inseparable from that of modern verse and, to some extent, of modern man. Yet though all readers of poetry know some of his early poems at least, few have more than a hazy impression of what the poet was like or what impelled him to take the direction he did. ' The Poet of Shadows ' developed too quickly to allow his readers to catch up with him, and not a few refused to embark when he set sail from the Lake Isle of Innisfree for the less contagious pleasures of an austere Byzantium.

Writings about him have tended to be either critical or factually biographical, with no bridge between. The more that is written, the more elusive he has become, as critics, friends, and biographers build up a variety of unconnected pictures. We are given the nervous romantic sighing through the reeds of the 'eighties and 'nineties and the worldly realist plain-speaking in

the 'twenties ; we have the business man founding and directing
the Abbey Theatre in broad day, the wan young Celt haunting
the twilight, and the occultist performing nocturnal incantations ;
we can choose between the dignified Nobel Prize winner and
Senator of the Irish Free State and their successors, the libidinous
old man and the translator of the Upanishads. These portraits
are not easily reconcilable, and the tendency has been, instead
of reconciling, to prove certain of them inessential or to split up
the poet's life into dozens of unrelated episodes.

Yeats is partly to blame. He wrote a great deal about himself,
but the autobiographical muse enticed him only to betray him,
abandoning him to ultimate perplexity as to the meaning of his
experiences. He spent much of his life attempting to understand
the deep contradictions within his mind, and was perhaps most
alive to that which separated the man of action lost in reverie
from the man of reverie who could not quite find himself in
action. Unsure which qualities were purely Yeatsian, he posed
and attitudinized, then wondered whether pose and attitude were
not more real than what they covered over. Afraid of insincerity, he struggled unsuccessfully to fuse or to separate the
several characters by whom he felt himself to be peopled. And
sometimes he yielded to the temptation of adopting convenient
simplifications and pretending that they left nothing out.

Autobiography did not come easy to a man who had grown
to literary maturity with Villiers de l'Isle-Adam's epigram ringing
in his ears, 'As for living, our servants will do that for us '. He
struggled into it against the grain, because he hoped it would
liberate him from the doubts and preoccupations that make it
possible to guess the centuries in which he lived. But this sense
of an ulterior responsibility drove him to seek always for patterns
and pictures, and to hack and hew at his life until it reached the
parabolical meaningfulness he found necessary. He must speak
for his generation as well as for himself, and reveal the truth
about both.

Then, too, there was his tendency to construct myths. ' I
know nothing but the novels of Balzac and the aphorisms of

Patanjali. I once knew other things, but I am an old man with
a poor memory ', he says in one of his essays, and then catches
himself up : ' There must be some reason why I wanted to write
that lying sentence, for it has been in my head for weeks '. He
does not usually break his myth as quickly as he makes it. On
the basis of having once learned the Hebrew alphabet and a few
Hebrew words he would say, ' I have forgotten my Hebrew ',
with an air of solemnity ; and Clifford Bax recounts that on
meeting the poet late in life, he was surprised to have Yeats
remark, ' Oh yes, I remember you ; they brought you up to
my rooms in a mattress like Cleopatra,' the only foundation for
the story being that Bax had once visited Yeats with heavy
gloves on. Talking to Edmund Gosse and Gilbert Murray,
Yeats explained how he had lost faith in an acquaintance when
he happened to observe that the man was followed, as he paced
the room, by a ' small green elephant '. ' And then ', the poet
added, ' I knew he was a very *wicked* man.' Similarly he gave
extravagant praise to his friends ; one of Lady Gregory's re-
castings of Irish legends is ' the best book that has come out of
Ireland in my time ' ; his *Oxford Book of Modern Verse* is full
of curious favouritisms ; the love of his youth is Helen of Troy.
Because he was a myth-maker his autobiography was never pure.

Another difficulty was that he wrote about himself late in life.
Though he thought

A man may put pretence away
Who leans upon a stick,

he was confronted by the same problem that made Goethe call
his autobiography *Poetry and Truth, or Truth and Poetry*, ' not
that any facts were to be reported inaccurately or invented, but
that his mature imagination, in which those facts were pictured,
could not but veil them in an atmosphere of serenity, dignity,
and justice, utterly foreign to his original romantic experience '.
Maud Gonne, who lived through many of the same events as
Yeats, remarked that his *Autobiographies* gave little indication
of the intensity and enthusiasm which raged in his youth ; the

self-possessed old man had buried the extravagant boy.

A final cause of the mistiness of the standard picture of Yeats is that he was even more obsessed with magic, occultism, psychical research, and mysticism, the whole *tradition à rebours*, than he allowed to appear, partly because of solemn vows of secrecy, partly because he was sensitive to mockery and convinced that he must use in his public writings only the most traditional aspects of his own thought. For many years he deliberately suppressed or only half disclosed many of his principal preoccupations, so that the reader who wishes to understand fully what any single work means must pass through a kind of initiation in those of his ideas that never went beyond the manuscript stage.

For if he was reticent in public, Yeats was indiscreet in private. He confided almost everything to his manuscript books, diaries, and letters, and from them another picture can be elicited, which joins together the disparate fragments and episodes of his life, and reveals him in quite a different light, the embroidered coat removed.

But this picture is one which few residents of his home town would recognize, for in Dublin he is too often a subject for anecdotes which reduce him to a pompous, lifeless man, incapable of having written a good line or even of having existed. Yet within that awful moat and the portentous bulwarks that suggest the Gothic revival rather than Gothic, lived the human being of whom his friend Frank O'Connor remarked : ' Every time I leave the old man I feel like a thousand dollars '.

The following pages set out to represent as fully as possible the development of Yeats's mind. We shall ask how he became a symbolist poet and why he adopted an Irish subject-matter ; we shall try to determine what lay behind his interests in occultism and in nationalism, and how these interests affected his work. The notion is sometimes advanced nowadays that a poet's development can be traced in terms of the literary tradition alone ; but whether we would or not, we shall be driven to answer many questions which seem at first to be beyond the literary pale :

what was his family like? where was he reared and educated?
why did he form certain friendships and not others? what effect
did his long, frustrated love affair have upon him? how did his
marriage alter his work?

We shall keep in mind, of course, that a poet has what Thomas
Nashe called a ' double soul'. The relation of the man and the
poet is close but it is not simple. A poem, even when it begins
with an actual experience, distorts, heightens, simplifies, and
transmutes, so that we can say only with many qualifications that
a given experience inspired a particular verse. Sometimes, however, it will be possible to follow the development of a poem out
of an experience and watch the creative process at close quarters.
At other times our method will lead to more general observations
as to why at a given time Yeats adopted a certain kind of treatment and a certain subject-matter and style. In pursuit of
nuances of development that are often hard to delineate, we
shall have to move back and forth between life and work, and
occasionally to diverge from chronology when the poet's state
of mind seems more accessible to some other approach.

No one will want the resultant picture to be prettified; we
have ceased to regard our poets as creatures apart, and the poets
themselves do not wish to be treated as such. In a lecture which
Yeats himself gave he explicitly asked for candid biography. He
had been discussing Lionel Johnson and said, according to the
rough notes which have survived:

I am speaking of him very candidly; probably he would not
[wish] to be spoken of in this way, but I would wish to be spoken
of with just such candour when I am dead. I have no sympathy with
the mid-Victorian thought to which Tennyson gave his support, that
a poet's life concerns nobody but himself. A poet is by the very
nature of things a man who lives with entire sincerity, or rather, the
better his poetry the more sincere his life. His life is an experiment in
living and those that come after have a right to know it. Above all it
is necessary that the lyric poet's life should be known, that we should
understand that his poetry is no rootless flower but the speech of a man,
[that it is no little thing] to achieve anything in any art, to stand alone
perhaps for many years, to go a path no other man has gone, to accept

one's own thought when the thought of others has the authority of the world behind it . . . to give one's life as well as one's words which are so much nearer to one's soul to the criticism of the world.

As a man Yeats could sometimes be timid and petty, and such qualities were not without their effect upon his verse. He could also be a hero, and to follow him from beginning to end of his life is to conclude that he was one of the true heroes of literature, who fought past weakness and conventionality only with the utmost labour. His life was a continual combat, and he chose the hardest battles when he might have chosen easier ones. As he himself remarked : ' Why should we honour those that die upon the field of battle ? A man may show as reckless a courage in entering into the abyss of himself.' Such courage we shall see him displaying again and again.

## CHAPTER II

# FATHERS AND SONS

The individual man of entire sincerity has to wrestle with himself, unless
transported by rage or passion ; he has so much mind to make up, with
none to help him and no guide except his conscience ; and conscience, after
all, is but a feeble glimmer in a labyrinthine cavern of darkness.

J. B. YEATS, *Early Memories*

### I. FROM THE RECTORY TO THE STUDIO

THE history of the Yeats family shows over three generations a kind of dialectical progression. The Reverend
William Butler Yeats (1806–62) was a deeply orthodox
Rector of the Church of Ireland ; his eldest son, John Butler
Yeats (1839–1922), became a complete sceptic ; out of thesis and
antithesis the poet William Butler Yeats (1865–1939), eldest son
in the third generation, erected an eccentric faith somewhere
between his grandfather's orthodox belief and his father's un-
orthodox disbelief.

Of the Rector we have scant information. Though urged
by his friends, he never published his sermons, and left no literary
traces. He is said to have been a remarkable man, and we know
that he had distinguished friends like Isaac Butt, the brilliant but
erratic barrister who was Parnell's predecessor as head of the
Irish Parliamentary party. As a boy the Reverend Mr. Yeats
was educated by his father, himself Rector of Drumcliff in
County Sligo in the west of Ireland, and afterwards went to
Trinity College and took orders. He became Rector of the
prosperous parish of Tullylish in County Down, and was respected and loved for his piety and humanity by his parishioners.
They would tell how during a cholera epidemic he risked his life
to visit and comfort the dying.

From the few facts at our disposal about the Rector we can

pick out some that are relevant to the intellectual history of the
Yeats family. At this period Protestant divines, particularly the
more intellectual ones, were in revolt against the deistic tendencies
of the eighteenth century and were seeking to infuse greater
emotionalism into their religion. In the Church of Ireland, as
in the Presbyterian Church, the younger men had turned evangelical. They put much emphasis upon the individual communicant,
and continually encouraged him to examine the reality of his
belief and to make faith a constant force in his life. The Reverend
Mr. Yeats, though he based his creed on the reasoned principles
of Butler's *Analogy*, preached in the evangelical way ; very likely
his son was right, however, in characterizing his evangelicalism as
'well-mannered'. To his fervid orthodoxy in religion the Rector
joined a heterodox way of life. The story is told of him that,
when he arrived fresh from Trinity College to serve as curate,
he rode about the parish with such skill that his outraged superior
wrote him that he had hired a curate, 'and not a jockey'. In spite of
official remonstrance he refused to give up sports or even dancing,
and was so dandiacal that he ripped three pairs of riding breeches
in a day because he insisted upon wearing them so tight. Later
it was to be rumoured, with uncertain truth, that he gave great
drinking parties.

We may follow this unusual clergyman a little farther because
of his strong influence upon John, his eldest son. Though his
parish was in Ulster, the Reverend Mr. Yeats always retained
his love for Drumcliff, where he had been reared, and for Dublin,
where he had gone to the University; with a prejudice which is
still common in Ireland, he remained 'unreconstructed' and never
considered himself a northerner. He had, indeed, a thorough
detestation for Belfast in particular, and transmitted to his son
the belief that as capital of the industrialized north it was the
seat of all intellectual vice.

When the matter of his children's education arose, the Rector
had many theories. He was convinced that his own intellectual
development had been hampered rather than helped by his
father's having educated him personally. His wife persuaded

him, notwithstanding, to begin the instruction of his eldest son, but this pedagogical effort failed dismally. John Butler Yeats has described in his *Early Memories*, a delightful, incoherent fragment of autobiography, how the Rector in sudden irritation boxed his ears, then shook hands with him and hoped he was not offended.

This experiment having failed, John was sent at the age of nine to a school at Crosby, near Liverpool, kept by Miss Emma Davenport. Here evangelicalism was no longer well-mannered ; hell was a whip to keep the children in line. Miss Davenport made sure that her pupils were ' desperately afraid ' of it, and threatened them with the vengeance of the Old Testament God. They slept with Bibles under their pillows and had orders to read them as soon as they awoke in the morning. ' It was the age of faith ', says John Butler Yeats of this period in his life. ' I believed every word to be the word of God, of that mighty God of whom our school-mistress was always speaking.'

After the children had completed Miss Davenport's school, the Reverend Mr. Yeats arbitrarily decided that they must learn discipline by being flogged. Unable to teach by this method himself, he sent them to a school kept by a Scotsman whose floggings were famous. ' That Scotchman brushed the sun out of my sky ', J. B. Yeats wrote later. The training went farther than the Rector had intended, for the schoolmaster was a man of independent mind, less orthodox than Miss Davenport, and he emphasized the power of the birch and by implication minimized that of God, so that John seems to have lost that spiritual reinforcement for the dictates of conscience which the Rector had given him at home. ' When I left that school for good,' he said, ' I felt myself to be empty of morals. There was a void within. The outer control had gone and it was a long time before the inner control grew up to take its place.'

Though orthodox morality and discipline were beginning to crumble for want of support, the boy retained still his respect for religion. His apostasy did not occur until his arrival in 1857 at Trinity College, where scepticism had begun to take root.

While at Trinity John Butler Yeats read Butler's *Analogy*, which was the most important book in his father's life. The Rector spoke of it constantly, and professed to be one of the two men in the world who correctly understood it. He had managed to placate the Dean of Dromore, who had planned to reject him for ordination because of his love for sports and dancing, by his profound knowledge of the *Analogy*. It was, then, the pillar of the Rector's faith, and John, knowing this well, suddenly amazed himself ' by coming to the conclusion that revealed religion was myth and fable ' ; ' this book that made my father a proudly orthodox man had shattered all my orthodoxy '. If we can trust his memory, it was in 1857 that his uncle Henry Yeats ' suddenly in accents of alarm said to me " Johnny, you are an atheist " and rushed from the room afterwards to come back and apologise, and I cared nothing, for suddenly I had realised that his accusation was true '.

For this change of heart, John Butler Yeats tells us, he had as yet no reasons, only ' poetic and artistic intuitions '. But at Trinity he came under the influence of John Stuart Mill and learned to back his intuitions with logic. Mill threw open for him all the doors of controversy which a religious education had kept closed. Yeats did not, however, argue with his father, or tell him that he had been converted to disbelief, but went on following the Rector's ambition for him to become a barrister. But the familial mould was beginning to break, and, his new convictions inside him, he must have started about this time to consider renouncing the dignified life of the barrister. In 1862 his father's death freed him from filial responsibility, and his inheritance was large enough to promise some years of financial independence. The next year he married Susan Pollexfen of Sligo. In the Pollexfen family, so silent, so instinctive, so deep-feeling, he sought an opposite to his own affable, argumentative, opinionative mind.

Little record exists of the stages of emancipation during the key years from 1863 to 1867, though his outward career is clear enough. In 1865, the year his famous eldest son was born, we find John Butler Yeats making a surprising speech to the Law Students' Debating Society of Dublin, of which he was Auditor. The members of this society were accustomed to upholding either side of any question for the sake of practice in debate. Yeats made the iconoclastic suggestion that the debates be held not for the sake of mere rhetorical finish but in a genuine pursuit of truth. From this speech, unusual in a man about to become a barrister, we may deduce that the prospect of defending clients right or wrong had begun to pall on him. Though we have no evidence, he must have already thought of turning art, his avocation since childhood, into a profession. Such a career, by its nature solitary and individualistic, would divide him from the public life which his father had lived as a rector and which would have been forced upon him as a barrister.

The next year (1866) J. B. Yeats was called to the bar ; had he wished to, he could easily have made a success, for he had distinguished sponsors. But about June, in the year 1867, he abandoned the legal profession entirely, and at the age of twenty-eight went to London to study painting at Heatherley's art school. Thus the web was torn at last, and for the first time he felt, as he afterwards declared, ' that I had become consciously a man, a person, a being detached and an individual, whereas till then I had only been a cog-wheel in some mysterious machinery that might grind me to powder '.

Like most filial defections this one was far from complete. John Butler Yeats could reject his father's religion but not his temperament. Though he changed the terms of reference, he shouldered the burden of the evangelical preoccupation with the problem of individual belief. He recognized, too, that the Rector, for all his ministering to the multitude, had been in reality a solitary man. He had been orthodox not through convention but conviction, and had been totally innocent of hypocrisy. ' He would lie neither to please the sentimentalists nor the moralists. What talent I have for honest thinking ', declared his son, ' I learned from him.' ' My father theorized about things and explained things, and that delighted me, not because I had any mental conceit but because I delighted then as I still do in reasoning.' In some respects, too, his father had been an artist, touching up incidents as he retold them ; he ' incessantly arranged and rearranged life, so that he lived in fairyland '. But above all else, he had never sought refuge, as did the conforming minds around him, in orthodoxy for its own sake.

Yet while his father had taught him to think, and John Stuart Mill had provided him with the ideal of the reasonable man, John Butler Yeats could not consider ratiocination altogether a blessing, for it got in the way of his art. Theorizing with him made not for enthusiasm and confidence, but rather for continual self-qualification and self-correction, for ' a web of grey theory '. When he arrived in London Pre-Raphaelitism was at flood-tide. All the promising young men went to Rossetti's house, and allegorical and narrative pictures were the fashion. Leighton and Millais came to Heatherley's art school to lecture and spread the new gospel. Yeats, fearing that he had begun ten years too late, worked feverishly to acquire skill in the new style. ' I was much under the influence of Rossetti and delighted in all his exaggerations. It enchanted me . . . to find in any stray model either the red hair or the curled lips or the columnar throat of the Rossetti woman.' He copied Watts's technique in figure-painting, and worked so hard as to hurt his eyesight over copies of Millais' woodcuts. His predilection was for the most passionate subjects, as we discover from an unpublished letter of January 15, 1869, informing Edward Dowden of his progress :

I have made two very rough designs for pictures. One is from Browning's [In a] Gondola — the lover says these words after he is struck by the assassins — ' Care not for the cowards but for thy beauteous hair that my blood hurt it not ' — these words are not accurate I fear. The other subject is from Job. Job's wife says to him ' Dost thou now retain thine integrity — curse God & die.' I have made her a large strong woman with chin thrust out, her features writhed with scorn & passion. She is of course middle aged which makes her wild rage more terrible. Tears are slowly following each other down her cheeks. This last is the part I care for. I have not yet drawn Job—but I think I shall make him a man drawing strength rather from the contemplation & sentiments of the mind & imagination than from the natural fortitude of the heart — a face like Mill's for instance — a sweet pathetic face would contrast with the coarse merely animal strength of the wife's — & besides be truer as I think to the real character of Job.

His conceptual skill attracted some attention at once. Probably it was the picture of Job and his wife which was shown to Rossetti, who sent three messengers to bring Yeats round to see him. The artist, however, did not go. Browning came to congratulate him on the design for ' In a Gondola ', but Yeats was out and did not return the call. He attributed his decision in both cases to timidity, but perhaps we are justified in seeing also a reluctance to endanger his personality by the acceptance of any orthodoxy, even an artistic one. A trip which he took to Antwerp and Brussels in 1868 may have upset his confidence in his English contemporaries, and in letters of the following year he is beginning to criticize Rossetti's school for substituting sensuousness for passion.

Gradually his faith in allegorical and narrative pictures dwindled, and he turned to portrait-painting where his doubts about Pre-Raphaelite principles were less pertinent, and where his psychological skill could help him. But too exacting theories were almost always his undoing ; he could never be satisfied, was constantly searching for the individual style as if for the Philosopher's Stone, yet it eluded him always. As his son wrote : ' Instead of finishing a picture one square inch at a time, he kept all fluid, every detail dependent upon every other, and remained a poor man to the end of his life, because the more anxious he was to succeed, the more did his pictures sink through innumerable sittings into final confusion '. On some occasions, when exigencies of time prevented his retouching, he was surprisingly successful. Those of his portraits which hang in the National Gallery in Dublin show, if not an original style, great vigour and sensitivity.

His influence was not to be artistic but intellectual. Nobody who met him was unimpressed by the old man who had an opinion about everything and information and eloquence to support it, and was always witty and intelligent even when inaccurate. Edward Dowden, G. K. Chesterton, Van Wyck Brooks, and others have testified to his personal charm and influence. But his most important legacy was to his eldest son, who in his forty-fourth year wrote his father that he had realized ' with some surprise how fully my philosophy of life has been inherited from you in all but its details and applications '. The feeling was not merely transitory : the poet, replying to a correspondent's congratulations on his seventieth birthday, wrote : ' I thank you very much for your generous letter. Something of what you say I have tried to do, I mean I have tried to create standards, to do and say those things that accident made possible to me, the accident being I suppose in the main my father's studio.'

## II. A SCEPTIC'S RELIGION

To determine what John Butler Yeats's intellectual framework was, we have to proceed as warily as he did in forming it. Once he had torn down the pillars of his father's religion, his mind, he says, was ' a contented negation ', and in later life he declared that ' when a belief rests on nothing you cannot knock away its foundations '. The obvious salvation for an agnostic who came to manhood in the late 'fifties and early 'sixties of the last century was to follow Matthew Arnold into a carefully upholstered ethicalism. This was the course pursued by Edward Dowden, a contemporary of J. B. Yeats at Trinity, who also came from a religious family. Dowden had prepared himself to take orders, but like Yeats, and possibly under his influence, he gave up his father's faith. In a letter to a friend Dowden ironically suggested that they write a book together to be called, ' How I Lost My Faith ', which should not be merely negative ' but adumbrate also the growing up of a positive creed which in some measure replaces the old faith. Running under jurymasts (when the true masts have gone by the board), is very common now-a-days.' Dowden, running under jury-masts, moved towards an ethical point of view which had for goal the highest development of character, the complete man of Goethe. But this was not J. B. Yeats's path.

Instead he struck out for himself, and repudiated immediately Dowden's way of thinking as too heavy, too moral, too intellectual. He writes Dowden as early as August 4, 1867, that he has little respect for conscience because it makes for timidity, and proposes, therefore, to substitute self-expression for it. In a letter of December 31, 1869, he insists upon the value of *personality*, individualized and indifferent to law, creed, or convention, as opposed to the more abstract, law-abiding, and moral *character* :

My Dear Dowden — It seems to me that the intellect of man *as man*, and therefore of an artist, the most human of all, should obey no voice except that of emotion, but I would have a man know all emotions. Shame, anger, love, pity, contempt, admiration, hatred, and whatever other feelings there be, to have all these roused to their utmost strength, and to have *all* of them roused, (two things you observe), is the aim, as I take it, of the only right education. A doctrine or idea with Catholicity in it is food to all the feelings, it has been the outcome of some strong and widely developed nature, and every other nature is quickened by it. Art has to do with the sustaining and invigorating of the Personality. To be strong is to be happy. Art by expressing our feelings makes us strong and therefore happy. When I spoke of emotions as the first thing and last in education, I did not mean excitement. In the completely emotional man the least awakening of feeling is a harmony, in which every chord of every feeling vibrates. Excitement is the feature of an insufficiently emotional nature, the harsh discourse of the vibrating of but one or two chords. This is what Ellis also meant by ' violent and untiring emotion '.

With you intellect is the first thing and last in education. With us, with me at any rate, and with everybody who understands the doctrine, emotion is the first thing and last. In haste, yours ever —

J. B. Yeats

In reading such a passage as this we have to bear in mind that J. B. Yeats was an accomplished debater and controversialist, and consequently took pleasure in stating his views in a fashion extreme enough to rouse his opponent to a vigorous reply. Dowden's respect for the intellect seemed to him excessive and he therefore challenged it, but with another correspondent he would have indicated that intellect was not excluded from his own system, but played an important part in his conception of personality. The distaste which he shows for it here is, however, of some moment. We can trace that distaste back through much transformation to his father's opposition to the rationalistic deism of the eighteenth century and preference for evangelicalism. Indeed, there is a touch of the ' new evangel ' about all J. B. Yeats's thought, especially after he becomes an artist. Previously he had talked constantly of John Stuart Mill and Comte, the rationalists who had been the priests of his university years, but after going to London he spoke more often of Blake and Whitman whom he read under Pre-Raphaelite influence. The forces of individualism and revolt which had driven Mill, swaddled in the utilitarian philosophy from infancy, to go to poetry for release in his early twenties, exerted their pressure on Yeats, who responded to them more fully than Mill because unconstricted by a formal system or the necessity for formal writing. He was determined, therefore, to keep intellect in its place, and creations of the intellect alone, like law or institutional religion, were pernicious because they obstructed harmony. Emotion was better than intellect as personality was better than character. This habit of contraposing two abstractions and then judging between them was typical of his method. Trained in logic and law, he worked by dichotomies, dividing the world up into them and then subdividing further and further, every division a part of the texture of his mind though his informality sometimes leads one to think him incoherent. His first dichotomies were based on affections and aversions, chiefly learned from his father, and his more subtle reflections frequently proceed from an attempt to turn these from prejudices to principles. He took over from the Rector, as foundation stones for his thought, a deep affection for Sligo and a thorough-going aversion for Belfast. Sligo represented the emotions, while Belfast represented the intellect in its most repellent form. He himself was between the two; hence he had not been thoroughly accepted at Sligo : ' I was the social man where it was the individual man that counted '. The Pollexfens, being deep, instinctive people, would have nothing to do with his theorizing and wondered at his affability. But by marriage with one of them, he had joined his sociability to their spirit that was ' buried under mountains of silence ', and thereby, in his poet son, had ' given a tongue to the sea-cliffs '. These statements, hardly more than impressions, form the basis for much of his esthetic theory, such as the fine apothegm that ' a work of art is the social act of a solitary man '.

Seeking always for the inner man, and reacting always against the parson's and barrister's ways of life, John Butler Yeats constantly exalts the poet in further dichotomizing the universe : ' poetry is the Voice of the Solitary Spirit, prose the language of the sociable-minded ' ; poets ' have to live in the hermitage of their own minds ' ; ' poets always know too much to give entertainment to any system of opinion '. In evaluating poets he says that Shakespeare so far exceeded Milton because Milton had too many opinions. On similar grounds he praises Rossetti for having avoided the men of Belfast, for having ' immersed himself in art and poetry, letting opinion go by the wind '.

For J. B. Yeats Shakespeare's age is the ideal ; then ' everybody was happy '. Unhappiness came after the French Revolution, which brought realism along with it. Shakespeare would not have been interested in realism, for he had discovered that the important part of life was the necessity of being true ' to thine own self '. Unfortunately the modern Englishman is in no way akin to the Englishman of Shakespeare's time ; instead he is commercial, proud of his empire rather than of his country, full of cold and abstract internationalism. The Irishman has more of the old naturalness, and instead of abstract internationalism has patriotism, a sentiment infinitely more profound because emotional and not theoretical.

But we need not look to J. B. Yeats for unadulterated praise

of his own countrymen.  He preferred, continuing his dichotomies, the old Ireland to the new, because the old aristocracy
was composed of true gentlemen.  The boast that ' there was no
gentleman the equal of an Irish gentleman ' was not altogether
idle in the early nineteenth century.  Masters and servants lived
in amity because it was accepted then that to serve was honour-
able.  The Ireland of his youth had much in common with
Shakespeare's age : ' conversation, idleness, the soul of romance
and of laughter ', everything but freedom of thought.  But
though freedom of thought was achieved later, ' the passion for
material success, and the remorseless logic it inculcates ' had by
that time destroyed the flower garden.  The only vestige of the
old system is to be found in the peasants of the west, who ' can
enjoy themselves in solitude, poetized, if I may use such a word,
by their religion, by their folk lore, and by their national history,
and by living under a changeable sky which, from north to south
and from west to east, is a perpetual decoration like the scenery
in some vast theatre '.  It is hardly necessary to add that this
picture of the Irish aristocracy and peasantry is itself a good
deal ' poetized ', with little resemblance to the Irish scene as
described by Sean O'Faolain or Frank O'Connor.

Yet such a systematization as we have been making is not
altogether just.  William Butler Yeats tells in his *Autobiographies*
how he also codified what he considered to be his father's social
and political principles, and emerged with ' a law-made balance
among trades and occupations ' comparable to the Elizabethan
system of degree ; but when he confronted his father with it
J. B. Yeats immediately opposed it on the grounds of liberty
and free trade.  This looks like self-contradiction but is not.
The artist was a believer in aristocracy, but he was also a disciple
of John Stuart Mill.  In the one case he had a family prejudice,
in the other an acquired conviction.  As situations arose he drew
upon prejudice or conviction, reinterpreting everything accordingly.  His statements were never intended to be absolute nor
his generalizations to be true out of their context, and his *ad
hoc* opinions were not to be mistaken for a political platform.

Dowden described J. B. Yeats's classifications as like his painting,
' perpetually growing and dissolving '.  His literary talents found
their best expression in the informal letter where, as in conversation, he could speak to a person and not to a page.  The moving
world must not be detained by theory.  What he wrote to his son
about the poet was also true of himself :

A poet should feel quite free to say in the morning that he believes
in marriage and in the evening that he now no longer believes in it ;
in the morning that he believes in God and in the evening that he does
not believe in God, the important thing being not that he keep his
mental consistency but that he preserve the integrity of his soul.  And
by soul I wish to use a word which includes all that we mean by senses,
passions, appetites, his memory of the past, his anticipations, joyous
or fearful, of the future.  This soul, this inner and outer self, in forcing
its way that it may preserve its integrity, must be permitted to make
every kind of change and every kind of experiment and venture.  On
no account must it be fettered, nor will this lead to lawlessness for every
soul of man carries with itself its own principle of order ; at least so
I think and so does every man who believes in the race and its destiny.

The *argumentum ad hominem* of the last sentence is characteristic
of this experienced debater.  One further passage is worth quoting, for we come near him now :

There are two kinds of belief ; the poetical and the religious.
That of the poet comes when the man within has found some method
or manner of thinking or arrangement of fact (such as is only possible
in dreams) by which to express and embody an absolute freedom, such
that his whole inner and outer-self can expand in a full satisfaction.
In religious belief there is absent the consciousness of liberty.  Religion
is the denial of liberty.  An enforced peace is set up among the warring
feelings.  By the help of something quite external, as for instance the
fear of hell, some feelings are chained up and thrust into dungeons that
some other feelings may hold sway, and all the ethical systems yet
invented are a similar denial of liberty, that is why the true poet is
neither moral nor religious.

Is not this his secret ?  Unable to rest easy with his scepticism,
yet opposed to faith, he exalted poetry as a form of knowledge
which was independent of both.  To have convictions was the

unhappy lot of the religious man and systematizer, to lack them was the curse of the sceptic, but to have them or have them not as he chose and felt was the source of the poet's fuller liberty. What J. B. Yeats was working towards was a psychological theory of value. For him the aim of poet and artist is ' the birth, the growth, and expansion of everliving personalities ', and these personalities are their works of art. By personality he means ' a man brought into unity by a mood, not a static unity (that is character) but alive and glowing like a star, all in harmony with himself. Conscience at peace yet vigilant ; spiritual and sensual desires at one ; all of them in intense movement.' Elsewhere he defines personality as ' the whole man, the great totality, an army, not a guerilla force '. Whether or not a work of art is valuable depends on whether the artist's personality is fully engaged in it.

And yet, though these definitions justify the label of ' psychological theory of value ', we grow conscious on reading them over that the net does not quite hold him. For he writes of personality with too much enthusiasm ; this word, which plays so important a part in his mind, sometimes takes on a strange aura, as when he declares that a poet's ' personality is glowing like a burning star — all its elements fused into a unity ', or, even more startlingly :

*Personality is neither right or wrong* — for it is divine — it transcends intellect and morality, and while it keeps to being pure personality we love it for it is *one with our very selves, and with the all pervasive Divine* — at least this I believe and contend. . . . Poetry is divine because it is the voice of the personality — this poor captive caged behind the bars.

Having reduced all to psychological terms, he is quite capable, as in the above passage, of giving psychology a theological twist. Words like ' all pervasive Divine ' slip easily, as he uses them, between their literal and figurative senses, and he perpetually reserves the right to fluctuate.

It is not altogether fanciful to conceive of all his thought as an evocation of his poet son. John Butler Yeats had cleared away the underbrush and demonstrated the right of poetry to continue to exist because its way of presenting knowledge was not that of scientific or philosophical speculation, and was independent of the truth or falsehood of religion. He had pointed the way, too, to what the next poet must think about. *Belief, doubt, style, personality, emotion, intellect*: these are the nuclei about which his thoughts resolve, and they are the magic words in the life of his son. They are all dependent, though with important qualifications, upon the individual consciousness, and the only criterion regularly offered for the development of that consciousness is fullness. The difficult task remained of sifting and formalizing the puzzling implications of these theories, and this work was complicated for the son by psychological factors which for a long time made for struggle rather than collaboration with his father.

## CHAPTER III

# THE PRELUDE

*Et ego in Arcadia vixi*

WHEN W. B. Yeats's first section of autobiography, *Reveries over Childhood and Youth*, appeared in 1915, his oldest friend, George Russell (A. E.), complained that this was no autobiography at all, but a chronological arrangement of pictures. 'His memories of his childhood are the most vacant things man ever wrote, pure externalities, well written in a dead kind of way, but quite dull except for the odd flashes. The boy in the book might have become a grocer as well as a poet. Nobody could be astonished if this had been issued as a novel, part one, to find in part two the hero had for some reason given up thinking of literature and become a merchant.' The objection is partly justified; Yeats, for reasons which will become clear later on, found it impossible and not altogether desirable to lay bare the 'foul rag-and-bone shop of the heart'. But the theme that forces its way through the fragmentary pictures is his dependence upon his father and his constant efforts to escape from that dependence. Had Gosse not already taken the title, said a friend who saw the book in manuscript, Yeats might well have called it 'Father and Son'.

Tension between father and son is a common enough phenomenon, but during the second half of the nineteenth century it became particularly noticeable. Victorian morality and religion had little faith behind them; the father, their defender, had much to answer for, and filial revolt runs like a Wagnerian *leitmotiv* through the literature of the period. The father is killed, attacked, lost, or hunted. One thinks of the uneasy conscience which harried Matthew Arnold throughout his life because he was unable to feel that a father-god dominated the world with the

same efficiency as Thomas Arnold had fathered Rugby and himself, and one remembers how he wrote book after book to keep
God in his heaven. ' Who doesn't desire his father's death ? '
cries Ivan Karamazov, and from the Urals to Donegal the
theme recurs, in Turgenev, in Samuel Butler, in Gosse. It is
especially prominent in Ireland. George Moore, in his *Confessions of a Young Man*, blatantly proclaims his sense of liberation
and relief when his father died. Synge makes an attempted
parricide the theme of his *Playboy of the Western World* ; James
Joyce describes in *Ulysses* how Stephen Dedalus, disowning his
own parent, searches for another father, and one of Joyce's most
moving poems is that which ends with the cry, ' Father forsaken,
forgive your son '. Yeats, after first handling the subject in an
unpublished play written in 1884, returns to it in 1892 in a poem,
' The Death of Cuchulain ', turns the same story into a play in
1903, makes two translations of *Oedipus Rex*, the first in 1912,
the second in 1927, and writes another play involving parricide,
*Purgatory*, shortly before his death.

For Yeats the problem of revolt against a father whose intellectual domination was so complete was complicated because
J. B. Yeats had himself revolted against the standard values of
the nineteenth century. The son was thrown into the position
of the counter-revolutionary, like the *avant-garde* in Paris today
who, wishing to escape the older generation and finding that the
older generation was Dadaist, surrealist, and rebellious, is obliged
to attack from the point of view of the conservative. Such a
position is always difficult for the young. Because of its difficulty, Yeats had a great deal of trouble in finding a basis for
self-expression.

From the time that he was old enough to understand his
family situation, he saw a father who was affectionate but intellectually dominating, filling the house with his personality and
with his opinions, though he would have called the latter by some
less contentious name. J. B. Yeats had little sense of financial
responsibility, and the financial burden was often very trying for
the family. ' Perennially hopeful ', as he described himself, he

had no mind for business, and would paint or draw all his friends or any ' good head ' for nothing. He was always convinced that the solution of his problems was just around the corner ; either he was about to master the secret of style or to win an order for a portrait from a wealthy judge. The unfinished portraits that lay about the studio were tributes to his conscientiousness as an artist but not as a good provider.

In the household father and mother afforded a distinct contrast : the man talked all the time and the woman hardly at all. Susan Pollexfen Yeats, the mother, is difficult to describe. She had few opinions about anything, but liked best of all to exchange ghost and fairy stories with some fisherman's wife in the kitchen. Sensitive and deep-feeling but undemonstrative, she always considered her birthplace, the romantic country of Sligo, the most beautiful place in the world, and she passed on the feeling to her children. Places associated with J. B. Yeats, like London and Dublin, had never the same charm for them or for her. She would have been happier had she never left Sligo, for in Dublin and London she never felt at home ; nobody in the cities told ghost or fairy stories. Instead she was always ill at ease with her husband's artistic and literary friends, who used a vocabulary to which she was unaccustomed and looked upon life in a theoretical, selective way to which she was unconsciously hostile. Mrs. Yeats had no interest in art, it is said, and never pretended to any ; she was never known to have entered her husband's studio. In her quiet way she stood for a different kind of life, where an ignorant peasant had more worth than a knowledgeable artist, and she secured her husband's respect for this point of view as she drew her children's love for her native home. Though not deeply religious, she did not accept J. B. Yeats's scepticism ; without objection from him she had her way in taking the children to church, teaching them to say their prayers, and having them confirmed.

The family moved impecuniously between London, Dublin, and Sligo, with Sligo as the principal residence during the first ten years of Yeats's life. The boy must have been aware that his mother's family looked askance upon John Butler Yeats and his profession, suspecting an irresponsible eccentricity in his indifference to money, in his lack of success, and in his search for an intangible goal. The Pollexfens had their faiths from birth; they were Protestants, though not devout, and Unionists, while J. B. Yeats, in spite of his Anglo-Irish upbringing, was a sceptic and a nationalist. In that atmosphere he was out of place, and so was his eldest son, who resembled him.

In a revealing passage in *Reveries*, William Butler Yeats confessed that he remembered little of childhood but its pain. He had from the first an unhappy time of it. His personal appearance was out of the ordinary; he was delicate, with a complexion so dark that he looked foreign or seemed about to die of a liver ailment. People would often think he came from India. His eyesight was bad, and he was eventually to lose the sight of one eye. In an unpublished autobiographical novel he refers to himself in the title, ' The Speckled Bird ', and quotes the Bible, ' Mine inheritance is as the speckled bird, all the birds of heaven are against it '. ' I wonder ', he says, ' why the other birds are so angry.' His awkwardness and physical weakness kept him from being a favourite of the Pollexfens, who were good athletes. To his father's indignation he did not learn to ride well, nor had he the physical courage with which J. B. Yeats made up for his own lack of horsemanship. The Pollexfens began to think Yeats mentally as well as physically defective when they could not teach him how to read.

Seeking refuge from the Pollexfens' disapproval of his awkwardness and from a keen sense of his physical inadequacies, the boy found what he wanted in reverie and solitude; he wandered by himself about the Sligo caves and dreamed the days away. He wrote later of these years to Katharine Tynan :

The place that has really influenced my life the most is Sligo. There used to be two dogs there — one smooth-haired, one curly-haired — I used to follow them all day long. I knew all their occupations, when they hunted for rats and when they went to the rabbit warren. They taught me to dream, maybe. Since then I follow my thoughts as I then followed the two dogs — the smooth and the curly — wherever they lead me.

The sociable father, so adept in conversation, so confident of his opinions, so hopeful of the future, had a great influence over a boy so lacking in these qualities. John Butler Yeats realized that his son was very malleable and decided to shape him. He took over his education and, finding him at nine years of age unable to read and a difficult pupil, he boxed his ears, like his father before him. Then in subsequent lessons he adopted the more effective method of terrorizing him by references to his ' moral degradation ' and his ' likeness to disagreeable people '. The Puritan conscience inculcated into Yeats by the Pollexfens responded ; he was filled with remorse over his sins, and, in a state of terror, he learned to read. But his timidity was not helped, his mind retained its restlessness and may even have increased it as a result of his inner rebellion. Certainly he never learned how to study successfully.

To rescue his self-esteem the boy cast about him for defences ; the chief defence had to be against his father, and he found it in the religious feelings which his mother accepted. He was full of thoughts about God and intensely religious by nature ; then one day his father's refusal to go to church in Sligo set him wondering about belief. Though he copied J. B. Yeats that day by staying at home, Yeats began, as he was later to state in his *Autobiographies*, to seek evidence to confute his father's scepticism. Watching the ants running about, he would say to himself : ' What religion do the ants have ? ' He thought he had found the evidence he needed at the age of nine or ten when the farm-hands had no answer to his question as to how calves were born ; he decided that only God understood this mystery and that therefore He must exist. These are the first signs of the rebellion against his father's scepticism which was to carry him in such strange directions. He said his prayers often to the understanding God.

Most of his early childhood was spent in the company of his mother, his brother, and his two sisters at Sligo, for his father was usually in London and could only occasionally visit them and join the intellectual excitement of the city to the physical life of Sligo. At the age of nine, in 1874, Yeats went with the family to England, where for two years John Butler Yeats took over his son's education, again keeping him often in a state of terror for pedagogical purposes. Yeats longed with his mother for Sligo. His experiences with schooling were particularly distasteful ; after suffering his father's insistent pedagogy for two years, he went in his eleventh year (January 26, 1877) to the Godolphin School, Hammersmith, for his first formal instruction. His mind was too addicted to reverie to enable him to do well in his lessons, and at games he was entirely inadequate. For the first time he was with boys of his own age, and they laughed at his awkwardness and bullied him because he was weak, because he was a poor student, and because he was not English. In defiance he became more Irish and more unhappy, and sought for out-of-the-way knowledge beyond the reach of the classroom.

To save himself from the small tyrannies of his fellow-pupils Yeats cultivated the best athlete in the school, Harley Cyril Veasey, so that Veasey fought his battles for him and eventually taught him a little about defending himself. But their relationship was not altogether that of hero and hero-worshipper ; Yeats made Veasey respect his mind and his knowledge, affecting to be intellectually much more mature than the athlete. Where with his father he had already started in a tentative way to become religious as a defence, with Veasey he outwardly assumed his father's scepticism, and used arguments from Huxley and Darwin heard at home to embarrass his orthodox friend. He would conveniently forget for the nonce how devoutly he said his prayers every evening. Another way he had to impress Veasey was to pretend that he was a tireless runner, so that at the end of a race, when the older boy was out of breath, Yeats would pose as untired and untiring. His energies turned towards science ; among other things he studied insects, then interested Veasey in accompanying him on entomological field trips, and made his recondite knowledge as impressive as possible. His father was delighted to see his enthusiasm for science, and bought geography and chemistry primers for him to study. When, in 1880, the young scientific rationalist refused, in spite of his mother's wishes, to go to church, his father supported his right to decide for himself. But a cross-current of superstitious belief underlay Yeats's scepticism, and, as his racing prowess was partly pretended, so his interest in science was not whole-hearted but calculated, as he later admitted, to assure him of his own wisdom. He was still rushing in several directions at once, and his father, who wanted him to be a scientist, was anxious lest he be diverted.

Late in 1880 the family's stay in England came to an end when, under financial pressure, they moved to Howth, a few miles from Dublin. The English visit left Yeats with a very unfavourable impression and he was happy to return. His father's influence, he says, was now at its height. J. B. Yeats read out poetry to the boy, as he had done continually for six or seven years ; his method in the past had been to awaken his interest with narrative verse and prose, Macaulay's *Lays of Ancient Rome*, Scott's *Lay of the Last Minstrel* and *Ivanhoe*. Now he would read from Shakespeare, Shelley, Rossetti, or Blake, but only the most passionate parts of play or poem ; a proud speech of Coriolanus, the child playing with the distaff of the Fates in *Atalanta in Calydon*, ' Rose Aylmer ', the opening speeches of *Prometheus Unbound*, a speech from *Manfred*, were characteristic selections. He taught his son that the highest form of literature was dramatic poetry, because the form most crammed with life and passion, and least tainted by beliefs.

By the light of these interests and precepts, Yeats's character began to solidify. No shopkeeper's son, but an artist's, he kept apart from boys who had not the same interests or background. At the Erasmus Smith High School in Dublin, which he attended from his sixteenth to his eighteenth year (from October 1881 to December 1883), he concealed his timidity by arrogance. At a meeting of a school debating society he pronounced himself to be on the side of Plato and of Socrates. He wore a Byronic tie and took to imitating the heroic walk which, in 1879, he and his father had seen Irving use in *Hamlet*. Perhaps in a further attempt to imitate Irving he developed the curiously rhythmical manner of speaking which is so difficult for those who tell stories about him to reproduce.

As a student Yeats did not distinguish himself. Poor in classics and good in science, he affected to despise the one and exalt the other. John Eglinton, then at the High School too, has written that Yeats would talk about Huxley and Spencer and avow himself a complete evolutionist. The authorities found him difficult to handle. To their annoyance he introduced chess into the classroom and spread throughout the school the art of playing it secretly. On one occasion he narrowly escaped flogging when he spent the whole time of a lengthy Latin examination in translating a short poem of Catullus into English verse. The headmaster was sure he would never amount to anything.

Meanwhile Yeats's day-dreaming continued unabated, and contributed to the psychological ' weakness ', as he later described it, which hindered concentrated study. When he was fifteen the awakening of sex, which came upon him ' like the bursting of a shell ', made his dreams so attractive that he wanted to be alone with them, and slept in a cave or among the rhododendrons and rocks of Howth Castle. There he dramatized himself as sage, magician, or poet, posing as Manfred, Prince Athanase, and the hero of *Alastor*. He was fascinated above all by his childish image of the magician, an image which is common enough in boyhood but which took hold of him with peculiar force. The boy who was awkward and timid and weak let his enraptured imagination dwell on the magician who could master the whole world by his mind. He wondered afterwards whether he had not written poetry ' to find a cure for my own ailment, as constipated cats do when they eat valerian. I was humiliated, and wrote always of proud, confident men and women.' Lonely and powerless himself, he painted in his mind's eye a hero both solitary and omnipotent.

Much of his day would be spent in a thicket some distance

from where three roads met in the middle of the rocky pro-
montory of Howth. Here were formulated his first esthetic
theories. Poetry was to provide a refuge from the unrest of the
world of action. ' The thicket gave me my first thought of what
a long poem should be ; I thought of it as a region into which
one should wander from the cares of life. The characters were
to be no more real than the shadows that people the Howth
thicket. Their mission was to lessen the solitude without destroying its peace.' He began an epic on Sir Roland in Spenserian
stanzas and set forth his theories in rhyme. The poet should deal
calmly, harmoniously, and sadly with love, not passionately with
war and suffering. He should load his rhymes with metaphor
so that they would move slowly with their precious freight :

> When to its end o'er ripened July nears
> One lurid eve befel mine history —
> No rime empassioned of envenomed years
> Or the embattled earth — a song should be
> A painted and be [-] pictured argosy
> And as a crew to guide her wandering days
> Sad love and change yea those that sisters be
> For they upon each others eyes do gaze
> And they do whisper in each others ears always.

The unpublished verse of the first two or three years of
creative activity reveals heterogeneous efforts in several styles.
The favourite scene is, as one would expect, soliloquy. There
are several attempts at play-writing, usually with Spenserian
characters (knights, shepherds and shepherdesses, enchanters and
enchantresses) and scenery (gardens, islands) and often with
Shelleyan attitudes. The hero is ' proud and solitary ', contemptuous of the crowd, Promethean, sad.

### AN OLD AND SOLITARY ONE

> They say I am proud and solitary yes proud
> Because my love and hate abideth ever
> A changeless thing among the changing crowd
> Until the sleep, an high soul changeth never

This crowd that mock at me, their love and hate
Rove through the earth and find no lasting home
Two spectral things that beg at many a gate
O they are lighter than the windy foam

Full often have I loved in olden days
But those I loved their hot hearts changed ever
To coldness some and some to hate — Always
I am the same, an high soul changes never

And often when I loved I fain would hate
And when I hated find for love a home
But have not changed though waxing old of late
But they are lighter than the windy foam

And therefore I am proud and sad forever
Until the sleep, an high soul changes never
The crowd, there love and hate hath never home
O they are lighter than the windy foam.


SCENE 1

Cyprian [speaks]
I live in this lake girt tropic island
Never a human eye has seen it
Never a boat has touched its magic strand
Long centuries ago I pitied man
And passed o'er the world a spirit of unrest
And rebellion 'gainst the race of Sleeping Gods
But men were mad and thought that they were blest
Misery was but a toll for living
That Olympian Zeus was good and slept
That the devil of the robber nation
Was good though they for all ages wept
Yet thou[gh] I am cursed with immortality
I was molden with a human nature
With the centuries old age came on me
And weary of flying from the wrath of nations
I long since crossed the mountain
Seeking some peace from the world's throbbing
And sought out a little fountain

Plaining because no nymph had decked his valley
And then I spoke to it a word of might
And it heard the oreads language
It spread a lake of glittering light
Then once more I spoke that tongue
And there rose a stately island
Bright with the radiance of its flowers
And I stood upon its dry streme.

His heroes are beginning to revolt, like Shelley's.

About the time these lines were written, in the middle of his eighteenth year, Yeats left the High School. His father had assumed that his son would follow a tradition of three generations of the Yeats family and go to Trinity College, but the young man refused. As he later acknowledged, he concealed from his father the real reason for his refusal. It was not, as he probably declared, because Trinity College was old-fashioned and uncongenial to his awakening spirit, but because he was unable to meet the entrance requirements in classics and mathematics. Yet he would have liked to go to the University, and his lack of an orthodox education was to dog him like a guilty conscience throughout his life and to result in an excessive respect for learning.

Having rejected Trinity, Yeats proposed to earn his living as an artist, with poetry as an avocation. His father encouraged him and sent him to the Metropolitan School of Art in Dublin from May 1884 through July 1885 ; then, through the early months of 1886, to the Royal Hibernian Academy School. Though none of his paintings of this period have survived, some pale, dreamy pastels that he sketched later indicate that he never arrived at any proficiency. He was discontented, for the pictures he liked were romantic ones like Turner's ' Golden Bough ', but at the art schools the principles of the anti-romantic French impressionist painters were dominant. Yeats wanted to paint in the manner his father had abandoned, that of the Pre-Raphaelites, but found himself weakly imitating his father's portrait style. He ' was too timid ', he says, ' to break away '. Had he possessed the courage, he would have liked to create pictures like tapestries in his painting as he was doing in his poetry.

The French impressionists, with whom, on the grounds that they painted from the life, he connected his father, were further associated in his mind with the rationalism of Huxley and Mill; since his father spoke of rationalism with sympathy, and since revolt was stirring in his own bones, he looked round him for authority to contest the paternal position. At the Art School he found a confederate even more determined in his opposition to the world of Herbert Spencer and Zola. This was George Russell, who a few years later took the *nom de plume* of A. E. and was destined to be, despite many vicissitudes, a lifelong friend. Russell was an anomaly in the Art School. While he was supposed to paint the model with the other students, a supernatural force seemed to guide his brush and produce a being from some extra-terrestrial world. In Russell's eyes the dense, molecular universe faded out before one that was magnificently free and vast, peopled by spirits not dissimilar to the sages in Puvis de Chavannes's paintings but wrapped in Corot's mists. For Yeats Russell was a godsend. Here was positive repudiation of the principles of the French school and of his father. The eye was not earthbound, the dream of the magician was no longer an absurdity, powers existed beyond his father's ken. John Butler Yeats disliked the friendship with Russell, but the two boys, both rebels against the actual, and wildly hopeful, were intimate at once. Yeats began to hate science with ' a monkish hate ', associating it with the paternal scepticism and with his own earlier youth, on which he now turned with fury. When John Eglinton reminded him that he had once said at the High School that ' Only two people can write an essay now-a-days : Matthew Arnold and Herbert Spencer ', Yeats angrily denied that Spencer had ever interested him. He urged Russell, who saw visions daily, to question the spirits and obtain from them confirmation of their beliefs and arguments with which he could confound Caesar. They began to compete with each other in writing long poetic dramas about magicians who could discourse like Shelley and proclaim their contempt of modern civilization from Asian thrones.

They did not have much poetic theory beyond the necessity of writing about and in favour of dreams. The manuscripts of these years may be searched in vain for a clear-cut use of symbolism ; the poet is still wrapped up in dreams for protection, and only dimly grasps that they may one day serve him as offensive weapons as well. Occasionally he seems half-way to allegory, but he does not quite arrive. In a group of miscellaneous poems is an interesting example of deliberate obscurity which may be given here because it shows the young poet laughing at himself and reminds us that he had an excellent sense of humour. It is contained in a letter written to a girl of his acquaintance :

My DEAR MARY CRONAN,

I send you the verses you asked for I have very few poems under a great many hundred lines but of those that I have this is the shortest and most intelligible its subject was suggested by my last two visits to Kilrock — I am afraid you will not much care for it — not being used to my peculiaritys which will never be done justice to until they have become classics and are set for examinations.

Yours truly,

W. B. YEATS.

PS. As you will see my great aim is directness and extreme simplicity.

A flower has blossomed, the world heart core
The petal and leves were a moon white flame
U gathered the flower, the colour lore
The aboundant measure of youth and fame
Many men gather and few may use
The secret oil and the secret cruse.

It is quite likely that his great aim was ' directness and extreme simplicity', virtues which his father would have exalted, even though the poet is not yet very successful. But he is steadily improving at his trade, and attempting ever larger projects. In the prefatory poem to his play, *Vivien and Time*, dated January 8, 1884, five months before his nineteenth birthday, the syntax is

sometimes tortured and the sense has little to recommend it, but
the poem is smoother than anything he had done before :

> I've built a dreaming palace
>   With stones from out the old
> And singing days, within their graves
>   Now lying calm and cold.
>
> Of the dreamland marble
>   Are all the silent walls
> That grimly stand, a phantom band
>   About the Phantom halls.
>
> There among the pillars
>   Arc many statues fair
> Made of the dreamland marble
>   Cut by the dreamers care.
>
> And there I see a statue
>   Among the maids of old
> On either hand, a goodly band
>   So calmly wise and cold.

In this play he used his magician more dramatically.   Reluctantly,
but with a sense of moral necessity, he surrendered his heroine
to the oncoming spectre of Time :

### ACT II, SCENE 2

*Room in the castle as in Scenes 2 and 3 of Act I.   Time : night, a pale*
*taper burning before the Magic Mirror.   Queen alone.*

> *Queen.*   The lily wristed asphodel has slept
>   These summers three, and I have quaffed full deep
>   The glorious cup of magic, till in drinking
>   That dred forbidden wine that once I dreamed
>   And read of only my soul gros
>   The image of the mighty viewless ones
>   No tis changed, sweet metamorphosis
>   To one great throbbing string that throbbing calls
>   Only one wild word, one wild word
>   Power, power outspeeding envy self
>   The only drink for my unceasing thirst

O word as the song of the sea to streams
Art thou to me, in thee I'd lose myself
Outgrowing human sense and human thought
As I have pity for the fleeting race
Of men who bend to every sudden blast
Of joy or grief or scorn and as they bend
Say it is human thus to bend, well then
So much less human I who shall not bend
Until upon the steeps the fountains rest
And 'fore the sun the flower lips are closed.

[*She starts and trembles.*

Some great spirit passes in the desert
Turning it enters by the city gate
I felt its influence through all my veins.
Tis swifter far than swiftest dream
Now t'as passed the sentries, t'is at the door
It is here.

The ambivalent attitude towards the lovely but overweening queen indicates that the poet now views the pursuit of power with more circumspection. His father liked the play and showed it to Dowden as proof that the young man was finding himself ; and a letter makes clear that *Vivien and Time* was rehearsed and possibly presented by Willie and a group of his friends at the home of a Judge Wright on Howth. The girl who played Vivien, Laura Armstrong, appears to have been the boy's first love.

During 1884 Yeats wrote more easily than ever before or afterwards, and gave himself up with enthusiasm to the drama. The next play, *Love and Death*, which is dated April 1884, was based upon a drawing done by John Butler Yeats in his Pre-Raphaelite days, and is the worst-written and most ambitious of the group. A god and a mortal are twin brothers ; the secondary plot which deals with the mortal is ill-conceived, but in the primary plot the daughter of a king falls in love with the god and, to make herself queen and thereby worthy of him, kills her father. The god at last appears, but, since no mortal can behold his glory and live, the queen is destroyed by her own love. At the end of the play everyone on the stage is dead : a mortality rate comparable to that in Thomas Kyd's works. Yeats is groping here towards his later use of the theme of father against child ; in the twin brothers who are mortal and immortal counterparts of one another, and in the mixture of ideal love and carnal murder in the queen's character, he shadows forth his later theory of the divided or double self.

From now on his development was swift. He applied himself conscientiously during 1884 to taming his unruly metrics. The poetic drama *Mosada*, the story of a Moorish enchantress burned at the stake by order of her unsuspecting boyhood sweetheart, shows Yeats still setting his scene in the most exotic clime, but also exposing the magician, not as in *Vivien and Time* to the ravages of old age, but to the inquisitors of the Catholic Church. This opposition is one that he was to employ continually for the next ten years to represent what he called the war of spiritual and natural order, all organized Churches typifying to his mind the latter. But these adumbrations of future themes are still primitive and half formed. His poetic imagination groups and relates and does not yet transmute ; dramatic episodes fit for a novel of Mrs. Radcliffe are hurled together to keep the passions as intense as possible. Thus we have the magic spell, the betrayal by the trusted friend, the sentence of death meted out by the unsuspecting inquisitor, the poisoning, the death scene and belated discovery of the lovers' identities. At the end the hero, overcome with grief at his beloved's death, is too proud and solitary to disclose to his attendants how thoroughly he is moved.

Yeats reached the climax of his youthful verse with his fourth play of 1884, *The Island of Statues*, which he finished in August of that year. He succeeded here in writing a picture play with Spenserian shepherds which, as the sub-title, *An Arcadian Fairy Tale*, suggests, was completely removed from the world. A shepherd and shepherdess succeed, after numerous *contretemps*, in overcoming the Circe of an enchanted isle, and in finding the flower which will restore to life the men who had been turned into statues. Once reanimated, the statues are given their choice as to whether to live on in Arcady or to return to the world.

They choose to remain Arcadians. In an epilogue the poet praises and defends their choice, exalting literature above life and song above science :

### AN EPILOGUE TO *THE ISLAND OF STATUES* AND *THE SEEKER*

*Spoken by a Satyr, carrying a sea-shell*

The woods of Arcady are dead,
And over is their antique joy ;
Of old the world on dreaming fed ;
Grey Truth is now her painted toy ;
But O, sick children of the world,
Of all the many changing things
In dreary dancing past us whirled,
To the old cracked tune that Chronos sings,
Words alone are certain good.
Where are now the warrior kings
Word be-mockers ? — By the rood,
Where are now the old kings hoary ?
They were of no wordy mood ;
An idle word is now their glory,
By the stammering schoolboy said,
In the verse of Attic story
Chronicling chimaeras fled.
The very world itself may be
Only a sudden flaming word,
'Mid clanging space a moment heard
In the universe's reverie.
Then nowise worship dusty deeds,
Nor seek — for this is also sooth —
To hunger fiercely after truth,
Lest all thy toiling only breeds
New dreams, new dreams ; there is no truth
Saving in thine own heart. Seek, then,
No learning from the starry men,
Who follow with the optic glass
The whirling ways of stars that pass —
Seek then, for this is also sooth,
No word of theirs — the cold star-bane
Has torn and rent their hearts in twain,
And dead is all their human truth.

Go gather by the humming sea
Some twisted, echo-harbouring shell,
And to its lips thy story tell,
And they thy comforters will be,
Rewording in melodious guile
Thy fretful words a little while,
Till they shall singing fade in ruth ;
For ruth and joy have brotherhood,
And words alone are certain good.
Sing then, for this is also sooth.
I must be gone — there is a grave
Where daffodil and lily wave,
And downy bees have ambuscade,
And birdly iteration is
Through all the well-beloved glade.
Farewell ; I must be gone I wis,
That I may soothe that hapless fawn
(Who's buried in the sleepy ground),
With mirthful songs till rise the dawn.
His shouting days with mirth were crowned,
And still I dream he treads the lawn,
Walking ghostly 'mong the dew,
Pierc'd by my glad singing through,
My songs of old earth's dreamy youth.
But ah ! she dreams not now — dream thou !
For fair are poppies on the brow :
Dream, dream, for this is also sooth.

Read with care, the poem reveals a curious irresolution. It sets up two forms of truth, one 'grey truth' which comes from scientific or other worldly knowledge, and the other the truth which is in 'thine own heart'; so far the distinction is clear and the preference is definitely accorded to truth in the heart. But we are also told not to hunger after grey truth lest all our toil only breed 'new dreams', while at the same time we are encouraged to dream. This implies that there are also two kinds of dreams, and that the second has more validity. By now the argument becomes puzzling, and what follows is even more so. The poem half suggests that words and dreams may be equated, a position which, if the words and dreams are a poet's, seems conventional enough ; but it then advances the further theory that the world itself may be ' only a sudden flaming word '. But if the world is a word, then the ' dusty deeds ' which the poet has till now disparaged partake of the nature of the word as much as dreams do. In short, if everything is but words, then the statement that ' words alone are certain good ' becomes meaning-less. Yeats suggests that words are not merely the signs of things, but things themselves, the stuff from which the universe is made. The animals did not exist until Adam gave them names. Such a position was too daring for the young poet, so he retreats in the rest of the poem to the land of the lotos-eaters, holding that poetry and dreaming are very pleasant sedatives. But the puzzling and startling suggestion about the relation between words, dreams, and the world—or, to put it more abstractly, between language, imagination, and reality—indicates that a strong wind was rising to make Arcady uninhabitable for the dark-faced boy with the black forelock that fell over his face.

## CHAPTER IV

## CLOUD AND FOAM

BETWEEN 1884 and 1888 Yeats left boyhood behind. When the young poet Katharine Tynan met him in 1885 he seemed to her ' all dreams and all gentleness ', but, unsuspected by her, he was violently extending his radius of interest and action, and as he dashed forward, trying to disregard the confusion which he inwardly felt. Previously he had been able to keep life and poetry simple, now he was besieged by a mob of ideas, uncertainties, and passions, which grew very difficult to control. In a letter which he wrote to her late in 1888, he described the alteration that had taken place in a few years' time :

I am sure the ' Island [of Statues] ' is good of its kind. I was then living a quite harmonious poetic life. Never thinking out of my depth. Always harmonious, narrow, calm. Taking small interest in people but most ardently moved by the more minute kinds of natural beauty. ' Mosada ' was then written and ' Time and Vivien,' which you have not seen. Everything done then was quite passionless. The ' Island ' was the last. Since I have left the ' Island ' I have been going about on shoreless seas. Nothing anywhere has clear outline. Everything is cloud and foam. ' Oisin ' and the ' Seeker ' are the only readable result. . . . The early poems I know to be quite coherent, and at no time are there clouds in my details, for I hate the soft modern manner. The clouds began about four years ago. I was finishing the ' Island.' They came and robbed Naschina of her shadow. As you will see, the rest is cloudless, narrow and calm.

What caused this change in his poetical climate ? We have already glimpsed some of the clouds in the distance : his disquietude about the scepticism imparted to him by his father, his feeling of guilt over his failure to follow his father to Trinity College, his inability to escape his father's style of painting though he disagreed with its principles; his league with George Russell in the battle of imagination against science; his growing need for self-assertion and self-expression. Now his energies flamed forth in three directions, ' in a form of literature, in a form of philosophy, and a belief in nationality '.

Of these three the form of philosophy was the most important and the most unusual. ' It was only when I began to study psychical research and mystical philosophy that I broke away from my father's influence.' He did not break away altogether, as he might have done by becoming a devout Christian, but far enough so that he and his father began to have quarrels. Yeats wanted to find intellectual support for his vague feelings of rebellion. With George Russell he was soon deep in occult study. Around the two eager young men gathered several others; one was Yeats's schoolfellow, Charles Johnston, son of a Protestant Member of Parliament from Ulster, who had planned to be a missionary; another was Claude Wright, who was to spend most of his life working for Theosophy; another was Charles Weekes, later to write mystical poems. All were parched by the desiccated religion which the Church of Ireland and the Presbyterian Church, now purged of their old evangelicalism, provided. ' An Irishman cut away from his priest is exceedingly speculative.' They all began to study European magic and mysticism and Eastern religion, and took a room in ' a dirty back street ' to be the headquarters of their new ' Dublin Hermetic Society '. They saw themselves as a small select group with infinite potentialities. In a country like Ireland, filled at that time with plots and counter-plots, they had their own conspiracy against the state of things.

The Hermetic Society met for the first time on June 16, 1885, with Yeats as chairman. Surviving notes of his opening address throw considerable light on his state of mind. He opens the meeting by announcing that the Society has been assembled to discuss the wonders of Eastern philosophy. The first paper will describe recent occult phenomena, and other papers will deal with the question of whether the Mahatmas of the Theosophists really

exist, and what their powers may be. The orator then warms
to his theme :

But is not European science answering all these problems ?  Are
there observed facts given that all the teachers and the schools of
Europe can reduce to no law, facts which they try to reason out of
existence as the professors of Genoa sought in the days of the telescope
of Galileo to reason the stars out of heaven with the metaphysics of
the schoolmen ?  Yes, there are the observed facts.  Our first two
papers this evening will deal with them.  But what is all this bother
about the immortality of the soul ? — it is great question whether the
soul be immortal or not.  Has not theology solved that ? — no !
Fairy tales and legends it has given as these days demand demonstration
and experiment — how can it prove anything ?  Science after science
is discovered and shakes mother church that cries let it be anathema.
Has not science solved it ?  Science will tell you the soul of man is
a volatile gas capable of solution in glycerine.  Take this for your
answer if you will.  Has spiritualism solved it ?  Where it is wise it
will tell you that year by year the footfall grows softer on the haunted
stairway, that year by year the mysterious breath becomes fainter and
fainter, that every decade takes something from the vividness of the
haunting shadow till it has grown so faint that none but the keenest
eyes can see the feeble outline and then it is gone it is dead dead forever.

Take this for your answer if you will, if you will not follow us
into the maze of eastern thought, but I warn you that on the road to
truth lurks many a dragon and goblin of mischief in wait for the soul.
Miracle hunger is one of them.  The dragon of the abstract is another,
devouring forever the freedom and the pride of life.  It beset Immanuel
Kant and compelled him on his daily constitutional to count his steps
and to try and breathe with his mouth shut.

We must not be deceived by the elaborate warning about pitfalls
into thinking that Yeats is sceptical as his father would have been
sceptical.  He is convinced that science has failed and hopeful
that another way of discovering truth exists.  Though he
waits for proof, he waits impatiently and with a certain amount
of deliberate credulity.  Like the young Goethe, he is ' desti-
tute of faith, yet terrified at scepticism ', a zealot in search of a
creed.

In the weeks that followed that first meeting the members
discussed the fourth dimension, Odic force, ' Esoteric Buddhism ',

and the like.  A Brahmin Theosophist named Mohini M. Chatterjee was invited to lecture to them.  'They spent their days in
battle about the absolute and the alcahest, and I think that none
read the newspapers, and am sure that some could not have told
you the name of the viceroy.'  They looked to the poets rather
than the scientists for truth, and discovered in the belief of Shelley
and Coleridge in the power of the imagination confirmation of
their conviction that miracles were still possible to man.

In this Society Yeats found the beginnings of an answer to
his father and his father's world.  Already he had made, he tells
us, a new religion of poetic tradition, a fardel of stories, personages, emotions.  Now, under his influence, the Hermetic Society
declared that ' whatever the great poets had affirmed in their
finest moments was the nearest we could come to an authoritative
religion, and that their mythology, their spirits of water and wind
were but literal truth '.  His one unshakable belief, he said later,
was that ' whatever of philosophy has been made poetry is alone
permanent, and that one should begin to arrange it in some
regular order, rejecting nothing as the make-believe of the poets '.
So far as this belief implied that poetry was a superior form of
knowledge, his father would have concurred, but he would have
objected violently to his son's attempt to formalize a new religion
and thus bind himself to an artificial pattern.

The poet's vague generalizations had more of the spirit than
of the substance of revolt ;  Yeats made up in vehemence for what
he lacked in certainty, and in passion for what he lacked in knowledge.  Occasionally his doubts seem to emerge in disguised form,
as in the dramatic poem, *The Seeker*, published in September
1885.  The hero of the poem, an old knight, has spent ' three-
score years of dream-led wandering ' in search of a spirit in a
wood.  At last he achieves his quest, and bowing down before
the spirit begs his reward :

> Now raise thy voice and speak !
> Even from boyhood, in my father's house,
> That was beside the waterfall, thy words
> Abode, as banded adders in my breast.

Thou knowest this, and how from mid the dance
Thou called'st me forth,
                    And how thou madest me
A coward in the field ; and all men cried :
Behold the Knight of the Waterfall, whose heart
The spirits stole, and gave him in its stead
A peering hare's ; and yet I murmured not,
Knowing that thou hadst singled me with word
Of love from out a dreamless race for strife,
Through miseries unhuman ever on
To joys unhuman, and to the — Speak ! Speak !

The spirit turns out to be no ineffable power, however, but a bearded witch whom men call infamy.

> *Knight.* I sought thee not.
> *Figure.* Lover, the voice that summoned thee was mine.

Yeats's attitude towards the mystic quest is that of the lion-hunter who pauses before shooting to remind his attendants that hunting is a dangerous and possibly foolish sport. But, for all that, occultism was his ' secret fanaticism '.

After occultism the second direction in which his energies flowed was towards a vigorous nationalism. In 1885 it was difficult not to be affected by the growing patriotic fervour of the times ; the dynamiters of the determined Irish Republican Brotherhood were blowing up English railway stations ; Parnell had unified the Irish party in Parliament and was bringing great pressure to bear on Gladstone, who introduced a Home Rule Bill for Ireland in 1886. Yeats's first contact with active nationalists (for his father, though a staunch nationalist, took no active part in the movement) was probably through Charles Hubert Oldham, the leader of a group of nationalists at Trinity College. In 1885 Oldham was chiefly responsible for founding the *Dublin University Review*, which published Yeats's first poems, and late in the same year he organized a discussion group called the Contemporary Club, where Yeats soon began to practise public speaking. Neither of these had an overt political object, but both had a nationalist tendency.

The major influence on him, however, was John O'Leary, who returned, late in 1884, from five years of imprisonment in England and long exile in France. O'Leary had been convicted of treason for taking part in an armed rising against the English in 1867, and, when asked by the judge if he had anything to say, had made an eloquent speech denying the right of an English tribunal to judge him for treason when England was not his country. He was treated brutally during his five years in prison, but neither then nor afterwards ever complained. When at last he was permitted to return to Dublin, his distinguished appearance, his sense of personal dignity, his upright character, and his slow but fearlessly honest and challenging mind, made him a nationalist rallying point. Young people in particular flocked to him as ' the veteran patriot ' and ' the old man ', though, as he smilingly declares in his *Reminiscences of Fenians and Fenianism*, he was but fifty-four years old.

Unlike most nationalists who had watched Parnell's rise to power, O'Leary had little belief in Parliamentary efforts to secure Irish Home Rule, and was not sanguine about the prospects of early independence. He liked to describe himself as ' very untransacting ' in matters involving immediate, violent action. In so far as he had any hatred, he directed it not against England but against English rule in Ireland. On occasion he was even known to assert that the English character was better, perhaps, than the Irish, but that the Irish could not turn English. He opposed terrorism and all unfair methods, saying, ' There are things that a man must not do to save a nation '. One of his major objectives was to build up national morale, a word he used very often which perhaps attracted him because of his own sense of self-discipline and dignity.

His nationalism was distinctive, also, in that he had a deep and somewhat discriminating interest in Irish literature. Much of his Fenian activity had consisted of editing a Fenian newspaper, and though his own literary style was abominable, he had always tried to maintain high standards in its columns. ' We protest against the right of patriots to perpetrate bad verses ', he declared on one occasion. When he returned to Ireland after his imprisonment and exile, O'Leary conceived of his mission as primarily an educative one, and therefore devoted himself to the broader issues of nationalism. Two speeches he gave in 1886, on 'What Irishmen Should Know' and 'How Irishmen Should Feel', are illustrative : in the first he recommended study of the classics, of English history ('it is well to learn from an enemy'), of Irish geography, history, poetry, and, what is more remarkable, of Irish folklore, a subject then considered a little newfangled. As to how an Irishman should feel, O'Leary declared that he should feel first of all that he was an Irishman, second, that Irish unity must be secured, and finally, that he should make some sacrifice for Ireland. These simple, unpolitical precepts, with O'Leary's moral force and revolutionary record behind them, had considerable effect upon Yeats, who up to that time had thought of the nationalist movement as an affair for politicians.

To all the enthusiastic young men and women, like Douglas Hyde, Katharine Tynan, and later, Maud Gonne, who clustered about him, O'Leary lent books and gave encouragement. To Yeats he lent Thomas Davis's poems, admitting that they were not the greatest poetry, but saying that they had converted him to the nationalist movement. Yeats was stirred to find a heroic figure upon whom poetry, even the mediocre poetry which he found Davis had written, could have such effect. The interest in fairy and folk tales, which he had learned from his mother in boyhood, now had the sanction of O'Leary's authority behind it. Through O'Leary, too, he joined a Young Ireland society, and said later with moderate hyperbole that from the society's debates, 'from O'Leary's conversation and from the Irish books he lent or gave me has come all I have set my hand to since'.

We can better understand the change that came over young writers in Dublin when O'Leary returned, by comparing the two first books of Katharine Tynan which appeared in 1885 and 1887. The first, *Louise de la Vallière*, but for two or three short poems, might have been written in England. But the second book,

*Shamrocks*, is almost exclusively Irish in subject-matter.

Yeats went through the same evolution. Early in 1886 he was working on a draft of a new tragedy, entitled variously *The Blindness*, *The Epic of the Forest*, and *The Equator of Wild Olives*. This play he says he had located in a crater of the moon, but his memory or myth-making sense deceived him, for the scene in the manuscript is Spain. Katharine Tynan, under O'Leary's influence, suggested that Yeats, too, should try his hand at an Irish subject, and very soon afterwards he began *The Wanderings of Oisin*, which was to set the tone for the Irish literary revival.

Whether or not to use Irish material was a much more debatable question then than it now seems in retrospect. Sir Samuel Ferguson had been writing dull narratives based on Irish subjects for many years, and Standish O'Grady had recently (1882) published prose versions of some of the old legends. But the standard view, supported by Professor Dowden at Trinity College, for example, was that the use of an Irish subject was unwise. When Aubrey De Vere asked his advice, Dowden suggested that he take Thomas à Becket rather than an Irish theme : ' As a fact, whether it ought to be so or not, the choice of an Irish mythical, or early historical, subject confines the full enjoyment of the poem to a little circle '. For a young poet to throw in his lot with literary nationalism instead of with the more traditional source-material of English verse required enthusiasm and determination. Yeats made his choice aggressively and was spoiling for a fight. In October 1886, he hot-headedly attacked Dowden for his well-known cosmopolitanism in the course of a review of the poetry of Sir Samuel Ferguson :

If Ireland has produced no great poet, it is not that her poetic impulse has run dry, but because her critics have failed her, for every community is a solidarity, all depending upon each, and each upon all. . . .

It is a question whether the most distinguished of our critics, Professor Dowden, would not only have more consulted the interests of his country, but more also, in the long run, his own dignity and reputation, which are dear to all Irishmen, if he had devoted some of

those elaborate pages which he has spent on the much bewritten
George Eliot, to a man like the subject of this article. . . .

I do not appeal to the professorial classes, who, in Ireland, at least,
appear at no time to have thought of the affairs of their country till
they first feared for their emolument — nor do I appeal to the shoddy
society of 'West Britonism' — but to those young men clustered
here and there throughout our land, whom the emotion of Patriotism
has lifted into that world of selfless passion in which heroic deeds are
possible and heroic poetry credible.

The denunciation is a little less heated than it sounds : Yeats
was rebuking Dowden for his lack of nationalist sentiment, but
was well aware that the man whom he defended, Ferguson, was
nationalist only in his use of Irish subject-matter, and in politics
was a unionist. We shall grow accustomed to finding loopholes
in the young man's extremism, loopholes which he carefully left
there. He and Dowden were soon friends again. But the article
is the first public appearance of the new Yeats, a passionate young
man ready to speak his mind and flesh his sword. He had chosen
to conquer his timid, shy personality by rushing into the world
with it instead of hiding in the thicket at Howth. He would write
*la littérature engagée.*

In March 1886 he published his first Irish poem, 'The
Two Titans, a Political Poem'. It is put in the framework of a
vision :

> The vision of a rock where lightnings whirl'd
>   Bruising the darkness with their crackling light ;
> The waves, enormous wanderers of the world,
>   Beat on it with their hammers day and night.
> Two figures crouching on the black rock, bound
>   To one another with a coiling chain ;
> A grey-haired youth, whose cheeks had never found,
>   Or long ere this had lost their ruddy stain ;
> A sybil, with fierce face as of a hound
>   That dreams.

The youth, though he has some resemblance to Yeats, is of course
Ireland, and the sibyl, to judge by the following description, is
England :

> She moveth, feeling in her brain
> The lightnings pulse — behold her, aye behold —
> Ignoble joy, and more ignoble pain
> Cramm'd all her youth ; and hates have bought and sold
> Her spirit.   As she moves, the foam-globes burst
> Over her spotted flesh and flying hair
> And her gigantic limbs.   The weary thirst
> Unquenchable still glows in her dull stare,
> As round her, slow on feet that have no blood,
> The phantoms of her faded pleasures walk ;
> And trailing crimson vans, a mumbling brood,
> Ghosts of her vanished glories, muse and stalk
> About the sea.

For a moment the young man drags his chain away from her, and

> With little cries of joy he kissed the rain
> In creviced rocks, and laughed to the old sea,
> And nodding to and fro, sang songs of love,
> And flowers and little children.

But the lightnings flash and he is dragged again before the possessive sibyl, who gloatingly watches his lips open and close as he imprints a mystical kiss ' on the dim brow / Of failure '. God or Fate, whom Yeats refers to non-committally as the ' Eternal Darkness ', has brought the youth to life to bring glory to failure.

This preposterous poem is chiefly of interest because of its partisan tone and its foreshadowing of *The Wanderings of Oisin*, which Yeats began a little later in 1886.   The allegory, as Gerard Manley Hopkins said, was ' strained and unworkable ',[1] but for the first time Yeats made use of an extended metaphor, so that the poem could not be taken merely as a picture ; the ulterior

---

[1] Hopkins was in Dublin in 1886, and wrote to Coventry Patmore of Yeats's *Mosada* and ' The Two Titans ' on Nov. 7 of that year : ' Now this *Mosada* I cannot think highly of, but I was happily not required then to praise what presumably I had not then read, and I had read and could praise another piece.   It was a strained and unworkable allegory about a young man and a sphinx on a rock in the sea (how did they get there ? what did they eat ? and so on ; people think such criticisms very prosaic, but common-sense is never out of place anywhere . . .) but still containing fine lines and vivid imagery.' *Further Letters of Gerard Manley Hopkins* (Oxford, 1938), 225-6.

meaning—the sub-title is ' A Political Poem ' — demands recognition but seems deliberately obscured, as if the poet did not want the reader to understand it too well. For a political poem ' The Two Titans ' is strangely apolitical ; Yeats makes one step to the side for every step forward, in a combination of assertion and qualification which was to dog him all his days. We may also find in the two titans, one representing weak youth, the other powerful age, an unconscious reference to the poet's conflict with his father ; and the mystical kiss, which has no corporeal object, suggests something of the sexual frustration which Yeats was beginning to find very troublesome. But above all, he is here for the first time identifying himself closely with Ireland, even to the point of representing his country by a young man instead of by the traditional Cathleen Ni Houlihan.

By early 1886, then, Yeats was both nationalist and occultist ; he had yet to choose decisively to become a poet. In this year of his coming of age in the legal sense he came of age poetically as well. After three years of getting nowhere under his father's tutelage in the Metropolitan School of Art and the Academy School, he defied J. B. Yeats's wishes and suddenly abandoned art. The decision was probably made while the artist was away in London trying to obtain commissions for portraits. It meant that the young man had renounced his efforts to follow the paternal pattern and would strike out for himself. Having rejected Trinity College, and having rejected art, he had put aside the less hazardous alternatives and must try to make his way by his writing. To take such a firm step he must have greatly increased in self-confidence, or rather, for we have to keep his continuing timidity in mind, in a kind of recklessness.

His poetic powers show their magnitude by October 1886, when the poems which he later entitled ' The Indian upon God ' and ' The Sad Shepherd ' were published in the *Dublin University Review*. But his first long work of importance was to be *The Wanderings of Oisin*, begun in 1886, finished in 1888, and published with O'Leary's help in January 1889. Narrative poetry was a new departure for him ; he wrote to Katharine Tynan that his ideas of a poem had greatly changed since he had written *The Island of Statues*, for that was a region, while *Oisin* was a ' series of incidents '. The change was significant of his increased scope and ambition. Though he adopted many elements from translations of the Irish original, he stamped *Oisin* with his own personality, and made it, to paraphrase Goethe, a part of the grand confession of his life. The poem is Irish in name and to some extent in scenery, otherwise Pre-Raphaelite in style but symbolist in method. The elaborate pictures suggest a Rossetti or Burne-Jones painting :

> His mistress was more mild and fair
> Than doves that moaned round Eman's hall
> Among the leaves of the laurel wall,
> And feared always the bow-string's twanging.
> Her eyes were soft as dewdrops hanging
> Upon the grass-blades' bending tips,
> And like a sunset were her lips,
> A stormy sunset o'er doomed ships.
> Her hair was of a citron tincture,
> And gathered in a silver cincture ;
> Down to her feet white vesture flowed,
> And with the woven crimson glowed
> Of many a figured creature strange,
> And birds that on the seven seas range.
> For brooch 'twas bound with a bright sea-shell,
> And wavered like a summer rill,
> As her soft bosom rose and fell.

*The Wanderings of Oisin* is divided into three parts, each of them a separate voyage. Yeats's life also fell into three main phases, at Sligo, at London, and at Howth, near Dublin. During the first Yeats chased after the two dogs and talked to the fishermen ; during the second he fought with the English schoolboys ; and during the third he secluded himself in the thicket and dreamed. Oisin, in the first book of the poem, is hunting with his fellow-Fenians around Sligo when Niam, daughter of the King of the Young, entices him to go with her to her kingdom. He finds there a world inhabited only by the young, and spends a hundred years in hunting and fishing. This century may be described as the Sligo period.

Then he makes a second voyage to a different kind of island, where ' rose a world of towers / And blackness in the dark '. Surely this is a symbolical England as seen through Irish eyes. Here is the castle of Manannan, the old god of the sea, his place taken now by a ' brown demon '. The demon has enchained a beautiful lady who, like the enchained young man in ' The Two Titans ', symbolizes Ireland. Oisin battles the demon for a hundred years but the demon's form is protean and ultimately unconquerable. After this second century Oisin and Niam go to the final island, that of forgetfulness, where, lulled by a bell-branch, Oisin dreams as Yeats had dreamed in the Howth thicket, until after another hundred years he is awakened by a starling. He resolves to return to Ireland to see his Fenian comrades, but the moment he touches the earth he becomes an old man.

In this poem for the first time Yeats used symbols with a sure hand. Besides the general symbolical relation of Oisin's life to his own, he included isolated symbols with great effect. In Book I he takes over from the Irish legend the hornless deer chased by a phantom hound, and the maiden with the golden apple followed by a beautiful youth ; these, like the pictures on the Grecian urn, are symbols of frustration as well as pursuit, for the chase is endless. In Book II, beside the symbolic portrayal of English oppression of Ireland in terms of demon and lady, there are two ' huge forms of stone ' who watch over the approaches to the second island ; one has his eye on the stars, the other on the churning waves, and they stand for the spiritual and physical man. Yeats did not intend that these symbols should be recognized. As he wrote to Katharine Tynan : ' In the second part of " Oisin " under disguise of symbolism I have said several things to which I only have the key. The romance is for my readers. They must not even know there is a symbol anywhere. They will not find out. If they did it would spoil the art, yet the whole poem is full of symbols — if it be full of aught but clouds.' But a week after the book was published, when the reviews had begun to come in, he wrote her again, as if dissatisfied with his own esotericism, ' Oisin needs an interpreter '.

One mystery about the poem remains. If Yeats takes over from the old legend only what suits his symbolic purposes, and if Oisin is in many ways Yeats himself, why should the hero, when he touches Irish soil, become an old man ? And similarly, why should the young man in ' The Two Titans ', who is also somewhat Yeatsian, have grey hair ? A letter which the poet sent to Katharine Tynan on September 6, 1888, just after he had finished *Oisin*, throws light on this premature decrepitude :

> I am not very hopeful about the book. Something inarticulate have I been, I fear. Something I had to say. Don't know that I have said it. All seems confused, incoherent, inarticulate. Yet this I know, I am no idle poetaster. My life has been in my poems. To make them I have broken my life in a mortar as it were. I have brayed in it youth and fellowship, peace and worldly hopes. I have seen others enjoying while I stood alone with myself — commenting, commenting, — a mere dead mirror on which things reflect themselves. I have buried my youth and raised over it a cairn — of clouds.

The statement has a histrionic ring. How can this young man of twenty-three talk as if he were an old man ? But Yeats is telling, in highly coloured language, the truth. Because he still felt the dream to be his natural element, he thought of himself as standing apart from all that he did when he left dreams behind. The gift of spontaneous composition had left him ; he had to premeditate everything for a long time. Underneath the aggressive denouncer of Dowden and the energetic organizer of the Hermetic Society were timidity and sensitiveness, as he well knew, but he was determined to conceal his weaknesses. To act naturally or spontaneously as other young men and women did would be to give himself away as a timid John-a-dreams. But not to act naturally or spontaneously is to give up his youth, to become detached from life like an old man. Reality withers him as it had withered Oisin.

' He had an uncanny faculty ', says Katharine Tynan, ' of standing aside and looking on at the game of life as a spectator.'

Perpetually contemplating his own actions as if from without, he grows self-conscious to an extreme point. In *The Wanderings of Oisin* he speaks of birds who ' pondered in a soft vain mood / Upon their shadows in the tide '. The very dew-drops are self-conscious in ' Miserrimus ', published in October 1886 :

> But naught they heard, for they are ever listening,
> The dewdrops, for the sound of their own dropping.

His self-consciousness is not that of Narcissus staring fondly at his own reflection, but that of the parrot in ' An Indian Song ', published in December 1886 :

> A parrot swaying on a tree
> Rages at his own image in the enamelled sea.

Yeats's battle with his father is merging into a battle with himself. This conflict, joined to his nationalist, occultist, and poetic activities, helped to produce the confusion of mind of which he complained to Katharine Tynan in the letter quoted at the beginning of this chapter.

To control the universe was no longer easy. Yeats realized that the poems he was now writing were poems ' of longing and complaint ', and he wanted to write instead poems ' of insight and knowledge '. But to do so he would have to arrive at a much more systematic arrangement of life than that he had so far achieved ; he would have to mould his intuitions into sources of hidden power and wisdom. All secrets became congenial to him, for secrets gave strength ; the first fascination of symbolism was that it did not altogether disclose the secrets upon which its use depended. Yet he was uneasy, and his letter describing the symbols of Oisin as pervading the poem shows him still diffident about letting the world know that he was using a symbolical method. One day he wants the symbols to be comprehensible only to him, and a few days later he feels that they should be interpreted to the public.

If we stop to examine Yeats's uneasiness, we begin to suspect that he thought symbolism a slightly illegitimate device. He had come upon it, not as Edmund Wilson asserts in *Axel's Castle*, through Arthur Symons's accounts of the school of Mallarmé, for Yeats had not yet met Symons when he wrote *Oisin*, but by an extension of his father's theories. J. B. Yeats had prepared the way by teaching his son that the only criterion in life as in art is the fullness or totality of one's personality. The external world's importance could therefore easily be reduced to the role of stimulus upon the self. From here it was but a short distance to the theory that the external world could be used to represent states of mind.

But J. B. Yeats was not himself a symbolist, and we have yet to decide why his son became one. With a temper as complex as that of the young poet, any one answer will not serve ; but among the factors no doubt Yeats's frequent failures in arguments with his father had something to do with his cultivation of his image-making faculty. He soon found that a picture, unlike a logical proposition, cannot be refuted. Frank O'Connor has described how, in the midst of an argument with George Russell in later life, Yeats would suddenly pull an image from his private phantasmagoria such as, ' But that was before the peacock screamed ', and puzzle and overbear his opponent. The method must have been even more necessary and effective when he was but an ill-read young man. A second factor lay in his dissatisfaction with himself and his consciousness of his own imperfections ; by symbols, especially traditional symbols, he could make his work less personal and identifiable. He was afterwards to warn Fiona Macleod that myths must be ' objective ', ' well born and independent ', rather than ' subjective, an inner way of looking at things assumed by a single mind '.

The use of symbols, then, was in part evasive. Goethe, whose mind in many ways resembled Yeats's, was conscious of the same characteristic, and when he was twenty-three told a friend that he ' always speaks figuratively, and can never express himself literally ; but that when he is older he hopes to think and say the thought itself as it really is '. But if Yeats adopted symbolism in part to compensate for psychological weaknesses, he was certainly conscious that its value transcended compensation. As he grew into maturity he wanted not merely to protect the inviolability of his own mind, but to ferret out more and deeper secrets which were withheld from logicians and literalists. He read mystical writers because they saw symbols in everything, and, with the same general purpose, he sought out those who said they could manipulate external nature by magic as the poet manipulated it by symbols. He would justify himself and his method. He rightly perceived that the question of symbolism went beyond poetry and esthetic theory, and knew that to use the magic wand he must master all the charms.

## CHAPTER V

## COMBATING THE 'MATERIALISTS'

OCCULTISM, the study of secrets too profound and dangerous to entrust to the ordinary man, was itself a magic word. While personal reasons impelled Yeats to depart from his father's incredulity, he would hardly have turned to occult research had a movement in that direction not been under way. All over Europe and America young men dropped like him, and usually without his caution, into the treacherous currents of semi-mystical thought. They refused to accept the universe that their scientific, materialist, rationalist, and often hypocritically religious elders tried to hand to them. Science had disproved orthodox conceptions of the making of the world and of man, and had implied a threat to every traditional attitude. Darwin had husked the world of meaning, and few could share Bernard Shaw's confidence in Lamarck's contention that the giraffe had secured its long neck by willing it. Matthew Arnold's even-tempered but desperate assurances of the adaptability of Christianity aroused little zeal.

Since Christianity seemed to have been exploded, and since science offered to Western man little but proof of his own ignominiousness, a new doctrine purporting to be an ancient and non-European one was evolved by a strange Russian lady. The new movement called itself Theosophy, and offered a ' synthesis of science, religion, and philosophy ' which opposed the contemporary developments of all three. Its founder, Madame Blavatsky, scouted the new evolutionary theories, and proclaimed with certainty that man had never been an ape. ' Modern science is ancient thought distorted, and no more ', she announced. At the same time she attacked all current religions, especially Christianity, and accused the priesthood of responsibility for modern materialism.  The 'priests in black gowns' had perverted doctrines originally true, and left of them only the husks to satisfy peoples hollow-eyed with spiritual starvation.  Modern religion, too, was ancient thought distorted and no more.  Philosophy was a less central target, but Madame Blavatsky carried on a running fight with Herbert Spencer.

To discover what was ancient thought undistorted, she supported the analogical method of the new science of comparative mythology.  Since about 1860 a great deal of research into the history of religion and myth had been carried out.  Max Müller was now publishing his translations of the wisdom literature of the East, d'Arbois de Jubainville was at work on Celtic materials, Sir James Frazer would soon publish *The Golden Bough* (1890).  Madame Blavatsky caught the infection early, and in her first book, *Isis Unveiled* (1877), asserted the similarity in fundamental beliefs of all religions, and attributed it to the existence of a secret doctrine which was their common parent.  Unlike Müller, Jubainville, and Frazer, she did not have to depend upon written literature for her knowledge.  She had access, she said, to an oral tradition, for the true and secret doctrine had never been allowed to disappear completely even from a degenerate earth.  In earlier ages there had always been an *élite* who had known of it ; Boehme and Paracelsus, for example, had even revealed a little of the arcana.  Now, she said, an ancient brotherhood was keeping the secret wisdom high in the mountain fastnesses of Tibet.  The members of this brotherhood, whom she habitually referred to as her ' Masters ', had little interest in propagating their doctrines ; enough for them that they should protect and perhaps enlarge upon what was already known.  Did they so desire, they could astonish the world by the mental powers which they had developed to a point far beyond the wildest dreams of the practitioners of the new ' telepathy '.  From time to time, indeed, they deigned to reveal a little to the outside world, and had shown certain things to Madame Blavatsky while she studied with them in Tibet, and telepathically afterwards.  Two masters in particular, Koot-Hoomi and Morya, had graciously indicated their willingness to transmit some of the secret doctrine to the world through the good offices of the Theosophical Society. As these mysteries were gradually revealed the world would slowly progress towards the greater spirituality that had been prophesied for it.

The impact of Theosophy was increased by the pretentious myths with which Madame Blavatsky sent forth into the world doctrines which she had put together from many sources. A system with smaller pretensions would have aroused less enthusiasm; the Tables of the Law, to win converts, had to be brought from Mount Sinai. Combining novelty and antiquity, the movement gathered force because it attacked atheism and at the same time supported anti-clericalism; because it attacked science, yet was careful to use the weapons of scientific language and confirmation whenever possible, and to fight only on carefully chosen battlegrounds; because it upheld fatalism, yet offered hope of progress; because it denounced modern man as fiercely as Nordau, but at the same time offered him the opportunity of becoming like a god. Spiritual evolution restored the hope which natural evolution had removed, and materialism was utterly condemned.

The tenets of *The Secret Doctrine*, as Madame Blavatsky called her chief work, are of interest because they brought Yeats into contact for the first time with a comprehensive cosmology. Whatever else may be said of Madame Blavatsky, she did try to hold the world in the palm of her hand, and made huge generalizations about man and the cosmos which were easier for him to credit, and more inviting, than the dogmas of the Churches. Madame Blavatsky's faith had three main articles : in the first place, there was an ' Omnipresent, Eternal, Boundless, and Immutable Principle on which all speculation is impossible '. This was a far cry from Dr. Arnold's personal God, and in practice the Theosophists paid little attention to deity. Secondly, Madame Blavatsky asserted the universality of the law of periodicity, of flux and reflux, or as she sometimes called it, of polarity. According to this doctrine, the world is a conflict of opposites ; good and evil are as in Manichaeism the contraries without which life cannot exist, but these are not the only opposites ; everywhere the armies clash, with now one, now the other triumphant.  Thirdly, she proclaimed the fundamental identity of all souls with the Universal Oversoul, implying that any soul might, under proper conditions, partake of the Oversoul's power, and proclaimed also the ' obligatory pilgrimage of every Soul through the Cycle of Incarnation in accordance with Cyclic and Karmic law '.

This last doctrine requires some elaboration.  According to Theosophical writings, the soul has seven elements or principles and its evolution proceeds through existences on seven planets, each with varying degrees of matter and spirit, earth alone having them in equal quantities.  There are seven races, and seven branch races, and seven root races, and the soul, passing through all these, has about eight hundred incarnations, ' like beads on a string '.  Heaven and Hell are real, but are to be considered as states, not places.

Though the Theosophists' principles are difficult to pin down, we may draw upon a summary of their theories of spiritual evolution made by Yeats's schoolfellow Charles Johnston in the *Dublin University Review* in 1885.  He had originally read the article as a paper before the Dublin Hermetic Society, where Yeats heard it.  According to Johnston, the soul passes through seven rounds, each being a passage round the seven planets and through all the races.  In the first round man is relatively ethereal, ' not intellectual but superspiritual ; spirituality in the Esoteric sense being direct or intuitive knowledge, as opposed to physical reason, or knowledge acquired by logic '.  The man of the first round ' inhabits an immense but loosely organized body '.

In the second round his body grows firmer and he is more physical, ' but still less intelligent than intuitive '.  In the next round he has more the form of a giant ape than of a true man, but his intelligence is much increased.  In the fourth round, which is the present round, ' he decreases in size ', and his intellect ' achieves enormous progress '.  In the fifth round his ' consciousness has to unite itself with the spiritual soul, and this union is termed final salvation '. During the sixth round ' humanity attains hardly conceivable perfection of body and mind, of intellect and spirituality '. The seventh round is ' altogether too godlike for man in the fourth round to forecast its attributes '.

Failure to become united to one's spiritual soul in the fifth round necessitates a return to further incarnations in the earlier rounds, but if the soul proceeds safely to the end of the seventh round it passes into ' nirvana, which is described as a sublime state of conscious rest in omniscience ', and becomes a planetary spirit. At the beginning of each round one of the planetary spirits incarnates, impresses moral ideas upon the races, ' and teaches to some receptive minds the outlines of the Esoteric wisdom which is handed down ' till the end of the round. From this incarnation at the round's beginning comes the idea of an anthropomorphic God.

Johnston's summary is not a complete one of Theosophical views about the soul and historical development, but gives a general notion of them. The Theosophists reinforced their doctrines with examples from Eastern religions, from European occultism, mysticism, philosophy, and, when it served their purpose, from science. They were fortunate to find in A. P. Sinnett an able propagandist for the English-speaking world. Sinnett was a wealthy English editor living in India. Madame Blavatsky overwhelmed him with phenomena — mysterious raps, tinklings of an astral bell, and so forth — which she said were made possible by her omniscient and, therefore, omnipotent Tibetan masters. The phenomena were trivial but to the eager Sinnett sufficient to prove the existence of powers heretofore unsuspected by respectable Englishmen. He called his book *The Occult World*, and with vigour and ' evidence ' defended the implications of the title. The phenomena he described, which competent witnesses had fully authenticated, were nothing, he said, compared with the real powers of the Tibetan Brotherhood, who had so easily exerted their wills over the broad Indian valleys and the towering Himalayan peaks. Of age undetermined, of a purity which decadent westerners could scarcely hope to fathom, the Masters busied themselves with preserving those secrets which priesthoods had corrupted and churches built with hands had concealed.

*The Occult World* acted at once upon the imagination of Yeats's friend, Charles Johnston, when he came upon it in 1884. ' When I first read this admirable little book ', he wrote later, ' the occult phenomena there described seemed to me wholly credible, and I found no difficulty at all in believing that powers commonly called miraculous should be possessed by men who had come to their full spiritual heritage.' Another schoolfellow, Claude Falls Wright, is said to have been inspired to go to Madame Blavatsky in 1884 and 1885 for teaching. She told him : ' Go back to your native Dublin and found a Lodge there '. Dubliners talked about the movement more and more ; one day shortly before Easter 1885, at the home of Edward Dowden, Yeats heard about Sinnett's second book, *Esoteric Buddhism*, which provided a doctrinal exegesis for the magical phenomena of *The Occult World*. Yeats was greatly excited by *Esoteric Buddhism*, and showed it to Johnston, who almost immediately joined the Theosophical Lodge in London, of which Sinnett was now president, and brought back accounts of its activities to his Dublin friends. Of *Esoteric Buddhism* Johnston wrote later : ' The entire reasonableness of the account there given of the life and growth of the soul, interwoven with the history of the world, came home with convincing force, and has remained with me ever since '. Johnston was then eighteen years old. Young Irishmen took to strange faiths with the same abandon as the Des Esseintes of the 'eighties in Paris to strange sins.

This setting of extravagant belief was disrupted in June 1885. The Society for Psychical Research, formed in 1882, had sent Richard Hodgson to India to investigate the truth of Sinnett's account of Madame Blavatsky's marvels. The Society, like its representative, was well-disposed towards occult phenomena, having been established to investigate with an open mind phenomena which scientists had too lightly dismissed. While acknowledging the validity of scientific evidence and procedures, the Society insisted with William James that at any rate the impossibility of supernatural manifestations had not been demonstrated.

Hodgson arrived in India just at the moment when two of Madame Blavatsky's servants decided as the result of a quarrel to betray their mistress. They told Hodgson of secret panels and other tricks she had used, and Hodgson returned to London and denounced Madame Blavatsky as a charlatan before the Society for Psychical Research. Charles Johnston, whom we can afford to watch because of his intimacy at the time with Yeats, was sitting in the audience, and heard Hodgson's report through with rising indignation. When F. W. H. Myers, an official of the Society, asked him his opinion of the address, the young man cried with all the certainty of youth that ' the whole thing was so scandalously unfair that, had I not been a member of the Theosophical Society, I should have joined it forthwith, on the strength of Mr. Hodgson's performance '. Oddly enough, Johnston was not alone in his fidelity. The very completeness of Hodgson's evidence turned Madame Blavatsky from a scheming adventuress into a persecuted Cassandra crying wisdom's wares to an insensate multitude.

Returning to Dublin, Johnston, with Wright and a few others, decided to throw in his lot with the ill-treated lady, and in April 1886 he obtained from Sinnett the charter for a Dublin lodge. George Russell was asked to join, but at that time he apparently disapproved of mysticism that was organized and refused. Yeats when approached also refused to join, having been shaken by Hodgson's charges and feeling unable to compete with his friends' zeal. He was, however, closely associated with the lodge and lectured to it from time to time.

He was still hesitating about becoming a Theosophist when he moved with his family to London in May of 1887. Madame Blavatsky had arrived a month before and within two weeks of her landing had founded a Blavatsky Lodge. Yeats went to call on her with a letter of introduction from Charles Johnston soon after he came to London, and was immediately persuaded to dismiss his doubts and join the lodge. She exercised a peculiar fascination on her visitors, and the poet, troubled as we have seen by his self-consciousness and lack of spontaneity, and filled with reverence for great personalities, was especially taken with her because she was so fully herself, so ' unforeseen, illogical, incomprehensible '. While with her he escaped from the restlessness of his own mind, as he wrote in the unpublished first draft of his *Autobiographies*, and he was reassured of the validity of his anti-materialist theories by the certainty and erudition with which she expounded them.

True, he was not altogether convinced of her occult powers. When her broken cuckoo clock hooted at him as he entered the house, he examined the mechanism to see if it were a trick. He wondered, too, why she did not refute Hodgson's charges. But these things did not trouble him much, for he saw in her a creature of myth who held in her head all the folklore of the world and much of its wisdom. The slender young Irishman with his enthusiasms and the fat Russian lady with her obsessions found common ground. ' She made upon me an impression of generosity and indulgence ', he wrote later. ' I remember how careful she was that the young men about her should not overwork. I overheard her saying to some rude strangers who had reproved me for talking too much, " No, no, he is very sensitive ".' She readily divined the young man's psychological difficulties. On one occasion he read a dull speech to the Theosophists, who received it coldly. Madame Blavatsky called him over and said : ' " Give me the manuscript. Now you go back and say your say about it." He did so, with the greatest success ', and was always grateful to her.

For about a year after her arrival in London Madame Blavatsky discouraged her over-eager followers from plunging too deeply into Theosophical depths, warning them of the danger of black magic. Yeats disregarded her injunction and took Katharine Tynan to a spiritualist séance, where he was so upset by the supernatural phenomena that he lost control of himself and beat his head on the table ; for his disobedience Madame Blavatsky

severely scolded him on his next visit to her.  But in 1888 the
Theosophists' demand for magical instruction was so great that
she resolved to form an Esoteric Section for the sincerest of her
' chelas '.  Yeats was delighted and joined the group soon after
it was formed.  He was eager to probe more deeply into Theosophical arcana, and he hoped, too, that the Esoteric Section would
give him the opportunity of proving to his own satisfaction, and
to the satisfaction even of sceptics like his father, that occult
phenomena were possible.  His friend George Russell characteristically took the opposite position, and wrote from Dublin in
great dismay to Madame Blavatsky, warning her of the danger
of changing the goal of the Theosophical Society from union
with the absolute to ' proving the phenomena of spiritualism,
table-rapping, and the evocation of spooks '.  In reply, she assured
Russell that the Esoteric Section would not practise magic but
would undergo that training necessary before magical power
might safely be entrusted to a member.  One would not learn
to perform miracles, only become ready to learn.

The section had strict rules.  Members had to take pledges
to renounce all vanity, to live a life of abstinence and asceticism,
and to devote themselves to the good of their fellow-men.  In
return, the Esoteric Section promised an undreamed-of change
in the personality.  The psychological development would be
immediate and at the beginning not altogether beneficent.  All
the powerful impulses of the soul, bad as well as good, would
rise to the surface ; only in this way could evil be expelled and
the ' soul be elevated and rendered capable of grasping and
making use of the higher knowledge '.

Yeats was of course extremely interested.  The bringing to
the surface of all the latent possibilities of his being was exactly
what he wanted ; he needed help to change his personality, to
purify himself of timidity, to learn to control others and himself,
to become the hero of whom he dreamed.  Still strongly under
paternal influence, he wanted to find out the ' law of his own
being ' and liberate his mind from inherited ideas and attitudes.
Since his father won the arguments about occultism that they

had together, he had lost his confidence, as he later confessed, but now he moved hopefully 'from speculation to the direct experience of the Mystics '.

The Esoteric Section gave him a system of arcane correspondences and symbols, establishing interrelationships between parts of the body, the seasons, colours, elements, and the like, giving the naked universe a garment at once mystical and personal. It inspired him, too, to go to Boehme and Swedenborg for further study. A journal which he kept during his membership shows him taking up the work conscientiously with, as might be expected, a more independent attitude than that of most of the members :

### ESOTERIC SECTIONS JOURNAL

About Xmas 1888 I joined the esoteric section of TS [Theosophical Society]. The pledges gave me no trouble except two — promise to work for theosophy and promise of obedience to HPB [Madame Blavatsky] in all theosophical matters, explained my difficulties to HPB, said that I could only sign on the condition that I myself was to be judge as to what theosophy is (the term is wide enough) and I consider my work at Blake a wholly adequate keeping of this clause. On the other matter HPB explained that this obedience only referred to things concerning occult practice if such should be called for. Since then a clause has been incerted [sic] making each member promise obedience subject to the decision of his own conscience. Last Sunday (this is Oct. 24 1889) at a private meeting of London esotericists — we passed a resolution that amounts to this

(1) We believe in HPB   (2) We believe in her teachers   (3) we will defend her, subject to our own consciences. I had some doubt as to whether I could sign this second clause. Mademoiselle Zambuca who probably thinks much as I do on this matter of Mahatmas left the section rather than sign. Still I think I was right in signing. I take it in this sense. ' I believe Madame Blavatsky's teachers are wholly righteous learned teachers and that I have in them all due confidence as from pupil to teacher ' Mlle. Zambuca and some who signed seem to have considered it as a committal to a particular theory of this matter. I tried to explain my view of the clause but somehow did not succeed. I as yet refuse to decide between the following alternatives having too few facts to go on,   (1) They are probably living occultists

as HPB says   (2) They are possibly unconscious dramatizations of
HPB's own trance nature   (3) They are also possibly but not likely,
as the mediums assert, spirits   (4) They may be the trance principle
of nature expressing itself symbolically.   The fraud theory in the most
provisional form I have never held for more than a few minutes as it is
wholly unable to cover the facts.   The four other hypotheses do cover
theirs.

I came to the conclusion that my view of the clause was right on
considering the Yankee insubordinate that made some such clause
needful and the statements, in some cases instructions, about there being
no need for any esotericist to commit himself on the question of the
masters but also came to the conclusion that owing to the extreme
vagueness of ES [Esoteric Section] resolutions, and the way various
members have various meanings, to keep a diary of all signings I go
through and such like, for my own future use, and always to state my
reasons for each most carefully and when in doubt as to the legitimacy
of my reasons to submit them to some prominent members in whom
I have confidence.

As to the personnel of sections (having seen these now together).
They seem some intellectual, one or two cultural, the rest the usual
amorphous material that gathers round all new things — All amorphous and clever alike have much zeal — and here and there a few
sparkles of fanaticism are visible.   This section will not in any way (I
believe) influence educated thought — for this as yet unattempted
propaganda the society has so far neither men nor method.   What
effects it has produced upon it are wholly owing to the inherent value
of the philosophy — the method of propaganda has repelled many
educated people.   In India things seem to go better and Moheni
[Mohini M. Chatterjee, the Brahmin who visited Dublin] made, while
over here, the one adequate appeal that has been made to cultivated
people but then he could not write decently.

Dec. 20th

Was at Esoteric Section meeting last Sunday reviewed with others
— Mrs. Besant, Burroughs, etc. — pledge — Mead whose intellect is
that of a good size whelp was a little over righteous as usual otherwise
meeting interesting.   A private soldier with intense face last addition.
Members taking a town each for propaganda by letter.   WB [W. B.
Yeats] Keep out of propaganda not by work.   The whelp may look
righteous in vain.

He was a little disappointed when no occult experiments were forthcoming, and decided to put pressure on Madame Blavatsky to authorize such experiments:

Dec. 20th [continued]

I proposed scheme for organization of occult research   matter referred to HPB.   HPB will refuse probably on the ground of danger by opening up means of black magic.

Dec. 30

Proposals for experiment accepted by HPB, last week.

Jan. 19th [1890]

Meeting of ES at Duke St.   Proposals for experiment accepted by section and Research Committee appointed with myself as sec.   New members seem turning up plentifully — some sparks of culture here and there.   What now shall research committee find to do with itself ?

On a Saturday a week or two after last entry we Research now Recording Committee made experiment in clairvoyance with Mouser as medium.   Mrs. Besant has the detailed account.

Several experiments in fact took place ; on one occasion the esotericists tried unsuccessfully to raise the ghost of a flower, on another to study the possibility of evoking certain kinds of dreams by sleeping with special symbols under their pillows. No miracles occurred, doubts rose in the minds of other members, and Yeats's committee seemed unlikely to further the Theosophical cause.   His last public appearance in the organization was probably in August 1890, when, with Annie Besant in the chair, he lectured on ' Theosophy and Modern Culture '.   Though the lecture was apparently acceptable, the experiments had tried Madame Blavatsky's patience too far.   Shortly afterwards her secretary, no doubt with her approval, asked him to resign.   The poet regretfully complied.

Notwithstanding his final excommunication, five or six years of Theosophy, three of them years of active membership under the organization's founder, had left their mark on Yeats.   He had been brought into contact with a system based on opposition to materialism and on support of secret and ancient wisdom, and was encouraged to believe that he would be able to bring together all the fairy tales and folklore he had heard in childhood, the poetry he had read in adolescence, the dreams he had been dreaming all his life. The Theosophists gave him support because they accepted and incorporated into their system ghosts and fairies, and regarded dreams and symbols as supernatural manifestations. A definition of the fairies such as Yeats made soon after leaving the Society, ' The fairies are the lesser spiritual moods of that universal mind, wherein every mood is a soul and every thought a body ', was entirely in accord with Theosophical doctrine. To the disciples of Madame Blavatsky the spiritual life, which could easily be equated with the imaginative life, was always at hand, always impinging upon matter. On one occasion a small Indian guest at Madame Blavatsky's house created a disturbance by complaining that a big materialist had sat on his astral body, which was reclining near him on the couch. The episode, ridiculous as it is to us and as it was to Yeats, still suggests how matter and spirit were interchangeable and interactive in the Theosophical outlook. It was on this canvas that he would paint.

As to specific doctrines, Yeats accepted tacitly most of what the Theosophists believed, though he understandably preferred to attribute the doctrines to Boehme, Swedenborg, and other reputable sources whom he was now inspired to read, rather than to Blavatsky. The God whom he referred to in ' The Two Titans ' as the ' Eternal Darkness ' is very like Madame Blavatsky's ' Omnipresent, Eternal, Boundless, and Immutable Principle on which all speculation is impossible '. As for the law of periodicity, of flux and reflux, Yeats tells us how, while he was writing *The Wanderings of Oisin*, he was greatly attracted by ' an elaborate metaphor of a breaking wave intended to prove that all life rose and fell as in my poem '. The conception of history as cyclical, and of a divine incarnation at the beginning of each round, is implicit in many of his early stories in *The Secret Rose*, and reappears in his writings during the rest of his life. He says little about reincarnation for some years, but seems to have accepted this principle too, and makes much of it later.  Whether the ideas took immediate effect or remained latent in his mind, they gave his thought a basis, and the work in which he afterward embodied his philosophy and theology, *A Vision*, is full of connections with Theosophy and is recommended as a text by present-day Theosophists.

Besides explicit ideas, Yeats was impressed also by the accoutrements of Theosophy : its air of secrecy, the mysterious *Book of Dyzan* which was constantly referred to in *The Secret Doctrine* but which nobody but Madame Blavatsky had ever seen.  He saw on her door the poorly drawn pictures of her masters, Koot-Hoomi and Morya, supposed to have been telepathically precipitated, and was moved to celebrate the Tibetan adepts in memorable lines :

> *Anashuya.* Swear by the parents of the gods,
>     Dread oath, who dwell on sacred Himalay,
>     On the far Golden Peak ; enormous shapes,
>     Who still were old when the great sea was young ;
>     In their vast faces mystery and dreams ;
>     Their hair along the mountains rolled and filled
>     From year to year by the unnumbered nests
>     Of aweless birds, and round their stirless feet
>     The joyous flocks of deer and antelope,
>     Who never hear the unforgiving hound.
>     Swear !

But perhaps above all else he admired Madame Blavatsky's bland assumption of her complete competence to deal with every department of human knowledge.

Yeats was of course aware that her phenomena might well be fraudulent, as he indicated in his ' Esoteric Sections Journal ', but he rightly considered the ' inherent value of the philosophy ' to be independent of the phenomena.  The occult and religious tradition compounded by Theosophy contained much that was sensible, even profound.  It made clear by examples more reputable than those of Madame Blavatsky, that reality could not be facilely explained as the perceptions of five senses and that scientific rationalism had ignored or superficially dismissed many most important matters. What Yeats now hoped to do was to systematize his knowledge, to put his intuitions and those of the great poets and mystics together, to perform experiments and demonstrate the existence of an occult world, to describe that world more exactly and stylistically than Madame Blavatsky had done. He had secured weapons for the attack on materialism. Theosophy had furnished him with shield and sword, and he went forth like Don Quixote, though with some hesitancy, to tilt at the windmills of modern life.

## CHAPTER VI

# ROBARTES AND AHERNE: TWO SIDES OF A PENNY

He goes like one on a secret errand.

WALTER PATER

OF all periods of Yeats's life the years from 1889 to 1903 are the most difficult to follow. He has so many interests and activities during this time, with so little obvious relation between them, that a strictly chronological account would give the impression of a man in frenzy, beating on every door in the hotel in an attempt to find his own room. But while he was somewhat confused, the maze was not without a plan, a clue to which can be found in his increasing self-consciousness. His inclination, which had begun much earlier, to pose before the world as something different from what he was, to hide his secret self, had come to the point where he saw himself as divided into two parts. This sense of a bifurcated self, to which we now turn, was not, as he thought it, unique. Many of his more sensitive contemporaries shared it, and if we think of the tendency as a general one we can avoid regarding Yeats as an anomaly, or his writings as a manifestation of the divided consciousness common in cases of hysteria.

We tread here on perilous ground, for what seems to be involved is a subtle change in mental climate during the nineteenth century. The nature of the change suggests itself if we take note of the different conceptions of personality which prevailed from the time of Byron at the beginning of the century to that of Wilde at the century's end. The Byronic hero, Manfred or the Giaour, was a man outwardly calm but preyed upon by passions which he could not keep his fiery eyes from showing, and by a secret sin that eventually destroyed him by its intensity. He scorned societal values, his life welled up within him as an uncontrollable force, driving him to revolution, incest, murder, suicide.

By the end of the nineteenth century this hero was brought under control. To the esthetes all passion was repugnant. They set up as their hero the man of great sensitivity who was above passion. Pater lived a cloistered life at Oxford and his Marius practised his Epicureanism as a *spectator ab extra*, and eventually, out of good taste as it were, became a Christian. In Wilde the artist revolted not against society but against life. Instead of having passions the artist had sensations, but even these in an abstracted, contemplative way. Whistler, in many things Wilde's mentor, had said that to ask the artist to paint life was like telling the player to sit on the piano. Wilde went a step further ; to ask a man to live life was also an impertinence. No, ' the first duty in life is to assume a pose ; what the second is no one yet has found out '. The pose is that manner which takes one furthest away from the passion and brutality of life. ' Create yourself ; be yourself your poem.' ' I treated art as the supreme reality and life as a mere mode of fiction.' No doubt the attitude was an overstatement, but it was a systematic one, with deep roots in the life of a man who went to court to prove that his conventional pose of respectability was true even though he knew it was not.

From Wilde's point of view the Byronic hero was a man who had insufficiently mastered life. Wilde was fully aware of his own divergence from the early nineteenth-century type of romanticism and explained it in this way : ' Byron was a symbolic figure, but his relations were to the passions of his age and its weariness of passion. Mine were to something more noble, more permanent, of more vital issue, of larger scope.' For Wilde, the ideal is not the man of unrestrainable passions, but the man whose passions have been tempered and refined into another self, which is consciously fabricated, *posed*. The measure of the greatness of the Wildean hero is the extent to which he has altered the raw material of his life into something quite different. So far as his passions emerge they are ignoble and uninteresting, part of an unpleasant, irrelevant reality, a subject for the naturalist and not for the true artist. Thus Wilde after his fall lamented ' that beautiful world of art where once I was King, and would have remained King indeed, had I not let myself be lured into the imperfect world of coarse uncompleted passion, of appetite without distinction, desire without limit and formless greed '.

The implication of the esthetes' conception of the artistic personality is that a man is really two men. There is the insignificant man who is *given*, whether by God, by society, or simply by birth ; there is the significant man who is *made* by the first. One evidence of this split, which goes beyond literature, is the verbal distinction that becomes common towards the end of the nineteenth century between personality and character, the former as in some way the conscious product of the latter. In literature the splitting up of the mind into two parts is accomplished near the end of the century by two books, *Dr. Jekyll and Mr. Hyde* (1885), and *The Picture of Dorian Gray*, published in magazine form in 1890. Though Stevenson was not of Wilde's school, his distinction between the civilized Dr. Jekyll and the animalistic Mr. Hyde is similar to that between Dorian Gray and his picture. The theme is taken up again in 1896 in Max Beerbohm's *The Happy Hypocrite*, where Lord George Hell, having fallen in love with a pure and innocent girl, woos her under the mask of a saint and under the name of Lord George Heaven.

Because Wilde was compelled by his sexual abnormality to lead a double life, he felt the split very acutely and founded much of his art upon the tension between the pose and the real self, the importance of being and of not being earnest. But his contemporaries understood the divided self too, without in most cases feeling the obligation to make quite so much of the division. The last decade of the century is thronged by extravagant *poseurs* like Lionel Johnson and Aubrey Beardsley ; even James Joyce, growing up in this atmosphere, says he felt compelled to cultivate ' the enigma of a manner '. The attempt to achieve a rarefied, synthetic self is implicit in Pater's extreme preoccupation with style, his method of rewriting innumerable times so that his finished phrase would resemble as little as possible the one that had come initially into his head.

In France there are signs of the same movement. Mallarmé was fabricating a separate life out of a perverse syntax and a verbal subtlety as different as possible from common speech. His disciple, Paul Valéry, develops the implications of the Mallarméan style in *Monsieur Teste* (1895). Teste is the abstract, Mallarméan man, the symbolist, stylist, mathematician, and Madame Teste the sociable, commonplace woman who, though married to him, understands him hardly at all; and we slowly recognize husband and wife for the two parts of Valéry's own mind.

The list could be multiplied indefinitely, but perhaps it is long enough to demonstrate that the notion of selfhood had changed drastically during the nineteenth century. If the self is binary or double-decked, whatever one's conception of the two parts may be, we may expect writers to anthropomorphize each part as Stevenson, Wilde, Valéry, Beerbohm, and others did. Now we may understand the popularity throughout this period of the pseudonym, for the pseudonym symbolized the duality which resulted from the dissociation of the personality. Consider the examples of Yeats's friends : W. K. Magee, George Russell, Oscar Wilde, and William Sharp. Magee's pseudonym, ' John Eglinton ', is explicable in terms of increased euphony or of a necessary reaction by a man of wide culture against the provincialism implied in the Irish name. With George Russell the pseudonym is carried a step further : ' A. E.' is derived from Aeon, a word which came to him in a vision as the name of the heavenly man, to whose state he aspired. Wilde, on leaving England, adopted the name of ' Sebastian Melmoth ', combining his sense of martyrdom and expiation, and eliminating ' amiable, irrepressible Oscar ', as he hoped, completely. In William Sharp, one of the most typical writers of the 'nineties, the pseudonym reached its furthest development. So seriously did Sharp take the pseudonym, so fully did he assume in 1894 the personality of

' Fiona Macleod ', that he wrote under her name books in a style different from his own, sent letters for her to friends in a feminine handwriting, complained to friends who wrote to her that they never wrote to him, and eventually almost collapsed under the strain of double life.

Yeats came to maturity in this atmosphere of doubling and splitting of the self, but his mental growth was parallel to that of other writers and did not derive from them. He did, it is true, see a dramatized version of *Dr. Jekyll and Mr. Hyde* in October 1888, and early in 1889 he met Oscar Wilde. Now, or perhaps a little later, he began to irritate George Russell by ' vigorously defending Wilde against the charge of being a poseur. He said it was merely living artistically, and it was the duty of everybody to have a conception of themselves, and he intended to conceive of himself.' Yeats noted everywhere about him confirmation of his sense of internal division. But as we have seen, that division had its origin in childhood with a revolt, which could only be a half-revolt, against his father and his father's world. He sought in vain the unself-conscious life which he associated with his mother's family. Hating his father's scepticism, he still could not escape it ; he would have liked to dream the days away, but he also wanted to be a success in the world. The inner struggle was dramatized by his difficulties with sexual desire ; he had a continual battle with his senses and was filled with self-loathing at what he thought was an unnatural and horrible state of mind. Thus many personal factors and many examples, and beyond these the spirit of the times, made him see his life as a quarrel between two parts of his being.

By 1884, according to George Russell, Yeats had already developed a theory of the divided consciousness. About that time he was greatly excited by a drawing of Russell's of a man on a mountain, startled by his own gigantic image in the mist. He used the theme from time to time in his verse, as in the lines about the parrot raging at his own image and the dewdrops listening to the sound of their own dropping, and was going to make it the subject of *The Shadowy Waters*. In the original plan of that play, as told to Russell, ' His hero was a world wanderer trying to *escape from himself*. He surprises a galley in the waters. There is a beautiful woman there. He thinks through love he can escape from himself. He casts a magical spell on Dectora. Then in the original version he found the love created by a spell was an empty echo, a shadow of himself, and he unrolled the spell seeking alone for the world of the immortals.' So far the division was chiefly connected with frustration and filial revolt, but on going to London in May 1887, Yeats found it to be more complex.

He was then almost twenty-two, painfully turned inwards, self-conscious and aware of the vast gulf between what he was in actuality and what he was in his dreams. Eleven years before, Bernard Shaw had made the same crossing of the Irish Sea, and had found similar difficulties in adapting himself. Shaw says, in his preface to his early novel, *Immaturity*, that he was too shy to accept invitations, and therefore hid his timidity under arrogance much as Yeats did : ' Clever sympathetic women might divine at a glance that I was mortally shy ; but people who could not see through my skin, and who were accustomed to respect, and even veneration, from the young, may well have found me insufferable, aggressive, and impudent'. Yeats, without the powerful epigrams with which Shaw drove the English before him, and by nature far more introspective and dreamy, was even more conscious of his own clumsiness. He remembered all his life how Oscar Wilde disapproved of the colour of his shoes, and felt that he was constantly committing *gaffes* :

I was always conscious of something helpless and perhaps even unteachable in my self. I could not hold to my opinions among people who would make light of them, if I felt for those people a sympathy. I was always accusing myself of disloyalty to some absent friend — I had it seemed an incredible modesty. Sometimes this timidity became inexplicable, and [is] still [in]explicable and painful to the memory. Some scholar in seventeenth century French poetry asked me to breakfast with him one Sunday in the Temple, and there was a younger Oxford [man] who shared his rooms. After breakfast I could not bring myself to go, though I wanted to go and though he and his friend to give me a hint began talking of church for which they had perhaps no liking, I was miserable and could not go. I called on some woman an old friend of my Father, and found her engaged with what looked like a committee. I felt certain I should not stay and yet, though I had even had experience with the same symptoms in others, I went away in utter misery when the meeting or whatever it was broke up. I never ventured to call again. Then something happened which by some caprice of the conscience is still the most painful of all my memories — even now I write in the hope of laying it at last. . . . I had introduced as a neophyte of my [magical] order a Dublin friend, a fellow student once at the Art School . . . afterwards somebody said there was an entrance fee of a couple of pounds. He said ' Well if one accepts a thing I suppose one should pay for it ' and laid the money down on the little table. I knew he was poor and that no poor man was ever asked to pay anything and yet I said nothing. I was like a man in nightmare who longs to move and cannot. I knew the woman who had asked him for the money well, and that if I said a word it would be returned and I did not speak. The thought of the moment returns again at night, with most bitter self accusation. I kept picturing him in Paris, where he was going to study and stinted in this or that because of his loss. I thought to send him the money myself, but I never had the money and presently I heard he was dead.

London made his shyness worse. To an Irishman, Yeats said later, ' England is fairyland ', and in the late 'eighties and 'nineties it very nearly was. Besides Madame Blavatsky and her extraordinary converts, the world of letters boasted individualists as remarkable as William Morris, Henley, Wilde, and a host of others who gave London under Victoria a literary atmosphere which it lost under the Edwardians. But to a poor Irishman, longing for recognition, it seemed alien and hostile. Yeats felt insignificant and out of place ; he had little education and not enough studious energy to remedy his lack ; he had published only in Dublin, and his second book of poems was still unfinished. Where Shaw cast his lot decisively for London and resolved to take it whether by storm or siege, Yeats often dreamed of beating a retreat to Sligo, and did, in fact, continually go to stay with his uncle George Pollexfen there. The early letters from the young man to Katharine Tynan, for the time his sole confidant, give a remarkable picture of maladjustment. He is always speaking of ' this hateful London '. ' London is always horrible to me.' ' It can give me nothing. I am not fond of the theatre. Literary society bores me. I loathe crowds. . . .'

Some of his dissatisfaction was caused by external circumstance. His family was very badly off, always poor and sometimes even hungry. Their house at 58 Eardley Crescent, Earl's Court, was drab and confining. Shortly after they arrived in London, his mother suffered a stroke which deprived her of her faculties and made her a permanent invalid for the remaining fourteen years of her life. Yeats would see his father sitting with his head in his hands before the fire, buried in gloom, and felt keenly his own dreamy indolence. He thought of returning to art, but dreaded it too much ; a friend of the family found a job for him, but with a unionist newspaper, and Yeats could not bring himself to accept it. To a considerable extent he buried himself in dreams and in books, and, when Katharine Tynan wrote to rebuke him for his lack of interest in other things, replied defensively :

I must write in this letter no more bookish news as I know you think me too little interested in other things. The real fact of the matter is that the other things at present for many reasons make me anxious and I bury my head in books as the ostrich does in the sand. I am a much more human person than you think. I cannot help being ' unhuman,' as you call it, these times. On the rare occasions when I go to see anyone I am not quite easy in my mind, for I keep thinking I ought to be at home trying to solve my problems — I feel as if I had run away from school. So you see my life is not altogether ink and paper.

He was, in fact, extremely unhappy, and made frequent mention in these letters of his ' dreadful despondent moods '. His desire to abstract himself was constantly thwarted, his worldly ambitions were unsatisfied, his sexual problems unsolved. He often referred to his bad health and even to physical breakdown. In this state he found writing verse, with its demands on intellectual energy and excitement, very difficult, and therefore turned to writing articles. He enjoyed the position of superiority of the critic, and made most of his articles in 1888 and 1889 vigorously nationalist. Like Shaw, who says he felt he ' was in a superior position as an Irishman, without a shadow of any justification for that patriotic arrogance ', Yeats made his Irishry into a refuge and a source of individuality which distinguished him from most of the London writers.

John Butler Yeats feared that his son's creative gifts would be lost in criticism, and urged him, if he could not get in the mood for poetry, to write stories. Into *Dhoya*, accordingly, Yeats put another of his half-symbolical autobiographies. ' Sometimes the barrier between myself and other people filled me with terror ', he wrote many years afterwards, and a little of the terror emerges through the thick enamel of this story. The hero, Dhoya, has from his earliest childhood been a slave, but his fits of passion become so frequent and dangerous that his masters let him go. He makes his home in a cavern on the west coast of Ireland, and falls more and more often into furies, as Yeats into fits of energy and depression, ' though there was no one but his own shadow to rave against '. These furies stop abruptly when he falls in love with a lady from the fairy world, but even with her his happiness is not complete, for she wishes not to love but to be loved. The story ends with her being taken from him, upon which, filled with despair, Dhoya mounts a black steed and plunges over a cliff to his death.

The story has many suggestions of psychological difficulties involving self-distrust, sexual fears, and a desire to burrow away from the world. Most of these Yeats was unconscious of, but in the next story, *John Sherman*, which he wrote in response to his father's demand for a tale about real people, he was fully conscious of what he was doing. In *John Sherman* it is clear that his real subject-matter is himself, and that he has cut himself definitely into two parts. His dreamy nature is symbolized by Sherman, a young man who prefers his little town of Ballah in the west of Ireland to every other place, and is empty of all ambition except to marry a rich woman so that he need do nothing but dream his life away. His counterpart is the energetic Reverend William Howard, a High Church curate, a lover of cities and man of the world. Like Yeats, Sherman is lured off to London for a time, and works as a clerk in his uncle's office there. He at last has the opportunity to marry a rich girl, but knows that with her his dream life is impossible. He therefore cleverly manages to turn his fiancée over to Howard, while he himself goes back to a childhood sweetheart at Ballah. There he will settle down to farming and dreaming.

The antithesis between Sherman and Howard was fairly completely worked out, though Yeats's sympathies were obviously very much on Sherman's side. He knew that he must either go back or go forward : Ballah or Sligo meant rest and peace, which he loved, while London meant turmoil and constant endangerment of his dreams. The traits of the two characters show the nature of the choice as it looked to Yeats at the end of 1888, when he was twenty-three : Sherman is rude and unconventional, while Howard is elegant and decorous ; Sherman is vaguely heterodox, Howard is a High Church curate ; Sherman is devious ; Howard conscientious and candid ; Sherman self-conscious, Howard self-possessed ; Sherman escapist, Howard worldly. Summing up the differences between them, Howard remarks to Sherman, ' Your mind and mine are two arrows. Yours has got no feathers, and mine has no metal on the point.'

When we remember that Yeats is both characters, we see that he himself had made no choice. He was aware of the fact and in the story symbolizes it in a chess game that Sherman plays against himself, right hand against left. Yeats had, in fact, come to that stage which he later described in *A Vision*, where man ' is suspended ; he is without bias,' and ' only a shock resulting from the greatest possible conflict can make the greatest possible change.'

The shock came on January 30, 1889, when Maud Gonne knocked on the door of the family's house. Yeats immediately fell in love, and the question was, which of his two selves should he show her ? He could not use duplicity, he had to show her his inmost heart, so with her he was John Sherman, the wild yet timid dreamer. But at the same time he knew that this ambitious beauty would be satisfied only if he were a master of men as well. The problem is stated in a story he wrote early in the 'nineties, called ' The Wisdom of the King '. A king, having fallen in love with a beautiful princess,

called her to him . . . and told her of her beauty, and praised her simply and frankly as though she were a fable of the bards ; and he asked her humbly to give him her love, for he was only subtle in his dreams. Overwhelmed with his greatness, she half consented and yet half refused, for she longed to marry some warrior who could carry her over a mountain in his arms. . . . He laid down his wisdom at her feet . . . and still she half refused.

In other words, the king shows himself to her as John Sherman, but it is with William Howard that she is prepared to fall in love.

Stated in less metaphorical language, Yeats's dilemma was that he was naturally dreamy, poetic, and self-conscious, and therefore unable to act with the spontaneity of the man of action. But he could not hope to attract Maud Gonne to a farm life in the west of Ireland ; no turning back to Sligo was possible any more. To win her, he would have to be the man of action, organizing and building for Ireland.

But this would be to deny his dreamy, ineffectual self and to play the part of another. Can true love be secured through artifice ? So long as love is unsuccessful it satisfies his dreaming nature ; once it is successful, it is no longer wholly honest. Had Maud Gonne accepted his love, as she did not, he would have feared that she loved him for qualities superimposed upon his natural ones. He imagined himself as trapping her, and was half pleased when she jumped out of the net.

For underneath he knew that his dreaming self was far from perfect ; he thought of himself as full of weaknesses, and felt that if she loved him, unaware of his weaknesses, she would be deceived. The only solution was to love her in vain. Because that intermediate state suited him, he glorified during the 'nineties

all indeterminate things. He would choose finally neither one
state nor the other, neither dream nor act, but the crepuscular
state between spirit and sense, where he was *not committed*. The
twilight demanded no decision. He filled his poems and stories
with dim, pale things, and longed to return to an island like
Innisfree, where his ' old care will cease ' because an island was
neither mainland nor water but something of both, and because
the return to Sligo, though he knew it now to be impossible,
would be a return to the prepubertal stage when his consciousness
had not yet been split in two. He buried himself in his mistress's
hair, or hid in a mystic symbol :

> And his neck and his breast and his arms
> Were drowned in her long dim hair. . . .
>
> Far-off, most secret, and inviolate Rose,
> Enfold me in my hour of hours ; where those
> Who sought thee in the Holy Sepulchre,
> Or in the wine-vat, dwell beyond the stir
> And tumult of defeated dreams ; and deep
> Among pale eyelids, heavy with the sleep
> Men have named beauty.

Whenever he tries to describe that other world which so
fascinates him, connected as it is with his dreams, he hedges.
What happens in Tir-nan-Ogh or the Land of Heart's Desire ?
Do Oisin and Niam sleep together, as in the Irish original, or
merely dance and travel and occasionally kiss ? Yeats will not
say. Sexual intercourse is natural, within the compass of any-
body, and worse still, within the province of that suspect man
of action. Can a unique passion be satisfied by a common
experience ? Do not all natural things wrong her image ' that
blossoms a rose in the deeps of my heart ' ? He prefers the state
of temptation or of half-seduction, with ' Niamh calling *Away,
come away* '.

One wonders how a young man in this state of mind could
act at all. Would not dream cancel out action and action dream ?
As a matter of fact, Yeats's father remarked after the move to

London that his son was spending a great deal of time in bed. But the poet had also evolved a stratagem which prevented him from being inert : he could, when necessary, leave the dreaming Sherman behind and take over the active role of Howard. Under the pressure of his new love he did this more and more often. Tentatively, but with increasing assurance, he adopted the role of Irish revolutionary. To guide himself when he played this part he had the twin doctrines of passion and failure. The great thing in life, as his father had taught him, is to express one's whole passionate self ; hence the active man throws himself with the utmost energy into what he does, and expresses himself always with reckless vehemence and confidence. But life does not reward the man of action with success ; he must end, like Oisin or like the young man in ' The Two Titans ', in failure. He must try to change Ireland or the world, or to win his mistress's favour, and fail, and in failure find apotheosis. Yeats makes a cult of frustration, and courts defeat like a lover.

> I became a man, a hater of the wind,
> Knowing one, out of all things, alone, that his head
> May not lie on the breast nor his lips on the hair
> Of the woman that he loves, until he dies.

So much a part of him did his theories of unsuccessful action and unsatisfied love become that in 1895 and 1896, when a beautiful married woman fell in love with him, he spent the first year in idealized chastity, meeting her only in museums and railway carriages ; and then, when they finally went to bed together, he kept expecting love to end until finally it did, and he returned to his former hopeless adoration of Maud Gonne and to his twilit state between chastity and unchastity. He was too ardent, underneath all his theorizing and idealizing, to be happy in this state, and so his poems are full of vague sorrow. ' I wander by the edge / Of this desolate lake.'

But his life was changing. Maud Gonne was a public figure, and to meet her on her own ground he had to spend far more time on public activities, so that the dream life, even though reinforced with the support of occult lore, became harder to keep intact. In view of the persistent parallelism between Yeats's life and works we should expect to find some reflection of this change in his writings. When he next separates himself into two parts, in some stories written in his thirtieth year, the antinomies are not the same as Sherman and Howard. Now he calls his two characters Michael Robartes and Owen Aherne, symbolic personages who recur in his writings during the rest of his life. Robartes is described as having a face that is ' more like a mask than a face '. His features are ' something between ' those of ' a debauchee, a saint, and a peasant '. He thus reflects Yeats's love affair with the married woman, then well under way, his occult bent and idealism, and his affection for the simpler life of Sligo. Robartes's counterpart, sometimes represented as simply the author, sometimes as Owen Aherne, is a pious Catholic on the verge of becoming a Dominican monk. Aherne is greatly tempted by Robartes, who tries to draw him into his Order of the Alchemical Rose, and thus into a world which fills him with terror. That Aherne is a Catholic is not to be understood as meaning that Yeats himself was strongly attracted to Catholicism ; he used that faith as a convenient symbol of conventional and prudent belief, an example of a traditional refuge which had drawn many converts among people he knew like Dowson, Beardsley, and Lionel Johnson. Catholicism offered a more dramatic contrast to the heterodoxy of Robartesism than Protestantism would have done.

Aherne is always on the verge of giving way to Robartes's temptations but always draws back in time; he is the conventional man, the refusing, abstract self which is counterposed to the daring, mysterious Robartes. Aherne has ' never looked out of the eye of a saint / Or out of drunkard's eye '. He is the public man, as Robartes is the private one. Where in *John Sherman* the title character is obviously the more essential to Yeats's personality, in these stories about Michael Robartes and Owen Aherne it is difficult to know which is primary. While Robartes in many ways resembles Sherman, he is addicted also to that

ceremonialism and ritualism which Yeats had previously attributed not to Sherman but to Howard. In other respects, too, the
opponents are different. Robartes is more active and aggressive,
and yet more full of dreams, than Aherne, who is contemplative
and withdrawn and yet favourable to conventional faiths and
ways. The distribution of characteristics is more complex than
in the earlier tale.

While this change could be interpreted as merely an elaboration of the story-teller's art, Yeats's almost constant use of
autobiographical material suggests that it reflects the change
which had taken place in his life between 1889, when he met
Maud Gonne, and 1896, when he wrote the stories about
Robartes. He was less certain now that he was by nature an
escapist like Sherman, for dreaming and writing poetry had
become more difficult for him now that he was organizing
nationalist groups and to some extent involving himself in Irish
politics. He had become much more independent, too, of his
father, for in the summer of 1895 he moved away from the family
and took rooms with Arthur Symons in Fountain Court ; then
a few months later, when his affair with the married woman began
in earnest, he moved into rooms of his own in Woburn Buildings.
The change is apparent in his letters to his father, which in 1894
still begin ' My dear Papa ', but in 1895 begin ' My dear Father '.
Yeats was the only one of the children to adopt the more formal
style of address.

The alteration within was reflected by an alteration without, in
manners and clothes. The manners were still far from perfect :
when he and Symons visited Edward Martyn at Tullyra Castle
in Galway in 1896, Yeats to Symons's horror proposed that they
toss a coin to see who should get the better room. But in general
he was much more at ease. In 1889 he shaved off the youthful
beard he had worn in Dublin, and changed to a moustache ; by
late 1896 he was clean-shaven. He and Symons resolved to dress
elegantly and inexpensively by wearing black. The pictures of
Yeats at this time show him to be every inch a poet, even to the
point of appearing theatrical. When late in 1893 Katharine Tynan

came to see him, she remarked the new tendency towards ' literary dandyism ' :

In the old Dublin days he was as untidy as a genius newly come from the backwoods. He was an art student then, and generally bore the stains of the studio. . . . He used to affect scarlet ties, which lit up his olive face. They were tied most carelessly. Ordinary young men who had been at school with him, and resented his being a genius, used to say that the carelessness was the result of long effort ; but one never believed them. Now he wears the regulation, London costume, plus a soft hat, and his ties are dark silk, knotted in a soft bow.

Yeats had now a considerable reputation, but nevertheless he continued to see himself as the divided man. He functioned in two spheres of activity, or, one might say, layers of reality. On the one hand he was a prominent public figure in the Irish nationalist movement ; on the other he was, like Robartes, a member of a secret order of occultists. Superficially they had little connection with one another, but he hoped nevertheless to unify them, and was always trying to find some public outlet for his secret work, and some secret group where he could apply his public nationalism. The severed halves of his selfhood, their characters varying with their creator's mounting years and experience, cried out for one another. We shall next survey his activities up to 1903 as Robartes and as Aherne, and then his efforts to combine these fluctuating personages into a well-integrated man.

## CHAPTER VII

# MICHAEL ROBARTES AND THE GOLDEN DAWN

Par ici, vous qui voulez manger
Le lotus parfumé, c'est ici qu'on vendange
Les fruits miraculeux dont votre cœur a faim.

BAUDELAIRE, 'Le Voyage'

ON March 7, 1890, a few months before his expulsion from the Theosophists, Yeats joined the Hermetic Students of the Golden Dawn and was thereby, he tells us, 'shaped and isolated'. This organization was founded in 1888, a year after Madame Blavatsky had founded her lodge, and its presuppositions about God, the universe, and man, were about the same as those of the Theosophists. One could, in fact, belong to both groups at once, as Yeats did for a time. In their procedure, however, the Hermetic Students emphasized the European tradition of Kabbalistic magic rather than the wisdom of the East. Unlike Madame Blavatsky, who continually warned her followers against the dangers of performing 'phenomena', the chiefs of the Golden Dawn encouraged members to demonstrate their power over the material universe. Great emphasis was put upon occult rituals and progressive initiations. Being a much smaller society and having less urge to proselytize, the Golden Dawn also succeeded in maintaining an atmosphere of secrecy far stricter than that of the Theosophical Society's Esoteric Section.

The 'order', as members called it, was one of a congeries of cults which grew up during the nineteenth century in Western Europe. The occult tradition was particularly strong in France, where towards the middle of the century Victor Hugo's friend, the Abbé Constant, who wrote under the name of Éliphas Lévi, awakened considerable interest by a series of books taking up every aspect of *la haute magie*. The core of Lévi's teaching was the Kabbalah, a collection of ancient Hebrew writings which occultists since the Middle Ages have treated as a kind of secret Bible. Besides offering a very complicated method of Biblical exegesis, the Kabbalah presents a cosmogony which has much resemblance to that of Neo-Platonism. The universe is considered to be a series of emanations or *Sephiroth* from an ineffable, boundless source ; the further from the source that the *Sephiroth* go, the cruder they become, until they form the world of matter, which is spirit in its lowest form. During and after the Renaissance many scholars, including Pico della Mirandola and Henry More, were strongly influenced by Kabbalistic doctrine.

In the nineteenth century, under the pressure of the interest in comparative mythology and religion, the Kabbalistic tradition was related in the literature of magic to other traditions. Lévi, for example, claimed to have discovered the secret relationship between the ten *Sephiroth* and the trumps of the ancient Tarot cards. Archaeological discoveries led to an infusion of Egyptian magic, while the Freemasons and Rosicrucians poured some of their legends and rituals into the cauldron. Throughout this farrago of myths and traditions runs the central conviction that the magician can ascend the Sephirotic ladder towards the source of spiritual and material power. He does so not by annihilating his individuality, like the mystic, but by the use of spells and symbols, by memorization and concentration, until at last he raises his mind to that flaming moment when it transcends itself. The mystic tends to exceed the orthodox framework of his faith, but the magician must keep to rituals and to ceremonies handed down by tradition, and proceed methodically with a hieratic, disciplined order.

Occult progress is achieved through study and practice, through self-purification and isolation. Its steps are symbolized by a series of initiations, each of them withdrawing the initiate further from his ordinary self and bringing him, as his mind is winnowed of impurities, more and more powerful and arcane knowledge. He learns to fix his mind, with an intensity previously unknown to him, upon the images he seeks to evoke. He goes about his daily tasks with new resources. He masters the formulae that give Faustian control over nature, and from the pride and isolation of his magic circle he affirms the limitless capacities of the human soul.

Secret societies are usually divided into two parts ; when the initiate has passed through the first part he has so purified, so trained his faculties that his earlier self is said to die. Now he enters on a new life, which is often symbolized by his receiving a new and secret name, and he pursues deeper realities. He can, like Glendower, call spirits from the vasty deep ; he has power to heal, to influence men and things, to transmit his thoughts over great distances. Nothing is now impossible for him, but he may rouse forces which are stronger than he. Evil spirits are ever ready to take advantage of his weaknesses, and the greater the powers he employs the more he is in danger of falling under their influence. While we may share Hotspur's impatience with magic, we must bear in mind that throughout history it has fascinated many intelligent people. Thus the Golden Dawn had prominent scientists, including the Astronomer-Royal of Scotland, and reputable men of letters, such as Arthur Machen and Algernon Blackwood, among its members.

For writers and artists the attraction of magic during the 'eighties and 'nineties was significantly strong. ' Artist, you are a magician ; Art is the great miracle, it alone proves our immortality ', wrote the renowned French magician, the Sâr Péladan. The poet Édouard Dubus visited Stanislas de Guaïta and under his magical influence wrote a play which far exceeded in quality anything he had done before. Enraptured and terror-struck, he exclaimed to a friend, ' Guaïta has enabled me to become a god '. Magic offered to the symbolists, many of whom studied it, a reinforcement of their belief in the power of word or symbol to evoke a reality otherwise inaccessible. ' Every true poet is instinctively an initiate, the reading of grimoires awakens secrets in him which he had always virtually known ', wrote

Charles Morice about the literature of the *fin de siècle*. The feeling of alienation from society, which beset so many artists of this time, caused them to seek spiritual citizenship elsewhere, whether in a realm of art to which they gave mythical autonomy, or in a spiritual realm too real for the mob to understand, where they might rule with their peers in splendid isolation. As the magician Stanislas de Guaïta put it in the preface to his book of poems, *Rosa Mystica*, in 1885 : ' Mysticism ? It is the love of our hearts for the dreams of our brains ; it is what makes the vulgar hate us, what makes us into outlaws ! ' The extreme example is Villiers de l'Isle-Adam's Rosicrucian play, *Axël*, where hero and heroine, both of them magicians, seek complete isolation from life and, to secure it, commit suicide.

By the end of the century Paris was swarming with cults. Jules Bois made a survey of *The Little Religions of Paris* in 1893, and found that they ranged from the Luciferians with their black masses and anti-Pope to the strange votaries of Auguste Comte who worshipped Humanity and used the armchair of Comte's mistress as their altar. But the movement that is most closely connected with the Golden Dawn, as a kind of French counterpart, began in Paris about 1883, when Stanislas de Guaïta, then a very young man, read Éliphas Lévi's *Dogma and Ritual of High Magic*. Guaïta, if we can believe his friend Maurice Barrès, feared that the English were attempting to take over (as a part of their imperial expansion, no doubt) the direction of the occult world, and so, with his friend the Sâr Péladan, he founded in 1888 a *Kabbalistic Order of the Rosy Cross*. He organized his society in the form of a college divided into three parts, which gave degrees in the Kabbalah. In 1890 Péladan seceded to form a schismatic *Order of the Catholic Rosy Cross, of the Temple, and of the Grail* ; his object was to reconcile Rosicrucianism and Catholicism, and to create an order of mages who would have a place in the Church hierarchy just above that of the clergy, the duties of the latter to be restricted to administering the sacraments. Occult battles now raged thick and fierce. In 1892 the Abbé Boullan, an unfrocked priest, accused Guaïta and Péladan of trying by magical means to poison him. Joris-Karl Huysmans rushed into the fray, declaring that Guaïta's black magic, which he had described in his novel *Là-Bas*, was infecting all Paris. Jules Bois also came to Boullan's defence and had inconclusive pistol duels with both Guaïta and Péladan as a result. Even the judicious Mallarmé was drawn into the controversy in the following year when Boullan died suddenly as the result, said his disciples, of a supernatural ambush, ' struck, if not from behind, from a great distance ', by the agency of Péladan and Guaïta. Jules Bois in the pages of *Gil Blas* demanded a full investigation of the causes of Boullan's death, and Huysmans, in a public letter, contended that the affair bore out his claim in *Là-Bas* that Guaïta and the Rosicrucians were practising black magic. Mallarmé, writing of the quarrel in an article in the *National Observer* which Yeats, who was also contributing to the newspaper, must have read, used the occasion to point out the close affinity between the artist and the magician. The writer is an ' enchanter of letters ' ; poetry is ' sorcery '.

Evoking, in an intended shadow, the unvoiced object, by allusive, never by forthright words, which in their turn are reduced to voiceless silence, calls for an endeavour close to that of creating ; it draws its verisimilitude from the fact that the operation is entirely contained within the limit of the idea. Now the idea of an object is put into play solely by the Enchanter of Letters, with such exactitude that it scintillates, indeed, under the illusion of being looked at. Line of verse, stroke incantatory ! and who henceforth will deny to the circle, which ceaselessly rhyme closes and opens, a similarity to the fairy's or the magician's rings amidst the grass.

Yeats took the same position, without any trace of Mallarméan irony, in an essay on ' Magic ' which he wrote in 1901 as a summary of his beliefs :

. . . All men, certainly all imaginative men, must be for ever casting forth enchantments, glamours, illusions. . . . Have not poetry and music arisen, as it seems, out of the sounds the enchanters made to help their imagination to enchant, to charm, to bind with a spell themselves and the passers-by ? . . .

And just as the magician or the poet enchants and charms and binds with a spell his own mind when he would enchant the minds of others, so did the enchanter create or reveal for himself as well as for others the supernatural artist or genius. . . .

I cannot now think symbols less than the greatest of all powers whether they are used consciously by the masters of magic, or half unconsciously by their successors, the poet, the musician, and the artist. . . . Whatever the passions of men have gathered about, becomes a symbol in the great memory, and in the hands of him who has the secret it is a worker of wonders, a caller-up of angels or of devils.

The interest in magic was not, then, so extraordinary as it might first appear, and in the setting of these French developments we can better understand the establishment of the Golden Dawn. That organization claimed very ancient beginnings and shrouded itself in the deepest mystery. To obtain an impression of the early days of the order, we may turn to its first public pronouncement, which appeared in Madame Blavatsky's review, *Lucifer*, on June 15, 1889 :

The Hermetic Students of the Rosicrucian G.D. in the outer.

The chiefs of the Second order fearing that the proceedings of certain men in the Northern Counties of England may by exhibition of pretended powers and Rosicrucian dignities lead students away from the Higher Paths of Mysticism, into Goetic practices, desire that all Fratres and Sorores of the G.D. will accordingly warn the unwary and uninitiated that no such persons hold any warrant from us, or possess our ancient and secret knowledge.

Given forth from the M∴ A∴

of

Sapiens Dominabitur astris
Deo Duce Comite ferro
Non omnis moriar
Vincit omnia veritas.

Published by order of the above : Sapere Aude, Cancellarius in Londinense.

The statement was typical of the hints that were being dropped around London of the new order. No one could guess what lay behind the impressive Latin titles and the pontifical tone.

The defections of several members have now exposed most of the secrets to the light of day. The GD is of course the Golden Dawn. The M∴ A∴ is the Mount Abiegnos, the Sacred Mountain which each Hermetic Student must symbolically climb. The Latin titles have the following equivalents :

| | |
|---|---|
| *Sapiens dominabitur astris* (the wise will rule the stars) | Fräulein Anna Sprengel of Nuremberg, Germany. |
| *Deo Duce Comite ferro* (with God as my leader, the sword as my companion) | S. L. MacGregor Mathers. |
| *Non omnis moriar* (I shall not wholly die) | Dr. W. Wynn Westcott. |
| *Vincit omnia veritas* (truth conquers all) | Dr. William R. Woodman. |
| *Sapere Aude* (dare to be wise) | another secret name of Dr. Westcott. |

Fräulein Sprengel was a German Rosicrucian who was said to have authorized the establishment of the new order. Mathers, Westcott, and Woodman were the triumvirate who governed it. All three were Masons and members of the *Societas Rosicruciana in Anglia* (Rosicrucian Society in England), an offshoot of Freemasonry devoted mainly to antiquarian research, but deeply interested, as Éliphas Lévi mockingly remarked of one of its founders, in ' external manifestations '.

The triumvirate invested the order with all the pomp and ceremony which they had learned in Masonry, and took over from the *Societas Rosicruciana* an elaborate system of grades, and a division into an outer and inner order. The dominating mind was that of MacGregor Mathers, who looked, Yeats says, ' a figure of romance ', and did many things which seemed miraculous. Mathers was a confirmed Celt and had taken the name of MacGregor in honour of an ancestor who fought for James IV of Scotland. His enemies alleged that Mathers considered that he himself was the king, but this Mathers indignantly denied. He apparently believed, however, that James IV was still alive. His wife, the sister of Henri Bergson, was his close collaborator in all his magical work. Mathers was an earnest student of the arcane tradition, and among his writings are translations of the Kabbalah and of the secret book of Abramelin the mage, and a pamphlet on the origin of the Tarot. After about 1894, when he moved to Paris, he acquired considerable reputation in occult circles there, and for a time gave masses for the goddess Isis at the Théâtre Bodinière under the auspices of Jules Bois. In the late 'nineties Mathers became so autocratic that in 1900 the Golden Dawn expelled him, Yeats playing a prominent part in the revolt. The order continued in England without his leadership, and in spite of faction and schism persists to this day. Mathers himself is said to have died a magician's death as the result of a psychic duel with Aleister Crowley, a former disciple, during the first World War.

Yeats joined the order in 1890 because MacGregor Mathers's magical powers deeply impressed him. The poet, in spite of his great interest in visions, had little clairvoyant ability, but early in his acquaintance with Mathers, the magician put the Tantric symbol of fire against his forehead, and Yeats slowly perceived a huge Titan rising from desert sands. He was greatly excited because this form of vision seemed to him to confirm his belief, still unsteady, in the supernatural, and he soon found that he could obtain even more remarkable results by trying Mathers's methods with others, especially with sensitive women. Soon he was experimenting upon all his friends and acquaintances, sometimes with remarkable success. Katharine Tynan mentions several ludicrous failures, but we have no reason to doubt Yeats's word that the symbols would often call up appropriate visions, as when he put a death symbol on the forehead of William Sharp, who without having seen the symbol immediately thought he saw a hearse passing outside. Instead of giving Yeats theories as Theosophy had done, the Golden Dawn gave him the opportunity and method for constant experimentation and demonstration. Yeats spoke of it later as the chief influence upon his thought up to perhaps his fortieth year.

The rituals of the order also fascinated him. Each member

was encouraged to meditate upon the central symbol of the Rose, the exact meaning of which was hard to determine, though it signified mainly the flower of love that blossoms from the cross of sacrifice. Yeats was entirely within his occult rights when, in the apostrophes or prayers — one knows not what to call them — to the rose in his second book of verse, *The Countess Kathleen and Various Legends and Lyrics,* he made it a symbol of beauty, of transcendental love, of mystic rapture, of the inner reality, of divinity. He was following the example of Guaïta, who had written in *Rosa Mystica* :

The Rose that I invite you to pluck — sympathetic friend who turn these pages — does not flower on the shores of far-away countries; and we shall take, if you please, neither the express train nor the transatlantic steamer.

Are you susceptible to a deep emotion of the intellect ? and do your favourite thoughts so haunt you as to give you at times the illusion of being real ? . . . You are then a magician, and the mystic Rose will go of her own accord, however little you desire it, to bloom in your garden.

But many of his friends were worried to see him veering, as they thought, so far from life. To John O'Leary's complaints Yeats replied in July 1892:

Now as to Magic. It is surely absurd to hold me " weak " or otherwise because I choose to persist in a study which I decided deliberately four or five years ago to make next to my poetry, the more important pursuit of my life. Whether it be or be not bad for my health can only be decided by one who knows and not at all by any amateur. The probable explanation however of your somewhat testy post card is that you were out at Bedford Park and heard my father discoursing about my magical pursuits out of the immense depths of his ignorance as to everything that I am doing and thinking. If I had not made magic my constant study I could not have written a single word of my Blake book, nor would *The Countess Kathleen* ever have come to exist. The mystical life is the centre of all that I do and all that I think and all that I write. It holds to my work the same relation that the philosophy of Godwin holds to the work of Shelley and I have allways considered myself a voice of what I believe to be a greater renaesance [*sic*] — the revolt of the soul against the intellect — now beginning in the world.

He was moving deeper into magical practice and theory, associating with magicians, performing invocations of spirits, calling up visionary forms, meditating on the rose. In the preface to the first collected edition of his poems, in 1895, he testified openly (but perhaps too rhythmically to be altogether convincing) to his occult interests :

This book contains all the writer cares to preserve out of his previous volumes of verse. . . . He has printed the ballads and lyrics from the same volume as *The Wanderings of Usheen*, and two ballads written at the same time, though published later, in a section named *Crossways*, because in them he tried many pathways ; and those from the *Countess Cathleen* in a section named *The Rose*, for in them he has found, he believes, the only pathway whereon he can hope to see with his own eyes the Eternal Rose of Beauty and of Peace.

W. B. YEATS

Sligo, March 24th, 1895.

The reason for this unusually bold statement of his position was that through the Golden Dawn he had begun to satisfy his cravings for a religion. He would soon speak more categorically than ever before of the power of the imagination to call up intangible forces, as in letters to Florence Farr in 1901, when he writes : ' All that we do with intensity has an origin in the hidden world, and is the symbol, the expression of its powers, and even the smallest detail in a professedly magical dispute may have significance '. Another statement is even more determined : ' We who are seeking to sustain this greater Order must never forget that whatever we build in the imagination will accomplish itself in the circumstance of our lives '.

To Yeats the order rituals seemed profound and beautiful, and he was particularly moved by the central myth, which was the mystical death and resurrection of the adept. In the earlier grades of the order the candidate was encouraged to think of this myth as primarily a Rosicrucian one : Christian Rosenkreuz, an adept of the fourteenth century, was said to have attained such spiritual perfection that after his death his body lay ' undecayed in tomb '. But in the later grades, as Yeats discovered in 1893, the order no longer spoke of Rosenkreuz but of Christ. In that year he attained the inner order of the Golden Dawn and, in the initiation of the Path of the Portal, he lay down in the tomb, died a symbolic death, and rose reborn in spirit, Christified.

We can only understand the extraordinary power of this strange mixture of paganism and Christianity over Yeats if we remember how dissatisfied he was with himself, how eager to be ' self-born, born anew '. The order dwelt a great deal upon this rebirth of the individual, which was achievable through magical practice and training, and compared it to the alchemical transmutation of base metal into gold, which they considered symbolical of the change of the dross of matter into the pure spirit of the perfected man. Yeats bound himself by a solemn oath to work towards this transmutation, using his order name (Demon Est Deus Inversus — a demon is an inverted god) which was itself an indication of man's dual nature :

[I,] Demon Est Deus Inversus[,] do bind myself that I will to the uttermost lead a pure and unselfish life, and will prove myself a faithful and devoted servant of the Order.

That I will keep secret all things connected with this Order and its secret knowledge from the whole world, equally from him who is a member of the first order of the GD as from an uninitiated person, and that I will maintain the veil of strict secrecy between the First and Second orders. . . . I further solemnly promise and swear that with the Divine permission I will from this day forward apply myself unto the GREAT WORK which is so to purify and exalt my spiritual nature that with the Divine Aid I may at length attain to be more than human, and thus gradually raise and unite myself to my Magus and Divine Genius, and that in this event I will not abuse the great power entrusted to me.

From the attempt to achieve personal transmutation it was but a brief step to the attempt to achieve a more general transmutation. The order taught that its doctrines should affect daily life. Many members of the Golden Dawn felt that they had the additional obligation of becoming ' a perfect instrument for the regeneration of the world '. As Florence Farr said, the true ideal of the adept is ' to choose a life that shall bring him in touch with the sorrows of his race rather than accept the Nirvana open to him ; and like other Saviours of the world, to remain manifested as a living link between the supernal and terrestrial natures '. Thus the golden dawn of the individual's transmutation was closely associated with that of the world's rebirth. MacGregor Mathers talked continually from about 1893 on of the ' imminence of immense wars ', which would precede the golden age, and Yeats even went so far as to collect prophecies of coming wars from many countries. We can see something of his enthusiasm at the prospect of an Armageddon in a letter written in 1896 by Stuart Merrill, who had just made Yeats's acquaintance, to a friend :

Yeats, who has a very clear idea of social questions, and who sees them from a lofty level, favours a union of superior forces for revolutionary action. He envisages revolution after an impending European war, like us all. He has even collected the prophecies of various countries on this subject, and all are agreed that the war will be unleashed during these next years. Oh ! to die before seeing it ! but since we shall see it, let us unite in behalf of the good !

The idea of revolution was of course in the air ; Pre-Raphaelites, esthetes, and socialists were all predicting it ; all hoped to be rid of the Victorian world, but Yeats gave the idea a supernatural slant. In a letter to Florence Farr of December 1895, he asked her, ' has the magical armageddon begun at last ? ' He thought, as he later declared, that ' Our civilization was about to reverse itself, or some new civilization about to be born from all that our age had rejected . . . because we had worshipped a single god it would worship many or receive from Joachim de Flora's Holy Spirit a multitudinous influx '.

These expectations entered into his tales of Michael Robartes, chief of the Order of the Alchemical Rose, which he wrote for the volume of prose stories, *The Secret Rose* (1897) ; they are also to be found in his verse in such lines as, ' Surely thine hour has come, thy great wind blows, / Far-off, most secret and inviolate Rose ? ' The use of a question-mark instead of a period, and the deliberately vague connotation of the rose, are the only indications of the survival of his earlier caution. He had a host of projects, some of them very practical, to bring about the transmutation for which he hoped.

## CHAPTER VIII

# OWEN AHERNE AND THE NATIONALISTS

When Pearse summoned Cuchulain to his side,
What stalked through the Post Office?

YEATS, ' The Statues '

CONCURRENT with Yeats's occult studies, but to his
mind so separate from them as at times to seem almost
the work of another man, were his nationalist activities.
In his first years in the nationalist movement he did not see clearly
what he could do for Ireland. Under O'Leary's influence he half
intended to start up some day a new Young Ireland movement
like that of Thomas Davis forty years before ; it would produce
nationalist literature, too, but of better quality, and would play
a less active role than Davis's group in practical politics, in which
Yeats had no interest. But after he moved with his family to
London in 1887 he gave up for a time, he says, all idea of organizational work. He continued to send Irish ballads as contributions
to O'Leary's newspaper, *The Gael*, and with Katharine Tynan,
Douglas Hyde, and others, put together under O'Leary's aegis
a little book, *Poems and Ballads of Young Ireland*, which appeared
in 1888 as the first sign of a common purpose among the young
Irish writers. The same year Yeats spent his holidays in Sligo
collecting fairy tales, and before 1890 he had edited several small
books of Irish fairy and folk tales. But these efforts were still
tentative.

A literary movement could have had little hope of arousing
popular enthusiasm during the years 1885 to 1890, when Parnell
was at the height of his power and everyone waited expectantly
for him to bring about Irish Home Rule by political methods.
During this period Parnell had complete control over the Irish
Members of Parliament ; they voted as he directed, and operated

as a powerful pressure group. Then in November 1890 Captain O'Shea won a divorce from his wife on the grounds of her adultery with Parnell, and before the year was out the Irish nationalists were divided and Parnell had lost the leadership of the party in the House of Commons. With a quarrelling representation in Parliament, Ireland could no longer expect favourable action on a Home Rule bill. All the patriotism which Parnell's earlier successes had encouraged was now ready to be diverted elsewhere.

From hateful London Yeats watched Parnell's last stand with enthusiasm. ' This Parnell business ', he wrote O'Leary after the divorce case, ' is most exciting. Hope he will hold on, as it is he has driven up into dust & vacuum no end of insincerities. The whole matter of Irish politics will be the better of it.' On Parnell's death in October 1891, he hastily wrote a poem, ' Mourn — and then Onward ', predicting that the nationalist movement should not now turn backwards.[1] He seems to have grasped instinctively that the time had come for him to act, and he had a new reason for wanting to work for Ireland on a larger scale than before. This impulsion came from his first meeting with Maud Gonne on January 30, 1889, a meeting which rever-

---

[1] The poem was published in the newspaper *United Ireland* on October 10, 1891 :

MOURN — AND THEN ONWARD

Ye on the broad high mountains of old Eri,
    Mourn all the night and day,
The man is gone who guided ye, unweary,
    Through the long bitter way.

Ye by the waves that close in our sad nation
    Be full of sudden fears,
The man is gone who from his lonely station
    Has moulded the hard years.

Mourn ye on grass-green plains of Eri fated,
    For closed in darkness now
Is he who laboured on, derided, hated,
    And made the tyrant bow.

Mourn — and then onward, there is no returning,
    He guides ye from the tomb ;
His memory now is a tall pillar, burning
    Before us in the gloom.

berated in his life like the sound of a Burmese gong in the middle of a tent. Three records of this dramatic event have survived ; the first, dated the same day, is an entry in the diary of Yeats's sister, Elizabeth :

Jan. 30. . . . Miss Gonne, the Dublin beauty (who is marching on to glory over the hearts of the Dublin youths), called to-day on Willie, of course, but also apparently on Papa. She is immensely tall and very stylish and well dressed in a careless way. She came in a hansom all the way from Belgravia and kept the hansom waiting while she was here. Lily noticed that she was in her slippers. She has a rich complexion and hazel eyes and is, I think, decidedly hand-some. I could not see her well as her face was turned from me. . . .
Jan. 31. Willie dined at Miss Gonne's tonight.

Yeats had just published *The Wanderings of Oisin and Other Poems*, and Maud Gonne had already read it, as he discloses in a letter to Katharine Tynan of January 31 :

Miss Gonne (you have heard of her, no doubt) was here yesterday with introduction from the O'Leary's ; she says she cried over ' Island of Statues ' fragment, but altogether favoured the Enchantress and hated Nachina. Did I tell you that William Morris likes the book greatly. . . .

The following day, February 1, he writes to O'Leary with greater elation :

Miss Gonne came to see us the day before yesterday. I dined with her & her sister & cousin last night. She is not only very handsome but very clever. Though her politics in European matters be a little sensational — she was fully persuaded that Bismarck had poisoned or got murdered the Austrian King or prince or what was it ? who died the other day. It was pleasant however to hear her attacking a young military man from India who was there, on English rule in India. She is very Irish, a kind of ' Diana of the Crossways.' Her pet monkey was making, much of the time, little melancholy cries at the hearthrug — the monkeys are degenerate men, not man's ancestors, hence their sadness & look of boredom & old age. There were also two young pigeons in a cage, whom I mistook for sparrows. It was you, was it not, who converted Miss Gonne to her Irish opinions. She herself will make many converts.

Neither of the young nationalists knew at the time, he being twenty-three and she twenty-two, what kind of project was possible, but both wanted to do something for their country. Yeats thought at first, when she confided to him her interest in the theatre, that he would satisfy his nationalist ambitions and hers by a series of dramas on Irish subjects which she would act on the Dublin stage. He had long intended to write a play on the Countess Kathleen O'Shea, subject of a west of Ireland folk tale. But Maud Gonne's flamboyant spirit was not to be put down so quietly ; she was looking, he wrote long afterwards, for some heroic action to consecrate her youth.

No ordinary career would have seemed adequate for Maud Gonne. She was said to be the most beautiful woman in Ireland, six feet tall, with the carriage of a goddess, and features at once perfect and full of charm. She had been brought up in the atmosphere of the Viceregal court, her father an officer in the British garrison in Dublin, but the spectacle of evictions of poverty-stricken Irish tenants by absentee English landlords had roused in her an unquenchable nationalism. Did she dream of becoming an Irish Joan of Arc ? Men began, at any rate, to see a resemblance. Yeats half thought that his mission was to make Ireland ready so that she might become, as he said to her, ' the fiery hand of the intellectual movement '. In a manuscript book of poems which he began to keep for her, he declared his belief in her messianic role explicitly :

> No daughter of the Iron Times,
> The Holy Future summons you ;
> Its voice is in the falling dew,
> In quiet starlight, in these rhymes,
> In this sad heart consuming slow ;
> Cast all good common hopes away
> For I have seen the enchanted day
> And heard the morning bugles blow.

Maud Gonne was, like Yeats, a romantic, which meant that she shared his ignorance of economics, history, sociology, and politics, but her devotion to the Irish cause was as fierce as his.

Like him, she thought of Ireland as the Shan Van Vocht, the poor old woman who had lost her four green fields ; they must be won back somehow, and she was not afraid of using war as the means. Yeats was vaguer about the means ; he was certainly less sympathetic to the idea of violence, and seems to have thought, in so far as he pondered the subject at all, that a concerted wave of opinion, the whole country fully united, would drive England from Ireland as a magician exorcizes an evil spirit. To accomplish this purpose the best men must be influenced, and in 1891 Yeats introduced Maud Gonne to the Golden Dawn, with the eventual object of carrrying on with her in Ireland a secret spiritual propaganda for the most profound minds only.

He soon realized that such a propaganda might not be sufficient to affect events, and shortly before Parnell's death in 1891 he decided to form literary societies. In his plans, he later confessed self-deprecatingly, ' there was much patriotism, and more desire for a fair woman '. He speaks in the first draft of his *Autobiographies* of how he justified his plans to his ' nervous mocking self by saying that Ireland which could not support a critical press must find a substitute. A moment later that nervous self would convict me of insincerity and show me that I was seeking a field of work that would not be demoralizing as I thought that even the most necessary politics were, not for all but mostly for her. . . .' Like other young men, he wanted to prove his courage and strength to his beloved and to himself. But we should not allow his own confession of a multiplicity of motives to blind us to the larger idealism which animated all that he did for his country.

At first he worked through a revived Young Ireland society with which he persuaded many smaller organizations to amalgamate, and we find him writing to O'Leary of Maud Gonne in 1891 : ' Help her to help on the Young Ireland League for what she needs is some work of that kind in which she could lose herself & she is so far enthusiastic about the League. Oldham who does not believe in it will probably try to damp her ardour.' But gradually the need for a group with a new name became evident. Yeats showed himself surprisingly practical and persuasive. With T. W. Rolleston he formed at the end of December 1891 the Irish Literary Society of London, and five months later, on May 24, 1892, he founded with John O'Leary's aid the National Literary Society in Dublin. The immediate object was to publicize the literature, folklore, and legends of Ireland. Young men who were bewildered by Captain O'Shea's divorce, and the split among nationalists that followed it, flocked to a movement which did not require them to take sides in the Parnell dispute and had no direct interest in politics. The nationalist press, whether Parnellite or anti-Parnellite, backed the movement solidly.

The success of the new societies in attracting members was extraordinary, and various projects were quickly developed. On Yeats's instigation the National Literary Society decided in September 1892 to stimulate interest in Irish things by starting small branch lending libraries throughout the country. These would serve as centres for national feeling as well as for education. Maud Gonne toured the country to start up the lending libraries, and founded three out of the seven that were eventually formed. Yeats planned to send a small travelling theatre to the library towns to perform plays on patriotic subjects, the first of which was to be on Robert Emmet. ' For the only time in my life I was a popular personage.'

The popularity could not last. Irish nationalism, developed by seven hundred years of hatred of the occupying authority, was exceedingly difficult to bridle. Yeats did not want his movement to be remembered, like that of Young Ireland, for fervour rather than talent. With all the vagueness of his intentions, he was sure of one thing, that Irish literature must not fall a prey to mere shibboleths, to what he later used to call the Shamrock and the Pepperpot. He was tormented by the fear that ' delicate qualities of mind ' might be destroyed in a mob movement. Fortunately he did not take up the alternative of art for art's sake, which would have excluded nationality from literature. If any generalized statement of his intentions during the early stages

of the movement may be made, it would be that he wanted art
to be dedicated to the service of heroic dreams, and that in Ireland
the dreams must be Irish ones.  With this conviction in mind,
he fought continually for a literary movement of the future
rather than of the past.  The new writers who wanted to deal with
Irish subjects without being fettered by catchwords found in
Yeats a defender and protector, and in the shelter of the courageous battle he waged by speech and written word against both
unionist indifference and the sanctified misconceptions of nationalism, an Irish literary renaissance began.

It is hard for anyone living outside of Ireland to understand
the kind of battles that had to be fought.  Yeats was surrounded
in the literary societies by men like the eloquent barrister, J. F.
Taylor, who thought that to dislike the poetry of Thomas
Davis or Thomas Moore was a kind of high treason, and by
Sir Charles Gavan Duffy, a leader of the Young Ireland movement of the 'forties, who had published in his youth an anthology
of poetry by Irish writers called *The Spirit of the Nation*, and
during forty-five years had never altered his conviction of the
greatness of the poems he had chosen.  Duffy, lately returned
from Australia with a knighthood, had a famous name and was
hard to deal with.  As for Taylor, Yeats noticed not only his
power to sway the multitude but also that the moving rhetoric
with which Taylor exalted bad writers was beginning to influence
Maud Gonne's thought, and the poet was jealous.

The fight began at the end of 1892 on the issue of choosing
books for the Irish libraries.  Yeats protested against the number
of books on Irish oratory, for he saw the potential danger to
style of disseminating old-fashioned rhetoric as the model for
young writers.  Taylor took the protest as an affront to his own
oratorical skill, and we can be sure that Yeats was at no pains to
conciliate him.  The barrister was supported by Sir Charles
Gavan Duffy and a group of young poetasters of the Pan-Celtic
Society, whom Yeats had antagonized because of some harsh
criticism of their work or of their Young Ireland models.  John
O'Leary and a group of young men who followed his judgment

supported Yeats, and the quarrels raged bitterly between the two factions, now on the issue of oratory, now on the quality of Young Ireland verse :

At some of our committee meetings questions, perhaps of merits of ' The Spirit of the Nation ' a volume of political verse then in its 50th edition, would often put our proper business aside, and passions rose so high at times behind Taylor and myself — O'Leary taking my side — that I have known strangers drawn by sport or sympathy to step into the room, and nobody have a mind disengaged enough to keep them out. The clever and better educated of those opposed to me did not think the literature of Young Ireland very satisfactory, but it was all Ireland had they said, and if we were to admit the defects England would take advantage of the admission. The argument would raise me to fury. . . . Others who believed perhaps as indeed thousands did ' The Spirit of the Nation ' was as great lyric poetry as any in the world would then say that I disliked it because I was under English influence — the influence of English decadent poets perhaps and I would reply that it was these, who lived with an argument over rights and wrongs, who could not escape from England even in their dreams. I took it all with a seriousness that amuses my more tolerant years.

Now a more important issue than that of the lending libraries arose. Yeats had formed a scheme of issuing a series of books of Irish interest with the two literary societies, in Dublin and London, as sponsors. T. Fisher Unwin had consented to publish them, and plans were going forward late in 1892 and early in 1893. Suddenly, before Yeats had been able to complete preparations, the scheme was taken out of his hands by Sir Charles Gavan Duffy. Yeats knew that Duffy's tastes, half a century out of date, would destroy the enterprise, and so fought savagely and with youthful tactlessness to regain control. But Duffy was stubborn, and as had been feared carried the New Irish Library to disaster.

Meanwhile Maud Gonne had found more exciting work in helping to prevent peasants' evictions. She disappointed Yeats by not taking sides in his quarrel with Taylor and Duffy ; he did not realize that from her point of view the production of good literature could be only a subordinate object. He resented the fact that she was now devoting her energies to trivialities like elections when he thought the forces he had set in motion made all political manœuvring insignificant. They quarrelled just before she went to France and he to Sligo, towards the middle of 1893. On his return to Dublin a few months later, he heard from O'Leary that the young men had turned against him. ' They repeated Taylor's continual attacks on my ignorance. I knew little of Burke, Swift, Grattan, and nothing of history, and the authors I did know, Blake, Keats, Shelley, and all the romantic school, they ignored or despised.' On O'Leary's telling him that he could do no more in Dublin for the present, Yeats departed for London in temporary despair.

He changed his scene but not his interest. From 1894 to 1899, when he began the Irish dramatic movement, London was his base for Irish work even though he made many trips to Dublin. He lectured to the Irish Literary Society in London and persuaded his scholarly friend Lionel Johnson to take part in it and give the movement intellectual backing. The three great volumes which Johnson announced that he was working on, dealing with ' Catholic ethics ', ' Catholic aesthetics ', and ' Catholic politics ', would keep the movement from seeming unscholarly and Protestant. Yeats was beginning to see more distinctly that his own role in the revival was to set standards for it ; he attempted to do this in part by his creative work, and in part by compiling, in 1894, *A Book of Irish Verse*, in which he set down formally and without bellicosity his opposition to the Taylor-Duffy school of criticism. He gave more space to Douglas Hyde, William Allingham, and Sir Samuel Ferguson than he gave to the old favourites of true-blooded Irishmen, Davis and Moore. The preface was modest and ingratiating :

This book is founded upon its editor's likes and dislikes, and everything it contains has given him pleasure. . . . He asks any patriotic critic, who is given to anger, to remember that he had only his temperament for a chart, and that the seas of literature are distraught with storms and currents, and full of the wrecks of Irish anthologies.

For the moment he had no new project on foot. He thought

much about Maud Gonne, and early in 1894 wrote *The Land of Heart's Desire* about her, thinking that what had caused her quarrel with him must be her longing ' for some impossible life, for some unwearying land like that of the heroine of my play '. He made numerous speeches to the Irish Literary Society in London.  Part of his task was, as we have noticed, to keep the movement intellectually respectable, and it was about this time or earlier that he ' had some difficulty in preventing our council . . . accepting a circular that began with the words " Ireland despite the dramatic genius of our people has had no dramatist like Shakespeare but a sub-committee of the Irish Literary Society has decided that the hour has come " '.  His own speeches were violent in their own way ; he attacked the unionists for aping English tastes, he attacked utilitarianism which he used like Carlyle as synonymous with materialism and English civilization, and he exalted patriotism and heroism.  He had his cult of passion to help him to cover his inner timidity with audacity ; on one occasion he gave a lecture in which he justified Swift's alleged use of false figures in *The Drapier's Letters* on the grounds that certain daimon-possessing men have been sent by God to utter ' truths of passion, that were intellectual falsehoods '.  Such talk was violent enough so that a judge resigned from the Society because of it.

Though his public speeches at this period were wilfully immoderate, Yeats was acquiring great skill as a speaker ; and at meetings of committees he was particularly expert in dominating. He astonished those who thought of him as an idle dreamer by his brilliant manœuvring, especially, as Bernard Shaw later remarked, in complicated situations.

Late in 1896 he entered into a different sort of nationalist work. About that time he was invited to join the Irish Republican Brotherhood.  The Brotherhood had been formed long before to bring about Irish independence, if necessary, by violent means, but at the time Yeats joined, though it occasionally sentenced enemies to death, the sentences were not carried out.  John O'Leary exercised a restraining hand upon its Dublin branch.

Yeats realized, however, that he might become involved in 'some wild conspiracy', but his despairing love for Maud Gonne had brought him to the point, he says, where he 'had come to need excitement, forgetfulness', and was 'ready for the sacrifice' if it proved necessary. The man who had asked him to join saw him through a ceremonious initiation, then resigned in a fright. Yeats stayed on.

At first he was not active, but at the end of 1896 he began to work with the Brotherhood to prepare the way for a centennial celebration for Wolfe Tone, and to gather funds for a proposed monument for him. The real purpose was to stage the greatest possible mass demonstration against British rule in Ireland. Maud Gonne had plans to go to America to collect money for the project by a lecture tour, but news came to her in Paris that the Dublin section of the I.R.B. had refused to authorize her trip. Yeats had been in France helping her to start up a Young Ireland society there, but he now returned to London, called a meeting of the London I.R.B. in his rooms, and had the necessary authorization passed.

The reason for the differences between London and Dublin branches of the I.R.B. was, he discovered, that they had taken opposite sides over the rights and wrongs of a political murder in America. He had a sensible impatience of internecine quarrels of this kind and managed to remain aloof from this particular quarrel. He thought that unity must be obtained above all else, and therefore formed a grandiose plan of using the Dublin Wolfe Tone Centennial Committee, which was an I.R.B. front organization, as a central council to bring together the two I.R.B. factions, Parnellites and anti-Parnellites, and any other groups he could persuade to join. The Dublin Committee would then proclaim itself an Irish Parliament, give orders to the Irish M.P.'s as their representatives in the British Parliament, and eventually declare Ireland's complete independence.

It was a time of impossible plans and this one was no more impossible than most. Yeats had a position of importance in the national as well as the literary movement — at that time it was difficult to distinguish between them — because he could claim with sincerity to be above factionalism. Having no label himself, he could mediate among those who did. Since his influence was greater in London than in Dublin, he had himself elected president of the '98 Centennial Association of Great Britain and France, as the English group was grandiloquently called. He secured a promise from a party of lukewarm unionists led by Lord Castletown to come into his projected Dublin council, and the nationalist politicians, he was sure, would have to join. Extremists would come in too if the council let it be known ' that it was ready to adopt unconstitutional means if it should seem at any time that success lay that way '. But his hope was that the existence of a body representing all, or almost all, Ireland would make force unnecessary. If they were faced by a unified front, the English would give way.

While he was developing these plans he went with Maud Gonne to Dublin in 1897 for Queen Victoria's Jubilee ; they were determined to make clear that the Queen's popularity did not extend to Irish soil. Maud Gonne delivered an incendiary speech to the crowd, telling how she had tried to decorate the graves of the Manchester Martyrs (Irishmen hanged for revolutionary activity thirty years before), and had been refused permission because of the Jubilee. ' In a low voice that yet seemed to go through the crowd ', she said, ' " Must the graves of our dead go undecorated because Victoria has her Jubilee ? " and the whole crowd went wild.' A riot started, and Maud Gonne wanted to join the rioters, but Yeats, to her great irritation, prevented her. He feared for her safety and for what might happen to his plans for an Irish Parliament if the crowd saw its Joan of Arc.

Preparations for the memorial to Wolfe Tone went ahead full blast. At last the demonstration was held, and, in the huge procession which marched to the laying of the cornerstone, all factions were represented as Yeats had hoped. By this time he knew, however, that his greater scheme had failed ; the Dublin council was composed of small politicians who shouted down their opponents and were quite incapable of taking political leadership or of forming the Irish Parliament he had wished to establish. But the Wolfe Tone celebration was an important factor in the healing of the split among the Irish Members of Parliament a year and a half later, and Yeats deserves some share of the credit for canalizing the public pressure which brought the two parties together.

After 1898 Yeats gradually dropped out of active politics and his nationalism became more purely literary. He had spent nine years of intense organizational work, at the expense of his art and his health, in an attempt to attain his goal, which was O'Leary's also, of a heroic, united nation. The adjectives are vague ; he had nothing to say about economic questions and little about practical politics. He was not concerned with the introduction of new Irish Home Rule bills in Parliament. His purpose was more general. 'When I started my movement', he wrote, 'I said to myself that I wanted to stiffen the backbone.' Not only Ireland's, we may surmise, but his own. He believed with O'Leary that no cause was worth winning if it had to be supported by demagogic arguments. When his colleagues in the national movement spoke, as Maud Gonne was beginning to, of their hatred of England, Yeats tried to transmute it into a hatred of the materialism that was associated with England. When the Taylors and Duffys praised excessively the works of the Young Ireland poets, Yeats brought to bear upon them higher canons of taste. Unlike his colleagues, he did not expect to be successful in the near future or even in his own lifetime ; the main thing, therefore, was to wage the struggle as heroically as possible. His rather misty but always heroic position is set forth in a speech he gave to a Wolfe Tone banquet in London on April 13, 1898 :

What I want to impress on all is that these '98 Celebrations are not going to pass away and be forgotten. My interest in them is that they will bring the union of the Gael nearer by persuading all parties and sections to work for a common object. We have struggled to keep from being identified with any party, and I think we have succeeded (*hear, hear*). This year will do much, not only for union, but much to reawaken our country after a great disillusionment. The political movement which has just passed away did some things that had to be done, but it left Ireland rent in pieces and full of an intense scepticism. It was utilitarian, and the Celt, never having been meant for utilitarianism, has made a poor business of it. . . .

He loves to roll the heroic names over his tongue :

Ireland is coming to her own and better self. She is turning to the great men of her past — to Emmet and Wolfe Tone, to Grattan and to Burke, to Davis and to Mitchel, and asking their guidance (*cheers*). She is turning, too, to subtler sources of national feeling than are in politics. . . . We hated at first the ideals and ambitions of England, the materialisms of England, because they were hers, but we have come to hate them with a nobler hatred (*applause*). We hate them now because they are evil. We have suffered too long from them, not to understand, that hurry to become rich, that delight in mere bigness, that insolence to the weak are evil and vulgar things. No Irish voice, trusted in Ireland, has been lifted up in praise of that Imperialism [of the Boer War] which is so popular just now, and is but a more painted and flaunting materialism ; because Ireland has taken sides for ever with the poor in spirit who shall inherit the earth (*cheers*). . . . We are building up a nation which shall be moved by noble purposes and to noble ends. A day will come for her, though not, perhaps, in our day. There is an old story that tells how sometimes when a ship is beaten by storm and almost upon the rocks, a mysterious figure appears and lays its hand upon the tiller. It is Mannanan, the son of Lir, the old god of the waters. So it is with nations, a flaming hand is laid suddenly upon the tiller (*loud applause*).

This speech sets no date for the revolution ; in fact the whole question of when and how liberty is to be attained is burked by the final metaphor. Mannanan is the *deus ex machina* whose sudden descent enables the poet to avoid the question, what is to be done this week or next ? One feels even that direct revolutionary action would be but a feeble response to this young man's idealism. The speech contains almost as much asbestos as flame.

In many of his struggles with extremists during the 'nineties Yeats would say that no one should discuss national issues unless

he could describe his Utopia. His own Utopia is pictured in a
speech which he gave in New York in 1904. It shows the effect
of Ruskin's *Unto This Last*, which deeply impressed Yeats as a
young man of twenty-three or twenty-four, and of William
Morris's *News from Nowhere* and the Fabian Socialists with whom
Yeats came in contact in the late 'eighties at Morris's house :

What is this nationality we are trying to preserve, this thing that
we are fighting English influence to preserve ? It is not merely our
pride. It is certainly not any national vanity that stirs us on to activity.
If you examine to the root a contest between two peoples, two nations,
you will always find that it is really a war between two civilizations,
two ideals of life. First of all, we Irish do not desire, like the English,
to build up a nation where there shall be a very rich class and a very
poor class. Ireland will always be in the main an agricultural country.
Industries we may have, but we will not have, as England has, a very
rich class nor whole districts blackened with smoke like what they call
in England their 'Black Country'. I think that the best ideal for our
people, an ideal very generally accepted among us, is that Ireland is going
to become a country where, if there are few rich, there shall be nobody
very poor. Wherever men have tried to imagine a perfect life, they
have imagined a place where men plough and sow and reap, not a place
where there are great wheels turning and great chimneys vomiting
smoke. Ireland will always be a country where men plough and sow
and reap.

So far Ruskin and Morris ; the rest is more characteristically
Yeatsian :

And then Ireland too, as we think, will be a country where not
only will the wealth be well distributed but where there will be an
imaginative culture and power to understand imaginative and spiritual
things distributed among the people. We wish to preserve an ancient
ideal of life. Wherever its customs prevail, there you will find the
folk song, the folk tale, the proverb and the charming manners that
come from ancient culture. In England you will find a few thousands
of perfectly cultivated people, but you will find the mass of the people
singing songs of the music hall. . . . In Ireland alone among the
nations that I know you will find, away on the Western seaboard, under
broken roofs, a race of gentlemen keep alive the ideals of a great time
when men sang the heroic life with drawn swords in their hands.

The isle will contain not socialists, but heroes, as Nietzschean as Celtic:

> Yes, we desire to preserve into the modern life that ideal, a nation of men who will . . . remember always the four ancient virtues as a German philosopher has enumerated them : First, honesty amongst one's friends. Second, courage amongst one's enemies. Third, generosity amongst the weak. Fourth, courtesy at all times whatsoever. . . . We seek to keep that old life living by keeping Irish living, and we seek to spread it where Irish is lost by putting it into plays and poems for those who only know English. . . . We all hope that Ireland's battle is drawing to an end, but we must live as if it were to go on endlessly. We must so live that we will make that old noble kind of life powerful amongst our people. We must be careful that we shall pass it on, fed by our example and not weakened by our example. It is not only necessary to be effective in one's own day, to be effective in the life and the politics of the hour, but it is even more necessary to do one's work in that day, in those politics, in that thought, so that we will pass on into the future the great moral qualities that give men the strength to fight, the strength to labour. It may be that it depends upon us to call up into life the phantom armies of the future. If we keep that thought always before us, if we never allow ourselves to forget those armies, we need have no fear for the future of Ireland.

How effective are these speeches as political oratory ? Today they seem very vague indeed, but Yeats was combating, beside the British, a type of nationalism which was also vague and to him pernicious as well, because it encouraged mass hatred and postulated that the ousting of the enemy would automatically make Ireland an earthly paradise. Yeats could not agree that the ends were more important than the means. He constantly ennobled the issues by trying, in accordance with his heroic ideal, to improve Ireland as well as to liberate her. But he could only maintain his position by continual conflict with uncomprehending extremists, and after the turn of the century, though he remained a patriot, he became isolated and embittered.

## CHAPTER IX

# SEARCH FOR UNITY

## I. AN IRISH MYSTICAL ORDER

HAD Yeats actually been the two persons he liked to imagine himself to be, the last two chapters would have supplied a comprehensive picture of his intellectual history during the 'nineties. But to divide oneself consciously into two parts implies that there is a *tertium quid* which does the dividing, and Yeats was fully aware that he was more than a partnership of mage and patriot. As a creative writer he could not afford to be completely possessed by any of his non-literary interests ; what he hoped to do, and increasingly succeeded in doing, was to mould both occultism and nationalism into his art. No sooner had he pulled himself into two parts and set them at odds than he wanted to make peace between them, seeking the centre that he fled from in a continual competition with himself.

This desire to fuse his interest occupied Yeats's mind a great deal. In 1919, reminiscing about his youth, he said that when he was twenty-three or twenty-four, ' this sentence seemed to form in my head, without my willing it, much as sentences form when we are half-asleep : " Hammer your thoughts into unity ". For days I could think of nothing else, and for years I tested all I did by that sentence.' The statement is a little too pat for us to give it complete credence, but his writings during the 'nineties mention unity often enough so that we can believe that he did, as he said, consciously work towards it.

The search for unity was in part defensive. Yeats was not sufficiently self-confident to disregard the continual condemnation of his interests by his father and many of his friends. John

Butler Yeats considered occultism to be absurd, and thought that his son was wasting in patriotic organizations energy which would better have gone into his poetry. Sometimes they came almost to blows over their theories. The son defended himself vigorously, but he felt the criticism keenly because his ' nervous mocking self ' was telling him the same things. Resisting his own scepticism, he set out to prove the value of his interests by showing that they informed both the spirit and subject-matter of his literary work. If he could demonstrate that everything he did was integrally part of his art and life, he would have more than adequate justification for occupations that might otherwise be held to be capricious.

We can see his efforts at combination very early. Most of what he writes becomes rather ostentatiously Irish and occult. Thus in 1888 he makes a collection of fairy tales in which he asserts that the Irish peasants, because of their distance from the centres of the Industrial Revolution, have preserved a *rapport* with the spiritual world and its fairy denizens which has elsewhere disappeared. He makes speeches declaring his belief in the fairies, though if hard pressed he will say that he believes in them as ' dramatizations of our moods '. In 1889 he begins *The Countess Cathleen*, which deals with a countess who sells her soul to the devil rather than permit Irish peasants to starve. Here he has united the Faustian pact with a nationalist description of Irish poverty under English rule. A later play, written in 1894, *The Land of Heart's Desire*, also brings the fairy kingdom, and thus the occult world, into contact with peasant Ireland.

From 1889 to 1893 Yeats was involved with Edwin Ellis, a minor painter and poet, in a three-volume edition of Blake's works, with a memoir and interpretation of the symbolism. He was pleased to find that Blake's ideas harmonized with those of the Theosophists and the Hermetic Students of the Golden Dawn, for he had now the authority of a great poet for using occult material. But he went farther still. On the shakiest evidence he persuaded himself that Blake's father, James Blake, had been born James O'Neil, an Irishman. Blake ' was, before all things,

an O'Neil', Yeats wrote. His writing ' has an Irish flavour '.
Erin has ' one of the highest places ' in *Jerusalem*. Next he
even suggested that Blake was a fellow-member of the Golden
Dawn :

It is possible that he received initiation into an order of Christian
Kabalists then established in London, and known as ' The Hermetic
Students of the G.D.' Of course this conjecture is not susceptible of
proof. He would have said nothing about such initiation even if he
had received it. The ' students ' in question do not name themselves
or each other, and the subject of their study is nothing less than
universal magic.

Blake, in short, bore an astonishing resemblance to Yeats, extending even to his initials (W. B. and W. B. Y.), and Blake had
succeeded in being Irish, mystical, and poetic. Here was a lofty
justifying precedent.

At the end of *The Countess Kathleen and various Legends and
Lyrics* Yeats put a direct statement in verse of his claim to be
considered as a poet in the Irish tradition, mystical interests and
all, on the ground that Ireland had always been a mystical land.
The argument is rather blurred but shows that he felt the necessity
of defending himself and that he intended to hold fast :

### APOLOGIA ADDRESSED TO IRELAND
### IN THE COMING DAYS

Know that I would accounted be
True brother of that company
Who sang to sweeten Ireland's wrong,
Ballad and story, rann and song ;
Nor be I any less of them,
Because the red rose bordered hem
Of her whose history began
Before God made the angelic clan,
Trails all about the written page,
For in the world's first blossoming age
The light fall of her flying feet
Made Ireland's heart begin to beat,
And still the starry candles flare
To help her light foot here and there,

And still the thoughts of Ireland brood
Upon her holy quietude.

Nor may I less be counted one
With Davis, Mangan, Ferguson,
Because to him who ponders well
My rhymes more than their rhyming tell
Of the dim wisdoms old and deep,
That God gives unto man in sleep.
For round about my table go
The magical powers to and fro.
In flood and fire and clay and wind,
They huddle from man's pondering mind,
Yet he who treads in austere ways
May surely meet their ancient gaze.
Man ever journeys on with them
After the red rose bordered hem.
Ah, fairies, dancing under the moon,
A druid land, a druid tune !

While still I may I write out true
The love I lived, the dream I knew.
From our birthday until we die,
Is but the winking of an eye.
And we, our singing and our love,
The mariners of night above,
And all the wizard things that go
About my table to and fro,
Are passing on to where may be,
In truth's consuming ecstasy,
No place for love and dream at all,
For God goes by with white footfall.
I cast my heart into my rhymes,
That you in the dim coming times
May know how my heart went with them
After the red rose bordered hem.

To state his combined nationalist and occult principles in
verse was not enough ; he must organize a group to support
them. We have seen how as early as 1891 he had thought of
starting a secret spiritual propaganda in Ireland with the aid of

Maud Gonne. Though he had temporarily abandoned the idea, it remained in his mind, and became suffused with vague theories of druidic worship and of the Celtic revival which were floating about France and the British Isles during the 'nineties. Might it not be possible to revive an ancient form of worship, not, of course, in its original form, but by combining druidism perhaps with Christianity as the Golden Dawn had combined Rosicrucianism with Christianity ? He was convinced, he says, ' that all lovely and loving places were crowded with invisible beings, and that it would be possible to communicate with them '. The direction of his thoughts can be seen in the stories of Michael Robartes which he wrote in 1896. Of one of these, ' The Adoration of the Magi ', he informed Fiona Macleod that he especially wanted her opinion, because it was ' a half-prophecy of a very veiled kind '. Some sort of cult is about to be born, and there is even the suggestion of a new annunciation ; ' another Leda would open her knees to the swan '.

Then the woman in the bed sat up and looked about her with wild eyes ; and the oldest of the old men said : ' Lady, we have come to write down the names of the immortals,' and at his words a look of great joy came into her face. Presently she began to speak slowly, and yet eagerly, as though she knew she had but a little while to live, and, in English, with the accent of their own country ; and she told them the secret names of the immortals of many lands, and of the colours, and odours, and weapons, and instruments of music and instruments of handicraft they held dearest ; but most about the immortals of Ireland and of their love for the cauldron, and the whetstone, and the sword, and the spear. . . .

In another story of the same date, ' Rosa Alchemica ', the veiled prophecy is made again and this time the cult is further elaborated, with four Celtic gods associated with the four elements of Cauldron, Whetstone, Sword, and Spear :

A time will come for these people also, and they will sacrifice a mullet to Artemis, or some other fish to some new divinity, unless indeed their own divinities, the Dagda, with his overflowing cauldron, Lu, with his spear dipped in poppy-juice, lest it rush forth hot for

battle, Angus, with the three birds on his shoulder, Bove and his red
swine-herd, and all the heroic children of Dana, set up once more
their temples of grey stone. Their reign has never ceased, but only
waned in power a little, for the Shee still pass in every wind, and
dance and play at hurley, and fight their sudden battles in every hollow
and on every hill ; but they cannot build their temples again till there
have been martyrdoms and victories, and perhaps even that long-
foretold battle in the Valley of the Black Pig.

The vague dream of an Irish cult slowly possessed Yeats's
mind. Late in 1896 a letter from George Russell to Fiona
Macleod informed her that ' My friend, Willie Yeats, has just
come by me wrapt in a faery whirlwind, his mouth speaking great
things. He talked much of reviving the Druidic mysteries. . . .
These stirring ideas of his are in such a blaze of light that, but for
the inspiration of a presence always full of enthusiasm, I would
get no ideas at all from him.' Russell was in fact as eager as Yeats,
for with a group of young Theosophical disciples he had been
seeing chiliastic visions of the coming world. In June 1896, he
wrote to Yeats :

DEAR W. B. Y.—
    I am not going to bother you about any damned thing this time
but simply to tell you some things about the Ireland behind the veil.
You remember my writing to you about the awakening of the ancient
fires which I knew about. Well it has been confirmed and we are told
to publish it. *The Gods have returned to Eri* and have centred themselves in the sacred mountains and blow the fires through the country.
They have been seen by several in vision. They will awaken the
magical instinct everywhere, and the universal heart of the people will
turn to the old Druidic beliefs. I note through the country the increased faith in faery things. The bells are heard from the mounds and
sounding in the hollows of the mountains. A purple sheen in the
inner air, perceptible at times in the light of the day, spreads itself over
the mountains. All this I can add my own testimony to. Furthermore
we were told that though now few we would soon be many, and that
a branch of the school for the revival of the ancient mysteries to teach
real things, would be formed here in time. Out of Ireland will arise
a light to transform many ages and peoples. There is a hurrying of
forces and swift things going out and I believe profoundly that a new

Avatar is about to appear and in all spheres the forerunners go before him to prepare.  It will be one of the kingly avatars, who is at once ruler of men and magic sage.  I had a vision of him some months ago and will know him if he appears.

To Russell, instructed in Theosophy and mystical writings, it was not extraordinary that at chosen moments the fingers of God and man should touch.  Shortly after the above letter he wrote another in which he described in detail the person and the residence of the avatar :

(Private)  The Celtic adept whom I am inclined to regard as the genius of the renaissance in its literary and intellectual aspects, lives in a little white-washed cottage.  I feel convinced it is in Donegal or Sligo.  There is a great log a tree with the bark still on it a few feet before the door.  It is on a gentle slope.  He is middleaged has a grey golden beard and hair (more golden than grey) face very delicate and absorbed.  Eyes have a curious golden fire in them, broad forehead. . . . . *Don't spread this about.*

He and his disciples were going to spend their next holiday searching for this venerable adept.

Yeats, on his side, wrote to Russell from London that he was convinced that a new cycle was about to begin, and that he and Russell were of it rather than of the cycle that was ending. Russell enthusiastically concurred : ' I agree with you that we belong to the coming cycle.  The sun passes from Pisces into Aquarius in a few years.  Pisces is phallic in its influence.  The waterman is spiritual so the inward turning souls will catch the first rays of the new Aeon.'

Filled with such ideas as these Yeats went to visit Douglas Hyde at Roscommon, and there began to give shape to his dream of a new form of worship for Ireland.  In the middle of Lough Key he found an island with an unoccupied castle in the middle of it.  This was what he wanted : he would turn this isolated place into the headquarters of a new cult through which truths of the spirit might be disseminated to the materialistic nations. The doctrines would be the same as those of Theosophy and the Golden Dawn, but associated here specifically with Ireland.

They ' would unite the radical truths of Christianity to those of a more ancient world '. To the ' Castle of the Heroes ' would come the finest men and women of Ireland for spiritual inspiration and teaching, and they would return, fortified by the supernatural powers which the Irish mystical order had concentrated, to act, in Florence Farr's words, as living links ' between the supernal and terrestrial natures '.

His principal coadjutor in organizing the new cult was to be Maud Gonne. She, like Yeats, believed strongly in spiritual forces, and thought of Ireland as a sacred, magical land. Many years afterwards she described their ambitions in this way :

> The land of Ireland, we both felt, was powerfully alive and invisibly peopled, and whenever we grew despondent over the weakness of the national movement, we went to it for comfort. If only we could make contact with the hidden forces of the land it would give us strength for the freeing of Ireland. Most of our talk centred round this and it led us both into strange places. . . .

They were then in their early thirties, so perhaps the project was not quite so naïve as it now appears. Maud Gonne thought that the order might work for separation of Ireland from Britain in the same way that the Masonic lodges in the north of Ireland were, she believed, working for union. It would use Masonic methods against the Masons, as another nationalist organization, the Clan na Gael, had done. Yeats, less political in his objectives, vaguely anticipated that the order would be able to aid the movement for national independence by its magical powers, but he had other aspirations as well. He hoped that it would provide him with an ' orderly background to work upon ', something that up to this time he had lacked and felt the need of, and that it would also supply a background for the Irish literary movement. He had another purpose which was even more practical. Driven almost frantic by loving in vain ' the most beautiful woman in the world ', he thought that in collaborating with Maud Gonne in this spiritual conspiracy his mind and hers would be so united that she would consent to become his.

The chief task was to prepare a rite for the order. ' An

obsession more constant than anything but my love itself was the need of mystical rites — a ritual, system of evocation and meditation — to re-unite the perception of the spirit, of the dream, with natural beauty.' It must not be written with conscious artistry, but obtained through the system which Mathers had taught to Yeats of concentrating on symbols and ' letting the will move of itself '. On the inner truth of the rite depended the order's spiritual sanctions, and Yeats and Maud Gonne devoted themselves with great ardour to its construction. They read John Rhys's *Celtic Heathendom* and various other works in order to fill in the background of pre-Christian Ireland ; they worked out parallels between the Irish gods and Graeco-Roman ones. But beyond this haphazard scholarship was their use of symbolic meditation. They would impel their imaginations to dwell on the ancient divinities, who would often obligingly seem to take definite shape and to enlighten them on various aspects of the other world. Yeats called this method of meditation ' vision ', but perhaps deliberate reverie would be a more accurate and acceptable designation.

He and Maud Gonne swore in other comrades to help in the secret work. George Russell, to whom Yeats attributed extraordinary clairvoyant powers, was a collaborator, as were William Sharp, always on the borders of trance, and his ardently Celtic *alter ego*, Fiona Macleod. Yeats went to Paris and enlisted the aid of MacGregor Mathers and his wife. A letter from Mrs. Mathers, dated March 16, 1897, shows how seriously the work was proceeding :

Nothing can be done until the most important part of the affair be accomplished, that of resurrecting the Gods and the ceremonies etc. ' SRMD ' [Mathers] is going to work at this but as you know, it may be a long and difficult business, and not a thing to be hurried at all. Anything of the kind got up without the solid foundation of Truth we will not have to do with, neither will you of course.

Towards the end of 1897 Yeats tried to hasten matters by organizing a group of enthusiastic Celts in London for the purpose of visionary exploration. Under his leadership the members would concentrate on a symbol and then tell each other what they saw, which was usually related to what they wanted to see ; by power of suggestion all the members of the group would gradually build up a sort of collective vision. An extract from the records of one such meeting describes what went on :

Those present were seated in a circle with the table of four elements in the centre. . . . D.E.D.I. [Yeats] performed a Celtic ceremony of invocation. This transported us to a mountainous district where in the midst of the hills we found ourselves before an ancient well. Leaning over the well on our left grew a mountain-ash tree laden with red berries that kept dropping, dropping into the water, so ripe that they seemed like drops of blood reddening the pool as they sank. Then appeared a venerable figure, luminous but human, the figure of a man with a white beard. He knelt beside the well and looked into the water. D.E.D.I. addressed him as ' Cuala ' and asked if he could tell us how he came to be here and connected with this well. Then looking with him into the water we saw that it was full of moving reflections, as of horses and chariots and battles in constant procession and we understood that once he had been involved in much stir and strife of the world and had then renounced it all in his pursuit of his Ideal. . . . Then S.S.D.D. [Florence Farr] discovered that to place the two forefingers crossed (right over left) upon the lips, touching both lips had a strangely restorative effect and in fact this sign is the salutation and key to the World of Heroes. Further investigation revealed that this is the world of Form and is associated with space as distinguished from the World of Spirit associated with cycles and periods. That this is the plane of Art. That its nature is airy. That the placing of the crossed fingers on the lips increases the power of concentration and of vision and also gives more heat and light. Saluting with the sign of the Ash-wand we returned as we came to the path through the wood where the Guardian waited to guide us. We noticed that the figure seemed less luminous and that we ourselves were much brighter, having absorbed light from the throne — and now it was twilight among the trees where before had been darkness. When we left the Guardian at his station we saluted with the X sign and again when we passed Manaanan for it seemed befitting ; and when at last we mounted through the dark Lethe-like waters we brought with us still the light from the throne. Two of our numbers had not brought enough of this light with them and when we reached the well, they noted the leafless ash-trees and the chill and cheerless aspect of the scene which was not so to the rest. So we all waited together till the ash-tree budded again and the scene assumed warmth and life. Then D.E.D.I. banished as before.

The chronological development of the order rituals is hard to determine, but a few dates can be established. In March of 1898 Yeats heard from Mathers that the magician had almost completed a ritual of initiation for the commencing grade. In July Yeats intensified his own efforts and began to keep an occult diary, which he continued until March 1901. He had various sleeping, half-waking, and day-dreaming visions ; for example, he saw ' two books full of pictures of marvellous and curious beauty ', and was told ' that one contained lost poems of Blake and the other something — whether doctrine or what I could not remember — that had influenced him '. In September he and Russell visited a haunted castle and compared the visions that they had there. Then in July 1899 he was working out the rites, dreaming of Maud Gonne, and writing *The Shadowy Waters*, a juxtaposition which as we shall see was of some significance. Some time afterwards he gave William Sharp a rough draft of the ' rite ', and in February 1900 they were seeking together to elaborate it. In March 1900, because of the quarrel in the Golden Dawn, Mathers was lost as a collaborator, and from this time on Yeats relied chiefly upon Maud Gonne, Russell, Sharp, and Fiona Macleod. Sharp and Fiona, for whose sake he called the order Celtic rather than Irish, took an active part by correspondence, but in July 1901 she wrote to Yeats suggesting a complete reconstruction of the rite, ' as for some reason we [Fiona and Sharp] both still feel either an inveterate hostility or an insuperable difficulty '. On January 15, 1902, Yeats writes to Lady Gregory that he has ' done a great deal of work ' on his magical rites, and has ' sketched them all out in their entirety '. After that, for reasons which will become plain, we hear no more of them.

In writing of the Irish mystical order in his *Autobiographies*, Yeats noted that his ' attempt to find philosophy and to create ritual ' for it was vain. The rituals, which have been preserved, confirm his statement. A great deal is said in them about the secret quest, but little information is given as to what the quest is after or how it should be carried out. His father had taught him to disregard ethical considerations, so the candidate is not encouraged to seek good or to be good, but rather to pursue ' the joyful imperishable thought, the last coming to himself, the truth that is his and not another's '. This was Yeats's own effort to discover his true individuality, but he does not suggest how the discovery can be made, for indeed he does not know. The candidate of the order passes through the initiations of the cauldron, the stone, the sword, and the spear, which symbolize his conquest of the four elements and their spiritual equivalents. One passage in the initiation of the sword is of some interest, because it shows how Yeats both seeks and shies away from unity, and foreshadows his later esthetic theories. Aengus and Edain are represented to the candidate as the contrary principles always at war in the world :

Now that he has heard their attributions so as to comprehend them, he must grasp the sword and go on ; leaving the eternal pursuit, whilst yet pursuing it, for the country where the contraries are equally true. The Candidate's Mind must become able to blend the two forces together, so as to create completeness, for without Aengus, when in the bower of glass, Etain was but a golden fly, Beauty without the Spiritual Intelligence. But still that union cannot be, still the eternal pursuit must go on, for life would cease to be life without it.

The last initiation is that of the Spirit, where the somewhat befuddled candidate is told ' of the Spiritual Life, the stilling of all choice, the end of the ways is the same, the incarnate is many, the discarnate is but one, all flames are in the flame '. He is now ready to be born anew. ' Active Spirit of the Divine Life wake in this man. Life that has descended illuminate him.'

What Yeats succeeded in saying throughout the rituals was principally that Irish life must have a basis in faith such as existing Churches could not provide ; farther than this he did not go. But at any rate the messianic Castle of the Heroes on the island

in Lough Key was a more socially responsible project than that
of the ' bee-loud glade ' on the isle of Innisfree to which he had
talked of retiring in 1890, and the spiritual strivings which went
into the six years' abortive attempt to institute a new form of
worship bore fruit in another field.

## II. AN IRISH MYSTICAL THEATRE

The external history of the Irish dramatic movement is well
known.  A handful of playwrights bent upon a national theatre
was joined by a group of actors with the same goal ; the plays
that were written for a small playhouse in a small country have
since been presented throughout the world.  The effect upon the
leading participants was overwhelming : Lady Gregory, a widow
in her late forties who had previously written nothing of special
value, revealed a considerable talent for comedy.  John Synge,
who had planned to devote his life to writing critical articles on
French writers for the English press, suddenly built a fantastic
drama out of Irish life.  George Moore and Edward Martyn,
and many lesser-known writers, found their outlook abruptly
altered.

The course of the movement can be briefly outlined.  In the
summer of 1898 Yeats and Lady Gregory secured Edward Martyn's
financial and literary help for the first productions of an Irish
theatre.  George Moore was persuaded to join the movement a
little later, and helped to rehearse the English company which
in May 1899 came to Dublin and gave Yeats's *Countess Cathleen*
and Martyn's *The Heather Field*.  In February 1900 three more
plays were presented, this time by Moore, Martyn, and Alice
Milligan.  A few months later, in October, an Irish heroic drama
by Yeats and Moore, *Diarmuid and Grania*, was produced along
with the first play ever written in Irish, worked from a scenario
of Yeats by Douglas Hyde.  In 1902 Yeats and Lady Gregory
collaborated on a series of Irish plays, and joined hands with a
small group of Irish actors, most of them amateurs, led by the
very talented brothers, Frank and William Fay.  By 1904 a

generous patron was found in Miss Annie Horniman, who bought the building which became the Abbey Theatre and who provided an annual subsidy. The theatre, backed by the state, continues to this day, though its periods of vigour are now more fitful.

Hardly any of the people involved in the theatre during its early days had any notion of the schemes that were forming in Yeats's mind, and to find these out one must go behind the scenes to the Irish mystical order. The order had as one of its purposes to serve as a background for literary work. Yeats's endeavours to found an order and to found an Irish theatre came about the same time, and the synchronization is significant. Occultism, or, to use a more generalized expression, spiritual ideas, underlie all his early plays and his theories of what the national theatre should be. It was not by chance that on the programme of his *Countess Cathleen*, the production of which in May 1899 started off the theatre movement, the sub-title was *A Miracle Play*. His original intention was to present a series of miracle plays, by which he meant plays not necessarily Christian but manifesting in one way or another the existence of an invisible world.

We can find evidence for this view in letters written to Katharine Tynan as early as 1890. In May of that year he wrote to her : ' If I was over in Ireland I would ask you to collaborate with me on that little Miracle Play I suggested to you on the Adoration of the Magi. I have written so much in dramatic form that I could perhaps help by working a little prose sketch in dialogue to be turned into verse by you.' Two months later he reverted to the subject, pleading as an excuse for not having written that ' I hoped to send you some notes or perhaps an abstract of the little " Mystery Play " on the Adoration of the Magi that I propose '.

Nothing came of this collaboration ; the Magi went into a short story, and later into a poem, instead. Meanwhile he wrote *The Countess Cathleen* (1889–92) and *The Land of Heart's Desire* (1894), both of them, from his point of view, miracle plays. In 1897 Yeats was beginning to get his plans for an Irish theatre

together, and he sent in that year an important letter to Fiona
Macleod :

I have just now a plan I want to ask you about.  Our Irish Literary
and Political literary organisations are pretty complete (I am trying to
start a Young Ireland Society, among the Irish here in Paris at the
moment) and I think it would be very possible to get up Celtic plays
through these Societies.  They would be far more effective than
lectures and might do more than anything else we can do to make the
Irish Scotch and other Celts recognise their solidarity.  My own plays
are too elaborate, I think, for a start, and have also the disadvantage
that I cannot urge my own work in committee.  If we have one or
two short direct prose plays, of (say) a mythological and folklore
kind, by you and by some writer (I may be able to move O'Grady,
I have already spoken to him about it urgently) I feel sure we could
get the *Irish Literary Society* to make a start.  They have indeed for
some time talked of doing my *Land of Heart's Desire*.

My own theory of poetical or legendary drama is that it should
have no realistic, or elaborate, but only a symbolic and decorative
setting.  A forest, for instance, should be represented by a forest
pattern and not by a forest painting.  One should design a scene,
which would be an accompaniment not a reflection of the text.  This
method would have the further advantage of being fairly cheap and
altogether novel.  The acting should have an equivalent distance to
that of the play from common realities.  The plays might be almost,
in some cases, modern mystery plays.  Your *Last Supper*, for instance,
would make such a play, while your story in *The Savoy* would arrange
as a story play of merely human tragedy.  I shall try my own hand
possibly at some short prose plays also, but not yet.  I merely suggest
these things because they are a great deal on my mind. . . . My
' Shadowy Waters ' is magical and mystical beyond anything I have
done.

The reason that Yeats appealed for aid to Fiona Macleod was
not only that she was devotedly Celtic but that she and William
Sharp, whose identity he did not at that time realize, shared his
occult theories.  Yeats, as the letter indicates, was willing to
adapt his views if that proved necessary, but he hoped that the
new dramas would serve as ' manuals of devotion '.  As he said
in the first draft of his *Autobiographies* : ' I wished my writings,
and those of the school I hoped to found, to have a secret sym-

bolical relation to these mysteries [of the Irish mystical order],
for in this way I thought there would be a greater richness, a
greater claim upon the love of the soul, devotion without ex-
hortation or rhetoric, should not religion hide within the work
of art as God is within His world and how can the interpreter
do more than whisper '. He was intensely excited by the prospect
of setting up a theatre to accomplish his aims, and wrote to
Florence Farr : ' We can make a great movement and in more
than magical things. . . .'

These statements give meaning to what might otherwise seem
merely fanciful remarks in Yeats's newspaper and magazine
articles at the time of the inception of the Irish theatre. In the
theatre magazine, *Beltaine*, he wrote in May 1899 : ' In the first
day, it is the Art of the people ; and in the second day, like the
drama acted of old times in the hidden places of temples, it is the
preparation of a Priesthood. It may be, though the world is not
old enough to show us any example, that this Priesthood will
spread their Religion everywhere, and make their Art the Art of
the People.' Discussing in the *United Irishman* John Eglinton's
theory of the role of the remnant or *élite*, Yeats said : ' They
are a small body, not more than one in five thousand anywhere,
but they are many enough to be a priesthood, and in the long
run to guide the great instinctive movements that come out of
the multitude '. We cannot tell (and Yeats himself was not sure)
whether he was speaking metaphorically or not, for his aspirations for the Castle of the Heroes and its effect on literature and
life were unlimited.

Whether the writer was a priest literally or metaphorically,
he held a position of great dignity, and Yeats was prepared to
defend him against all comers. The dramatist, since he carries
on a secret tradition, has the right to decide what the people
should have rather than the people themselves or their clergy.
This conviction had a profound influence on the development of
the theatre, for soon after the production of plays had started the
issue of ecclesiastical censorship arose. George Moore was prepared to compromise, but not Yeats, who boldly declared :

I believe that literature is the principal voice of the conscience, and that it is its duty age after age to affirm its morality against the special moralities of clergymen and churches, and of kings and parliaments and peoples. . . . I have no doubt that a wise ecclesiastic, if his courage equalled his wisdom, would be a better censor than the mob, but I think it better to fight the mob alone than to seek for a support one could only get by what would seem to me a compromise of principle.

Ireland was to be a holy land full of holy symbols, not in the orthodox clergyman's sense but in the poet's sense, which was also the mystic's sense ; here alone in a degenerate Europe would spiritual realities be understood.

All Yeats's early plays reflect these yearnings and beliefs. *The Shadowy Waters*, begun in 1885 and started over in 1894 after Yeats had seen *Axël*, was formed, as he said, largely out of certain visionary experiences. The plot shows a fundamental uncertainty in his mind during the 'nineties. For years he had sought to persuade Maud Gonne to renounce her political activities and pursue with him the reality beyond the veil, where love transcends itself and 'is made / Imperishable fire under the boughs / Of chrysoberyl and beryl and chrysolite, / And chrysoprase and ruby and sardonyx '. The difficulty of finishing the play, which was not published till 1900, was the difficulty of knowing what he meant. He wanted his beloved in the flesh, but felt that a love so overpowering and noble as his must have some loftier goal. For this reason he had worked with her upon the Irish order, seeking to attain with her the inner reality and to make their minds one, and hoping vaguely and vainly that their bodies would become one in the process. Villiers de l'Isle-Adam, handling a similar problem, had solved it by having his lovers kill themselves rather than spoil by consummation their perfect passion. Yeats hedged by sending off Forgael and Dectora on a ship which might lead to death but would probably bear them, clasped in one another's arms, to the world where appearances were true.

His other early plays fit even more easily into the pattern of the miracle play than *The Shadowy Waters*, where the only miracle is Forgael's magic playing of the harp. *Cathleen Ni Houlihan*, written in 1902 for Maud Gonne to act, is a powerful rewriting of the theme of *The Land of Heart's Desire* in terms of nationalism ; just as the fairy child lured Maire Bruin away from her husband, so Cathleen Ni Houlihan (the symbol of Ireland) wins Michael Gillane away from his prospective bride. Though Maud Gonne acted the role of Cathleen, she was really the prototype of Michael Gillane, for Yeats felt that she had given herself to Ireland instead of to him. He was able to treat this theme sympathetically by making the love of Ireland no mere patriotism but a transcendental passion, saying of the play : ' It is the perpetual struggle of the cause of Ireland and every other ideal cause against private hopes and dreams, against all that we mean when we say the world '.

The *Hour-Glass*, also written in 1902, is sub-titled *A Morality*, and is built around a text which occurs in the Irish mystical order rituals in somewhat altered form. The wise man of the play is called upon by his students to explain the meaning of the sentence, ' There are two living countries, the one visible and the one invisible ; and when it is winter with us it is summer in that country. . . .' A complete sceptic, he is suddenly confronted with an angel of God, and compelled like Dr. Faustus to mend his ways. Another play which Yeats worked out in the same year with Lady Gregory, *The Travelling Man*, was sub-titled *A Miracle Play*, and also dealt with the theme of a sceptic confronted by undeniable miracle.

Two other plays written in 1902, *Where There Is Nothing* and *The Pot of Broth*, fit into the same pattern but with a difference. *Where There Is Nothing* is an attempt to write a realistic drama about a mystic. The hero does not sail away on a symbolical ship towards symbolical shores, as in *The Shadowy Waters*, but applies himself to altering life on earth. Paul Routledge does not proceed, however, with Yeats's secrecy and caution ; he feels a mission to destroy in the sight of all men the falsehoods he sees about him : ' I want to pull down all this — what do you call it ? — the thing, the building of the world — to put a crowbar under the gate and a grappling-iron over the towers and uproot it all '. Under the pressure of this desire, and in search of a life free of civilized falsehoods, Paul joins a group of gipsies and marries one of them in a pagan ceremony. For the wedding feast he buys enough porter to inflame the neighbourhood in the vague hope of using drunkenness to abolish the old values ; then, deciding that the true way lies elsewhere, he enters a monastery. After a few years there he starts a new revolt among the monks, and gives a sermon asking for the elimination of laws, cities, and churches, of all that is organized and therefore vicious. Eventually a superstitious mob kills him.

The play is a bad, clumsy one, but repays study because, as Yeats said, he put a great deal of himself into it, more perhaps than in any other work since *John Sherman*. We must not suppose that he has completely identified himself with the hero ; rather he seems to have asked himself the question, What would happen if I said and did all the things I have dreamed of saying or doing ? If I acted without self-qualification and self-distrust ? Paul Routledge is a kind of anthropomorphosis of Yeats's secret desires, and Paul's violence is indicative of his creator's growing restlessness with his way of life. In another respect, too, the play is revealing. Paul is a very serious young man, but he is in search of laughter : ' I have taken to the roads, because there is a wild beast I would overtake . . . a very terrible wild beast, with iron teeth and brazen claws that can root up spires and towers. . . . That wild beast is laughter, the mightiest of the enemies of God.' Yeats, too, was in search of laughter, of release from the appalling seriousness of his frustrated bachelorhood. Though he had always had an excellent sense of humour, he had so far rigorously excluded it from his writing. Now he began to think of putting it into his work.

The first product of the new trend was *The Pot of Broth*, a trivial little comedy. A tramp persuades a gullible peasant woman that by dropping a magic stone into a pot of hot water she can make a wonderful soup. This play is also a miracle play, but *manqué*, for the miracle does not come off and the credulous woman is laughed at. The tramp's stone is not the philosopher's. *The Pot of Broth* was the last play of this genre that Yeats wrote until many years later : after 1902 a great change occurred in his way of thought. But even if the change had not occurred, he would hardly have been able to continue much longer with his first formula of what the theatre should be. The theatre audience, to which he was more responsive than he pretended, needed more substantial fare, and in 1903 John Synge, with his *Shadow of the Glen*, diverted the movement from Yeats's half-religious intentions. Yeats, without renouncing his own position, accommodated himself.

As a result, the successful fusion of his occult and national interests in the dramatic movement was short-lived, but certain effects of the fusion endured. The Abbey Theatre, to use its later name, was preserved from the facile comedies of manners which were popular in England and in other Dublin theatres. The subject-matter had to be Irish, and Irish in a self-respecting sense ; the stage Irishman was banished. Because for Yeats the materialistic middle class was the enemy of all he wished to accomplish, the plays of his movement rarely deal with that class, but almost always take up some aspect of peasant life or of Irish legend. It may be complained with some justice that the theatre was too carefully sheltered from features of modern life which Yeats considered degrading because they could not form part of his visionary dreams. But certainly the exalted view of the writer as a missionary among the heathen which he developed and fostered gave the movement the independence from excessive contemporaneity that made possible Ireland's outstanding contribution to twentieth-century drama.

## CHAPTER X

# MAKING A STYLE

I made my song a coat
Covered with embroideries.

YEATS, ' A Coat '

I F, as Yeats said, ' The self-conquest of the writer who is not a man of action is style ', the process of self-conquest was for him a very slow and arduous one.  George Moore, who worked closely with him at the end of the century, asserted that Yeats's style gave only a slight notion of his personality, which was really more varied and inclusive than either his prose or verse disclosed.  Moore prophesied that Yeats must therefore eventually cease altogether to write as he exhausted the small literary area to which he had staked his claim.  What Moore did not realize was that Yeats, during the 'nineties, had not one style but two, that he used one to undercut the other, and that as a result he was less committed to any one way of writing than he appeared.  The same uncertainty which made him set up a tension in his life between opposing conceptions of his personality, and a further tension between the principles of opposition and fusion, affected all his thought and kept him for a long time from deciding unequivocally upon a manner of expression.  As a result his literary craft was unusually flexible and adaptable, but it was many years before he had developed an inflection that was stamped ineradicably as his own.

We can better understand the enormous importance which he attached to style if we remember that it was his father's obsession too.  John Butler Yeats had broken away from the Pre-Raphaelite style of painting but was not prepared to make the radical departures from orthodox technique which the French impressionists had carried out.  Lacking the confidence that success or membership of a school might have given him, he laboured day and night to find a method that would be entirely his own. In 1890, for example, he decided to abandon portrait-painting altogether, and for about seven years made nothing but pencil sketches. Then in 1897 he seized the paint-brush once again, convinced that his salvation lay there. He moved restlessly on, always seeking the formula that seemed to be attainable by one more stroke but yet escaped him.

His son had wanted to return to the Pre-Raphaelite style of painting, as we have seen, and in poetry, too, W. B. Yeats for a long time adhered to the esthetic principles of Rossetti and William Morris. Their elaborate rhythms suited their strange subjects, and closed off hermetically the world of their poems from the contemporary world ; the Pre-Raphaelites quickly allied themselves in his mind with hieratic magicians, and an ornate style was like a mysterious ceremonialism. A passage which he wrote about Oscar Wilde tells a good deal about himself :

In London he took to the aesthetic movement, in verse to the style of Rossetti, and in prose to that of Pater, and the slow-moving elegance — born of toil and sedentary — became all the more marvellous in his eyes, because it was not his natural expression. He was fascinated by it, as I was fascinated when as a boy of fourteen I stood motionless on the street wondering if it was possible to ask my way in what would be recognized at once as fine prose. It was so hard to believe, after I had heard somebody read out let us say Pater's description of the Mona Lisa, that ' Can you direct me to St. Peter's Square Hammersmith ' was under the circumstances the best possible prose.

Yeats, it will be recalled, was caught up by Pre-Raphaelitism as early as his seventeenth or eighteenth year, when he said that a poem should be ' a painted and bepictured argosy '. When late in 1885 he became a nationalist and hoisted over his fleet the green flag, the change was one of subject-matter alone. *The Wanderings of Oisin*, while far more skilful than any extended work he had done earlier, had the same unhurried, unassertive manner full of metaphor and ready to dawdle at any attractive spot along the way. He spoke in this poem with obvious delight

of words ' glorious as Asian birds / At evening in their rainless
lands '.  The style is unlike that of an earlier work, *The Island
of Statues* for example, only in that it is more heavily lacquered.
His metaphors are deliberately imprecise ; actual observation
can hardly be said to play any part in such lines as :

> And like a sunset were her lips,
> A stormy sunset o'er doomed ships.

The description, evocative as it is, seems better suited to one of
Rossetti's women than to Oisin's lady.

Yeats was becoming expert at this way of writing, but as it
grew easy for him he became suspicious of it.  Had he not written
to Mary Cronan in his late boyhood that his aim was ' directness
and extreme simplicity ' ?  These were virtues which his father
was always seeking and upholding, for his father contended that
the artist, whatever his style, must have life for a basis and never
diverge very far from it.  Towards the end of 1888, when *Oisin*
was completed, we find the poet devising various expedients as
brakes upon his inclination to write elaborately of elaborate
subjects.  The principal one was to deal with peasant life and
employ peasant speech.  He considered also sleeping upon a
board, and, more practically, he wrote the *Countess Cathleen*
(with its many peasant characters) twice over in prose before
writing a line of verse, hoping thereby to avoid ' every rhetorical
trick and cadence '.  His alarm is manifested in a poem written
about 1891, ' To the Rose upon the Rood of Time ', where he
prays that the search for beauty will not destroy his appreciation
of common things :

> Red Rose, proud Rose, sad Rose of all my days,
> Come near me while I sing the ancient ways —
> Cuchullin battling with the bitter tide ;
> The druid, grey, wood nurtured, quiet eyed,
> Who cast round Fergus dreams and ruin untold ;
> And thine own sadness, whereof stars grown old
> In dancing silver sandaled on the sea,
> Sing in their high and lonely melody.

Come near, that no more blinded by man's fate,
I find under the boughs of love and hate,
In all poor foolish things that live a day,
Eternal Beauty wandering on her way.

Come near, come near, come near — Ah, leave me still
A little space for the rose-breath to fill,
Lest I no more hear common things that crave,
The weak worm hiding down in its small cave —
The field mouse running by me in the grass,
And heavy mortal hopes that toil and pass,
But seek alone to hear the strange things said
By God to the bright hearts of those long dead,
And learn to chant a tongue men do not know.
Come near — I would before my time to go,
Sing of old Eri and the ancient ways,
Red Rose, proud Rose, sad Rose of all my days.

The extraordinary structure of this poem, in which he summons the Rose only to bid her come not too close, merits examination, because it holds the secret of Yeats's methods of composition. ' I even do my writing by self-distrusting reasons ', he confessed in a private diary some years later ; as a result each poem pictures a struggle, and, especially at this period, the poet avoids as far as he can choosing between his attraction and repulsion by an idea. In later life he would try to resolve the opposition ; as he wrote to Dorothy Wellesley forty-five years later :

We have all something within ourselves to batter down and get our power from this fighting. I have never ' produced ' a play in verse without showing the actors that the passion of the verse comes from the fact that the speakers are holding down violence or madness — ' down Hysterica passio '. All depends on the completeness of the holding down, on the stirring of the beast underneath. Even my poem ' To D. W.' should give this impression. The moon, the moon-less night, the dark velvet, the sensual silence, the silent room and the violent bright Furies. Without this conflict we have no passion only sentiment and thought. . . . About the conflict in ' To D. W.', I did not plan it deliberately. That conflict is deep in my subconsciousness, perhaps in everybody's.

But in the 'nineties the conflict appears to master him ; he swings one way and then the other without decision, and fails to inspire the reader with confidence. The conflict is of course deeper than technique, but the technique exemplifies it.

Often the same poem will contain signs of both styles, for they were not irreconcilable, as in the concrete details of the first stanza and the fancy metaphors of the second stanza of ' The Lake Isle of Innisfree'. We can see the two manners more distinctly contraposed by comparing stanzas of two ballads, ' The Ballad of Moll Magee ' (published in January 1889), and ' Father Gilligan ' (published in July 1890) :

### THE BALLAD OF MOLL MAGEE

Come round me, little childer ;
    There, don't fling stones at me
Because I mutter as I go,
    But pity Moll Magee.

My husband was a fisher poor
    With shore lines in the say ;
My work was saltin' herrings
    The whole of the long day.

### THE BALLAD OF FATHER GILLIGAN

And then, half-lying on the chair
    He knelt, prayed, fell asleep ;
And the moth-hour went from the fields,
    And stars began to peep.

They slowly into millions grew,
    And leaves shook in the wind ;
And God covered the world with shade,
    And whispered to mankind.

In the first, which he called in a letter to O'Leary a ' mere experiment ', Yeats is aiming at a folk ballad, though the simplicity does not ring true, especially in an inversion like ' fisher poor '. In the second he attempts an artificial, literary ballad with equal maladroitness, as in the trite line, ' And stars began to peep ', and the clumsy line, ' He knelt, prayed, fell asleep ', which Yeats later altered.  Each style seems slightly contaminated by the other, as if he did not yet fully understand either.

In London Yeats came under the influence of a group of poets whom in 1891 he was largely responsible for organizing into the Rhymers' Club.  The Rhymers furnished much of the talent for the *fin de siècle* reviews, *The Yellow Book* and *The Savoy* ; among the members were Ernest Dowson, Victor Plarr, Richard Le Gallienne, Aubrey Beardsley, John Davidson, Lionel Johnson, Arthur Symons, and Ernest Rhys.  One thing they all had in common, an admiration for the traditions of Rossetti in verse and of Pater in prose.  For a time Yeats was heavily, though never whole-heartedly, affected by them.  He was especially friendly during the years 1890 to 1895 with Lionel Johnson, and after that till the end of the century with Arthur Symons, with whom he shared lodgings in the last months of 1895 and in January 1896, at Fountain Court in the Temple.  The tiny Johnson, wasting away in drink, made a cult of dignity ;  he loved words like ' hieratic ' and ' magnificence ', and Yeats never forgot such of his remarks as, ' Life must be a ritual ', ' One should be quite unnoticeable ', ' I wish those people who deny the eternity of punishment would recognize their unspeakable vulgarity '.  He made Yeats conscious of his own ignorance, telling him, ' I need ten years in the wilderness, you need ten years in a library ' ; and in 1893 he presented him with a copy of the works of Plato and made him read it.  Johnson's poetry, while rather dull, had a chiselled coldness about it which Yeats greatly admired.  As for Symons, who liked women too well to be friendly with the ascetic Johnson, he had a great deal of information about the contemporary French writers ;  he knew most of them personally and had translated some of their works. It may have been his accounts of Mallarmé's *mardis* that encouraged Yeats to have his own famous Monday nights at home at Woburn Buildings.  Yeats helped Symons with the writing of *The Symbolist Movement in Literature* (1899), a book which was not profound but made the term 'symbolist' fashionable in England. Symons, while he gave Yeats a clearer picture of contemporary developments in literature than the poet, with his imperfect knowledge of French, could have secured by himself, acknowledged in the dedication to his book that he had little to teach Yeats about symbolism.

The Rhymers were highly polished craftsmen with little interest in anything but literature, particularly melancholy lyrical poetry. They talked of Catullus and Herrick as their models, but were too disconsolate to try to imitate their spirit. Johnson supplied a theoretical justification : ' Nothing of importance could be discovered, he would say, science must be confined to the kitchen or workshop ; only philosophy and religion could solve the great secret, and they said all their say years ago ; a gentleman was a man who understood Greek '. Symons declared : ' We are concerned with nothing but impressions '. Poetry was autotelic ; it had to do only with cadence and beauty of phrase. The Rhymers would have concurred in Yeats's remark to Russell in a letter of about March 1898 : ' It is bad morals not to obey to the utmost the law of one's art for good writing is the way art has of being moral & the only way '.

Where did Yeats stand in relation to these futile, convinced young men ? He was certainly impressed by the artistic skill of some of them, especially Dowson and Johnson, and a little awed by them. To the Rhymers he must have seemed an occasionally inspired provincial, poorly educated and full of uninteresting theories. In a newspaper article which he wrote in 1892 Yeats described one of their meetings where he had tried to set forth his own views :

I well remember the irritated silence that fell upon a noted gathering of the younger English imaginative writers once, when I tried to explain a philosophy of poetry in which I was profoundly interested, and to show the dependence, as I conceived it, of all great art and literature upon conviction and upon heroic life. To them literature had ceased to be the handmaid of humanity, and become instead a terrible queen, in whose service the stars rose and set, and for whose pleasure life stumbles along in the darkness.

Though at the Rhymers' Club meetings in London Yeats opposed
art for art's sake with his own theory ' that literature must be
the expression of conviction, and be the garment of noble
emotion, and not an end in itself ', he evidently had a secret
ambition of emulating and surpassing his fellow-poets on their
own grounds of style and craftsmanship. Early in his stay in
London Edwin Ellis had given him the first minute criticism of
his work which he had received, and made him aware that scope
and intention were no more important than ' the management
of a cadence '. His methods of composition became as a result
exceedingly painstaking, as we can see in the following drafts
of a poem :

> Impetuous heart give heed to my rime
>   The tale of tales may never be told
> Cover it up with a lonely tune
>   Cover it up with a fitful dream
> Give help to my heart great journeyman
>   Who hid away the infinite fold
> With the pale stars and the wan moon
>   And in thy

> O heart tell not in tale or rime
>   The hidden things that may not be told
>     Wrap them about with a lonely tune
>       Wrap them about with a fitful dream.
> O help my heart great journeyman
>   Who cover away the infinite fold
> With the pale stars and the wandering moon
>   And to thy

> Give heed impetuous heart to my rune
>   Your sorrowful thoughts may never be told
> Cover your love with a lonely tune
>   Cover your hope with a fitful dream.

> Give help to my heart great journeyman
>   Who hid away the infinite fold
>     With the pale stars and the wandering moon
>       And the things that are with the things that seem.

Impetuous heart be still be still
   Your sorrowful things may not be told
      Cover your love with a lonely tune
         Cover your hope with a fitful dream.

Impetuous heart be still, still,
   For He has hid the infinite fold
      With pale stars and the wandering moon
         The things that are in the things that seem.

Impetuous heart be still, be still,
   Your sorrowful thoughts may not be told,
      Cover your love with a lonely tune,

For he who could bend all to His will
   Has covered the door of the Infinite fold
      With the pale stars and the wandering moon.


### THE LOVER TO HIS HEART

Impetuous heart be still, be still,
   Your sorrowful love may never be told ;
      Cover it up with a lonely tune ;
He who could bend all things to His will
   Has covered the door of the infinite fold
      With the pale stars and the wandering moon.
                  Nov. 19th [18]94

The poem changes slowly from the first version, which is a
conventional plea to deity (under the metaphorical title of ' great
journeyman ') for help in concealing his sorrow ; it becomes
more compact and at the same time more remote and suggestive,
less compromisingly personal. But even in the last of these
drafts the metaphors and rhythm were still too placid. Two years
later Yeats returned to the poem and rewrote it from a new and
more energetic point of view for *The Savoy*: he removed deity
and put in its stead the elements of fire, water, and air, freeing the
poem from any perishable religious connotation and charging his
doctrines with symbolical overtones. The images have been
made active and contrasting, and the rhythm has been daringly
loosened:

Be you still, be you still, trembling heart ;
Remember the wisdom out of the old days :
*Who trembles before the flame and the flood,*
*And the winds blowing through the starry ways,*
*And blowing us evil and good ;*
*Let the starry winds and the flame and the flood*
Cover over and hide, for he has no part
*With the lonely, proud, wingèd multitude.*

Yet there was danger that the wingèd multitude might be identified with angels, too exact a reference for this kind of verse ;
the words in the fifth line were too abstract, and the astonishing
syntactical manœuvre of the last six lines had not been fully ex-
ploited. Yeats took care of these defects before publishing the
poem in its final form in *The Wind among the Reeds* (1899) :

TO MY HEART, BIDDING IT HAVE NO FEAR

Be you still, be you still, trembling heart ;
Remember the wisdom out of the old days :
*Him who trembles before the flame and the flood,*
*And the winds that blow through the starry ways,*
*Let the starry winds and the flame and the flood*
Cover over and hide, for he has no part
*With the proud, majestical multitude.*

Only by infinite patience did the poet achieve such skill in
his art.

It is an over-simplification, but a useful one, to state that in
London Yeats took up the position of his Dublin friends as to
the importance of a heroic and nationalist subject-matter, while
in Dublin he made much of the position of the London Rhymers
as to the importance of technique. We are justified in discovering
general correlatives of these different emphases in the two styles
which he put against each other. The one was simple, based
more in theory than in fact on Irish peasant dialect ; the other
was elaborate and resembled that of the English Pre-Raphaelites
and Rhymers. The first emphasized content by making the form
inconspicuous, the second elaborated the form and obscured the

content.   Feeling for a time that he was too much drawn to the second, Yeats forced himself to write peasant stories where ornateness would destroy the authenticity.   In 1893 he published *The Celtic Twilight*, which contained such passages as this from a chapter called ' Village Ghosts ' :

In a cottage at the village end of the bogeen lived a house-painter, Jim Montgomery, and his wife.   They had several children.   He was a little dandy, and came of a higher class than his neighbours.   His wife was a very big woman.   Her husband, who had been expelled from the village choir for drink, gave her a beating one day.   Her sister heard of it, and came and took down one of the window shutters — Montgomery was neat about everything, and had shutters on the outside of every window — and beat him with it, being big and strong like her sister.   He threatened to prosecute her ; she answered that she would break every bone in his body if he did.   She never spoke to her sister again, because she had allowed herself to be beaten by so small a man.

This is not good writing, but can be defended as good discipline.

From the end of 1893 until early in 1896 Yeats spent little time in Ireland ; in London during these years he wrote more and more elaborately.   Pater's death in 1894, and Lionel Johnson's work on a biography of him, encouraged him to make some unsuccessful efforts to imitate Pater's prose rhythms :

While I thought these things, a voice cried to me from the crimson figures : ' Into the dance, there is none that can be spared out of the dance ; into the dance, into the dance, that the gods may make them bodies out of the substance of our hearts ' ; and before I could answer, a mysterious wave of passion, that seemed like the soul of the dance moving within our souls, took hold of me, and I was swept, neither consenting nor refusing, into the midst.   I was dancing with an immortal august woman, who had black lilies in her hair, and her dreamy gesture seemed laden with a wisdom more profound than the darkness that is between star and star, and with a love like the love that breathed upon the waters ; and as we danced on and on, the incense drifted over us and round us, covering us away, as in the heart of the world, and ages seemed to pass, and tempests to awake and perish in the folds of our robes and in her heavy hair.

Yeats chooses words here in much the same way as in *The Wanderings of Oisin*, as a protective cover ; he makes skilful use of verbal repetitions and rhythmical pairs of adjectives and nouns to drug the reader's senses. The satanic implications of the crimson figures, the incense, and the black lilies are so heavily suffused with the pale Pre-Raphaelite glow as to lose most of their Satanism. In content this prose is very thin.

The verse which he writes at the same time is in an equally ornate style, but more successfully executed, as in this extreme example dated in manuscript September 24, 1895 :

### MICHAEL ROBARTES BIDS HIS BELOVED BE AT PEACE

I hear the Shadowy Horses, their long manes a-shake,
Their hoofs heavy with tumult, their eyes glimmering white ;
The North unfolds above them clinging, creeping night,
The East her hidden joy before the morning break,
The West weeps in pale dew and sighs passing away,
The South is pouring down roses of crimson fire :
O vanity of Sleep, Hope, Dream, endless Desire,
The Horses of Disaster plunge in the heavy clay :
Beloved, let your eyes half close, and your heart beat
Over my heart, and your hair fall over my breast,
Drowning love's lonely hour in deep twilight of rest,
And hiding their tossing manes and their tumultuous feet.

No word has any explicit meaning ; we neither know nor feel compelled to ask what are the Shadowy Horses of Disaster ; the four cardinal points have a conventional relation to the four capitalized abstractions (Sleep, Hope, Dream, endless Desire), and danger is coming from the capitalized symbols (the Horses of Disaster) ; but the poem is carefully contrived so as to leave undefined the danger which Robartes cannot help but express even while seeking to forget it. Yeats wrote the poem to a lady whom he called in manuscript notes ' Diana Vernon ' ; he began to court her in 1895 while he was still in love with Maud Gonne, and he hoped to shelter himself from pursuing cares and responsibilities and from his helpless passion in her arms.  The style was suitably escapist, but he had too many cares and responsibilities to remain for long in the ' deep twilight of rest '.

When he found that this elaborate manner was infecting even some short stories about the poet Hanrahan, which were supposed to be in peasant dialect but were actually farther from it than the stories of *The Celtic Twilight*, Yeats came to the conclusion that he had reached a crisis in his artistic development.  Probably about this time he wrote to Fiona Macleod to ask her which of his two styles she preferred.  He tells in his *Autobiographies* of his perplexity : ' I had for some time been troubled about my work.  I had written " Rosa Alchemica " and many slow-moving elaborate poems, and felt I had lost my old country emotions of the *Countess Cathleen* and of the early poems.'  He consulted Diana Vernon, who was ' psychic ', and she advised him to shun ' the solar ray ' and ' live near water '.  ' " Solar ", according to all that I learnt from Mathers, meant elaborate, full of artifice . . . whereas " water " meant " lunar " and " lunar " all that is simple, popular, traditional, emotional.'  Her words were in his mind when he went with Arthur Symons to visit Edward Martyn at Tullyra Castle in Galway.  The visit proved important for several reasons.  Not far off the Galway coast are the Aran Islands, and Yeats now plotted out a novel which would alternate between Aran and Paris ; its hero would talk with peasants in Aran and work with mystical cults in Paris, thus affording opportunity for both the simple manner and the elaborate one.  To gather background material Yeats made two trips in a fishing boat to Aran and was greatly impressed by the folk and fairy tales he heard there.

While at Tullyra, too, he met Lady Gregory, who invited him to visit her at Coole which was close by.  He spent part of the summer there, and, being in ill-health, did no literary work but went with Lady Gregory to peasants' cottages collecting more peasant stories.  Never had Yeats been a more enthusiastic supporter of the peasantry.  When he returned to London, he talked of little else.  George Moore, on making his acquaintance about this time, was informed that it was only from the peasants that 'one could learn to write, their speech being living speech, flowing out of the habits of their lives, struck out of life itself'. Later in the same year Yeats was in Paris and met John Synge, who was planning to write critical articles on contemporary French literature. Yeats persuaded him that Symons had already covered the field and urged him to go to Aran and learn style from the peasants. Eventually Synge followed his advice.

Whenever Yeats swings strongly in one direction we must be wary of him. Though he gives the impression in his *Autobiographies* that he had now returned entirely to the folk tradition, we find that, after the excellent reception of *The Secret Rose* in 1897, he wrote to O'Leary on May 30: 'It is at any rate an honest attempt towards that aristocratic esoteric Irish literature, which has been my chief ambition. We have a literature for the people but nothing yet for the few.' Indeed, he would not have propagandized his friends so violently had he not also been propagandizing himself ; it was no easy matter to get back to the soil. Near the end of the century the effect of the propaganda becomes evident. By this time, however, other factors had entered in, so that the interest in peasant speech may best be considered as one of a complex of symptoms of a growing disaffection with Pre-Raphaelitism in verse which paralleled his father's break away from Pre-Raphaelitism in painting a quarter of a century before. Yeats learned from the Aran Islanders but he also learned from actors and actresses, for from 1899 he had the opportunity of testing the power of his writings upon a theatre audience. It became apparent at once that the lavish beauty in which he had indulged during the 'nineties would not serve with an impatient audience. Not only did he rewrite drastically his old plays, but he also turned for the first time to writing prose dramas. For two years he collaborated with George Moore, helping him first with a revision of a play of Edward Martyn (*The Tale of a Town*), and then writing in full-scale collaboration an Irish heroic drama, *Diarmuid and Grania*, which has happily not been published. Though Yeats hated

Moore's style, he respected his skill in construction, and Moore must have constantly forced the sacrifice of some bewitching prose rhythm for the sake of the plot. Some heated correspondence passed between them on the subject. Inevitably they quarrelled and broke apart, and then in 1902 Yeats wrote a great number of plays with Lady Gregory, who had a very good ear for country dialect and natural speech. Meanwhile he indefatigably attended rehearsals, talked with actors, and tried to work out a new theory for the speaking of verse. He carried on a long correspondence on the subject with the knowledgeable Irish actor, Frank Fay, and a series of demonstrations with the actress Florence Farr. Yeats would lecture on the method of verse-speaking and she would recite to the accompaniment of a specially designed instrument vaguely like a lute which they called the psaltery. The defect of the method was that it exalted sound above sense, but even so it gave Yeats the rare opportunity of frequent oral tests of his work.

The effect of these activities was to reduce the extravagances of his two styles both in prose and verse, and to effect an unstable marriage between them. The change in his prose, a less straight-forward one, can be seen in a passage from an essay on the psaltery which he wrote in 1902 :

I cannot tell what changes this new art is to go through, or to what greatness or littleness of fortune ; but I can imagine little stories in prose with their dialogues in metre going pleasantly to the strings. I am not certain that I shall not see some Order naming itself from the Golden Violet of the Troubadours or the like, and having among its members none but well-taught and well-mannered speakers who will keep the new art from disrepute. They will know how to keep from singing notes and from prosaic lifeless intonations, and they will always understand, however far they push their experiments, that poetry and not music is their object ; and they will have by heart, like the Irish *File* [minstrels], so many poems and notations that they will never have to bend their heads over the book, to the ruin of dramatic expression and of that wild air the bard had always about him in my boyish imagination. They will go here and there speaking their verses and their little stories wherever they can find a score or two of poetical-minded people in a big room, or a couple of poetical-minded friends sitting by the hearth, and poets will write them poems and little stories to the confounding of print and paper. I, at any rate, from this out mean to write all my longer poems for the stage, and all my shorter ones for the Psaltery, if only some strong angel keep me to my good resolutions.

The manner of writing here displayed, while in many ways very pleasing, is not altogether satisfactory. Its main characteristics are graciousness and evasiveness. After reading the paragraph we are prepared to give it general consent simply because the author has cautiously left nothing for us to attack. We cannot tell how much he believes what he says and how much he is simply expounding a beguiling fancy. The paragraph abounds in non-committal expressions ; Yeats does not exactly advocate or predict the use of the psaltery ; he merely is 'not certain' that he will not see a psaltery movement arise. Then, too, he smiles slightly at us, and perhaps the smile means that we should not take this urbane man too seriously. He writes with the confidence of the author who is making no assertions to which his reader will not consent ; he seems to say, if you do not believe in the psaltery, and indeed, perhaps you are right, you will certainly not deny that verse today is badly spoken. No one need wonder that shortly after writing the essay he gave up the psaltery.

We will not pause to illustrate his increased skill in handling peasant speech in his comedies, which were admittedly minor works ; in his principal prose essays he used that devious way of writing which he had evolved so that his growing cautiousness about his own ideas could be successfully concealed under an appearance of taking the reader into his confidence. At his best he writes very well within this framework, especially in matters peripheral to the point ; but he usually commits himself definitely only to the most general propositions. The technique is very adroit ; he interrupts the flowing rhythm often enough with a short phrase or a change in sentence structure, so that we are never afraid as in reading 'Rosa Alchemica' that he has anaesthetized us ; he introduces simple words and phrases, such as ' a couple of ', ' here and there ', ' a big room ', which suggest common speech without descending, as in *The Celtic Twilight*, to the awkwardness of excessive simplicity. There is no doubt that this way of writing is effective, but it is not very bold. It consorts better with the theatre director who must think of his audience than with Paul Routledge trying to tear down the world. Half-consciously aware of his circumspection and accommodation, Yeats had many doubts about his prose style to the end of his life, and in old age made a great effort to alter it.

Prose, he said later, has not ' those simple forms that like a masquer's mask protect us with their anonymity '. Because verse had that advantage, it moved ahead of his prose, growing more limber, firm, and courageous, and throwing off some of the fainting rhythms. We can gather some of his changing theories of verse from his correspondence. In a letter to George Russell probably dating from 1898, he urges him to eliminate from his poem ' Carrowmore ' the word ' ere ', as being ' a conventional bit of poetic diction ', and suggests changing two lines because ' out of the natural order of the words '. Writing Russell in 1900, he criticizes the description of a goddess as vague : ' I think I would myself avoid it in poetry for the same reason that I would avoid " haunted " & because vague forms, pictures, scenes, etc., are rather a modern idea of the poetic & I would not want to call up a modern kind of picture. . . . All ancient vision was definite and precise '.

*Definite and precise* : the words suggest anything but the poetry of *The Wind among the Reeds*. A letter to Fiona Macleod in 1901 carries his theories a little further ; he advises her to seek in her style for ' utter simplicity ', a ' self-effacing rhythm and language ', an expression that is ' like a tumbler of water rather than a cup of wine '. In his own verse, he says, he has to make ' everything very hard and clear. . . . It is like riding a wild horse. If one's hands fumble or one's knees loosen one is thrown.' The formula which he phrased in later life as ' the natural words in the natural order ' is beginning to dom-

inate his technique in ' Adam's Curse ', published in December
1902 :

> We sat together at one summer's end,
> That beautiful mild woman, your close friend,
> And you and I, and talked of poetry.
>
> I said, ' A line will take us hours maybe ;
> Yet if it does not seem a moment's thought,
> Our stitching and unstitching has been naught.
> Better go down upon your marrow-bones
> And scrub a kitchen pavement, or break stones
> Like an old pauper in all kinds of weather ;
> For to articulate sweet sounds together
> Is to work harder than all these, and yet
> Be thought an idler by the noisy set
> Of bankers, schoolmasters, and clergymen
> The martyrs call the world.'

This verisimilitude is a new development for Yeats in lyrical
verse.  He is remarkably successful in reproducing for the first
time ordinary conversation in selected, heightened form ; words
like ' marrow-bones ', ' kitchen pavements ', ' bankers, school-
masters, and clergymen ', which he would once have rigorously
excluded, now appear without undermining the tone.  But the
ending of the poem reminds us that he has still not gone over
definitely to his mature manner, for it reverts almost to the
technique of *The Wind among the Reeds* (1899) :

> We sat grown quiet at the name of love ;
> We saw the last embers of daylight die,
> And in the trembling blue-green of the sky
> A moon, worn as if it had been a shell
> Washed by time's waters as they rose and fell
> About the stars and broke in days and years.
>
> I had a thought for no one's but your ears :
> That you were beautiful, and that I strove
> To love you in the old high way of love ;
> That it had all seemed happy, and yet we'd grown
> As weary-hearted as that hollow moon.

Even here, however, the loosening of rhythm in the next to last line, the somewhat abrupt ' for no one's but your ears ', and the imperfect rhymes of the last two couplets show that Yeats was pulling away from his earlier method.

He felt that he was changing. Writing to Lady Gregory in January 1903, he said : ' You need not be troubled about my poetical faculty. I was never so full of new thoughts for verse though all thoughts quite unlike the old ones. My work has got far more masculine. It has more salt in it.' But he did not anticipate the sudden admixture of new ingredients into his life and work which came a few weeks later.

## CHAPTER XI

# THE END OF YOUTH

> And what of her that took
> All till my youth was gone
> With scarce a pitying look?
> How could I praise that one?
>
> YEATS, ' Friends '

IN 1903 a wind storm did considerable damage to Lady
Gregory's estate in Galway, and in a little book of verse,
*In the Seven Woods*, printed in July of that year, Yeats
refers to the disaster :

I made some of these poems walking about among the Seven
Woods, before the big wind of nineteen hundred and three blew down
so many trees, & troubled the wild creatures, & changed the look of
things ; and I thought out there a good part of the play which follows.
The first shape of it came to me in a dream, but it changed much
in the making, foreshadowing, it may be, a change that may bring a
less dream-burdened will into my verses.

His allusion to the climate and natural scenery is so insistent as
to suggest that he may have been thinking of something else,
and perhaps we may guess what was in his mind.

The rather scattered references which have been made to
Maud Gonne should not give the impression that Yeats's interests
were ever very far away from her. Since January 1889 his life
and everything he did had been coloured by his love, which was
always unsuccessful but never decisively discouraged. His letters
make clear that he was very deeply in love, and not merely
playing at the role of modern troubadour. So on November 30,
1891, he writes to Russell :

I have seen Miss Gonne several times & have, I think, found an
ally in the cousin with whom she is staying. An accidental word of

the cousin's showed me that they had been discussing me together & reading my poems in the vellum book, & yesterday the cousin gave me a hint to go to Paris next spring when Miss Gonne did — so you see I am pretty cheerful for the time until the next regiment of black devils come.  Tomorrow Miss Gonne is to be initiated into GD — the next day she goes to Paris but I shall see her on her way through London a couple of weeks later — she promises to work at the Young Ireland League for me this winter.  Go & see her when she gets to Dublin & keep her from forgetting me & occultism.

The vellum book, which Yeats had presented to her, contained such poems as these :

### DEDICATION OF 'JOHN SHERMAN AND DHOYA'

We poets labour all our days
To make a little beauty be
But vanquished by a woman's gaze
And the unlabouring stars are we ;
So I, most lovely child of Ir,
Rising from labour bow the knee
With equal reverence to the fire
Of the unlabouring stars and thee.

Dublin, Sept. 1st, 1891


He who bade the white plains of the pole
From the brooding warm years be apart ;
He has made me the friend of your soul,—
Ah he keeps for another your heart.

Dublin, October 1891


### YOUR PATHWAY

Archangels were I god should go
Unhook the stars out of the sky,
And in a sudden hurry fly
And spread them in a shining row,
A shining pathway as were meet ;—
I had alone my life for thee—
Tread gently, tread most tenderly,
My life is under thy sad feet.

Dublin, July 5th, 1891

These are not the poems by which a woman is won, but they demonstrate his sincerity. Maud Gonne knew about almost all his secret activities ; she had been initiated into the Golden Dawn, though she had soon resigned ; she had also been a member for a time of the Irish Republican Brotherhood, into which she persuaded a London doctor to initiate her in spite of the rule against women members. As we have seen, she was Yeats's main helper in reviving the Druidic mysteries. His nationalist work was closely linked with her. She had even taken part in the dramatic movement for a time as an actress and as vice-president of the Irish Theatre Society. But not only was she involved in the same secret and public organizations ; she was his confidant for every plan and ambition, and he told her all, thinking that once she knew she would become his. Maud Gonne gave him little inkling of much of her character.

Because he considered his to be the perfect love, for five years he had nothing to do with other women, but, wrestling with his senses, thought of himself as an Arthurian Knight dedicated to his lady's service unto the death. Then, in 1894, he half escaped from the toils. The lady whom he called in manuscript notes ' Diana Vernon ' was a beautiful, sensitive, and very unhappily married novelist. She was charming and of good family, and her love was flattering and consolatory. She gave him to understand that she had many lovers, he says in the first draft of his *Autobiographies*, and, thinking that wrong, he suggested that they become lovers. At the same time, he did not know how to conduct the affair, for since childhood he ' had never touched a woman's lips '. First they plotted to run away together, but on the day when Diana Vernon came with a friend to his rooms to make final arrangements, Yeats, who had gone to buy cakes for tea, discovered he had forgotten his key and could not let them or himself in. With Maud Gonne never far from his mind, he must have had a strong half-conscious repulsion to the elopement.

The love affair was carried on at first with great timidity on both sides, as Yeats smilingly confessed many years afterwards.

From late in 1894 he met Diana Vernon frequently, and they resolved not to give vent to their passions until Diana's elderly mother had died and their elopement would not cause her mother pain. Then Diana decided to ask her husband for a separation, expecting that he would be indifferent, but instead he was astonishingly put out and went to bed ill. So she told Yeats it would be ' kinder to deceive him '. Still nothing happened until two friends in whom they had confided intervened and told them that, since elopement was out of the question, they should no longer curb their love.

Yeats accordingly left the flat he shared with Arthur Symons at Fountain Court and, probably in January 1896, took rooms at Woburn Buildings, near St. Pancras's Church. He went with Diana Vernon to buy furniture, and remembered their embarrassed conversation about the size of the bed, each additional inch of space increasing the expense. Yeats was extraordinarily nervous but Diana was very sympathetic, and at last the affair got well under way. It lasted, he says, nine or ten months, or possibly a little less ; he was always somewhat discontented, as we can tell from his sorrowful love poems, 'Michael Robartes Bids His Beloved Be at Peace ', and ' Aedh Gives His Beloved Certain Rhymes ', and never surrendered wholly to his new love. Then one day came the first letter for many months from Maud Gonne and tore him apart. Diana Vernon soon saw that something was wrong, and when she discovered the truth visited Woburn Buildings no more for many years.

The obsession for Maud Gonne came back to him now with its old fury. His family wanted him to forget her ; a good friend like Russell warned him that she would never marry him, and Yeats replied admitting that he had no reason for hope ' except a few omens '. The strain was almost more than he could bear. He lived as he said on tiptoe, and was continually on the verge of physical collapse. At Coole in the summer of 1897 he was almost too weak to dress himself. In a manuscript book of about this time we find the pathetic entry :

SUBJECT FOR LYRIC

O my beloved you only are
    not moved by my songs
Which you only understand
You only know that it is
    of you I sing when I tell
    of the swan on the water
    or the eagle in the heavens
    or the faun in the wood.
Others weep but your eyes
    are dry.

II

O my beloved.   How happy
I was that day when you
came here from the
railway, and set your hair
aright in my looking glass
and then sat with me at
my table, and lay resting
in my big chair.   I am
like the children o my
beloved and I play at
marriage — I play
with images of the life
you will not give to me o
my cruel one.

He confided mainly in Lady Gregory, for he had to confide
in someone, and his letters during these years make frequent
anxious references to the degree of Maud Gonne's friendliness
or unfriendliness at their last meeting or in her last letter.  Though
she steadily refused to marry him she kept writing to him, as he
later said, with 'no sense of the mischief she was doing', and never
allowed their relations to lapse.   Once he saw her in Dublin and
she seemed half willing to yield.   He wrote an incoherent letter to
Lady Gregory who was then in Italy, and she returned at once and
offered to give him money to marry.   'Do not leave her until

she has consented', Lady Gregory said, but Yeats answered :
' No, I am too exhausted, I can do no more.'

The state of mind between hoping and having, desire and
fufilment, brought him to those shadowy waters of vague pain
and to the quicksands of the poetry of *The Wind among the
Reeds*, a poetry where one sinks down and down without finding
bottom.  If we combine this mental turmoil with ill-health we
have some idea of the acute suffering Yeats went through during
what might have been his happy youth.  Failure in his personal
life clouded all his successes in literature and in organizations,
and his health, for mental or physical reasons, was frequently
near the breaking-point.  He badly needed someone to look after
him and guard him from the irregular existence of a bachelor.
A London pathologist, who knew him from 1890 in the Golden
Dawn, suspected that he had tuberculosis, and many years later
believed the suspicions were confirmed when he X-rayed Yeats,
though by that time the disease had gone.

Whether the malady was nervous strain or tuberculosis, or,
as seems likely, a combination of the two, the cure was due to
Lady Gregory.  She gave him a permanent home at Coole for
his summers, with a definite, unalterable routine, and when he
went to London her bounty followed him in great packages of
food and wine.  She lent him money, too, rather against his will,
which he was not in a position to repay for many years.  By
1902, when he wrote five plays with her help and stayed much
of the year at Coole, he had become much stronger physically,
and to this recovery is probably attributable some of the new
firmness in his verse.

But the old attraction remained.  He and Maud Gonne met
often in Dublin now and he could not stop loving her.  He
thought she would never marry anyone, but would devote her
life to the salvation of Ireland, and on that theme he wrote
*Cathleen Ni Houlihan* in 1902 for her to act.  But the heavens
were frowning.  One night in February 1903 he went to give a
lecture, and just before he was about to speak he was handed a
letter in her familiar handwriting.  Maud Gonne wrote, however,

an unfamiliar message : she had just married Major John MacBride in Paris.

For a moment, 'the ears being deafened, the sight of the eyes blind / With lightning', Yeats did not know what to do. Then he went through with his lecture, and afterwards members of the audience congratulated him on its excellence, but he could never remember a word of what he had said.

Now we may grasp the full significance of his remarks on the big wind which ' blew down so many trees, & troubled the wild creatures, & changed the look of things '. The forest he had planted with so much tenderness and care toppled suddenly and left

> Roots half hidden under snows,
> Broken boughs and blackened leaves.

He was broad-awake and thirty-seven years old, half of his life over. What would he do now that his most cherished dream was gone ?

## CHAPTER XII

# A NEW DIVISION

Moi-même, que je haïs comme une épouse.

Valéry, *Ébauches de Mon Faust*

Myself wars on myself.

Yeats, *Deirdre*

As he puts the 'nineties resolutely behind him the defect of Yeats's work during the first half of his life becomes apparent in retrospect, and can be partially traced to psychological causes. The relations between poetry and the poet are admittedly not even and precise ; any good poem, when completed, has to some extent escaped out of the poet's life into an independent existence, so that the act of creation is also an act of separation. Yet the danger of not allowing for this separation is probably less with minor verse, where the creative process has not worked at white heat, and Yeats's early verse was no more than minor. If we look closely at either his early prose or his early poetry, we are compelled to notice that, instead of solving the problem of creation, he had largely dodged it. What the problem was we can see in part from studying his psychological difficulties in youth, and in part from examining his later solution. Given his sense of a divided mind, Yeats had to try to achieve in his verse what Coleridge called the ' balance or reconcilement of opposite or discordant qualities '. His shortcoming in the 'nineties was that he conceived of his art, not as a balance or reconcilement, but as a see-saw, sometimes between scepticism and belief, sometimes between natural and supernatural love, sometimes between action and the dream, sometimes between the peasant and aristocratic traditions. In later life, as will become clear, he welded such oppositions together, but earlier he conceived of his artistic method largely as an absorption of contrary impressions which he liked to believe were often visions or like visions. As in his poem, ' To the Rose upon the Rood of Time ', he saw no inconsistency in beginning the poem by summoning the rose, then partially repelling it, and then summoning it once more. He received and portrayed emotions episodically, unifying them mainly by technical devices. Later he was to abjure this method as ' sensuality ', because it pretended ' that we can linger between spirit and sense '. These were not the only opposites between which he lingered, but the word ' sensuality ' is a good description for verse which is too readily assumed to be entirely mystical.

The world which Yeats builds up in the 'nineties is therefore not really an independent world at all, but a skilful evasion, neither here nor there. His professed object was, like Mallarmé's, to evoke an unseen reality ; and symbols were the only way to do it. But in practice Yeats used the symbols primarily to hide this world rather than to reveal another one. George Russell pointed out that the land of his friend's early verse was not the ' Land of the Living Heart ' but the ' Many-Coloured Land ', and his remark may be translated as meaning that the poet was not concerned with truth but with concealment by decoration. As we have observed in the poems, ' To my Heart, bidding it have no Fear ', and ' Michael Robartes bids his Beloved be at Peace ', Yeats makes his passion unrecognizable by subduing and obfuscating it ; he escapes from personal statement but, his freedom secured, has nowhere to go. Early in his acquaintance with Katharine Tynan he had written to her that they both needed to substitute the landscape of nature for the landscape of art, but the press of his personal failure in love made this impossible.

We must, indeed, conclude that Yeats's attitude towards Maud Gonne had a great deal to do with the state of mind that generated his early poetry ; the fact that his love was centred on a woman so beautiful as to be a symbol of beauty seemed to justify his uncertainty as to how she would finally act towards him. In an affair of the heart, closely connected with the enterprise of writing verse, he left the decision to another, and then wrote poems in which he hid his plight ; he was like a man who carries a heavy burden on his back and tries to dress so that it will not show. Symbolism, instead of providing a means for balance and reconcilement, furnished an elaborate robe to cover a wretched young man. This, then, was the effect of his life upon his verse : just as he accepted Maud Gonne's supremacy in his love affair, so he could adopt no masterful attitude towards the symbols of which she made one. Instead of manipulating his symbols, he drowned himself in them. The result is that they are imperfect symbols, if we accept symbols in Baudelaire's sense as the means by which man can penetrate the temple of nature. Yeats's ' shadowy horses' and ' majestical multitude' are elaborate metaphors which suggest a symbolical meaning that they do not sustain. They are pegs to hang moods on, but other pegs would do just as well. Yeats himself recognized that his early verse had not done what he intended, when he wrote in 1908 : ' I had set out on life with the thought of putting my very self into poetry, and had understood this as a representation of my own visions and an attempt to cut away the non-essential, but as I imagined the visions outside myself my imagination became full of decorative landscape and of still life '. We need only look at his father's imperfectly painted but shrewdly conceived portraits of him during the 'nineties to understand ; the pictures show him with a yielding, passive body, his face bathed in softness and shadow. There was point in James Joyce's remark that Yeats's early poems were ' onanistic ', that is, that they were self-indulgent and not truly creative.

Some men, John Butler Yeats once wrote to Dowden, are born in full armour ; others have to develop slowly, and Yeats was of the latter sort. He moved ahead by trial and error, only gradually learning his own potentialities. Frequently he failed, but usually found instruction in his failures. Thus his early efforts to bring his thoughts into unity in the Irish mystical order and then in the dramatic movement were not successful, the first because the revelations which he hoped to receive from the other world did not come, the second because he leaned over sideways to embrace what the Abbey Theatre now disrespectfully calls P.Q. (Peasant Quality). He was later to return to both, but with a less naïve point of view. The mystical rituals would eventually be transformed into the elaborate machinery of the *Vision*. The endeavour to find spontaneity and escape from deliberateness in the folk tradition would be successful for Yeats when, as an old man, he achieved a real instead of an artificial simplicity. This was not to be done by immersion in the folk tradition, but by better understanding of himself.

The period which now begins for him is primarily a theoretical one, as dangerous in its way as the laxly emotional one which had preceded it. Instead of simply representing his inner conflict in various half-instinctive projections, he tries now to expose it to theoretical investigation. He moves from the twilight to the cold of dawn before the sun appears. The alteration was so considerable that George Russell, who wrote an essay on him in 1902 entitled ' The Poet of Shadows ', had to attach a note in 1906 saying that his essay no longer applied. The years from Maud Gonne's marriage in 1903 to Yeats's own in 1917 provide a curious parallel to those from 1895 to 1903. The poet felt called upon to rebel against his own past, as he had done repeatedly since his revulsion against science in late childhood, and particularly against the vague unity in his life and work which he had tried to attain near the century's end. In order to mend his soul, he had to split it again into pairs of opposites ; these pairs, as will now be abundantly clear, were constantly changing according to his mood and interest. Since he was older, however, the results were different from what they had been before. While we investigate this redivision of himself, it should be borne in mind that as early as 1906 the counter-process of reuniting had begun, and that Yeats was conscious of both processes of fission and fusion and was attempting to find a rational justification for the peculiar method of self-development which he had earlier come upon instinctively.

The first years were evidently the most difficult for him. His *Autobiographies* end in 1902, and from that date until December 1908, when he began a diary, we have no direct recording of his thought or life.  During almost six years he wrote only one lyric, ' O do not Love too Long '.  In a man notoriously indiscreet about self-revelation (his wife would banteringly christen him ' William Tell ') the silence about these years is significant. His fists were tightly clenched.

Most of the facts we know or can guess.  Early in May 1903 he had a talk with Maud Gonne and they remained friends.  The same month his book of essays, *Ideas of Good and Evil*, was published, and his letters about it indicate that he already considered it inadequate.  To Russell he writes : ' The book is only one half of the orange for I only got a grip on the other half lately ', and his letter to John Quinn, a New York lawyer and patron of the arts, is even more decisive : ' I feel that much of it is out of my present mood, that it is true, but no longer true for me.  I have been in a good deal better health lately, and that and certain other things have made me look upon the world, I think, with somewhat more defiant eyes.  The book is . . . too lyrical, too full of aspirations after remote things, too full of desires.  Whatever I do from this out will, I think, be more creative.  I will express myself, so far as I can express myself in criticism at all, by that sort of thought that leads straight to action, straight to some form of craft.'

In November of the same year Yeats went to America on a lecture tour which lasted into 1904.  For the first time in his life he was far away from friends and relations, and could test himself in new surroundings.  He took the tour very seriously, and worked hard to perfect his oratorical method.  In the old days he had deprecated oratory, but now he spoke of it with respect. The trip obviously afforded him an occasion to reconsider his way of life.  On his return people noticed a change in him ; as one of his friends commented, he was *externalized*.

This alteration must be held in mind as we try to follow Yeats's mind in its writhings and twistings over the question of Maud Gonne's marriage, which remained the most important event of his life for many years.  Rejection of his love had come too late for him to mollify its shock, as most men do, in the pattern of other experiences. Yeats, until his thirty-seventh year, had remained in his love affair a wide-eyed boy. Even the liaison with Diana Vernon had from beginning to end a self-conscious purity about it. He had never surrendered to his instincts with any full confidence, and generally had repressed them, preferring to remain faithful to the most beautiful woman in the world, who, if she would not marry him, yet assured him of her affection, and had told him she was not interested in marrying anyone. Then he saw John MacBride, a dashing major of the Irish Transvaal Brigade in the Boer War, but no poet, no occultist, no learned man, in fact, no perfect lover, take the rose he had so long striven for in vain.

Was the blame his or hers ? Could his fifteen-year-old conception of her character be at fault ? Was it not rather some defect in his own soul that he had lost her ? Some quality of MacBride's that had won her ? Yeats blamed his own timid, critical intellect for restraining his impetuous nature so that when he should have embraced he had feared and qualified and idealized. He had lost the capacity for acting on instinct which men like MacBride, lacking the critical mind, possessed. Maud Gonne's marriage was therefore an indictment ; instead of condemning her, he condemned himself, ' took all the blame, out of all sense and reason '.

The five plays which date from 1903 to 1910 are filled with this sense of guilt at having separated himself from ' the normal, active man '. The first of these, *On Baile's Strand*, was written on the theme of father against son which was close to Yeats's heart as it was to Matthew Arnold's. Yeats had handled the theme before in a short verse narrative, but into his new treatment he put ' heart-mysteries ', as he admitted near the end of his life. Though the armed combat is between Cuchulain and the stranger who will not give his name, the real struggle is between the warrior Cuchulain, instinctively loving and hating, and the crafty king Conchubar who forces Cuchulain to slay unwittingly his own son. Cuchulain's tragic fate, like Yeats's own, is caused by his listening to the voice of apparent reason ; instead of following his own impulse to make friends with the unknown warrior, he allows Conchubar to persuade him that the cry of his heart is witchcraft, and discovers too late the identity of his opponent. Yeats never explained this meaning of the play, said indeed that he had forgotten what his symbols meant except that the fool and blind man, who constitute a kind of chorus to the main action, are the shadows of Cuchulain and Conchubar. Thus he divided himself into four parts, the warrior and his opposite, the fool ; the wise man and his opposite, the helpless blind man ; and put all his raging bitterness into blind man and fool who steal the bread from the ovens while Cuchulain, overcome with grief at what he has done, battles madly with the waves.

The King's Threshold, completed in 1903, the same year as On Baile's Strand, is a less complicated picture of poet against the world. The quarrels in the Irish theatre movement no doubt had something to do with pushing the theme into Yeats's consciousness. Seanchan the bard goes on a hunger strike to resist the efforts of the King to restrict the rights of the poets. Again the imprudent individualist, with his high, laughing verse, battles with the politic King and his dour practicality. The antithesis is clearer still in Deirdre, begun in 1904 and finished in 1907. Here Naisi, the ' young, famous, popular man ' has carried off the King's bride because of his ' insolent strength of youth ', but is at last trapped and killed by order of the jealous, crafty, patient King Conchubar. Naisi is not John MacBride, nor King Conchubar Yeats, but Naisi is the qualities in Yeats which MacBride's success made Yeats realize he had suppressed, as Conchubar is the qualities which MacBride made Yeats realize he had overly exalted. ' I give you the championship because you are without fear ', says the stranger to Cuchulain in The Golden Helmet (1908), and the speech in the poetic version of the same story, The Green Helmet (1910), makes the partisanship clear :

. . . I choose the laughing lip
That shall not turn from laughing whatever rise or fall,
The heart that grows no bitterer, although betrayed by all ;
The hand that loves to scatter ; the life like a gambler's throw. . . .

The issue was battled out in earnest in the early drafts of *The Player Queen*, begun in 1907 after the completion of *Deirdre*. Here two lovers, Yellow Martin and Peter, expound their philosophies, which are really the philosophies of Yeats in the nineteenth and Yeats in the twentieth century, respectively :

*Peter.* She cannot be found anywhere.

*Yellow Martin.* Not found ! Not found ! Oh, my God ! What has happened to her ! She has hidden herself, drowned herself maybe.

*Peter.* She will come back when she is hungry.

*Yellow Martin.* You don't know what she is capable of. She is capable of killing herself, that she might look up through the roots of the grass and see my misery.

*Peter [sings].* ' Woman's delight is the death of her best-beloved,
Who dies in tears and in sighs.' [William Blake]

*Yellow Martin.* Here am I all out of my mind, and you sing your verses at me. Is there nothing in life that you do not take as a game ?

*Peter.* Because I take all things lightly, I am a master of all [*stands up, puts arm on poet's shoulder affectionately*]. If you would only listen to me. Here am I, with all my trifling, with my empty head, and I have won, and tired of, half a dozen women, while you were losing one. Love is an art — a science, if you will. You treat it as if it were the inspiration of heaven. Why do you not give way to her a little, pretending to think her right when you know she is wrong.

*Yellow Martin.* But she wants to play a part that she can't play, and that nobody wants if she could play it. Such a wild part. I must not let her hurt herself. Love is a part of wisdom. I have to bring her mine, my wisdom. How else can we be the two halves to make one perfect whole ?

*Peter.* No, no. Love is not a part of wisdom, but of gaiety and love. My dear Martin, it is we light lovers who understand love. We make of ourselves what a woman wishes.

*Yellow Martin.* But I wish her to be all the perfection I can imagine, and would be no less myself.

*Peter.* Seem a little, play a little. If you are jealous try to seem trustful and happy. If you are full of gloom because she was cross with you seem lighter than a swallow. If you think her foolish, pretend that she is wisdom itself.

*Yellow Martin.* But I love, and she would not think me worthy of her love if I did not show myself strong enough to be her master.

*Peter.* But only we who love lightly, keeping always our gaiety, are
masters.    Love masters you, and so you are despised.
*Yellow Martin.* But I love her, what else can I do ?

If we try to assemble the terms of the dichotomy of the personality as Yeats now sees it, we find such oppositions as these :
spontaneity against craft, light-heartedness against seriousness,
pretence against sincerity, natural mastery against artificial
authority, and, as we shall see, mask against face.   The relation
of Michael Robartes to Aherne during the 'nineties had been
primarily that of tempter to tempted, but now an active combat
and rivalry are at work.   The elements cannot co-exist :  they
collide and seek to destroy each other.

Among the qualities which he now extols, most are instinctive,
though, complicating the pattern, some are not.   The respect for
instinct was not new, for Yeats had always had it and would not
have left London so often for Sligo and then for Coole Park if he
had not.   But the shock of Maud Gonne's marriage emphasized
to him how much a part of his being the way of the serpent had
become ; till then he had not realized how tortuous his mind's
workings were.   The world must not know how deeply he had
been hurt.   A young man who has been jilted puts injured pride
in place of love and conceals his wound.   Yeats, feeling as always
with unusual intensity, had gone on with his lecture the night
the dreadful news arrived, and now savagely pursued his theatre
work and writing though he was no longer an inhabitant of the
same world.   His feet sinking in the sands, he continued to hold
up the sky.   But in his writings he held emotion out at arm's
length, putting it in the mouths of legendary characters who are
more animate fractions of himself than living people.   No matter
what happens, they keep their sufferings inarticulate, and act
boldly and decisively.   The tight-lipped restraint with which
long before he had endowed the hero of *Mosada* now became a
constant feature, even a hallmark, of his work.

For his present mood the miracle play was no satisfactory
vehicle, being incapable of containing either earthly passion or a
tragic theme.   It was also too closely tied up with the early days

of the theatre and with the Irish mystical order, and thus with
Maud Gonne. After 1902 Yeats put it aside for many years and
took to Irish heroic tragedy ; he had now

> Nothing to make a song about but kings,
> Helmets and swords, and half-forgotten things
> That were but memories of you,

as he wrote to Maud Gonne later. The kings never forget their
royal rank. Cuchulain, discovering the identity of the warrior
he has killed, does not cry out as in the old Irish saga, holding
the dead boy in his arms : ' Here is my son for you, men of
Ulster '. Instead, he speaks no word ; he shakes with grief, and
rushes off stage to do battle with the sea. The passion is in the
silence, and in the heroic personality that turns to madness rather
than to lamentation and tears.

In *The King's Threshold* the same heroic attitude enables
Seanchan to resist the blandishments of his friends and foes, and
of his own weaker nature, and at last by his implacability to bring
the King to his knees. Deirdre and Naisi, the Tristram and Iseult
of Irish legend, maintain the heroic pose by playing chess while
waiting for the King to wreak his vengeance on them, and after
Naisi's murder Deirdre, who has found the pretence of indifference most difficult to maintain, is able to feign a calm resignation
that she does not feel until she gains Conchubar's permission to
perform the last rites for her lover and commits suicide over his
body behind the curtain. We do not see her weep ; the heroic
pose holds back her tears as the curtain covers her death. King
Conchubar, too, has the pose ; he has been for seven years
' watching my own face / That none might read it '. Yeats stated
his theory in an essay on Synge which he wrote in 1910 :

When Oedipus speaks out of the most vehement passions, he is
conscious of the presence of the Chorus, men before whom he must
keep up appearances, ' children latest born of Cadmus' line ' who do
not share his passion. . . . Nothing happens before our eyes. The
dignity of Greek drama, and in a lesser degree of that of Corneille
and Racine, depends, as contrasted with the troubled life of Shakespearean drama, on an almost even speed of dialogue, and on a so

continuous exclusion of the animation of common life, that thought remains lofty and language rich.

He was at last finding reasons for what he had been doing for many years.

To grasp at the same time the psychological genesis and the meaning of his doctrines we must turn back and forth between his life and work. His policy of concealment of his more intimate self now became much more definite than it had been before. His timid, sensitive nature, his keen sense of personal failure, he enveloped for the world's view in the habiliments of arrogance and power. He will let no one, except Lady Gregory and one or two other woman friends, observe the soul which, as we shall later see, he was all the time trying to improve. Not till many years afterwards did he describe himself as he truly was at this period, ' one that ruffled in a manly pose / For all his timid heart '. The word that begins to occur constantly in his writings during the first decade of the century is ' mask ', a word which lent dignity and a kind of traditional sanction to his theories of the pose. He first used it prominently in verse in a song he wrote in August 1910, for *The Player Queen* :

### THE MASK

' Put off that mask of burning gold
With emerald eyes.'
' O no, my dear, you make so bold
To find if hearts be wild and wise,
And yet not cold.'

' I would but find what's there to find,
Love or deceit.'
' It was the mask engaged your mind,
And after set your heart to beat,
Not what's behind.'

' But lest you are my enemy,
I must enquire.'
' O no, my dear, let all that be ;

What matter, so there is but fire
In you, in me ? '

As the poem appears in the *Collected Poems*, out of context, it
has the tone of a Cavalier poet, but an early draft shows a little
more of what was in Yeats's mind :

I would know who you are,
My beloved said to me,
Put off that mask of burning gold,
That mask with emerald eyes,
That I may know who you are,

I will not put away my mask,
It is the mask of burning gold,
It is the mask with emerald eyes,
That makes your heart beat so quickly,
I would be praised by the beating of your heart,

But my beloved answered me,
I do not know if you are a friend or if you are an
enemy.

It is a mistake to give all one's heart :

True love makes one a slave
Less than a man
The light lover is always love's master
So much the more is he man.

So Peter, the light lover, sings in an early draft of *The Player
Queen*.

The doctrine of the mask is so complex and so central in
Yeats that we can hardly attend to it too closely.   Even at this
early stage of its development it has multiple meanings and is a
variable concept.   To start with its simplest meaning, the mask
is the social self.   Browning had spoken of ' two soul-sides,
one to face the world with ', and one to show the beloved.
But Yeats's doctrine assumes that we face with a mask both the
world and the beloved.   A closely related meaning is that the
mask includes all the differences between one's own and other

people's conception of one's personality. To be conscious of the discrepancy which makes a mask of this sort is to look at oneself as if one were somebody else. In addition, the mask is defensive armour : we wear it, like the light lover, to keep from being hurt. So protected, we are only slightly involved no matter what happens. This theory seems to assume that we can be detached from experience like actors from a play. Finally, the mask is a weapon of attack ; we put it on to keep up a noble conception of ourselves ; it is a heroic ideal which we try to live up to. As a character in *The Player Queen* affirms : ' To be great we must seem so. . . . Seeming that goes on for a lifetime is no different from reality.' Yeats used to complain that English poets had no ' presence ', because they insisted upon looking too much like everyone else ; a poet should be instantly recognizable by his demeanour. The poet looks the poet, the hero looks the hero ; both may be deceiving others and they may even be practising a form of deception upon themselves.

If the mask seems at first to be the conception of a timid man, it cannot be dismissed as such. A draft of *The Player Queen* shows that Yeats is eliciting all the ambiguities in the notions of the mask and the theatre, and insisting upon a relation between reality and the dream which makes the latter no mere capitalized abstraction but a driving force in life.

*Player Queen.* I remember your own words, what you said the other day. I know that you were timid about your own thoughts, and nothing seems true that we find out for ourselves. Only the most delicate mind can discover the truth, and that mind is always hesitating. The truth comes to us like the morning lost in clouds hesitating . . . we are only confident about the ideas of others. But there must be people like me to take up your thoughts, to believe in them because they are not our own, to put them on our faces like a mask. . . . Let me become all your dreams. I will make them walk about the world in solid bone and flesh. People looking at them will become all fire themselves. They will change, there will be a Last Judgment in their souls, a burning and dissolving. . . .

*Yellow Martin.* No, no, I am older than you, and I know what the people want. They want Noah's wife and characters of that kind.

Aren't they just like her themselves ? She won't go into the ark.
Is she not just like themselves, tame and quiet and peaceable and her
thoughts on household things — I mean after she's been beaten.

In his devious way Yeats is coming at the problem of identity
and is puzzling over such questions as : Can we discuss a man
apart from his dreams and aspirations ? Can a man think of
himself without thinking of how he appears to others ? Is not
every man an actor ? Who does not wear a mask ?

A paradox is of course implicit in Yeats's belief that the mask,
a word which he chose deliberately because it was a creation of
artifice, could be filled with instinct and passion. Like every
artist, he believed that the best of him was in his work rather
than in his life. But the theory must be understood in part, also,
as one of desperation ; he was so removed, he thought, from
natural passions that he had to recover them somehow. As he
wrote in 1909 : ' I think that all happiness depends on the energy
to assume the mask of some other self ; that all joyous or creative
life is a re-birth as something not oneself, something which has
no memory and is created in a moment and perpetually renewed '.
For a bald record of his feelings at this time we must be grateful
to a quarrel Yeats had with Lady Gregory and her son Robert.
Edmund Gosse had written her an insulting letter. Yeats, to
whom Gosse had always been a faithful friend, did not condemn
him as quickly and instinctively as the Gregorys expected. To
justify himself Yeats wrote Robert Gregory a letter which he
probably never sent. In it he lays himself bare :

MY DEAR ROBERT : I want you to understand that I have no instincts
in personal life. I have reasoned them all away & reason acts very
slowly & with difficulty & has to exhaust every side of the subject.
Above all I have destroyed in myself by analysis instinctive indignation. When I was twenty or a little more I was shocked by the conversation at Henley's. One day I resolved if the conversation was as
bad again I would walk out. I did not do so & next day I reasoned
over the thing & persuaded myself that I had thought of walking out
from vanity & did not do so from fear. As I look back I see occasion
after occasion on which I have been prevented from doing what was

a natural & sometimes the right thing, either because analysis of the emotion or action of another or self distrustful analysis of my own emotion destroyed impulse. I cannot conceive the impulse, unless it were so sudden that I had to act at once, that could urge me into action at all, if it affected personal life. All last week the moment my impulse told me, that I should demand with indignation an apology from Gosse my analysis said ' you want to do a passionate thing because it stirs your pride.' I was once told by a relation that my father had done some disgraceful thing — of course it was absurd & untrue — & I found with amused horror that I was coldly arguing over the proba- bilities, & explaining (to myself I am glad to say) why it could not be true. In impersonal & public things — because there this distrust of myself does not come in I have impulse. I would have explained it by saying that it is the world I have been brought up in — you have always lived among defined social relations, I only among defined ideas — but then my family seems to me to have more than enough of the usual impulses. I even do my writing by self distrusting reasons. I thought to write this note in the same way as I wrote the others. And then I said ' I am explaining myself to Robert Gregory. I am afraid to write to him directly or speak to him directly & so I am writing this note thinking that some chance may show it to him. So I will write it as if to him. Since then while writing it I have thought this an insincerity, for I have understood that I am trying to put myself right with myself even more than with you.

I want you to understand that once one makes a thing subject to reason, as distinguished from impulse, one plays with it, even if it is a very serious thing. I am more ashamed because of the things I have played with in life than of any other thing.

All my moral endeavour for many years has been an attempt to recreate practical instinct in myself. I can only conceive of it as of a kind of acting.

One thing I want you to understand & that is that I was never influenced by any fear of a quarrel with Gosse. There were moments, when thinking over that letter which I believed to have been posted, I thought that Gosse would probably prevent my getting that pension. I never hesitated on that ground. I can say with sincerity I was simply thinking the matter out in an impersonal way & talking of it that I might think the better, & trying to remember kind acts by Gosse while weighing my letter.

But after all nothing that I have written will interest you. You will merely say ' He is thinking of himself & not of my mother who has been insulted by Gosse.' Yes & you will be right. That is just the trouble only the self I have been thinking of is not self interest.

August 2, 1910

A few days after writing this letter he wrote the poem called ' The Mask ', which has already been quoted. He was busily building bridges to connect himself with humanity.

In the violence of ' theatre business, management of men ', Yeats sought to wear his fiery mask and thereby to reassociate himself with ' the normal active man '. He was also looking for something to think about besides his disappointment in love. Into the dozen or so fairly important quarrels in the theatre movement from 1903 till 1911 he threw himself with something like abandon. The issue was in almost every case national art versus nationalist propaganda. Yeats found chauvinism and mob-spirit rising before him in a dozen shapes ; now it was the actors refusing to play Lady Gregory's *Twenty-Five* because they said it would stimulate emigration to America ; now it was the audience objecting to Synge's *Shadow of the Glen* and then, more violently, to his *Playboy of the Western World*, for giving a picture of Ireland which was considered derogatory. Yeats fought every fight, sometimes by public speeches, sometimes by letters to newspapers and articles, sometimes by private persuasion, and with his supporters succeeded in stemming the tide. He became a terrible man in combat, who could compel by sheer force of personality, or, as he would have put it, by power of his mask, a jeering crowd into silence. He commanded all the forensic weapons, from the appeal to nationalism (' The author of *Cathleen Ni Houlihan* addresses you '), patronizing contempt (' You have disgraced yourselves again '), to angry insult (' You're dogs ! ') ; on one occasion he suddenly recited in his majestic manner the magic name ' Charles . . . Stewart . . . Parnell ', and then, the crowd once quiet, proceeded with a speech that had nothing to do with Parnell. Behind the scenes he compromised a great deal, but at the footlights he was inflexible.

These quarrels, and one over the founding of a new art gallery, embittered him as the quarrels of the National Literary

Society and Irish Literary Society had not.  The reason was that in the 'nineties his great hopes for his country had stifled his irritation with his countrymen ;  he had worked almost incessantly for a national ideal connected in his mind with his beloved and with his own development ;  he had hoped to transmute Ireland and himself and to win Maud Gonne in the process. Now, in the time of the shattering of idols, he was angry with Ireland as with himself and with Maud.  He searched for explanations of the stupidity and ill-will of his enemies, and too easily believed he could find most of them in class distinctions.  Lady Gregory, his well-born friend, helped to confirm his prejudice ; she read to him Castiglione's *Courtier*, and in 1907 invited him to join her and her son Robert in a tour of northern Italy, where the results of the patronage of artists by the great dukes were everywhere to be seen.  It is at this period that Yeats makes ludicrous attempts to ally himself with the aristocracy ;  someone looked up his family coat of arms for a book-plate and delighted him with the information that, on his father's side of the family, he had aristocratic blood in his veins.  He told one acquaintance that the Duke of Ormonde was not of the *real* Butlers ;  and he is said to have declared to George Russell that if he had his rights he would be Duke of Ormonde, only to have his mystical friend reply :  'In any case, Willie, you are overlooking your father'.  Feeling keenly his cleavage from society, Yeats tried to ally himself with the aristocracy by blood and with the peasantry by sympathy.  The main target of his attacks was the middle class, which had neither family tradition nor a belief in anything beyond the material world.  It was acquisitive, priest-ridden, ready to take up shibboleths ; in many ways it was like the Belfast men whom his father and grandfather had condemned, but Yeats was the first to turn that condemnation into active hatred. His hopes for the Ireland to be were not lost, but gave way to a new emphasis upon his despair for the Ireland before his eyes. Maud Gonne complained to him of his class hatred, and he wrote but did not publish four lines which show how closely his emotional and intellectual life were linked together :

> My love is angry that of late
> I cry all base blood down
> As though she had not taught me hate
> By kisses to a clown.

But, though he answered her criticism, he was secretly half-aware
that he was overdoing his hatred.[1]

Not only the base-blooded middle class felt the sting of his
arrogant personality. He quarrelled savagely with his sister over
the management of a small hand-press. J. B. Yeats wrote to
remonstrate in the name of family affection, but his son replied
to the effect that he no longer had need of family affection and
quoted Nietzsche, whom he had read in 1902 and 1903. The father
would have been more sympathetic had he realized that his son's
attitude had Maud Gonne rather than Nietzsche at the bottom of
it ; as it was, he wrote a stern letter of rebuke :

> As regards the other matter in your letter. As you have dropped
> affection from the circle of your needs, have you also dropped love
> between man and woman ? Is this the theory of the overman, if so,
> your demigodship is after all but a doctrinaire demigodship.
>
> Your words are idle — and you are far more human than you
> think. You would be a philosopher and are really a poet — the con-
> trary of John Morley, who is really a philosopher and wants to be a
> statesman. Morley is never roused except when some pet synthesis is
> in jeopardy.
>
> The men whom Nietzsche's theory fits are only great men of a sort,
> a sort of Yahoo great men. The struggle is how to get rid of them,
> they belong to the clumsy and brutal side of things. . . .

One can be grateful that J. B. Yeats, though he had aristocratic
prejudices too, stood always on the side of humanity. A better
instance of his paternal acumen is in a letter which he wrote to
Dowden in 1911, saying that he did not want his son to be
Dowden's successor as Professor of English Literature at Trinity
College, at that time a possibility : ' In the first place he is

---

[1] In his poem, ' The People ', which grew out of this quatrain many years later,
he confessed as much :

> And yet, because my heart leaped at her words,
> I was abashed, and now they come to mind
> After nine years, I sink my head abashed.

naturally conservative & very conservative & I dont want to see that side of his character developed — I would rather keep him in the ranks down among the poor soldiers fighting for sincerity & truth '. It is odd to think of the poet, whom we have watched as a revolutionary, although one with many reservations, as now a conservative, but his father's fears were well grounded. A revolutionary who puts spiritual ennoblement above political or economic gains is apt to find himself, like Carlyle in later life, on the side of the Tories.

In the 'nineties Yeats had had a cult of passion and perfect love ; the passion remained, but now he tended towards pure hatred. As his wife was later to remark, everything had to be either geese or swans to him. He wrote in 1906 to Stephen Gwynn complaining of the mild policies of two Dublin magazines, *The Shanachie* and *A Celtic Christmas* : ' Damn all Celtic Christmases now and for ever. What Dublin wants is some man who knows his own mind and has an intolerable tongue and a delight in enemies.' He fancied himself in this role, although he was far from assuming it entirely.

There was another way in which he had changed. The mask was too fiery to be ascetic. In 1903 Yeats brought to an end the years of self-denial, and sought comfort once more with Diana Vernon ; subsequently he had affairs with Florence Farr and with a woman in London. Asceticism had been his sacrifice to Maud Gonne ; she had rejected it, so he thought he would put on wantonness instead. The change in his life is reflected in his verse, which for the first time introduces a sexual theme without occult or Pre-Raphaelite camouflage. One can find it in both of the plays written just after Maud Gonne's marriage, *On Baile's Strand* and *The King's Threshold* ; in neither of these is it indispensable, but Yeats wanted to speak out. Barach the fool cries to Fintain the blind man, in *On Baile's Strand*, of a blighted love that resembles Yeats's own :

It's a woman from among the Riders of the Sidhe. It's Boann herself from the river. She has left the Dagda's bed, and gone through the salt of the sea and up here to the strand of Baile, and all

for love of me. Let her keep her husband's bed, for she'll have
none of me. Nobody knows how lecherous these goddesses are.
I see her in every kind of shape but oftener than not she's in the
wind and cries 'give a kiss and put your arms about me'. But no,
she'll have no more of me. Yesterday when I put out my lips to
kiss her, there was nothing there but the wind.

*The King's Threshold* is less personal :

> You're fair to look on,
> Your feet delight in dancing, and your mouths
> In the slow smiling that awakens love.
>
> .    .    .    .    .
>
> Go to the young men :
> Are not the ruddy flesh and the thin flanks
> And the broad shoulders worthy of desire ?

*Deirdre* shows an increasing boldness :

> What's the merit in love-play,
> In the tumult of the limbs
> That dies out before 'tis day,
> Heart on heart, or mouth on mouth
> All that mingling of our breath,
> When love longing is but drought
> For the things come after death ?
>
> . . . you know
> Within what bride-bed I shall lie this night,
> And by what man, and lie close up to him,
> For the bed's narrow, and there outsleep the cockcrow.

Miss Horniman, the generous, cultured spinster who was giving
the Abbey Theatre its financial backing, had to exert all her
self-control to keep from protesting against some revisions Yeats
made in *The Shadowy Waters* in 1907 :

> *1st Sailor.* I am so lecherous with abstinence
> I'd give the profit of nine voyages
> For that red Moll that had but the one eye.

The effect of the new way of thinking about life, of what
Synge called in a phrase that Yeats liked 'the shock of new

material ', was to accelerate the alteration in the style of both his
prose and verse that he had begun to make at the end of the
nineteenth century.  The prose style became a little harder and
firmer, less obviously evasive ; but it remained graceful, with all
anger adroitly excluded.  The poetic style drew further away
from it, being forceful and direct, with all weakness and vacillation excluded.  A letter to Russell in 1904 about a small collection
of verse by Russell's friends and followers was Yeats's fullest
statement of his change of heart :

> Some of the poems I will probably underrate . . . because the
> dominant mood in many of them is the one I have fought in myself
> & put down.  In my ' Land of Heart's Desire ', and in some of my
> lyric verse of that time, there is an exaggeration of sentiment & senti-
> mental beauty which I have come to think unmanly.  The popularity
> of ' The Land of Heart's Desire ' seems to me to come not from its
> merits but because of this weakness.  I have been fighting the pre-
> valent decadence for years, & have but just got it under foot in my
> own heart — it is sentiment & sentimental sadness, a womanish intro-
> spection . . . this region of shadows is full of false images of the
> spirit & of the body.  I have come to feel towards it as O'Grady feels
> towards it sometimes & even a little as some of my stupidest critics
> feel.  As so often happens with a thing one has been tempted by and
> is still a little tempted by I am roused by it to a kind of frenzied hatred
> which is quite out of my control. . . . We possess nothing but the
> will & we must never let the children of vague desires breathe upon
> it nor the waters of sentiment rust the terrible mirror of its blade.  I
> fled from some of this new verse you have gathered as from much
> verse of our day knowing that I fled that water and that breath. . . .
> Some day you will become aware, as I have become, of an uncontrol-
> lable shrinking from the shadows and as I believe a mysterious com-
> mand has gone out against them in the invisible world of our energies,
> let us have no emotions, however absurd, in which there is not an
> athletic joy.

And this opposition to disembodied emotion led directly to his
new opposition to disembodied expression.  As Yeats wrote to
John Quinn on September 16, 1905, he was now including
' homely phrases ' and ' the idiom of common speech ' in his
verse ;  he was happy to have succeeded in putting ' creaking

shoes ' and ' liquorice root ' into what had been ' a very abstract passage '. ' I believe more strongly every day ', he declared, ' that the element of strength in poetic language is common idiom, just as the element of strength in poetic construction is common passion.'

Here was a great advance in theory over the esotericism and elaborateness which he had espoused in the middle 'nineties. The poems written according to these new esthetic doctrines in the 1910 volume, *The Green Helmet and Other Poems*, are very close to speech, usually arrogant speech :

> Why should I blame her that she filled my days
> With misery, or that she would of late
> Have taught to ignorant men most violent ways,
> Or hurled the little streets upon the great. . . .

> I had this thought awhile ago. . . .

> How should the world be luckier if this house,
> Where passion and precision have been one
> Time out of mind. . . .

> Out yonder, where the Race Course is. . . .

> Sickness brought me this
> Thought, in that scale of his. . . .

The pronoun ' I ' is used oftener, sometimes in epigrams so bitter as to make new enemies :

> TO A POET, WHO WOULD HAVE ME PRAISE CERTAIN
> BAD POETS, IMITATORS OF HIS AND OF MINE
> You say as I have often given tongue
> In praise of what another's said or sung,
> 'Twere politic to do the like by these ;
> But where's the wild dog that has praised his fleas ?

The monosyllabic end rhymes are intentionally abrupt :

> There's something ails our colt
> That must, as if it had not holy blood,

> Nor on an Olympus leaped from cloud to cloud,
> Shiver under the lash, strain, sweat, and jolt
> As though it dragged road metal.

There can be little doubt that Yeats's Pegasus during this period did drag road metal. His lyrics have often an irritating air of bravado and snobbery about them. His dramas show the effect of much theorizing : the author's ideas about his characters dominate them, and the subject-matter of *On Baile's Strand*, *The King's Threshold*, and *Deirdre* is all too human to allow for this kind of treatment. In spite of his principle of common language and common passion, his personages are close to arrangements and abstractions and even in tragic circumstances do not assume altogether human life. Something seems to be wrong with their breathing ; they suffer, especially in *Deirdre*, from an overdose of royal blood, and in the other plays also they are too often lop-sided. Yeats had come close to a tragedy of humours, how close the list of characters in an early draft of *The Player Queen* shows :

*Yellow Martin*. Oversincere. In love with Player Queen, but incapable of giving way to her caprices, incapable of wearing a mask.
*Peter*. A light lover, gives way to every caprice, always wears a mask.
*Player Queen*. Values nothing in life but the mask.

We could make similar abstract patterns for the earlier plays. Yeats evidently saw the difficulty, and in *The Player Queen* left Ireland altogether for an abstract country ; he was soon to use masks to achieve the necessary distance from life so that his characters would not demand so pressingly as in the Irish legends to be entirely human. In his earlier treatment, however, we feel an equivocation between formalized and realistic drama.

These, then, were Yeats's efforts from 1903 to 1910 to formulate anew the antithesis as he conceived it in his own mind between Cuchulain and Naisi on the one hand, and their antagonists on the other. The theory of the mask bulked large in this work, giving the opposing self a symbolical form. Yeats was too human, however, to be wholly absorbed by any theoretical scheme of binary fission, whether the parts were called Robartes and Aherne, Cuchulain and Conchubar, or even mask and face. Beyond either of these pairs was another Yeats who was not royal and not above putting to bed a drunken friend ; a Yeats not reckless who refused a duel on the grounds that the laws of the country forbade it ; a Yeats who was not passionate as Tristram but terrified by the possibility of an illegitimate child, who was not wise as Solomon but in need of the advice and affection of friends, in short, a man like other men. This Yeats often returned lonely to the Nassau Hotel in Dublin, and could not always find, even in Lady Gregory, a kindred spirit. Perhaps we may see him in the play, *The Green Helmet*, when Cuchulain, thinking he is about to sacrifice his life, comforts his wife Emer :

*Cuchulain.* He played and paid with his head and it's right that we pay him back,
    And give him more than he gave, for he comes in here as a guest ;
    So I will give him my head.           *[Emer begins to keen.*
      Little wife, little wife, be at rest.
    Alive I have been far off in all lands under sun,
    And been no faithful man, but when my story is done
    My fame shall spring up and laugh, and set you high above all.
*Emer* [putting her arms about him]. It is you not your fame that I love.
*Cuchulain* [tries to put her from him]. You are young, you are wise, you can call
    Some kinder and comlier [*sic*] man that will sit at home in the house.
*Emer.* Live and be faithless still.

In the midst of the soul-splitting Yeats began to devote a great deal of time and thought to effect a new unity which would be more inclusive and impregnable than that he had built up during the 'nineties. We must retrace our steps a little to survey this development.

## CHAPTER XIII

# SPIRITS AND MATTER: TOWARDS HARMONY

*Tous ceux qui ont fait de grandes choses les ont faites pour sortir d'une difficulté, d'un cul-de-sac.*

HENRI MICHAUX

I T would be difficult to believe in the increasing intricacies of Yeats's psychological convolutions if he did not bear witness to them so often in both public and private writings. Along with redividing his personality he set himself the task of achieving a unity which he had intentionally made as difficult of achievement as possible. For this purpose he had two methods : one was to strive, in general terms, for spiritual rehabilitation ; the second was to work out a theory which would reconcile the opposites within himself. Either way he hoped that unification would mean transmutation, so that he would no longer be a prey to continual suspicion of his own ideas, beliefs, and powers.

The search for this transmutation becomes noticeable about 1906, when he prefaced a volume of his collected poems with an apologia which testified to his renewed efforts to be reborn :

I am a little disappointed with the upshot of so many years, but I know that I have been busy with the Great Work, no lesser thing than that, although it may be the Athanor has burned too fiercely, or too faintly and fitfully, or that the *prima materia* has been ill-chosen.

Some of my friends, and it is always for a few friends one writes, do not understand why I have not been content with lyric writing. But one can only do what one wants to do, and to me drama — and I think it has been the same with other writers — has been the search for more of manful energy, more of cheerful acceptance of whatever arises out of the logic of events, and for clean outline, instead of those outlines of lyric poetry that are blurred with desire and vague regret. All art is in the last analysis an endeavour to condense as out of the flying vapour of the world an image of human perfection, and for its own and not for the art's sake, and that is why the labour of the alchemists, who were called artists in their day, is a befitting comparison for all deliberate change of style.

That he was gathering himself together at the same time as in *Deirdre* he was pulling himself apart is evident from a letter to Lady Gregory of June 27, 1907 : ' I feel that I have lost myself — my centre as it were, has shifted from its natural interests, and that it will take me a long time finding myself again.  Miss Horniman wants me to resign from the theatre entirely, but I am reluctant to do that. . . .'  As a point of departure he resolved in 1907 to revise all his works in prose and verse and for the first time to publish them together in a collected edition.  He rewrote as indefatigably as ever, and then anticipated his readers' complaints by declaring that the changes were more than merely stylistic ones :

> The friends that have it I do wrong
> Whenever I remake a song
> Should know what issue is at stake :
> It is myself that I remake.

In the same year, as part of the same effort, Yeats began *The Player Queen*, in which for the first time he left Ireland for a purely mythical land where he could work out some of his psychological difficulties.  We have already seen how he developed his theories in the opposition of such characters as Yellow Martin and Peter, but he went further.  Each character was to seek his own opposite or antithetical self ; thus the actress who normally played the role of Noah's wife would aspire to play the role of the queen.  The characters would be tragic or comic in so far as they became or failed to become their antithetical selves.

But an old problem arose again, how to end the play.  Once the characters had turned into their antithetical selves did they ever lapse back ?  Or was eventually some reconciliation effected between the old selves and the new ?  Blake had affirmed that in Beulah contrarieties are equally true, and Yeats was looking for an exegesis of this idea. The bent of his thoughts can be observed in a note in his diary in 1909 on an intended revision of an early story, ' The Tables of the Law ' :

What does the woman in Paris reveal to the Magi ? Surely some reconciliation between face and mask ? Does the narrator refuse this manuscript & so never learn its contents. Is it simply the doctrine of the Mask ? The choosing of some one mask ? Hardly for that would be the imitation of Christ in a new form. Is it becoming Mask after Mask. Perhaps the name only should be given ' Mask & face ' — yet the nature of the men seems to prepare for a continual change — a phantasmagoria, one day one god & the next another.

He was not at all sure what sort of reconciliation was possible ; the choosing of a single mask would be too serious an arrest of the changing world and mind. The difficulty was the old one of the Irish mystical order, — how to define the grail in symbolical or psychological terms, — since any other definition would involve presuppositions about religious truth that Yeats was not prepared to make. As we can now see, the mask had come to occupy in his system during the first decade of this century the position which the rose had held in it during the 'nineties. Both were fluctuating symbols which somehow contained, he felt, the solution to his difficulties. The difference was that the rose was remote, perhaps inaccessible, while the mask fitted securely on the face ; the rose was soft, the mask hard. He was harassed by the same uncertainty with the new symbol as with the old one, but he was bringing all his faculties to bear to dominate it. He did not work out a satisfactory theory, however, for many years.

At the same time that he pondered these abstract problems he tried to remake himself more directly. For a time, especially from 1906 to 1909, he studied again with the Golden Dawn, where the transmutation of the self was, as we have seen, the central doctrine. Yeats had not swerved from his one consistent belief that the human mind had power to control the universe, to make and unmake reality. He kept trying order methods for several years, but without great success. In 1906 he wrote to his fellow-member Florence Farr that he had begun ' eastern meditations, but with the object of trying to lay hands upon some dynamic and substantializing force as distinguished from the eastern quiescent and supersentualizing state of the soul — a movement downwards upon life not upwards out of life '. The next year he drew on Golden Dawn symbolism when rewriting with Lady Gregory's help his early mystical play, *Where There Is Nothing*. The dying hero, Martin Hearne, cries out :

> Ah, that is blood ! I fell among the rocks. It is a hard climb. It is a long climb to the vineyards of Eden. Help me up. I must go on. The Mountain of Abiegnos is very high — but the vineyards — the vineyards !

For the members of the Golden Dawn, it will be remembered, the Mountain of Abiegnos was the mountain of spiritual struggle, to be ascended only by those who had sufficiently purified themselves. George Moore, watching the curtain come down on this scene in the revised play, which had as title *The Unicorn from the Stars* (a symbolical name for the soul used in the order), said to the man next to him, ' Poor Yeats ! He's dead ! ' But, though the play was certainly a bad one, Yeats was earnestly climbing the mountain with his hero and attempting greater accomplishments. That he had his own spiritual ascent in mind in Martin Hearne's speech is evident from a symbolic meditation which he wrote in July 1909 in connection with his order work :

> Imagine yourself as being led through a forest or other wild place at nightfall by the light of a star — the only star visible — this is the morning or evening star — ♀ [Venus] the star of the side of the vault through which the initiate enters — you come to a mountain side. This mountain the central mountain of the world, is represented in old prints as having a flat top on which is Eden, a great walled garden. The birds of the night cry one by one. You can go no further but are lost among confused cries of birds of the night & in the gathering darkness. You make the sign of the rending of the veil, & say Pawketh. There is a light suddenly & mouth of cave appears which shines with light. You approach the cave & cry out the word שׁיה (Shieh) & make the sign, O & T. The cave is seven sided, & the walls

are carved with Egyptian or earlier figures. In the middle of that cave is a sarcofagus. You make the sign of 5 = 6 & lie down in the pastos. Around are three figures one of whom places on the breast the rose, one places in the right hand the tree sign & one in the left the lotus. You gaze upward at the rose & say ' O Rose of Rubies grant to me the knowledge of 7 earth keys & the power over these. Let me know what I have been — what I am & what I shall become. Then think of yourself as passing into deep sleep & as you sleep cry out ' O rose take me up into thy joy.' Think of the soul as ascending into a world of light & knowledge where the meaning of life will become clear. Rise into the supernal Eden.

The sarcophagus here described is that of Christian Rosenkreuz, who had achieved the conjunction of rose and cross, their ' mystic marriage ', and was thus for Yeats a convenient prototype of the reconciler of opposites.

Further encouragement for the spiritual quest came from complete reconciliation in 1909 with Maud Gonne, ' the first of all the tribe ', who had been separated from her husband. With some of his old love Yeats felt some of his old thoughts return, and he used the Irish mystical invocations again till he found that the life had gone out of that dream. Their relations, she soon told him, could be those of a spiritual marriage only. Yeats wrote in his diary in bewilderment :

What end will it all have — I fear for her & for myself — she has all myself. I was never more deeply in love, but my desires, always strong, must go elsewhere if I would escape their poison. I am in continual terror of some entanglement parting us, & all the while I know that she made me & I her. She is my innocence & I her wisdom. Of old she was a phoenix & I feared her, but now she is my child more than my sweetheart. . . . She would be cruel if she were not a child, who can always say ' you will not suffer because I will pray.'

Though reconciliation seemed very important to Yeats, who was tenacious of old associations, Maud Gonne was not of much help to him in his new work.

At the same time that he was filling his mind with symbols and evocations, and especially after the disquieting reconciliation with Maud Gonne, Yeats went into long sieges of self-criticism from 1908 to 1910. In December 1908 he began a diary in which he could put his dissatisfaction with his life and his attempts at reformation. Part of it was published eighteen years later, but many personal passages were omitted, including the letter to Robert Gregory already quoted. The most frank of the suppressed portions throw light on Yeats's spiritual condition :

The other day in Paris I found that for days I lost all social presence of mind through the very ordinary folly of a very ordinary person. I heard in every word she spoke ancient enemies of vanity & sentimentality & became rude & according[ly] miserable. This is my worst fault. . . . I must watch myself carefully, recording errors that I may become interested in their care. Perhaps I should seek out people I dislike till I have conquered this petulant combativeness. It is always inexcusable to lose one's self possession. It always comes from impatience, from a kind of spiritual fright at someone who is here & now, more powerful even if only from stupidity. I am never angry with those in my power. I fear strangers, I fear the representatives of the collective opinion and so rage stupidly & rudely, exaggerating what I feel & think.

[1909] . . . I notice that my old childish difficulty of concentration is as great as ever. I can evade it, in a thousand ways, I can return to a subject again & again but I cannot give it many minutes at a time.

I dare say that these notes, if some chance eye light on them, may seem morbid, but they help me to understand myself & I remember hearing a man of science once argue that all progress is at the outset ' pathological '. I know that I have already made moral gains. [This paragraph was later published, but out of context.]

Yeats had little of that quality of self-pity in which his father sometimes indulged :

I do not listen enough. . . . It is not merely that I talk for if I were silent in a room I still do not really listen. A word suggests something and I follow that. I am always like a child playing with bricks in the corner.

August 7 [1909]

My work is very near to life itself but I am always feeling a lack of life's own values behind my thought. They should have been there before the strain began, before it became necessary to let the work create its values. . . .

I know myself to be utterly indiscreet. Now it is that strange intoxicating thing the sense of intimacy now it is an unrestrained sense of comedy that lays hold of me & in either case I forget all discretion. This & my indolence are the most humiliating faults I have — for indolence I have disciplines which may gradually conquer it but for the other nothing. I cannot say to anyone ' Tell me all for I need the discipline of a great secret because of my indiscretion, & the old secrets are no longer new enough to stir the imagination.' When they are new they have all their dangerous time, my own through sympathy & those of others through my sense of comedy. . . .

O master of life give me confidence in something even if it be but in my own reason. . . .

Why do I write all this ? I suppose that I may learn at last to keep to my own in every situation in life. To discover & create in myself as I grow old that thing which is to life what style is to letters, moral radiance, a personal quality of universal meaning in action & in thought. . . .

> But every powerful life goes on its way
> Too blinded by the sight of the mind's eye
> Too deafened by the cries out of the heart
> Not to have staggering feet & groping hands.

Intense though his desire to improve himself was, Yeats was a poet ' but no saint ', as his wife was later to remark to him ; the search for moral radiance did not perceptibly change his conduct, but it did lend an added sense of responsibility to his work. The diary is notable because its tone gradually changes from self-recrimination to self-justification, indicating a growth, too, in confidence.

He needed still a fresh impetus, and the Golden Dawn failed ultimately to supply it because it was too much a part of his old thought. The visions which he could produce through symbolic meditations were limited, as he came to realize ; the impersonal and inhuman forms which he evoked through Golden Dawn methods were totally unlike the richly individualized super-natural beings of the peasant tales. Then, too, they became difficult for him to evoke. He admits as much in the epigraph to the new volume of poems, *Responsibilities* (1914), where he quotes Khoung-fou-tseu,

> How am I fallen from myself, for a long time now
> I have not seen the Prince of Chang in my dreams.

In a poem of the same year, if we may accept it as biographical evidence, he says that the ' reed-throated whisperer ' comes to him ' not now as once / A clear articulation in the air, / But inwardly ', and in ' Lines Written in Dejection ' (dating probably from 1915), he is more emphatic :

> When have I last looked on
> The round green eyes and the long wavering bodies
> Of the dark leopards of the moon ?
> All the wild witches, those most noble ladies,
> For all their broom-sticks and their tears,
> Their angry tears, are gone.
> The holy centaurs of the hills are vanished ;
> I have nothing but the embittered sun ;
> Banished heroic mother moon and vanished,
> And now that I have come to fifty years
> I must endure the timid sun.

His symbols had lost their power in part because of over-use, but also because he had abandoned projects of which they had once been a part. For a certainty the castle in Lough Key would never be the Castle of the Heroes ; there would be no Irish mystical order and no magical rites. The future of Ireland, in spite of Maud Gonne's attempts to revive his flagging enthusiasm, did not stir him as much as in the past, and the Irish gods were accordingly of less interest. As for the project of a mystical theatre, that too seemed gone, for the Abbey was presenting realistic plays. Yeats made an effort to revive his earlier dramatic conceptions in 1910 and 1911, rewriting his *Hour-Glass* and *Countess Cathleen* for a second company to perform at the Abbey ; but nothing permanent came of the venture. As for his writing of new plays, that stopped abruptly after 1910 except for *The Player Queen* (which he had begun in 1907), and did not recommence for six years. There was no more interest payable on the old capital.

Yet the restless efforts to perfect his character and to find a new source of literary and spiritual energy were rewarded. Beginning seriously in 1909, and especially from 1911 on, Yeats's imagination was captured by a branch of supernaturalism of which up to that time he had known little : the phenomena of spiritualism. As a young man, it will be recalled, he had gone with Katharine Tynan to a spiritualist séance which had upset him for days. After that he had accepted the magician's bias against passive mediumship, which the Blavatsky Lodge and the Golden Dawn alike considered immoral because it implied surrender instead of control of the will. But about 1909 he grew interested again ; in 1911 he met a remarkable American medium during a lecture tour in America, and in that latter year he decided to take up spiritualism in earnest. The Celtic gods were relegated in favour of the international dead. Perhaps the gates of ivory and of horn would at last spring open at his call.

Everything about spiritualism was fascinating to him, from the small number of collaborators to the darkened rooms and atmosphere charged with suspense and hidden drama. Where the success of his symbolic visions had depended largely on his power to repress his scepticism, here he found spirits eager to convince disbelievers with manifold proofs of their posthumous existence and power to communicate. He could make the continual experiments which he loved. Latently sceptical by nature, but craving the irrefutable evidence of the supernatural which would finally lay his doubts at rest and prove that a child's refusal to follow his father's scepticism was more than a son's champing against paternal authority, Yeats threw himself with his old gusto and tenacity into psychical research.

He wanted a great deal from the spirits : they must furnish him with a new influx, a supernatural basis for his thought and writing such as the Golden Dawn and its offspring, the Irish mystical order, had given him from 1890 to 1903. They must supply evidence for the existence of another world interlinked

at points but not identical with man's.  They must prove that the
soul survives the body's death.  He hoped that, in addition, they
would give him advice about future actions and wisdom and
insight into death and life.  Perhaps they would, as he suggested
in some unpublished papers, reunite ' the mind & soul & body
of man to the living world outside us '.  Perhaps they would
solve his problem of the relation between face and mask.

Yeats did not go entirely blind and believing into the kingdom
of the shades, but he was undoubtedly more credulous than an
impartial observer would have been.  He felt that he had a great
deal at stake.  His approach was comparable to that of the Society
for Psychical Research, the president of which, Dr. Everard
Feilding, became his friend.  This attitude may be fairly described
as a predisposition to believe and a desire to find fair evidence
which would convince people lacking the predisposition.  Yeats's
principal inves igations were in three fields :  (1) the authenticity
of an alleged miracle ;  (2) the power of a medium or automatic
writer to transcend the boundaries of her own mind and knowledge ;  (3) the nature of a particular spirit and of the after-life.
His less formal goals were expressed in such questions as, ' Am
I to marry Maud Gonne ? ' which he asked mediums on more than
one occasion.  But he was always hesitant, in such matters, about
putting their advice into practice.

These investigations overlap in time, and we may take up
first the research into the miracle.  In May 1914 Yeats, Feilding,
and Maud Gonne went to the little town of Mirabeau, near
Poitiers, to see a picture of Christ which had begun to bleed.
The priest impressed them as honest, and neither Yeats nor
Feilding accepted the later official verdict that the miracle was
not authentic.  Yeats, with his fondness for pagan parallels,
suggested to Feilding that the statue of Adonis might have bled
similarly in the market-place.  He wrote up a lengthy report of
the miracle but did not publish it.

Meantime he had come upon important evidence of the kind
he needed.  In the spring of 1912 he first met a young woman
whose automatic writing seemed to call upon resources far

beyond those of her own mind. Although her conscious know-ledge of languages was confined to French and a little Italian, her automatic writing contained words and phrases and answers to questions in Greek, Latin, Hebrew, German, Welsh, Pro-vençal, Irish, Chinese, Coptic, Egyptian hieroglyphs, and several other languages. In addition, spirits of obscure dead people took possession of her hand and wrote down facts about themselves which she could not possibly have known. The spirit of a dead London policeman, for example, related his suicide of a hundred years ago. No newspaper had published the account and Yeats could corroborate it only by consulting confidential police records to which the automatic writer did not have access. Confronted by much material of this kind, Yeats subjected her from 1912 to 1914 to a variety of tests, trying to discover any possible conscious or unconscious fraud. He would ask questions mentally to see if she could divine them telepathically and reply to them. At length he decided that he had irrefutable evidence that a living mind could serve as a medium for departed spirits, and that these spirits preserved their identities after death. In June 1914 he wrote up the elaborate notes he had kept from the beginning as a ' Preliminary Examination of the Script of Miss X ', and would probably have revised and published it had she not shunned publicity. The defect of the essay is that Yeats seems too easily convinced that the powers involved are those of departed spirits and not the abnormal capacity of the medium's mind.

While the investigations with ' Miss X ' were going on, he had been attending séances with great regularity, and at the home of Mrs. Wreidt, an American medium living in Hampstead, he was first accosted by a spirit named Leo Africanus, the Italian geographer and traveller, who showed great astonishment when Yeats said he did not know him. Leo Africanus professed to be his attendant spirit or guide.

The possibility of such a being Yeats had long accepted ; he had heard unknown voices in his childhood, he had been half-convinced that Madame Blavatsky's masters might have, as she professed, some independent existence. He had often declared his own kinship with the illustrious dead. That daimons exist and possess or guide men he had asserted, for metaphorical purposes at any rate, as early as 1895 in an essay on Verlaine. While he was therefore receptive to the notion that a specified spirit might have a peculiar relation to himself, he could not at first understand how Leo Africanus — whose geographical interests seemed so much at variance with his own — could be that spirit. Then after much consultation of reference books he discovered that Leo Africanus had been a poet among the Moors. Fascinated, Yeats told his friends about the discovery with the same burst of enthusiasm that he had once shown over the Golden Dawn method of symbolic vision ; and one night at his rooms a medium to whom he had mentioned Leo's communications suddenly seemed to be controlled, and spoke in Leo's name.

She gave Yeats the key he had been seeking. Speaking through her, Leo Africanus said that he was Yeats's opposite, that ' by association with one another ' they ' should each become more complete '. Leo Africanus ' had been unscrupulous ' while Yeats was ' over-cautious and conscientious '. Yeats must write a letter to him as if he were still living among the Moors or Sudanese, put into it all his difficulties, and afterwards answer it in Leo's name. Leo would ' overshadow ' Yeats as he wrote the reply and set at rest all his doubts.

Yeats followed directions, and the resultant exchange of letters, which has not been published, shows how warmly he welcomed this new theory that his opposite, instead of being solely a mask, a conscious product of his own mind with slight independence of its creator, might be a spirit or daimon with a full personality of his own. The discovery, if it could be confirmed, would be of first importance. It meant that the conflict which Yeats had visualized as internal and psychological might be an external battle between a living man and a dead one, between this world and the next. Thus he would have supernatural sanction for the pose he had built up since childhood ; the mask would be filled with cosmic drama. He would have, too, an explanation of the strange power and purity which he could experience only when writing verse.

The relation of man and daimon is worked out in the exchange of letters between Yeats and Leo Africanus. Leo explains it in this way :

In my life I travelled over much of the known earth. I . . . was often in danger, & all but always in solitude, & so became hard & keen like a hunting animal, & now for your good & my own I have chosen to linger near, your contrary mind. . . . If I have been sent to give you confidence & solitude it is because I am a brooding & braggart shade, & even in this I am not wholly stable, for at times I am aware of a constraint upon my thoughts or my passion deepens because of one who is remote & silent & whom I wile [*sic*] I lived in Rome I was forbidden to call Mahomet.

The implication is that God may also play a share in the conflict of man and daimon, but Leo is vague about it. He goes on to assert that he stands in the same relation to Yeats as Christ to the pagan world, an idea which lay dormant in the poet's mind for many years :

I know all or all but all you know, we have been over the same books — I have shared in your joys and sorrows & yet it is only because I am your opposite, your antithesis because I am all things furthest from your intellect & your will, that I alone am your Interlocutor. What was Christ himself but the interlocutor of the pagan world, which had long murmured in his ear, at moments of self abasement & death, & thereby summoned.

The difficult but crucial question for Yeats to decide was whether Leo Africanus was an image or a phantom ; was he really the ghost of a dead poet from Fez or was he a creation of the living man's ? In either case, how much autonomy did he have ? On these questions Leo himself hedged, in one place asserting of himself and other spirits : ' We are the unconscious as you say or as I prefer to say your animal spirits formed from the will, & moulded by the images of Spiritus Mundi ', and in another place advising : ' Yet do not doubt that I was also Leo Africanus the traveller '. Yeats did not commit himself definitely about the image or phantom, but used both theories in October 1915 when he wrote the first synthesis in didactic verse of his new philosophy. The poem was called ' Ego Dominus Tuus ' ; it is a dialogue of Hic and Ille, or, as Ezra Pound used to say, of Hic and Willie.    Ille, representing Yeats, says :

> By the help of an image
> I call to my own opposite, summon all
> That I have handled least, least looked upon.

He explains that Dante, because of his lecherous life, felt compelled to write of ' the most exalted lady loved by a man ', and that Keats, because he was ' the coarse-bred son of a livery-stable keeper ', developed his ' luxuriant song '.    In both instances the opposite seems to be the artist's own creation, but in the concluding lines of the poem Yeats leans towards a more supernatural hypothesis :

> I call to the mysterious one who yet
> Shall walk the wet sands by the edge of the stream
> And look most like me, being indeed my double,
> And prove of all imaginable things
> The most unlike, being my anti-self,
> And standing by these characters disclose
> All that I seek ; and whisper it as though
> He were afraid the birds, who cry aloud
> Their momentary cries before it is dawn,
> Would carry it away to blasphemous men.

The word ' anti-self ' is intended to serve as a more theoretical and abstract one than the symbolical ' mask ', but it does not really clarify matters very much.

Yeats did not publish ' Ego Dominus Tuus ' until late in 1917, and then only after he had made sure that he could protect himself.    For this purpose he studied a great deal in Henry More, in Swedenborg, in Flournoy, Maxwell, and other writers on psychical research.    At last he published the poem in a little book, *Per Amica Silentia Lunae*, where his prose is almost as metaphorical as verse :

When I come home after meeting men who are strange to me, and sometimes even after talking to women, I go over all I have said in gloom and disappointment.  Perhaps I have overstated everything from a desire to vex or startle, from hostility that is but fear ; or all my natural thoughts have been drowned by an undisciplined sympathy.  My fellow-diners have hardly seemed of mixed humanity, and how should I keep my head among images of good and evil, crude allegories ?

But when I shut my door and light the candle, I invite a Marmorean Muse, an art, where no thought or emotion has come to mind because another man has thought or felt something different, for now there must be no reaction, action only, and the world must move my heart but to the heart's discovery of itself, and I begin to dream of eyelids that do not quiver before the bayonet : all my thoughts have ease and joy, I am all virtue and confidence.  When I come to put in rhyme what I have found it will be a hard toil, but for a moment I believe I have found myself and not my anti-self.  It is only the shrinking from toil perhaps, that convinced me that I have been no more myself than is the cat the medicinal grass it is eating in the garden.

How could I have mistaken for myself an heroic condition that from early boyhood has made me superstitious ?

This prose is full of Yeats's old trick of evasion.  He has effectively covered his tracks ; the use of the word ' superstitious ' instead of  mystical ' or ' religious ' will prevent the reader from supposing that the writer has not anticipated the sceptical attitude. But he does not really think of himself as superstitious, or if he does, he thinks more highly of superstition than his reader does. He seeks not so much to convince the reader as to take him in.

Another unpublished dialogue written about 1915 or 1916 comes at similar problems from a different angle.  It is called ' The Poet and the Actress ', and the poet (who bears some resemblance to Leo Africanus) tries to persuade the actress to accept the gift of a black box, which he says contains a mask given to her by the poets and artists at Fez.  She protests that her features are quite good enough without it, but the poet says that the great drama in which she should act expresses, not the external battles with which Ibsen and Shaw are concerned, but the internal battle in the soul, where ' one of the antagonists does not wear a shape known to the world or speak a mortal tongue '.  To express this greater combat, where ' the dream and the reality may face one another in visible array ', a symbolic phantasmagoria is necessary, and the poet therefore urges the actress to hide her external appearance with the mask.  She replies that he has almost convinced her, but convinced or not she will never wear the mask and the poet can pack it straight back to Fez.  ' There is no mask,' the poet replies, ' I have never been in Fez.'

In thus turning the dialogue into an extended and elaborate metaphor, Yeats makes it impossible to object to his theory of the supernatural mask.  He had done the same in *Per Amica Silentia Lunae*.  The fact is that the spirits aroused in him only sporadic certainty, as he confessed in his letter to Leo Africanus :

You wish me to [tell] what leaves me incredulous, or unconvinced. I do not doubt any more than you did or the Alchemists of Fez the existence of God, & I follow tradition for the last time explicitly stated in Swedenborg & in Blake, that his influence descends to us through hierarchies of mediatorial shades & angels.  I doubt however, though not always, that the shades who speak to me through mediums are the shades they profess to be.  The doubt is growing more faint but still it returns again & again.  I have continually to remind myself of some piece of evidence written out & examined & put under a letter in my file.  How can I feel certain of your identity when there has been so much to rouse my suspicion.

Like ' The Magi ' in his poem of that name, Yeats is always in need of a second miracle to reassure him about the first.  Leo Africanus is slightly contemptuous, and rebukes him for being influenced by the scientific tradition, and for trying to persuade sceptical friends instead of breaking away into a life of his own as Swedenborg, Blake, and Boehme had done.  ' You seek ', Leo charges, ' to meet not your own difficulties, but the difficulties of others.  Entangled in error, you are but a public man.'  But since Yeats has once been able to put vague intuitions into his verse, and has had some inklings of the truth about things, Africanus will reveal to him a little of what he wants to know. Disdaining to prove his own existence, the spirit gives an account of what has happened to him since death.  At first he passed through crisis after crisis of his past life, ' but now I judged all

& judged myself '. Gradually the form and colour of these crises changed, and he began to take possession of living beings. The errors of mediums, he declares, are due to the fact that when the medium is not pure the possessing shade loses control and is himself possessed either by the medium's unconscious mind or by other spirits.

But Yeats, after writing out the letters to and from Leo Africanus, is not satisfied that the daimon has overshadowed his hand as was promised, and ends with a postscript to Leo expressing his continued doubt and his continued belief :

I am not convinced that in this letter [written as if from Leo by Yeats] there is one sentence that has come from beyond my imagination. . . . I have been conscious of no sudden illumination. . . . Yet I am confident now as always that spiritual beings if they cannot write & speak can always listen. I can still put my difficulties.

This picture of Yeats, shooting one way and facing another, has to be emphasized because he was aware of it and it bothered him. Was he never to pierce the trembling veil, never to know what he deeply felt and thought in his own person, always to slip from belief to unbelief to belief again ? Could he ever reconcile Robartes and Aherne ? He struggled, but could not, try as he would, escape from the position that his father aptly expressed in a letter to him of September 7, 1915 :

You will remind me that Blake was a mystic. I know that Blake's poetry is not intelligible without a knowledge of Blake's mystical doctrines. Yet mysticism was never the *substance of his poetry, only its machinery*. . . . The substance of his poetry is himself, revolting and desiring. His mysticism was a make-believe, a sort of working hypothesis as good as another. He could write about it in prose and contentiously assert his belief. When he wrote his poems it dropped into the background, and it did not matter whether you believed it or not, so apart from all creeds was his poetry. I like a poem to have fine machinery, but if this machinery is made to appear anything more than that, the spell of the poetry is broken.

Unable to give full consent to the doctrines of psychical research, Yeats more and more inclined to the use of myth and metaphor

which somersaulted over the question of literal belief. Imagina-
tively or actually, one way or the other, Leo Africanus and all
other ghosts existed, and Yeats filled his poetry with them.
Metaphor made irrelevant the questions, was there a mask ? had
the poet been in Fez ? Most of the lyrics in *Responsibilities* (1914),
the first volume to show the effects of prolonged psychical research,
are more artful than those in *The Green Helmet* (1910). The poet
speaks less often in his own person but uses beggars, hermits, and
fools to voice with safety opinions about life and after-life that he
is not prepared to guarantee. The volume is full of indecision
about most of the matters with which it deals ; Yeats introduces
his ghosts cautiously, unwilling to say for sure that the ghosts of
his ancestors can hear him :

> Pardon, old fathers, *if* you still remain
> Somewhere in ear-shot for the story's end,

or that the ghost of Parnell has revisited Dublin :

> *If* you have revisited the town, thin Shade,

or that his dead friends among the Rhymers have achieved
immortality :

> Since, tavern comrades, you have died,
> *Maybe* your images have stood,
> Mere bone and muscle thrown aside,
> Before that roomful or as good.

' The Three Beggars ' and ' The Three Hermits ' come to no
conclusion about life or death. In ' The Hour Before Dawn '
the poet will not decide whether it is better to sleep for ever or to
stay awake for a lifetime.

Whatever his doubts about doctrine, however, the poems
show a considerable improvement in method. If metaphor is
sometimes a slide between conflicting opinions, it sometimes
furnishes a sudden image which resolves the conflict. The first
use is evident in ' The Three Hermits ', where, while two of
the hermits dispute about life after death, the third, ' Giddy
with his hundredth year / Sang unnoticed like a bird '. The

poem is amusing and no more. But in ' A Memory of Youth ',
the man and woman who have failed to find unity are suddenly
united by an image :

> We sat as silent as a stone,
> We knew, though she'd not said a word,
> That even the best of love must die,
> And had been savagely undone
> Were it not that Love upon the cry
> Of a most ridiculous little bird
> Tore from the clouds his marvellous moon.

Here the image is no mere picture to complete a scene, but a
violent reconciler which tears the clouds apart. Another poem
shows the same technique, again with a bird as the symbolic
catalyst ; the speaker in ' Paudeen ' is filled with indignation at
the malice and stupidity of his Irish neighbours, when he hears
two curlews cry :

> and suddenly thereupon I thought
> That on the lonely height where all are in God's eye,
> There cannot be, confusion of our sound forgot,
> A single soul that lacks a sweet crystalline cry.

The vision now comes like lightning ; no elaborate magical
machinery is necessary to set it off, the cry of a most ridiculous
little bird is sufficient. It is a secularized vision, and, instead of
alternating between opposites, it transcends them. The poem
' Friends ' presented the same problem in more difficult form ;
Yeats wanted to celebrate the three women, Lady Gregory,
' Diana Vernon ', and Maud Gonne, who had been most important in his life. His debt to the first two was obvious, but
what of Maud Gonne, who had taken ' All till my youth was
gone / With scarce a pitying look ? ' He is repelled as much
as attracted : ' How should I praise that one ? ' But suddenly
the reconciling image comes :

> When day begins to break
> I count my good and bad,
> Being wakeful for her sake,
> Remembering what she had,

> What eagle look still shows,
> While up from my heart's root
> So great a sweetness flows
> I shake from head to foot.

The emotion that flows from his heart's root, like sap in a tree, is a resolution that transcends argument.

The function of reconcilement is brought up in several of the poems in the volume. The speaker in ' Running to Paradise ' says that in Paradise ' the king is but as the beggar '. In ' The Mountain Tomb ' Yeats celebrates Father Rosicross who, as we have noted, had solved the quarrel of opposites by achieving the mystic marriage of rose and cross ; Rosicross is thus the symbol of the reconcilement. ' The Three Beggars ' hints at the method of achieving such images ; the title characters struggle for a treasure and, because they are lost in the conflict, lose it, while in the waters near by a philosophical crane expatiates on the proper method of attaining success : ' maybe I shall take a trout / *If but I do not seem to care* '. The crane, like the poet, must wear a mask of indifference to his principal concern.

In relation to Yeats's artistic problems, ' The Cold Heaven ' is the most significant poem in the book and points the way to his later development. The heaven which he now sees in vision is not that which he had imagined in the 'nineties, a pretty heaven of ' embroidered cloths ', but a cruel and remorseless one of burning ice ; for a staggering instant he beholds himself shorn of all his accomplishments and defences, with no memory left except that all-important one of love crossed long ago, for which he feels inexplicably compelled to take all the blame. The poem ends in terror :

> Ah ! when the ghost begins to quicken,
> Confusion of the death-bed over, is it sent
> Out naked on the roads, as the books say, and stricken
> By the injustice of the skies for punishment ?

In comparison with an early poem, like ' To the Rose upon the Rood of Time ', ' The Cold Heaven ' exhibits a great advance in force. The former also ended with a question :

> Surely thine hour has come, thy great wind blows,
> Far-off, most secret, and inviolate Rose ?

but the question there is a kind of prayer. In ' The Cold Heaven ' the question at the end forces itself out like an exclamation ; instead of reluctantly admiring the poet's facility, we are swept into the poem, and find his reaction dramatically possible and meaningful for ourselves.

' We sing amid our uncertainty ', Yeats wrote in *Per Amica Silentia Lunae*. Much uncertainty can be found in ' The Cold Heaven '. Neither Dante nor the writer of the apocryphal book of Enoch, who probably affected the poem, nor Ruysbroek whose statement that the mystic ecstasy is ' not this or that ' Yeats incorporated in one of the lines, would have used the point of interrogation ; they would have used declarative statement. But Yeats's problem was to admit doctrine (the idea of a heaven) and doubt (the divergence from the Christian conception of heaven, and the possibility that heaven may be only a state of mind), and then to transcend them by directing the emphasis away from them to the emotional state of the speaker. Through dramatic metaphor Yeats was able to escape a large share of the responsibility for his fictions despite the title of the volume, and at the same time to attain a more powerful mode of expression. Though he said in ' A Coat ' that he had given up his old coat, embroidered with mythologies, and was now ' walking naked ', nakedness had itself become an artifice for him. His search now will be for a variety of dramatic situations in which to pretend to be naked. To some extent this solution still seemed a partial evasion of his anxious struggle to escape from scepticism to direct belief. He continued to long for the day when Abramelin the sage would read to him from his sacred book and make all plain.

## CHAPTER XIV

# ALL CHANGED, CHANGED UTTERLY

*Transmutemini, transmutemini de lapidibus mortuis in lapides philo-
sophicos vivos.*                                              ROBERT FLOOD

THE generality of spirits, if we may put Leo Africanus aside for the moment, have one trait in common, — a strong family sense. Thought in the astral envelope is simplified, so that the spirits who inhabit there have kept only those poignant memories and affectionate longings that by their intensity can defy the tomb. They return to earth to search for a brother, a father, a wife, or a child, and remember only such basic associations as these. The family is indeed the one social unit which survives the stopping of the breath and the stiffening of the limbs.

So much the dead confirmed for Yeats about the living, and along with the supernatural influx into his verse came a great deal of family feeling. We have noticed with what uncertainty he regarded his theories about self and anti-self, an uncertainty which was fully justified, for they grossly over-simplified the complexities of life. To explain Lady Gregory's light comedies as the result of her desire to escape a life too full of judgment, *The Eve of St. Agnes* as Keats's reaction to his humble upbringing, or *The Divine Comedy* as Dante's opposition to his debauched life — contentions which Yeats made in *Per Amica Silentia Lunae* — could hardly seem for long an adequate psychology. To use the explanation at all Yeats had to clothe it in his richest, most metaphorical prose. To avoid using it, to escape from abstraction in his writings about himself, he drew on the strong family sense which he and the spirits shared and which roused in him no nervous doubts.

He had reason to be proud of his family, and on better grounds than the aristocratic lineage to which he sometimes laid claim. By this time the Yeatses were comparable in their achievement to the family of William Morris, with whom they had been friendly during the late 'eighties and 'nineties. For all his shortcomings, John Butler Yeats was in his best portraits a good artist, and Jack Butler Yeats, the poet's brother, was capturing in his paintings the fantastic, humorous spirit of the west of Ireland as no one had done before ; Lily and Elizabeth Yeats, sisters of the poet, were publishing fine hand-printed books at their Cuala Press. Amidst the turmoil of the world and of Ireland, the family proceeded serenely on its way in the service of art and craftsmanship, living by values more fundamental than those of politicians and generals. So far as national politics were concerned, Yeats was out of things and had been for some years. The parliamentarians, the bourgeoisie, the new men were running the world, and running it badly. In his poem, ' September 1913 ', he acknowledged the failure of his youthful dream, saying bitterly : ' Romantic Ireland's dead and gone, / It's with O'Leary in the grave '. The family was an island, and Yeats turned to it as he had once turned to the islands on Lough Gill and Lough Key.

Since 1908 his father had lived in New York and refused to come home, and no doubt this sense of separation had much to do with Yeats's growing consciousness of family ties. As the oldest and most prosperous child, he sent money generously from a very modest income to his impoverished father. The whole family urged the old man to return, but John Butler Yeats, secure in the admiration of such American disciples as Van Wyck Brooks and Alan Seeger, kept postponing the date of the embarkation for Ireland, and his return faded into the future like the secret of style.

But a change came over the relations of father and son ; imperceptibly the painter treated the poet more as an intellectual peer, and asked his opinion on esthetic matters with evident respect. In turn W. B. Yeats was greatly impressed by his father's letters, which were almost all devoted to esthetic problems. He began to see at last that his father's exaltation of personality, his use of psychological terms, his belief in a totality of being in which intellect was only a part, and his insistence that the poet should be free of his beliefs, implied that poetry was an alogical method of discourse ; and he instinctively understood that his father's theories had made his own symbolical method a necessity as well as a possibility. It had taken him many years, however, to understand how the method would work for him. Spurred by this discovery that his father and he were collaborators rather than opponents, he began to make a collection of J. B. Yeats's letters with the intention of having his sisters publish them, and he repeatedly urged his father to write an autobiography to give permanence to family traditions.

What was worthy of respect in his father beyond his theoretical discoveries was the harmony of his personality ; John Butler Yeats had not to act through the elaborate mechanism of the mask, but naturally, and W. B. Yeats lamented his inability to do likewise. The artist was always himself, without being self-conscious, while the poet could rarely act directly. Yeats may have been satirizing his own failing when late in 1912 he wrote ' The Dolls ', where the doll-maker's house is thrown into an uproar by the complaints of the dolls at the introduction of a real baby into the house.[1]

What bridge could there be between his private doll-house and the mainland ? The question had long vexed him ; he did not want to be a mere maker of dolls, he wanted to fill his work with life ; and now, regardless of his theories, he wanted to live as other men lived, as his father for instance had lived. He had reached middle age and had no family of his own, no son to whom he might one day write as his father was writing to him. He needed affection and love, and the steadying effect of married life. None of his love affairs had been mentally satisfying for long, and he was not always able to find even physical relief. As a beggar cries in a poem written on March 5, 1913 :

[1] As if the poem had been prophetic, a young woman who had been his mistress in London intermittently from about 1909 suddenly telegraphed him in May 1913 that she was pregnant. Yeats did not know what to do, so he consulted a medium who said ' Deception ! ' and proved to be correct.

' Time to put off the world and go somewhere
And find my health again in the sea air,'
*Beggar to beggar cried, being frenzy-struck,*
' And make my soul before my pate is bare.

' And get a comfortable wife and house
To rid me of the devil in my shoes,'
*Beggar to beggar cried, being frenzy-struck,*
' And the worse devil that is between my thighs.'

Lady Gregory and another close friend, the novelist Mrs. Olivia
Shakespear, aware of the difficulties of bachelorhood, urged him
to get married, but he felt himself to be still tied to Maud Gonne,
and she had never divorced her husband. He sought advice
from mediums but did not take it.

Yet his house must somehow be put in order, and he decided
to write an autobiography. Lady Gregory had already started
upon her memoirs of the early days of the Irish theatre, and
Katharine Tynan had published her *Twenty-Five Years : Reminiscences* in 1913, with several dozen of Yeats's early letters
included without his permission. More important, George Moore
had published *Hail and Farewell*, his mischievous reminiscences
of the Irish literary movement. The book intermixed praise and
blame for Yeats so cleverly that at first he did not take offence,
but slowly it dawned on him that Moore had subtly made his
whole movement ridiculous. At the end of *Responsibilities* (1914),
Yeats placed a poem which expressed his feelings about Moore
though without mentioning his name. What did Moore know
of the mystical basis of the theatre, of the spiritual qualities of
Yeats's life and writings ? The poem ended,

all my priceless things
Are but a post the passing dogs defile.

But he did not stop at rejoinder. He would issue his own memoirs
as an apologia, both for himself and for his family. The book,
written in 1914 and published in 1915 under the title of *Reveries
over Childhood and Youth*, is full of recollections of his mother's
half-legendary relatives, whom he celebrated also in the prefatory

poem to *Responsibilities*, and in fragmentary pictures shows the young poet as timid and sensitive, a good deal dominated by his father, though Yeats was careful to say nothing that would hurt his father's feelings. The memoirs were human and uncontroversial, coming down to about his twentieth year ; for a time he went no further because too many living people and too many intimate memories were involved in the rest of his youth.

It must be understood that during the period when he was writing his *Reveries* he was also attending séances and working out the first drafts of *Per Amica Silentia Lunae*, which incorporated his notions of the relation of opposites in this life and of the ontology of the after-life. His recollections of the past were intended, like his occult theories, to help him in the present. What he needed to find was a new art form which would enable him to write plays again, not merely abstract plays like *The Player Queen*, which was still unfinished, but plays of genuinely human interest ; and he needed, too, a better systematized statement of his religious or occult beliefs which would enable him to use them as background rather than as plot. He wrote his father that he was arranging his thought into a ' religious system ', and in a diary note he says that in the new Ireland a counter-religion would carry more weight than mere anti-clericalism. From various hints we can be sure that the religious system had for its central doctrine the union with one's opposite of which Yeats had talked so much, and that he mistily conceived of the union as altering the qualities of self and anti-self as hydrogen and oxygen react in combination to form water.

Such a system would have no meaning if its founder had not first-hand knowledge of this reaction and concomitant synthesis. Yeats could reasonably consider his symbolical method, in which the symbol emerged from the conflict of opposites and transcended it, as a literary extension of his theories of spiritual development. He was beginning to feel, too, that the change of thought and style which he had tried to bring about in his work since 1903 had been realized in every direction. He had reason for his growing confidence. In a diary note dated Christmas 1912 he stated succinctly his present theory of art :

First Principles

Not to find one's art by the analysis of language or amid the circumstances of dreams but to live a passionate life, and to express the emotions that find one thus in simple rhythmical language. The words should be the swift natural words that suggest the circumstances out of which they rose.

To see how far he had come we may set against this manifesto one he had made thirteen years before in an essay called 'The Autumn of the Flesh'. It is almost the exact contrary :

I see, indeed, in the arts of every country those faint lights and faint colours and faint outlines and faint energies which many call ' the decadence,' and which I, because I believe that the arts lie dreaming of things to come, prefer to call the autumn of the flesh. An Irish poet [A. E.] whose rhythms are like the cry of a sea bird in autumn twilight has told its meaning in the line, ' The very autumn's weary and it's time to quit the plough.' . . . Man has wooed and won the world, and has fallen weary, and not, I think, for a time, but with a weariness that will not end until the last autumn, when the shares shall be blown away like withered leaves.

In putting his principles into practice, to use ' a speech so natural and dramatic that the hearer would feel the presence of a man thinking and feeling ', Yeats had signal assistance from Ezra Pound. Pound had breezed into England in 1908, confident and full of information about obscure literature, persuaded that Yeats was the best poet writing in English but that his manner was out of date. The poet must be a modern man, Pound insisted ; he must be clear and precise, he must eliminate all abstractions and all words which sense did not justify as well as sound. Everything must be hard and concrete, a statue of Epstein, not a musical composition of Debussy.

Pound himself was a very mixed personality. His instincts, as he once remarked, were to write in the manner of the 'nineties, but he curbed and scorned them. He was now very much the man of the new movement, the organizer, busy from the time of his arrival in separating both living and dead poets into the readable and the unreadable. His strong prejudices were directed particularly against all that seemed to him stodgy, such as the poetry of Wordsworth, and on one occasion he is said to have challenged a reviewer in *The Times* to a duel for having ' too high an opinion of Milton '.

Pound and Yeats got along well from the first, with the younger man assuming towards the older a mixed attitude of admiration and patronage. ' Uncle William ', as he called him, was making good progress but still dragging some of the reeds of the 'nineties in his hair. Pound set himself the task of converting Yeats to the modern movement, and had many opportunities from 1912 to 1915 to apply pressure. In 1912 he impudently altered without permission some poems which Yeats had given him to send to *Poetry* magazine ; Yeats was infuriated but then forgave him. During the winters of 1913–14, 1914–15, and 1915–16, Pound acted as Yeats's secretary at a small cottage in Ashdown Forest in Sussex, reading to him, writing from his dictation, and discussing everything. It was Pound who, hearing that Yeats had spent six or seven years trying to write *The Player Queen* as a tragedy, suggested that it might be made into a comedy, with such effect that Yeats completely transformed the play at once. In Ashdown Forest Pound would have liked to read contemporary literature to Yeats, but ' Uncle William ' insisted on *Sordello* and Morris's Sagas. Pound would frequently urge Yeats to make changes in words or lines so as to get further away from the 'nineties ; the older poet asked him to go through his verse and point out to him which words were abstractions, and was surprised at the large number that were so marked. He made a renewed effort to purge his verse of its weaknesses in *At the Hawk's Well*, his first play in six years, which he dictated to Pound early in 1916. The improvement is readily noticeable ; the new verse is more spare, the images are exactly delimited by the words, every shadow is removed. The tone, too, is definitely that of Yeats and of no one else :

> I call to the eye of the mind
> A well long choked up and dry

> And boughs long stripped by the wind,
> And I call to the mind's eye
> Pallor of an ivory face,
> Its lofty dissolute air,
> A man climbing up to a place
> The salt sea wind has left bare.

The play shows the effect of the young American's stimulating influence in its dramatic form as well as its style. During the first winter that Pound acted as his secretary Yeats was working on an essay to prove the connection between the beliefs of peasants, spiritualists, Swedenborg, and Henry More ; his thoughts were full of ghosts, witches, and supernatural phenomena. Pound, on the other hand, had a project of his own. He was the literary executor of Ernest Fenellosa, a scholar who had spent many years in Japan studying the Noh drama. It was very exciting to Yeats, always on the lookout for new ways of using occult research, to hear that the Japanese plays were full of spirits and masks, and that the crises in the plays usually occurred when a character who had appeared to be an ordinary mortal was suddenly revealed to be a god or spirit. He must have been reminded of his poetic images which, if he succeeded in giving them symbolic force, suddenly took on a character that they did not have in nature. As for masks, he had already begun to experiment with them in some productions of his plays, but till now had lacked a definite method. The ritual dance also fascinated him because it was pure image. He was delighted to learn from Pound that the Noh was ' one of the great arts of the world, and . . . quite possibly one of the most recondite '.

The art of allusion . . . [wrote Pound] is at the root of the Noh. These plays, or eclogues, were made only for the few ; for the nobles, for those trained to catch the allusion. In the Noh we find an art based upon the god-dance, or upon some local legend of spiritual apparition, or, later, on gestes of war and feats of history ; an art of splendid posture, of dancing and chanting, and of acting that is not mimetic. . . . It is a symbolic stage, a drama of masks — at least they have masks for spirits and gods and young women. It is a theatre of which both Mr. Yeats and Mr. Craig may approve.

A little school of devotees of the Noh plays grew up in London, including Pound, Yeats, Arthur Waley, and Edmund Dulac. Pound began publishing his translations of the plays in magazines and then in a small volume, with a preface by Yeats, at the Cuala Press. The difficulty was that none of the devotees had ever seen a Noh play, but late in 1915 Pound discovered, living in poverty in a backstairs room, the Japanese dancer Ito, who had acted in the Noh in Japan. The stage was now set for Yeats, and he threw himself into the development of a new form of drama, based upon the Japanese but suited to European conventions, with music and dancing allied to drama. A note of exultation appears in his first essay on the subject ; at last he had a form of drama where all could be symbolic, instead of merely half symbolic as in his Irish heroic dramas and his early miracle plays :

. . . I have invented a form of drama, distinguished, indirect, and symbolic, and having no need of mob or press to pay its way — an aristocratic form. . . .

All imaginative art keeps at a distance, and that distance once chosen must be held against a pushing world. . . .

Therefore it is natural that I go to Asia for a stage convention, for more formal faces, for a chorus that has no part in the action and perhaps for those movements of the bodies copied from the marionette shows of the 14th century.

And a later essay makes it even more clear that he has returned to his theory of drama as almost a secret ritual, shaped by arcane wisdom which only initiates will understand :

I want to create for myself an unpopular theatre and an audience like a secret society where admission is by favour and never to many. . . . I desire a mysterious art, always reminding and half-reminding those who understand it of dearly loved things, doing its work by suggestion, not by direct statement, a complexity of rhythm, colour, gesture, not space-pervading like the intellect but a memory and a prophecy : a mode of drama Shelley and Keats could have used without ceasing to be themselves, and for which even Blake in the mood of *The Book of Thell* [*sic*] might not have been too obscure. . . . I seek, not a theatre but the theatre's anti-self, an art that can appease all within us that becomes uneasy as the curtain falls and the house breaks into applause.

The theatre's anti-self : — everything Yeats touches now he tries to turn into a symbol which is pure and self-sufficient, beyond question though it issues from much questioning.

Ireland was not forgotten. ' Perhaps some day a play in the form I am adapting for European purposes shall awake once more, whether in Gaelic or in English, under the slopes of Slieve-na-mon or Croagh Patrick ancient memories. . . .' The first play in this new form which Yeats wrote was *At the Hawk's Well*, another in his series on Cuchulain ; and its terse, vivid diction stamped him as a modern poet even in the mind of such a fastidious critic as T. S. Eliot, who attended its performance in a drawing-room.

Though the play is on Cuchulain, it has no single source in the Cuchulain legends and is purely symbolic, the kind of drama that Yeats had wanted to create in the 'nineties but for which he had then lacked method. The hero comes, as a young man, to the well of immortality, which symbolizes wisdom, and finds there an old man who has sat by the well for fifty years trying to drink of it, but always foiled by the hawk woman who guards the well. While they wait together for the water to bubble up, the woman is possessed by the hawk and dances a magic dance which lures the hero away from the well and puts the old man to sleep. Cuchulain returns from his fruitless pursuit of the hawk woman to find the well dry and to learn that the people of the hills are roused against him and that the rest of his life must be continual warfare. The chorus grimly concludes that he who searches for wisdom must lead a bitter life.

Yeats had at last found an adequate medium for his dramatic talents ; the collision which we have observed in his earlier dramas between humanity and pattern no longer occurs when the actors wear masks, when they speak a highly specialized language, when a chorus announces that all is set within the mind's eye, and when the climax is a symbolic dance. An autobiographical element in the play is difficult to overlook : the old man who has been patiently waiting at the well for fifty years is Yeats's intellect (he was exactly fifty at the time of writing the play), as the young Cuchulain is his instinctive self. We are back with our old friends Aherne and Robartes, Conchubar and Cuchulain, but one change in their attitude towards each other is significant. For the first time they are not in opposition but are both intent upon the same goal. A few years earlier Yeats would have made them quarrel and fight and thus lose the precious water. Each is now led astray, for neither reason nor instinct had enabled Yeats to drink of the well of wisdom, and each is deluded by the hawk which symbolizes logic and abstract thought. The play ended in the first draft : ' Accursed the life of man — between passion and emptiness what he longs for never comes. All his days are a preparation for what never comes.' Yeats had ended his *Reveries over Childhood and Youth* with the same thought :

For some months now I have lived with my own youth and child-hood, not always writing indeed but thinking of it almost every day, and I am sorrowful and disturbed. It is not that I have accomplished too few of my plans, for I am not ambitious ; but when I think of all the books I have read, and of the wise words I have heard spoken, and of the anxiety I have given to parents and grandparents, and of the hopes that I have had, all life weighed in the scales of my own life seems to me a preparation for something that never happens.

Yet a great deal had happened, and his feelings were not merely chagrin. He was not the same timid clumsy boy who twenty-five years before had put on a pose so he could face the world. He was not the same over-sensitive young man who had built in his imagination the perfect love, the Castle of the Heroes, an Ireland made spiritual. It seemed to him that he had turned into a well-mannered public man, with a spare, limber style the reverse of his youthful manner.

Shortly after finishing *At the Hawk's Well*, Yeats felt far enough removed from the period before 1903 to continue his autobiography, and in 1916 and 1917 he wrote with the idea of posthumous publication an account of his busy youth. ' I will lay many ghosts ', he wrote to John Quinn, ' or rather I will purify my own imagination by setting the past in order.' It was indeed a catharsis, for in the first draft he confessed all his faults and misfortunes. This manuscript contains much information which Yeats chose to omit from the reticent version he published in 1921 and 1922.

The act of writing everything down, even if it was later to be modified, implied courage and will and the attainment of a distance from himself, which was made possible largely by his realization of the great transformation that had come over him and his work. He did not carry his account into the twentieth century, for to do so would have too much involved his present thoughts, but he could now look back on his first thirty-five years from the perspective of another man. Just as he had at last discovered, in the Noh plays, the theatre's anti-self, so in his confident moments he felt that he had found and become his own anti-self. His theorizing of so many years seemed to have reached its fulfilment ; he had lived his pose so long as to be successfully fused into it.

We should expect to find in his verse and plays more evidence of this sense of having arrived, and perhaps we may see it in his work in 1916 and 1917, when he begins to write about miracles as he had not done since 1902. His poem, ' Easter 1916 ', is a good example. At first Yeats had been indignant with the Dublin insurrectionaries for needlessly sacrificing their lives, but gradually their death became ennobled in his mind and seemed an illustration of his theories. In July 1916 he said in a note to his bitter poem, ' September 1913 ' that it ' sounds old-fashioned now '. He had not foreseen the recent events. ' The late Dublin Rebellion, whatever one can say of its wisdom, will long be re-membered for its heroism.' The rebels were men whom he had known, Pearse whose school he had visited, MacDonagh whose poems he had read, Connolly who had joined him and Maud Gonne in the demonstrations against England and the Queen in the late 'nineties, MacBride, the ' drunken, vainglorious lout ' who had taken Maud Gonne away from him. All had seemed to him ordinary people, but they had suddenly found their heroic opposites, not like Yeats by effort and discipline, but by the sudden

violence of a great action.  On September 25, 1916, he wrote their
eulogy :

> I write it out in a verse —
> MacDonagh and MacBride
> And Connolly and Pearse
> Now and in time to be,
> Wherever green is worn,
> Are changed, changed utterly :
> A terrible beauty is born.

The same kind of miracle finds its way into his next play,
*The Cat and the Moon* (1917).  Here a blind man and a lame man
come to St. Colman's Well to be blest.  The saint asks the blind
man, who symbolizes the soul, whether he wishes the sight of
his eyes or the state of blessedness; the blind man chooses sight.
But the lame man, who symbolizes the body, chooses blessedness
in preference to the healing of his lameness.  The blind man,
having beaten the now blessed lame man, runs off and leaves him
with the saint, who mounts on the cripple's back and assures him
that he is a miracle.  The lame man is gradually persuaded that
this is indeed the case, and suddenly drops his crutches and breaks
into a dance.  As Yeats explained the ending, ' when the lame
man takes the saint upon his back, the normal man has become
one with his opposite '.  Thus self and anti-self were reconciled
and Yeats had a miracle much more esoteric than any he had
written about in his early plays.  Regardless of the presence of
the saint, the reconcilement of opposites was for Yeats a secular
miracle, the key to his verse, his private system, and his life.

But no theorizing about face and mask and the miracle of
transmutation, and no autobiographical apologias, could hide
from him the fact that his personal life was still inadequate.  An
old bachelor in spite of his new style and method, he filled many
of his poems during these years with laments for his lost youth,
as in ' The Wild Swans at Coole ' :

> All's changed since I, hearing at twilight,
> The first time on this shore,
> The bell-beat of their wings above my head,
> Trod with a lighter tread.

He was still, for all his literary skill, an unsettled, sensitive, lonely man in need of companionship.

Marriage seemed the solution to many problems : it would give him a family, a home, and peace of mind in which to work. After the death of MacBride Yeats went to Paris and proposed to Maud Gonne on condition that she give up politics. As he had anticipated, she refused, and he then became infatuated with her beautiful adopted niece, Iseult. After some months of deferring her reply to his proposal of marriage, however, Iseult decided against it.

Yeats was luckier than he knew. He had long had more than a casual interest in Georgie Hyde-Lees, a friend of Mrs. Shakespear and Ezra Pound. They had first met in 1911, and he had several times visited her and her family for week-ends, finding in her a charming companion and a kindred spirit in his occult studies. She had become interested in psychical research by reading a book of Lombroso, and from time to time after her first meeting with Yeats she helped him to check the authenticity of information given him by mediums. In 1914 she joined a group of Rudolf Steiner Theosophists, and that same year Yeats suggested that she become a member of the Golden Dawn. He sponsored her and saw her through her initiation.

Miss Hyde-Lees, with her remarkable subtlety and sense of humour, seemed to be specially fitted for organizing a lyric poet's errant life. Yeats was greatly attracted to her and felt that she would be able to help him to move forward. On October 21, 1917, after a short engagement, they were married.

A few days after their marriage, Mrs. Yeats for the first time in her life attempted automatic writing. There were a few meaningless lines, and then suddenly she thought that her hand was seized by a superior power. In the fragmentary sentences that were scribbled on the paper her amazed husband saw the rudiments of the system which he had spent his early life trying to evoke through vision, and his middle age trying to formulate through research. Here, in his own home, was miracle without qualification. The bush was burning at last.

## CHAPTER XV

# ESOTERIC YEATSISM: THE FLOWERING
# OF A DREAM

Which book spak muchel of the operaciouns,
Touchinge the eighte and twenty mansiouns
That longen to the mone, and swich folye,
As in our dayes is nat worth a flye ;
For holy chirches feith in our bileve
Ne suffreth noon illusion us to greve.

CHAUCER, *The Franklin's Tale*

. . . I, being driven half insane
Because of some green wing, gathered old mummy wheat
In the mad abstract dark and ground it grain by grain
And after baked it slowly in an oven ; but now
I bring full-flavoured wine out of a barrel found
Where seven Ephesian topers slept and never knew
When Alexander's empire passed, they slept so sound.

YEATS, ' On a Picture of a Black Centaur by Edmund Dulac'

HAD Yeats died instead of marrying in 1917, he would have been remembered as a remarkable minor poet who achieved a diction more powerful than that of his contemporaries but who, except in a handful of poems, did not have much to say with it. Had he not married but lived on in bachelorhood, he would probably have continued his indefatigable attendance at spiritualist séances and made minor elaborations in his rather confusing theories of the mask and of life after death. His prose would have continued to come forth in the same beautiful, bottomless style as in *Per Amica Silentia Lunae*, published just before his marriage, built up out of evasion so skilful that the reader is never sure whether he is being presented with a doctrine or with a poem in prose. Only too aware of the unreliability of his own conclusions, Yeats would probably have devoted himself chiefly to plays and narrative verse. If bachelorhood had continued, we may reasonably assume also that personal problems would have gone on operating, as they had done for many years, as brakes upon his mind.

Marriage to Georgie Hyde-Lees released his energies like a spring. He fell deeply in love with his wife and knew for the first time the happiness of a relatively uncomplicated relationship with another person. He was astonished to find himself playing the role of husband and, after February 1919, of father, without feeling that it was a role at all. ' The marriage bed ', he wrote later, ' is the symbol of the solved antinomy.' Certainly it was so for him, and the ecstasy of the solution shines through the worldly humour of the poems, ' Solomon and the Witch ' and ' Solomon to Sheba ', which he wrote in 1918. A great serenity came over Yeats as he emerged from the isolation and eccentricity of bachelorhood into peace and harmony. His wife was kind and self-sacrificing ; she understood his strange mixture of arrogance and diffidence, and behind the pose which he put on before strangers found him deeply human. For his part, Yeats kept no more diaries of his mental difficulties, wept no more over a barren passion, and no longer thought of himself as shut out from common experience. Eighteen years before, when George Russell's first son was born, Yeats had written in his letter of congratulation : ' I think that a poet, or even a mystic, becomes a greater power from understanding all the great primary emotions & these one only gets out of going through the common experiences & duties of life '. A newly acquired sense of strength enabled him now to write lyric after lyric in which he spoke, with fresh confidence, in his own person. He would say a few years later in a letter to Tagore that as husband and father he felt ' more knitted into life '.

Marriage was a humanizing and normalizing experience, but in no sense a prosaic one. Nothing that had happened to him before was more dramatically exciting than the automatic writing of his wife, which he felt put wisdom at last within his reach. He gave up his obsession for going to séances where he had never been able to learn very much, and stopped his work on a further elaboration of Henry More's theory of the after-life, which was to have been a sequel to *Per Amica Silentia Lunae*. So great was his excitement that he even offered to give up poetry altogether, but the reply that came from the automatic writing said, with a dash of practical wisdom : ' No, we have come to give you metaphors for poetry '. He had always considered himself lucky, and perhaps the best of his good fortune was to find himself married not only to an exceptionally intelligent and sympathetic woman, but to the Sibyl herself.

Not that Mrs. Yeats, a friendly, witty young woman, relished the idea of being the Sibyl ; she insisted that her part should not be made public, and after the first excitement had worn off was often bored with her exhausting task. Automatic writing is chiefly a matter of suspending conscious use of the faculties. Many persons with no ' psychic gift ' are occasionally surprised to find that without thinking they have unconsciously scribbled a meaningful phrase or drawn a meaningful picture on a piece of paper. A few can prolong this automatism over considerable periods, relaxing the will so that they have the sensation that their hand is controlled by a more powerful hand. The script that results has many of the characteristics of dreams, being full of images, fragmentary, run together, by turns coherent and incoherent. In the excitement of marriage Mrs. Yeats discovered that she possessed this ability to suspend her conscious faculties, and would sit down for two or three hours a day with her tireless husband, he putting the questions and she replying to them in automatic script in a notebook. Certain spirits with incongruous names claimed to be dictating to her, and Yeats liked to refer to them as the ' communicators ' and never wholly gave up the idea that they were indeed spirits. The sceptic need not, however, believe that anything more than the unconscious mind was involved in the automatic writing, though some of the attendant manifestations, such as the sudden smell of roses in the room, are difficult to explain. Since husband and wife would discuss the communications afterwards, their conscious minds no doubt had considerable effect upon the direction which the automatic writing would take, but this effect was never sufficient to prevent the revelations from being exceedingly cryptic.

By the end of November 1917 the first part of *A Vision*, as Yeats called the completed book, had been outlined. Human personality was classified into twenty-eight types, or, to use his phraseology, into twenty-eight phases of the moon, each phase being pictured as one of the spokes of a Great Wheel. The classification was based upon the amount of subjectivity or objectivity, words for which Yeats substituted the symbolic abstractions, *antithetical tincture* and *primary tincture*. He vacillated in his definition of these terms, quoting the colloquial meaning of ' objective ' in Murray's Dictionary as ' all that " is presented to consciousness as opposed to consciousness of self, that is the object of perception or thought, the non-ego . . . treating of outward things and events rather than inward thought . . . the actual facts, not coloured by the opinions or feelings of the writer " '. Yeats dodged the difficult philosophical question of whether objective reality had any existence apart from the apprehension of the beholder ; it involved problems of the origin of the world into which he was not prepared to go, but the psychological bias learned from his father encouraged him to minimize the importance of the external world. At phase 15, where the moon is full, subjectivity is at its height ; as the moon wanes subjectivity decreases and objectivity increases, until at phase 1, where the moon is dark, objectivity is greatest. Any individual can be typed or classified as belonging to one of the twenty-eight phases, and Yeats soon began to put his friends and enemies into their appropriate phases as Dante had done in the *Divine Comedy*.

Any human soul passes through all twenty-eight phases in a series of incarnations, although at full moon and dark of the moon (phases 15 and 1) the soul takes on the form of a spirit rather than of a man. In a further sense, — and here the system becomes more complicated, — ontogeny recapitulates phasogeny ; that is, the soul may be said to pass through all the phases within a single lifetime, beginning with the completely unindividualized or objective state of infancy (phase 1), rising to the full individuality or subjectivity of maturity (phase 15), and sinking back at last into ' second childhood and mere oblivion ' (phase 28), where it dies and then after a period begins the round once more. The Shakespearean life-span of seven ages grew to twenty-eight in Yeats's scheme. Usually Yeats discusses the phases as a series of incarnations rather than as the stages of a single lifetime, though one may accept either explanation in reading the didactic poem, ' The Phases of the Moon ', which he wrote in 1918 to expound this portion of his system :

. . . . .

   *Aherne.* Sing me the changes of the moon once more ;
    True song, though speech : ' mine author sung it me.'
   *Robartes.* Twenty-and-eight the phases of the moon,
    The full and the moon's dark and all the crescents,
    Twenty-and-eight, and yet but six-and-twenty
    The cradles that a man must needs be rocked in :
    For there's no human life at the full or the dark.
    From the first crescent to the half, the dream
    But summons to adventure and the man
    Is always happy like a bird or a beast ;
    But while the moon is rounding towards the full
    He follows whatever whim's most difficult
    Among whims not impossible, and though scarred,
    As with the cat-o'-nine-tails of the mind,
    His body moulded from within his body
    Grows comelier. Eleven pass, and then
    Athene takes Achilles by the hair,
    Hector is in the dust, Nietzsche is born,
    Because the heroes' crescent is the twelfth.
    And yet, twice born, twice buried, grow he must,
    Before the full moon, helpless as a worm.
    The thirteenth moon but sets the soul at war
    In its own being, and when that war's begun
    There is no muscle in the arm ; and after,
    Under the frenzy of the fourteenth moon
    The soul begins to tremble into stillness,
    To die into the labyrinth of itself !

. . . . .

All thought becomes an image and the soul
Becomes a body : that body and that soul

> Too perfect at the full to lie in a cradle,
> Too lonely for the traffic of the world :
> Body and soul cast out and cast away
> Beyond the visible world.

The fifteenth phase which Robartes is describing is the link between the *Vision* and Yeats's poetic method. This ' phase of complete beauty ' is inhabited only by spirits ; no human life is possible there. Though Yeats does not explicitly say so, it is clear that to this phase belong the symbols of poetry, caught up into reconcilement. ' Thought and Will are indistinguishable ', he writes elsewhere of the phase, ' contemplation and desire ' are ' united into one '. ' Chance and Choice have become interchangeable without losing their identity. As all effort has ceased, all thought has become image, because no thought could exist if it were not carried towards its own extinction, amid fear or in contemplation. . . .' Robartes next pictures the phases that follow the fifteenth :

> And after that the crumbling of the moon.
> The soul remembering its loneliness
> Shudders in many cradles ; all is changed,
> It would be the world's servant, and as it serves,
> Choosing whatever task's most difficult
> Among tasks not impossible, it takes
> Upon the body and upon the soul
> The coarseness of the drudge.
>
> *Aherne.*                          Before the full
> It sought itself and afterwards the world.
> *Robartes.* Because you are forgotten, half out of life,
> And never wrote a book, your thought is clear.
> Reformer, merchant, statesman, learned man,
> Dutiful husband, honest wife by turn,
> Cradle upon cradle, and all in flight and all
> Deformed because there is no deformity
> But saves us from a dream.
>
> *Aherne.*                          And what of those
> That the last servile crescent has set free ?
> *Robartes.* Because all dark, like those that are all light,
> They are cast beyond the verge, and in a cloud,

Crying to one another like the bats ;
And having no desire they cannot tell
What's good or bad, or what it is to triumph
At the perfection of one's own obedience ;
And yet they speak what's blown into the mind ;
Deformed beyond deformity, unformed,
Insipid as the dough before it is baked,
They change their bodies at a word.

.    .    .    .    .

When all the dough has been so kneaded up
That it can take what form cook Nature fancies,
The first thin crescent is wheeled round once more.

Having passed phase 28, where all individuality is lost, the soul begins the cycle again.

Yeats's psychology is much more elaborate in *A Vision* than in *Per Amica Silentia Lunae* or any of his earlier works. The soul, to use a word which he avoids as often as possible because of its theological bias, is not merely subjective or objective (antithetical or primary), but contains both qualities in varying proportions. Instead of being divided into Self and Anti-Self, as in *Per Amica Silentia Lunae*, it is split into Four Faculties, or two pairs of contraries : Will and Mask, Creative Mind and Body of Fate. In the second edition of *A Vision*, where he was in better control of his material, Yeats defined these chiefly by metaphor, but in the first edition he made some rough definitions :

1. *Will*, originally *Ego* in the automatic script, is ' the first matter ' of the personality, the basic choice which determines the individual's phase.

2. *Mask* is the Will's opposite or anti-self, ' the image of what we wish to become.' There are two possible masks, one true and one false, and the Will may choose the wrong one. Yeats implies that the two masks of any given phase are pre-determined.

3. *Creative Mind* is ' intellect, as intellect was understood before the close of the seventeenth century — all the mind that is consciously constructive,' that part of the mind which acts on external events. Like the Mask, it may be true or false.

4. *Body of Fate* is ' the physical and mental environment, the changing human body, the stream of Phenomena as this affects a particular

individual, all that is forced upon us from without, Time as it affects sensation.' If any reality exists outside us, it lies in the Body of Fate.

The mind of man is a kind of resolution of the energies of these Four Faculties. Some critics have described the system as completely determinist, and Yeats himself liked to talk as if it made everything predestined ; but we soon realize that it does not work that way at all. Man may choose between several alternatives, such as between True and False Mask and True and False Creative Mind ; his phase may not be the phase of his age, in which case he will have to make voluntary adjustments ; as we shall see in analyzing the later edition of the *Vision*, the doctrine of the Thirteenth Cycle was to make the will even more free.

Reading the *Vision* we are conscious of many echoes of Yeats's previous work and interests. The mixture has a different taste but the ingredients have been used before. ' What I have found indeed is nothing new ', Yeats insisted in *A Vision*. There are numerous connections between his system and traditional occult systems with which he was familiar. The Four Faculties, for example, are a variation of a familiar quarternary, which appears in the four elements of magic, in the four humours of medieval medicine and psychology, in the Four Zoas of Blake, in Yeats's Irish mystical order, and, of course, elsewhere. The opposition of objectivity and subjectivity has an evident relation to the active and passive forces, or positive and negative ones, which form an important part of the teachings of the Golden Dawn and most other occult and mystic systems. The twenty-eight-phase lunar cycle is common enough in astrology, as the quotation from Chaucer at the beginning of this chapter indicates. The cycle is reminiscent, too, of the Dark Fortnight and Bright Fortnight of Brahminism. As for the conception of the Four Faculties moving about a wheel, we need look no further than the Zodiac and the astrological analysis of an event or personality according to the influence of dominant planets. But the amazing aspect of the Yeatsian system is that it is not merely a pot-pourri like Theosophy and the Golden Dawn teachings, but a fairly

successful fusion into an original pattern, and here the influence
of the unconscious mind of Mrs. Yeats in building up images was
almost as important as that of Yeats in bringing into unity with
the images the fragmentary theoretical revelations that came with
them. In the end everything is stamped with his personality and
brought into line with his work.

On December 6, 1917, a new symbol corollary to the lunar
symbolism was introduced into the automatic writing. This was

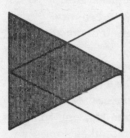

a spiral, which Yeats preferred to call a
gyre (and pronounced with a hard ' g '), or
whirling cone, or, using an Irish and Scots
word, a ' pern ' or spool. Then two such
cones were drawn in the script and related
to European history, which was considered
to pass like the human soul through a cycle
from subjectivity to objectivity. These
cones were imagined as interpenetrating,
whirling around inside one another, one subjective, the other
objective. They provided Yeats with a splendid image to represent the antinomies which had always been present in his mind.
The cones were not restricted to symbolizing objectivity and
subjectivity ; they were also, he said, ' beauty and truth, value
and fact, particular and universal, quality and quantity, the bundle
of separated threads as distinguished from those that are still in
the pattern, abstracted types and forms as distinguished from
those that are still concrete, Man and *Daimon*, the living and the
dead, and all other images of our first parents '. This symbol
was a much more successful one than the mask which he had been
using earlier in the century, for the relation between mask and
face was difficult to visualize. Yeats thought that he had discovered in this figure of interpenetrating gyres the archetypal
pattern which is mirrored and remirrored by all life, by all movements of civilization or mind or nature. Man or movement is
conceived of as moving from left to right and then from right to
left ; no sooner is the fullest expansion of the objective cone
reached than the counter-movement towards the fullest expansion

of the subjective cone begins.  For example, if we apply the cones to history, at the time of Christ objectivity was at its fullest expansion ; the self was struggling to escape from personality, to be lost in ' otherness ', while at the time of the Renaissance subjectivity was at its fullest expansion, and great personalities were everywhere realizing themselves to the utmost.  In our time history is swinging back again towards objectivity, for the cycles continue in eternal recurrence.  Mass movements, such as democracy, socialism, and especially communism, are for Yeats evidences of this shift towards objectivity, when every man tries to look like his neighbour and repress individuality and personality.[1]

The interpenetrating gyres have an obvious sexual symbolism, which Yeats welcomed because it anchored the gyres in the earth. They have, too, a striking resemblance to the seal of Solomon, which is basic in magical invocations ; in the seal one triangle represents water and the other fire, and in union they sometimes symbolize that marriage of spirit and matter which is the magical beatitude.

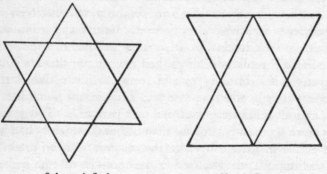

Solomon's Seal                    Yeats's Gyres [2]

[1] As he wrote to Russell just after the Russian Revolution : ' I consider the Marxian criterion of values as in this age the spearhead of materialism & leading to inevitable murder '.

[2] Yeats's conjoined gyres do not, however, transcend the flux of life ; they are, he says, ' pursuit and illusion ', reality being in a sphere which contains them.  The sphere is discussed in later chapters.

This is by no means a full treatment of the architecture of *A Vision*, but it is perhaps enough to indicate that esoteric Yeatsism was an adaptation, reduced to a few essentials and thereby made unusually coherent, of traditional occult ideas. Many problems arise which he does not solve ; for example, he can tell us no more than Leo Africanus about the exact relation between Will, Mask, and Daimon. He slides warily past the question of what causes individual differences, whether it is the action of the Daimon, the man's free will, or the success with which Mask and Will come to terms, or the action of other spirits, or the effect of earlier lives. Yeats suggests that all these may play their share, but does not commit himself any further.

A more basic question which rises in the mind of the reader is, Did Yeats believe in esoteric Yeatsism ? It cannot be answered simply. As a man he sometimes believed in his system and sometimes did not ; at first he had more confidence in the ' communicators ' of the automatic writing as being spirits beyond space and time than he afterwards retained. As a poet he largely accepted his father's position that the poet must be free of dogma and formula. But he feared that the real reason for his reluctance to use the *Vision* in verse might be his timidity, and therefore wrote a few poems explicitly didactic, based on the system, to salve his conscience. But in most of his verse he proceeded with his usual craft so that, while the metaphors for poetry which the communicators had brought him often appear, it is hard to find specific passages which are incomprehensible to someone who has not read *A Vision*. For instance, the musician's song in *The Only Jealousy of Emer*, a play which he wrote in 1917 and 1918, alludes to the series of incarnations necessary to bring the soul to the beauty of the fourteenth phase, at which Eithne Inguba (inspired by Iseult Gonne), the mistress of Cuchulain, is classified. Yeats would not have written the song in this way without his system, but the song is not dependent upon the system for comprehension :

> How many centuries spent
> The sedentary soul

> In toil of measurement
> Beyond eagle or mole,
> Beyond hearing or seeing,
> Or Archimedes' guess,
> To raise into being
> That loveliness ?

The same independence of the system exists in ' An Irish Airman Foresees his Death' (1918), where the airman is a symbol of subjective life, and 'In Memory of Major Robert Gregory', written in the same year, where Gregory is identified with the Renaissance man who comes near the full moon of the historical cycle. These poems are wholly exoteric, but in ' Shepherd and Goatherd' (1918) the theory of *A Vision* that the after-life is the gradual unwinding of life's memories — a proposition put forth also by Leo Africanus — is in evidence in the description of life after death :

> He grows younger every second. . . .
> He unpacks the loaded pern
> Of all 'twas pain or joy to learn,
> Of all that he had made. . . .
> Knowledge he shall unwind
> Through victories of the mind,
> Till, clambering at the cradle-side,
> He dreams himself his mother's pride,
> All knowledge lost in trance
> Of sweeter ignorance.

Here too, however, the meaning was public enough.

He is quite capable of over-simplifying his system, as in ' The Double Vision of Michael Robartes', where he asserts that he has no free will but is controlled by mechanical spirits which are themselves controlled ' by some hidden magical breath ', as Leo Africanus was controlled by Mahomet. He could also turn the system to humorous use, as in ' Under the Round Tower' (1918); here his subject-matter is the inter-action of the two cones, but he makes them into a dance of sun and moon in a round tower (the sphere), the wild dream of a beggarman :

He stretched his bones and fell in a dream
Of sun and moon that a good hour
Bellowed and pranced in the round tower ;

Of golden king and silver lady,
Bellowing up and bellowing round,
Till toes mastered a sweet measure,
Mouth mastered a sweet sound,
Prancing round and prancing up
Until they pranced upon the top.

The poem is not made less slight by the knowledge of its secret meaning. Similarly, a considerable number of symbols of the transcendence of the antinomies appears in these poems of *The Wild Swans at Coole* and *Michael Robartes and the Dancer*, but the *Vision* cannot be credited with having supplied these ; rather it reinforced their use by theoretical justification. Thus in ' Demon and Beast ', a white gull symbolizes the poet's sense of joyful freedom as he imagines himself beyond the gyres of hatred and desire. Swans are used in several of the poems, but one of these, ' The Wild Swans at Coole ', antedates Yeats's marriage and evolution of the *Vision*. Only in ' The Phases of the Moon ' is the material of the automatic script presented directly as a mystical system, and here Yeats, with his old deviousness, represents himself as not knowing the system which Robartes and Aherne expound, and makes Robartes say :

And now he [Yeats] seeks in book or manuscript
What he shall never find.

With the *Vision* to sustain him, we need not be astonished to find Yeats beginning to prophesy again, as he had not done since the 'nineties. Then he had believed that the new epoch would be a golden age, heralding, as in *The Secret Rose*, a heroic Ireland, or, as in *Where there is Nothing*, a finer world. But there was little in the post-war era to inspire him with such hopes. From January 1919 to May 1921 war raged in Ireland between the English forces, including the notorious Black and Tans, and the Irish patriots. Yeats and Lady Gregory were both deeply moved by the 'troubles', she writing articles for a liberal English review condemning the government's policies, and Yeats writing, among other things, a still unpublished poem to Robert Gregory, raging bitterly at the deeds of the British soldiery. He had had little to say about the first World War, its issues being too abstract and international for his mind, but he shared in the feeling that 'many ingenious lovely things are gone'. As in 1914 he had envisaged a heaven of burning ice instead of 'embroidered cloths', now he gave utterance to a chiliastic prophecy of the transvaluation of values, but saw in it only evil :

### THE SECOND COMING

Turning and turning in the widening gyre
The falcon cannot hear the falconer ;
Things fall apart ; the centre cannot hold ;
Mere anarchy is loosed upon the world,
The blood-dimmed tide is loosed, and everywhere
The ceremony of innocence is drowned ;
The best lack all conviction, while the worst
Are full of passionate intensity.

Surely some revelation is at hand ;
Surely the Second Coming is at hand.
The Second Coming ! Hardly are those words out
When a vast image out of *Spiritus Mundi*
Troubles my sight : somewhere in sands of the desert
A shape with lion body and the head of a man,
A gaze blank and pitiless as the sun,
Is moving its slow thighs, while all about it
Reel shadows of the indignant desert birds.
The darkness drops again ; but now I know
That twenty centuries of stony sleep
Were vexed to nightmare by a rocking cradle,
And what rough beast, its hour come round at last,
Slouches towards Bethlehem to be born ?

This poem could not have been written with such prophetic authority without the *Vision*, and the 'widening gyre' is obviously the gyre of objectivity there discussed. But an awareness of the system was more useful for writing than it is for reading the poem. Yeats was careful not to require knowledge of his prose from the reader of his verse, and has made it possible to suppose that the gyre is merely the falcon's flight. The symbol has more connotative power if its esoteric meaning is understood, but the extra connotations can be ignored. It is more necessary that we be familiar with the ancient, traditional myth of a second coming, to which Yeats has given a new slant, than that we understand the novel myth of the gyres.

For the most part, then, the *Vision* supplies only additional connotations for the symbols in Yeats's verse. But the poet was not satisfied to so restrict its use ; scarcely had the automatic writing begun when he decided to make a prose book out of it. Characteristically, he determined to present it to the public as if it were a secret, and his fertile imagination began to tailor a myth to cover ' those bare symbolic bones ', themselves a myth. For this purpose he brought back to life Michael Robartes ; the story he evolved was that Robartes, while travelling in the Middle East, had unexpectedly found in the religious beliefs of an Arab tribe called the Judwalis an explanation of diagrams which he had long before seen in a Latin work of Giraldus Cambrensis. Fascinated by his discovery, Robartes spent twenty years among the Judwalis learning their system and then returned to England to ask his friend Owen Aherne to edit his papers and publish them. But their old quarrel was renewed when Aherne, a loyal Catholic, refused to give any credence to the system beyond that which he would accord to a Platonic myth. Robartes was angry and decided to ask Yeats to prepare the material for publication, and the poet agreed.

This fantastic story, or its rudiments, had already evolved by four months after the commencement of the automatic writing, for in January 1918 Yeats asked Edmund Dulac to cut a medieval-looking woodcut of Giraldus Cambrensis, which would really be a portrait of Yeats, and later used this as a frontispiece for *A Vision*. He began to make rather coy references to the Robartes papers in his notes to Cuala Press editions of his poems.

From 1917 to 1919 he laboured to put the whole of the system into the form of a dialogue between Robartes and Aherne, but dialogue proved too clumsy as the automatic writing grew in detail and complexity. An excerpt from these papers, dated 1919, shows Yeats a little puzzled as to what claim to make for his system's importance and significance :

*Robartes.* I have lived so much alone or among men who could not understand their own philosophy reshaped to the needs of my European mind that I must find someone to talk to. Say to yourself that it is all a classification and when I have shown you how every soul contains the rudiments of the soul that follows in the chain assume that God created all from the same stuff and that they are but a series of little wooden medals which show when we put them together the continuous grain of the tree that they were cut from and that I am as mad as though I believe that medal could grow into medal. It is only my idiosyncrasy perhaps that I prefer to believe that God created the world through the souls of men and angels.

*Aherne.* I shall but return to my catechism the more gladly from granting to your incarnations that form of belief I grant to a play upon the stage.

*Robartes.* Nor is it a moment for believers to quarrel about the form of their belief, the great mass of men even those who go to places of worship have in reality given up the souls immortality. I mean, that they do not consider it a premise for reasoning upon important matters. In a few years[,] for it is already established to the student, they will believe once more. When that time comes it will be understood that just as a man can investigate the laws by which the ocean moves in a cup of water we can investigate by studying our own minds the final destination of the soul. In that day the system of Aquinas will be weighed and that of Ben Luka who thinks not more inaccurately because he thinks in pictures and the world will have plenty of time to choose.

The spectacle of the world choosing between Thomism and Yeatsism was of course removed before publication. In the first edition of *A Vision*, Robartes and Aherne appear only in the introductory chapters and a few notes, and in the final edition, when Yeats was more confident and willing to speak in his own person, they occupy an even smaller role.

Work on this book occupied a great deal of Yeats's time from 1917 to 1925, and sometimes Mrs. Yeats, fearing for his creative gifts, would refuse for extended periods to do any more automatic writing. But to Yeats the system increased steadily in importance ; he was exalted and exulting as never before. With *A Vision* he had a system comparable in its elaborateness to Blake's ; sometimes it seemed to him a new religion with which he could deny his father's scepticism ; always it was a point of reference for all his thought and action. In a sense it was a huge projection of his own life, filled with autobiography and rationalization of his personal crises and temperament, his own soul sitting for model for all the twenty-eight phases. It was a far more satisfactory system than that he had evolved in *Per Amica Silentia Lunae*, the furthest extension of his thought before his marriage, for instead of seeing life as an opposition of two principles he saw it now as a pitched battle fought by a whole city-full of faculties, gyres, phases, cycles, principles, spheres, spirits, and daimons, ' displaying the conflict in all its forms '. That the system appeared eccentric did not worry him overmuch, for he felt that it had enough tradition behind it. He saw more clearly that his earlier posing and masking had been attempts to make his life and work converge into a symbolism ; there was truth as well as malice in the rumour that George Moore was now spreading, that Yeats was going to live in a tower in the west of Ireland to cultivate a ' Poetic Personality '. Yeats knew that now he could live more and more in a world of his own creation, which without the automatic writing he would probably never have brought into being. He was proud of his accomplishment, and his half-humorous description of himself in several poems of this period as Solomon is half-serious too. Though the Black and Tan war reminded him that the night could still ' sweat with terror as before / We pieced our thoughts into philosophy ', the universe seemed to be coming at last within the sphere of influence of his magician's wand :

> Such thought — such thought have I that hold it tight
> Till meditation master all its parts,

Nothing can stay my glance
Until that glance run in the world's despite
To where the damned have howled away their hearts,
And where the blessed dance ;
Such thought, that in it bound
I need no other thing,
Wound in mind's wandering
As mummies in the mummy-cloth are wound.

The power to classify is the power to control, and a new sense of strength comes into his writing. The ideal phase in *A Vision*, the phase ' where Unity of Being is more possible than at any other phase ', is shortly after the full moon, phase 17, and here Yeats classifies himself along with Dante, Shelley, and Landor. We shall not be surprised to find that Unity of Being is a variant of his father's old ideal of ' personality '. It is the result of a struggle, for the mind is beginning to burst into fragmentary images, and consequently ' The being has for its supreme aim . . . to hide from itself and others this separation and disorder ', hence the pose and mask. The men of phase 17 are naturally ' partisans, propagandists and gregarious, yet because of the *Mask* of simplification, which holds up before them the solitary life of hunters and of fishers and " the groves pale passion loves ", they hate parties, crowds, propaganda '. Everyone was given a phasal number ; in the Yeats household at Oxford in 1920 and 1921, as L. A. G. Strong has described it, the poet would often shoot some searching question at an unsuspecting guest whose answer would reveal where he could be typed in the lunar cycle. Mrs. Yeats and John Butler Yeats belonged to phase 18, where unity is beginning to break up, though a ' wisdom of the emotions ' is still possible. Lady Gregory was in phase 24, where codes of conduct must dominate ; and George Russell, in spite of his vigorous objections, was put in phase 25, where the self accepts ' some organized belief '. Ezra Pound was originally in the highly subjective phase 12, but Yeats moved him among the humanitarians of the late objective phases after seeing him feed all the cats at Rapallo. So it went, with the dead as well as the living.

*A Vision* thus became a justification ; most of Yeats's acquaintances were consigned to less attractive phases of the moon than his own, where they could not hope to attain to the state of Unity of Being which is the most satisfying condition to be attained in life. Yeats is proud of his own Unity of Being, and in the essay, ' If I were Four-and-Twenty ', part of which has been quoted earlier, a note of self-gratulation can be detected in his language :

One day when I was twenty-three or twenty-four this sentence seemed to form in my head, without my willing it, much as sentences form when we are half-asleep : ' Hammer your thoughts into unity.' For days I could think of nothing else, and for years I tested all I did by that sentence. I had three interests : interest in a form of literature, in a form of philosophy, and a belief in nationality. None of these seemed to have anything to do with the other, but gradually my love of literature and my belief in nationality came together. Then for years I said to myself that these two had nothing to do with my form of philosophy, but that I had only to be sincere and to keep from constraining one by the other and they would become one interest. Now all three are, I think, one, or rather all three are a discrete expression of a single conviction. I think that each has behind it my whole character and has gained thereby a certain newness — for is not every man's character peculiar to himself : — and that I have become a cultivated man.

He was now able to rephrase his ' lover's quarrel with the world ' in more general terms ; being a man of phase 17, and born into an age which is at phase 22 of its historical cycle, he is doomed to belong to ' a tragic minority '. From 1919 to 1922 Yeats rewrote that first draft of his *Autobiographies* which he had written in a mood of self-purgation before his marriage ; with *A Vision* in mind he put reticence upon his narrative and suffused it with the serenity of the man who has achieved Unity of Being. Memories which had seemed all-important a few years before, such as the intertwining of Maud Gonne with all his thought and action during his youth, he now considerably reduced in scale ; his desperate search for the secrets of the occult world was played down and fitted into unity ; the crises in his fortunes were, as he said, smoothed over. He had removed many of his particularities and turned himself into that man of phase 17 whom, once he had posited, he had decided to resemble ; and the book was no longer a mere autobiography, but a ' political and literary testament ', he wrote in 1920 to Lady Gregory, ' intended to give a philosophy to the movement. Every analysis of character, of Wilde, Henley, Shaw & so on builds up my philosophic nationalism — it is nationalism against internationalism, the rooted against the rootless people.'

So we see him slowly welding himself and his surroundings into his myth. He is not merely a poet, but the symbol of a poet, and as he thinks of himself in these terms his gestures become more noble and his speech more considered. The normal processes of life do not stop, of course ; he retains his old friendships and the need for them, and has, for example, alternate quarrels over politics and reconciliations with Maud Gonne. But, as his principal interest, he surrounds himself with material objects which become part of his secret ritual. One of these was the Norman tower, Thoor Ballylee (Ballylee Castle) in Galway, which he had bought in 1915. He wrote of it to John Quinn on July 23, 1918 : ' I am making a setting for my old age, a place to influence lawless youth, with its severity and antiquity ' ; and a year later he remarked that he was reluctant to accept a teaching position in Japan which had been offered him, because his tower needed ' another year's work under our own eyes before it is a fitting monument and symbol '. In 1922 he made several poems about the castle where with his family, which now included a son and daughter, he lived. The tower and many of its furnishings took on deep significance. For example, the winding stair which leads up the tower was an emblem of the spiritual ascent, with some side reference to the visionary gyres, which could be conceived of as the antinomy of spirit and matter or of heaven and earth. A sword given him by a Japanese named Sato was a symbol of life, its silk-embroidered sheath a symbol of beauty ; while outside in the garden flowered ' the symbolic rose '. The Yeats touch turned all to symbol.

We can understand what has happened if we remember that the rose was one of the symbols he used in the 'nineties, but then it was always far off and remote, while now it grew on his property. Those other vague, unpossessed emblems of his youth, such as ' the wind among the reeds ', which represented the spirit breathing upon mankind, had entirely given way before the solidity and private ownership of tower and stair. This is not the symbolism of an exile or pariah, but of a man of means and position. Yeats heads the sections of his ' Meditations in Time of Civil War ' as ' *My* House ', ' *My* Table ', ' *My* Descendants ', 'The Road at *My* Door'. That old Castle of the Heroes of which he had once dreamed as a kind of ethereal temple of the spirit is now, in 1922, a microcosm, where he and his family live, and where life is condensed and controlled by the machinery of symbolism. Who can say now where the work begins and the life ends ? The world, once so hostile, lies docile at his feet.

CHAPTER XVI

# SAILING TO BYZANTIUM

WITH his new burst of intellectual vigour came material success. When Yeats returned to his own country in the spring of 1922, after several years of residence chiefly in England, he found himself a famous man. Queen's University, Belfast, gave him an honorary degree in July, and Trinity College, Dublin, so often the subject of his denunciations years before, gave him another in December. At the end of the year President Cosgrave appointed him, as a reward for his services to Ireland, to the Senate of the newly formed Free State. In 1924 he was awarded the Nobel Prize for Literature and could think of himself as a writer of European importance.

Yet the poems which he wrote from 1922 to 1927, and published in 1928 in *The Tower*, are full of a bitterness which seems irrational in the face of all these successes. His father's death in New York in 1922 probably had something to do with it. Then, too, he was perhaps a little disappointed to find that the convergence of his life and work into a symbolism did not make themes for poetry easier to come by or composition less arduous. No static unity was possible for him ; he had to submit every integration to ' the shock of new material ', destroying and then rebuilding. The most obvious pressure on him was the furious Irish civil war which broke out in June 1922 as the result of De Valera's refusal to accept the treaty signed by Arthur Griffith and others with Lloyd George, which guaranteed the independence of Ireland under the Crown. The war lasted until about the end of May 1923, and affected Yeats deeply, for he had always closely identified his country's troubles with his own. At Thoor Ballylee in 1922 the symbolical tower seemed likely to be attacked by unsymbolical men and weapons at any moment, and husband and wife frequently ran to the window to look out when sounds of gunfire were especially close. In October 1922 Yeats wrote from Dublin of ' a drift towards conservatism perhaps towards autocracy. I always knew that it would come, but not that it would come in this tragic way. One wonders what prominent man will live through it. One meets a minister at dinner, passing his armed guard on the doorstep & one feels no certainty that one will meet him again.'

Besides this anxiety for his country, Yeats was full of bitterness about old age ; for many years he had been blind in one eye ; now he felt deafness coming on and told himself that he was too old to dash with his former abandon into impossible projects. Were he twenty-four instead of fifty-four, he wrote as early as 1919, he would propose to the nation his new doctrine of Unity of Being. But he had not given up his hopes for some immediate outlet for his ideas, and on January 6, 1921, wrote to Lady Gregory : ' I would prefer to stay out of Ireland till my philosophy is complete & then to settle there and apply its doctrine to practical life '. After his return to Ireland in 1922 he was restless and excused himself for his practical inactivity on the grounds of old age. Though the excuse was not wholly satisfactory he began to use it often, and deliberately exaggerated it for the purposes of poetry, wishing, as usual, to swing the pendulum as far as possible. Thus in June 1922 he wrote querulously to Mrs. Shakespear : ' I am tired & in a rage at being old, I am all I ever was & much more but an enemy has bound and twisted me so I can plan & think as I never could, but no longer achieve all I plan & think '. In his salad days he had demonstrated his power by building up organizations and movements. Now he had acquired knowledge but was not moving men's minds. As usual he framed the problem as an opposition, and it was in his mind when in 1923 he wrote the splendid sonnet, ' Leda and the Swan '. This myth had held his mind since his first use of it in ' The Adoration of the Magi ' in 1896, where he had prophesied that ' another Leda would open her knees to the swan ' and begin a new age. The bird's rape of the human, the coupling of god and woman, the moment at which one epoch ended and another began, the antinomies engendering breast to breast : in the act which included all these Yeats had the violent symbol for the transcendence of opposites which he needed. After celebrating it in verse almost as miraculous as the event described, the poet suddenly demands whether copulation has resolved, if only for an instant, that last antinomy of knowledge against power :

> Being so caught up,
> So mastered by the brute blood of the air,
> Did she put on his knowledge with his power
> Before the indifferent beak could let her drop ?

Could power and knowledge ever exist together in this world, or were they, as he had reason to suspect, contraries ever at war ? Was wisdom the ripe fruit obtainable only when the sense of taste was gone ?

But Yeats's feeling of senile decay, if we may find this auto-biographical element in the poem as it is in his letters, was a little premature ; at fifty-seven he still had a great deal of energy and was annoyed with himself for being sedentary and putting on weight. He took exercises to stay the hand of time. During the civil war, the sight of the ' affable Irregular ', a man of action, at his door, filled him with envy. The defence was clear though not altogether adequate : he was an artist. He dramatized his feelings in several poems, consoling himself in one :

> The soul's own youth and not the body's youth
> Shows through our lineaments.

Had he become a man of action, his dissatisfaction would have been greater :

> I turn away and shut the door, and on the stair
> Wonder how many times I could have proved my worth
> In something that all others understand or share ;
> But O ! ambitious heart, had such a proof drawn forth
> A company of friends, a conscience set at ease,
> It had but made us pine the more.   The abstract joy,
> The half-read wisdom of daemonic images,
> Suffice the ageing man as once the growing boy.

The argument was perfectly true but did not altogether convince him, and as honour and distinction came to him he began to feel as much uneasiness as pride. A well-fleshed senescence was hardly the ideal of his Promethean youth.

The role of Senator suited his mood of dignity and wisdom, and appeased, but only partially, his desire for some practical outlet for his energies. Friends like Maud Gonne have insisted that it made him conservative, but this tendency had begun long before. What was important to Yeats was that he regained the sense of participation in Irish affairs which he had not had for many years. As a Senator he was in the thick of intrigue, albeit official intrigue, full of secrets, and happy to be building a new Ireland. ' Here ', he wrote to Mrs. Shakespear, ' one works at the slow exciting work of creating the institutions of a new nation —all coral insects but with some design in our heads of the ulti- mate island. Meanwhile the country is full of arms & explosives ready for any violent hand to use. Perhaps all our slow growing coral may be scattered but I think not — not unless Europe takes to war again, & starts new telepathic streams of violence and cruelty.' He did not, however, have much opportunity to speak on subjects of which he had knowledge, and rather than betray his ignorance in economic and administrative matters, generally kept silent : ' My work in the Senate interests me, a new tech- nique which I am learning in silence — I have only spoken once & then but six sentences & shall not speak again perhaps till I am (if I shall ever be) at ease with it '. His colleagues, old confident bankers with endless facts at their disposal, overwhelmed him a little so that he could not hope to turn the Senate into a forum for his ideas. He distinguished himself in writing a new Copy- right Act and in helping to develop a new Irish coinage, but these were minor matters.

His pursuit of wisdom went on, however, with gathering intensity. In the chapter, ' Dove or Swan ', which he was writing for *A Vision*, he hoped not only to interpret the past but to predict the future on the basis of the movement of the gyres. For the purpose he did not depend on the communicators' fragmentary revelations but read a great deal of history and related material. In a letter of 1921 he mentions reading Eugénie Strong's *Apotheosis and After Life*, a book which furnished many of the symbols for his poems on Byzantium, and then remarks : ' I read many books of this kind now, searching out signs of the whirling gyres of the historical cone as we see it & hoping that by their study I may see deeper into what is to come '. The automatic script had offered no help about the future, but his cyclical theories should enable him to foretell accurately. On August 26, 1924, he is bringing his work together : ' I am meanwhile writing daily on the philosophy. At present I am concentrating the history of the world into twenty pages or so, & then I shall do the same for the next world. Both will seem better so abbreviated.' The new revelation, he thought, must inaugurate a subjective, pagan era opposite to the objective one of Christianity, an annunciation to some new Leda by a swan rather than to some new Mary by a dove. Such a movement would be distinguished by its great personalities, he hoped, and, looking about him for signs of the impending millennium, Yeats saw in Mussolini's spectacular new regime in Italy personal government at its height and a burst of powerful personality such as he anticipated for the new era. Fortunately he did not go so far as to accept Fascism explicitly, but he came dangerously close. He extolled the virtues of government by an *élite* for Ireland, but had too much rebelliousness in his nature to be merely a supporter of the party in power. At the same time he had a hearty distaste for the opposition party of the Irish republicans, for they represented to him democracy and mob-rule, the worst tendencies of the cycle that was ebbing out. As a result of this perilous flirtation with authoritarianism, Yeats's political speeches of this period are not pleasant reading. On August 2, 1924, he spoke with cautious satisfaction at a public banquet of the curtailment of liberty which he foresaw :

' There will never be another war,' that was our opium dream. That is all gone, and Ireland celebrates its coming of age in such a different world. We do not believe that war is passing away, and we are not certain that the world is growing better. We even tell ourselves that the idea of progress is quite modern, that it has been in the world but two hundred years, nor are we quite as stalwart as we used to be in our democratic politics. Psychologists and statisticians in Europe and America are attacking the foundations, and a great popular leader [Mussolini] has said to an applauding multitude ' We will trample upon the decomposing body of the Goddess of Liberty '. It is impossible not to ask oneself to what great task of the nations we have been summoned in this transformed world where there is so much that is obscure and terrible. I see about me the representatives of nations which have suffered incomparably more than we have, more than we may ever suffer. Our few months of war and civil war must seem in their eyes but a light burden. To them, as to us perhaps, it seems that the world can never be the same. Is it not possible perhaps that the stream has turned backward, and that a dozen generations to come will have for their task, not the widening of liberty, but recovery from its errors ; that they will set their hearts upon the building of authority, the restoration of discipline, the discovery of a life sufficiently heroic to live without opium dreams ? Certainly whatever happens it is to the older Nations that our new Nation must look for example and for guidance.

But Yeats's oratory was not a complete expression of his personality or philosophy. He still hoped to introduce *A Vision* directly into the political scene ; ' thought is nothing without action ', he wrote wishfully, and added that if readers would master his system ' the curtain may ring up on a new drama '. Perhaps some new conspiracy might be fomented which would better embody his ideas than any existing institution or organization. Early in 1924 he went with his wife to Stockholm to receive the Nobel Prize, and afterwards, when a beautiful woman came up and asked him a question, his hopes bubbled out :

We are going to change the thought of the world, I say, to bring it back to its old truths, but I dread the future. Think what the people have made of the political thought of the eighteenth century, and now we must offer them a new fanaticism. Then I stop ashamed, for I am talking habitual thoughts, & not adapting them to her ear, forgetting beauty in the pursuit of truth, and I wonder if age has made my mind rigid and heavy.

At last, in June of the same year, this would-be revolutionary managed to find a sort of conspiracy. A group of young men came to see him bursting with ardour to start a revolutionary literary review, but without a programme. Yeats persuaded them to found their policy on one of the major doctrines of *A Vision*, the immortality of the soul. ' My dream ', he said in a letter, ' is a wild paper of the young which will make enemies everywhere & suffer suppression & hate a number of times, for its logical assertion with all fitting deductions of the immortality of the soul.' Accordingly he wrote but did not sign the leading article of the review, which was called *To-Morrow*. The article, not elsewhere reprinted, is a flamboyant mixture of paganism, anti-clericalism, and Yeatsism :

### TO ALL ARTISTS AND WRITERS

We are Catholics, but of the school of Pope Julius the Second and of the Medician Popes, who ordered Michaelangelo and Raphael to paint upon the walls of the Vatican, and upon the ceiling of the Sistine Chapel, the doctrine of the Platonic Academy of Florence, the reconciliation of Galilee and Parnassus. We proclaim Michaelangelo the most orthodox of men, because he set upon the tomb of the Medici ' Dawn ' and ' Night,' vast forms shadowing the strength of ante-diluvian Patriarchs and the lust of the goat, the whole handiwork of God, even the abounding horn.

We proclaim that we can forgive the sinner, but abhor the atheist, and that we count among atheists bad writers and Bishops of all denominations. ' The Holy Spirit is an intellectual fountain,' and did the Bishops believe that Holy Spirit would show itself in decoration and architecture, in daily manners and written style. What devout man can read the Pastorals of our Hierarchy without horror at a style rancid, coarse and vague, like that of the daily papers ? We condemn the art and literature of modern Europe. No man can create, as did Shakespeare, Homer, Sophocles, who does not believe, with all his blood and nerve, that man's soul is immortal, for the evidence lies plain to all men that where that belief has declined, men have turned from creation to photography. We condemn, though not without sympathy, those who would escape from banal mechanism through technical investigation and experiment. We proclaim that these bring no escape, for new form comes from new subject matter, and new subject matter must flow from the human soul restored to all its courage, to all its audacity. We dismiss all demagogues and call back the soul to its ancient sovereignty, and declare that it can do whatever it please, being made, as antiquity affirmed, from the imperishable substance of the stars.

Yeats was right in foreseeing the failure of *To-Morrow*, but not in thinking that the failure would be magnificent. The review, with its heretical but vague policies, collapsed after two issues had roused considerable notoriety.

We may reasonably ask why Yeats was suddenly so preoccupied with his doctrine of the immortality of the soul. The fact is that, now that he was finishing the first edition of *A Vision*, he saw clearly that by removing God from the universe and turning all life into cycles, he had deprived his system of any teleological basis for conduct except that, if one lived a harmonious life, one might expect more harmonious future lives and perhaps, — though here he was indefinite, — escape eventually from the cycle of rebirth. He could not define good and evil except in terms of complete or incomplete self-expression, returning to his father's theory of personality as the ultimate reality. Consequently, that 'virtue might not lack sanction', he emphasized the immortality of the soul. The best summary of his position at this time, and for Yeats a remarkably straightforward one, is in a passage which he later removed from *A Vision* :

It is possible that the ever increasing separation from the community as a whole of the cultivated classes, their increasing certainty, and that falling in two of the human mind which I have seen in certain works of art is preparation. During the period said to commence in 1927 . . . must arise a form of philosophy, which . . . will be concrete in expression, establish itself by immediate experience, seek no general agreement, make little of God or any exterior unity, and it will call that good which a man can contemplate himself as doing always and no other doing at all. It will make a cardinal truth of man's immortality that its virtue may not lack sanction, and of the soul's reembodiment that it may restore to virtue that long preparation none can give and hold death an interruption. The supreme experience,

Plotinus' ecstasy, ecstasy of the Saint, will recede . . . and men may be long content with those more trivial supernatural benedictions as when Athena took Achilles by his yellow hair.  Men will no longer separate the idea of God from that of human genius, human productivity in all its forms.

The form of philosophy which would be ' concrete in expression ' and ' establish itself by immediate experience ' would be either the *Vision* or a system like it, more symbol than philosophy.  To Yeats, communism, socialism, fascism, and democracy were all myths, for only myths could ' rouse great masses to action ', and now myth would be pitted against myth, ' victory resting with that most deeply rooted '.

These principles were not easily applicable to the contemporary Irish scene, and they help to account for the ineptness of even the best of Yeats's Senate speeches.  He had an excellent opportunity for a great oration when a bill was introduced to make divorce illegal.  The issue was an important one : Catholic pressure for the bill was intense ;  an important cause was at stake.  Yeats could have defended divorce simply on the grounds of established, traditional practice ;  or he might have made the defence Milton had made, that divorce was human and natural and that opposition to it was a clerically fostered superstition as well as a serious restraint on individual liberty.  Yeats touched on all these points in his speech on June 11, 1925, but offhandedly, like a man who is afraid that his arguments are not good enough.  As for liberty, he was hamstrung here because of his growing hostility to democracy, and the liberty which he demanded was the liberty of a privileged class rather than of a human being.  He insisted upon speaking as a man of the world and Anglo-Irishman rather than as a man of letters or a man of conviction.  His peroration, in which he extolled the Protestant minority, was his only burst of eloquence, and this was in the service of class rather than of principle :

I think it is tragic that within three years of this country gaining its independence we should be discussing a measure which a minority of this nation considers to be grossly oppressive.  I am proud to con-

sider myself a typical man of that minority. We against whom you
have done this thing, are no petty people. We are one of the great
stocks in Europe. We are the people of Burke ; we are the people of
Grattan ; we are the people of Swift, the people of Emmet, the people
of Parnell. We have created the most of the modern literature of this
country. We have created the best of its political intelligence. Yet
I do not altogether regret what has happened. I shall be able to find
out, if not I, my children will be able to find out whether we have
lost our stamina or not. You have defined our position and given us a
popular following. If we have not lost our stamina then your victory
will be brief, and your defeat final, and when it comes this nation may
be transformed.

In prose, however sounding the periods, this was snobbery, but
when Yeats turned to verse he could take the same thought,
purge it of pettiness, and put the full weight of that heroic personality who was protagonist of his poems behind it :

> It is time that I wrote my will ;
> I choose upstanding men
> That climb the streams until
> The fountain leap, and at dawn
> Drop their cast at the side
> Of dripping stone ; I declare
> They shall inherit my pride,
> The pride of people that were
> Bound neither to Cause nor to State,
> Neither to slaves that were spat on,
> Nor to the tyrants that spat,
> The people of Burke and of Grattan
> That gave, though free to refuse. . . .

Although in politics he had, as he once wrote, ' no gift to set a
statesman right ', in verse he escaped from temporary prejudices
and eccentricities.

As he finished *A Vision* in 1925 he began to read more deeply
in philosophy than, fearing to spoil his own system, he had done
before, and he found, particularly in Plotinus and Plato, a feeling
of wisdom and pure contemplation which seemed what he had

always desired. From them (though he disagreed with them), from his age and natural dignity, his position as Nobel Prize winner and Senator, and his sense of fulfilment in having finished *A Vision*, he drew strength for the three mighty poems of 1925 and 1926 : ' The Tower ' (October 7, 1925), ' Among School Children' (June 14, 1926), and 'Sailing to Byzantium' (September 26, 1926). These poems seem to have his whole life behind them. In ' The Tower ' he asserts his conclusions against those of Plato and Plotinus, and does so successfully because he makes his theories into what they basically were, — a defiant, Faustian cry of the infinite power of the mind of man :

> And I declare my faith :
> I mock Plotinus' thought
> And cry in Plato's teeth,
> Death and life were not
> Till man made up the whole,
> Made lock, stock and barrel
> Out of his bitter soul,
> Aye, sun and moon and star, all,
> And further add to that
> That, being dead, we rise,
> Dream and so create
> Translunar Paradise.

But the main problem of the poem is that contrast between his young muse and his old age which, now that he was past sixty and ailing, had real foundation in fact :

> What shall I do with this absurdity —
> O heart, O troubled heart — this caricature,
> Decrepit age that has been tied to me
> As to a dog's tail ?
>             Never had I more
> Excited, passionate, fantastical
> Imagination, nor an ear and eye
> That more expected the impossible. . . .

His conclusion, emerging from the antinomy, is to devote himself entirely to wisdom :

Now shall I make my soul,
Compelling it to study
In a learned school
Till the wreck of body,
Slow decay of blood,
Testy delirium
Or dull decrepitude,
Or what worse evil come —
The death of friends, or death
Of every brilliant eye
That made a catch in the breath —
Seem but the clouds of the sky
When the horizon fades ;
Or a bird's sleepy cry
Among the deepening shades.

The problem of the poem is solved, but in actual life Yeats's pursuit of wisdom could never be so single-minded. In ' Among School Children ' the structure of the poem more thoroughly reflects the total complexity. The scene is a schoolroom which Yeats is inspecting. As he looks at the children and hears from a nun about the modern educational methods, he is struck by the contrast between the children and himself, now sixty years old. His mind is carried back to a day in his youth ; when his beloved (Maud Gonne, though he does not name her) told him of an incident in her school days, they had seemed suddenly, momentarily blended together by sympathy into a sphere or the yolk and white of one shell. This image of opposites reconciled points the way towards the poem's conclusion, but lasts only an instant ; the recollection makes him wonder whether Maud once resembled these children, and suddenly her image as she must have been when a child floats into his mind. It gives way to the image of her as an old woman. Both she and he, though handsome once, are now old scarecrows.

Filled with horror at the contrast, the poet says that no mother, if she could see her son at sixty years, would consider motherhood worth while. Even the greatest philosophers, Plato, Aristotle, and Pythagoras, are but ' scarecrows when their fame has come ', and their greatest achievements are nothing. What then is left ? In the next to last stanza he declares that only images escape the disintegration of age ; the mother worships an image of her son (not his flesh and blood) just as the nun worships an image of God. Only such images are real : they are ' self-born ' ; being perfect and unageing, they mock man's enterprise ; and they are the symbols of heavenly glory. In the final stanza the poet imagines heavenly glory a place, or more likely, a state, where body and soul are united as he and his beloved had seemed united that day long before. Triumphing in his theme, he changes in the last stanza from declarative statement to apostrophe or secular adoration of the completed symbol of heavenly glory :

> Labour is blossoming or dancing where
> The body is not bruised to pleasure soul,
> Nor beauty born out of its own despair,
> Nor blear-eyed wisdom out of midnight oil.
> O chestnut-tree, great-rooted blossomer,
> Are you the leaf, the blossom or the bole ?
> O body swayed to music, O brightening glance,
> How can we know the dancer from the dance ?

In ' Sailing to Byzantium ' Yeats reached the climax of this period by creating richer and more multitudinous overtones than before. He attempted here to evoke a symbol — in the poem as a whole and also in the symbolic bird spoken of in the poem — which would have a life of its own into which he could put himself :

### SAILING TO BYZANTIUM

#### I

> That is no country for old men.   The young
> In one another's arms, birds in the trees,
> — Those dying generations — at their song,
> The salmon-falls, the mackerel-crowded seas,
> Fish, flesh, or fowl, commend all summer long
> Whatever is begotten, born, and dies.
> Caught in that sensual music all neglect
> Monuments of unageing intellect.

### II

An aged man is but a paltry thing,
A tattered coat upon a stick, unless
Soul clap its hands and sing, and louder sing
For every tatter in its mortal dress,
Nor is there singing school but studying
Monuments of its own magnificence ;
And therefore I have sailed the seas and come
To the holy city of Byzantium.

### III

O sages standing in God's holy fire
As in the gold mosaic of a wall,
Come from the holy fire, perne in a gyre,
And be the singing-masters of my soul.
Consume my heart away ; sick with desire
And fastened to a dying animal
It knows not what it is ; and gather me
Into the artifice of eternity.

### IV

Once out of nature I shall never take
My bodily form from any natural thing,
But such a form as Grecian goldsmiths make
Of hammered gold and gold enamelling
To keep a drowsy Emperor awake ;
Or set upon a golden bough to sing
To lords and ladies of Byzantium
Of what is past, or passing, or to come.

We shall have to distinguish some of the overtones. Byzantium is a holy city, because it is the capital of Eastern Christendom, but it is also Yeats's holy city of the imagination as Golgonooza was Blake's. Byzantium is more effective for symbolic purposes than Golgonooza, for Yeats needs only to divert it from the traditional meaning it already has and is not required to explain it from the beginning. The protagonist of the poem is not Yeats but may be described as a symbol of Yeats and of the artist and of man. In his apostrophe to the sages,

O sages standing in God's holy fire
As in the gold mosaic of a wall,

the use of the connective ' as in ' prevents our knowing whether
the sages are primarily images in the mosaic and secondarily
sages in God's holy fire or the reverse ; the painted figures
and transfigured saints symbolize each other with exact equiva-
lence, for an image is in the world of art as holy as a sage.  God
in the poem stands less in the position of the Christian God than
in that of supreme artist, artificer of eternity and the holy fire ;
he is thus also the poet and the human imagination which is sometimes in Yeats's system described as the maker of all things.  As
for the emperor, Yeats reminds us in *A Vision* that the Byzantine
emperor was himself a god as well as a man.  Finally the golden
bird, symbol of the reconciliation of opposites, symbolizes : (1)
the poem itself, the created artifact ; (2) the protagonist, who
fades into it ; (3) the poet, who becomes what he creates.  The
poem is a veritable chorus of symbols, all contributing to what
Yeats had long ago declared as his endeavour, ' to condense as
out of the flying vapour of the world an image of human perfection, and for its own and not for the art's sake '.

'Sailing to Byzantium' is full of echoes of Yeats's other
works, of his reading, and of his experiences.  In a sense he had
been writing it all his life.  The image of the soul clapping its
hands he remembered from his reading of Blake in his 'twenties ;
Blake had seen the soul of his dead brother rising to heaven,
' clapping his hands for joy '.  His imagination had been taken
by the Byzantine mosaics which he had first seen at Ravenna with
Lady Gregory in 1907, and later in Sicily with his wife in 1924.
The phrase, ' perne in a gyre ', he had used in ' Demon and
Beast ' (written in 1918) ; the ' tattered coat upon a stick ' was
reminiscent of the scarecrow imagery he had used a few months
before in ' Among School Children '.  The juxtaposition of fire
and music in the third stanza may be traced back to his statement
in *Per Amica Silentia Lunae* that ' In the condition of fire is all
music and all rest '.  The phrase, ' gather me / Into the artifice
of eternity ', goes back to ' The Tables of the Law ' (1895), where

he had written of ' that supreme art which is to win us from life and gather us into eternity like doves into their dove-cots '. As a boy in London, Yeats had stared for hours at Turner's picture of ' The Golden Bough ' in the National Gallery. The bird is a common symbol in his work, but in its particular application here a talk Yeats gave on art in 1908 is curiously close. The *Irish Times* reported him as saying on that occasion :

> The President had just quoted a reference from some author about ' Art for Art's sake.' When he (Mr. Yeats) wrote ' Kathleen ni Houlihan ' he did not write it to make rebels. All he meant was that he, like every other artist, wrote that play to express his own feelings at a certain moment, to express them without thought of anybody else, to express them as the bird expresses itself when it sings. The bird was not trying to preach to anybody, the bird did not moralise to anyone ; it gave no lessons — it merely sang its song. All artists were precisely the same. ' Art for art's sake ' meant art for the sake of sincerity, for the sake simply of natural speech coming from some simple, natural child-like soul.

Not only were the phrases deeply imbedded in his mind ; the subject, too, was part of his habitual thought. Here, for example, is a sketch of a poem he wrote for the initiation into the highest grade of the Golden Dawn in 1915:

### FOR INITIATION OF 7–4

We are weighed down by the blood & the heavy weight of the bones
We are bound by flowers, & our feet are entangled in the green
And there is deceit in the singing of birds.
It is time to be done with it all
The stars call & all the planets
And the purging fire of the moon
And yonder is the cold silence of cleansing night
May the dawn break, & gates of day be set wide open.

But he had to secure a dramatic structure and the more dense and powerful Byzantine symbolism before the idea took on full poetic significance.

Lyrical poetry at this pitch and on this theme could not long be sustained. The poem gathers its tension from the dramatic conflict of passion and wisdom.  But though wisdom conquers, its victory is almost Pyrrhic.  The poet has sailed to Byzantium, but his heart, ' sick with desire ', is full of Ireland, and he cannot speak of the natural life without celebrating it.  Searching for the monuments of unageing intellect is as much a *pis aller* as a goal, and the eternity into which the poet longs to be gathered is described with deliberate ambivalence as an artifice.  His prayer and ambition are also impure ; those personages to whom he prays, being figures in the mosaics or sages in God's holy fire, or both, are already removed from life, but he wishes to escape even further.  He asks, therefore, not to become a sage like them, but to be turned into a beautiful, mechanical bird which will have wisdom placed in its mouth by its fashioner.  He will be liberated not only from life but from all responsibilities by being trans-muted into an image, which, in turn, will sing not of the world of eternity but of time.

Such a fate could only satisfy Yeats momentarily.  Having sailed to Byzantium, he was ready to re-embark.  But the pursuit of wisdom from 1917 to 1926 had changed the look of things.  Returning to Ireland he would find a ' new intensity ' in ' all visible and tangible things ' which was ' not a reaction from that wisdom but its very self '.

## CHAPTER XVII

# RIGHT MASTERY OF NATURAL THINGS

Every thought is like a bell with many echoes.

YEATS, *Wheels and Butterflies*

HEALTH now became a major concern. Twice during the years from 1926 to 1932 Yeats was close to death, the first time in Dublin in October 1927, when he hardly expected to recover from congestion of the lungs ; the second time at Rapallo in December 1928, when he contracted Malta fever and was critically ill for almost four months. Minor ailments, beginning with a slight rupture from exercise followed by what he called the ' ignoble complaint ' of measles in 1926, combined with almost chronic lung trouble and high blood pressure to make the process of living more difficult and more precious. As death moved perceptibly closer, Yeats's mind turned in self-defence, as it were, towards life ; the moods of his poems changed and a stream of blood imagery poured into his verse like a transfusion. He turned to love poetry, which he had not written in any quantity since the 'nineties, and at first made his reminiscences his subject in ' A Man Young and Old ', but gradually became less autobiographical, as in ' Twelve Poems for Music ', which he sought to make ' all emotion and all impersonal '. He by no means abjured the pursuit of wisdom, but he declared firmly now that the wisdom he had in mind was not the saint's wisdom, and that beatitude, if it implied total escape from the wheel of reincarnation, attracted but did not win him. For him the antinomies, even if transcended, must be present ; the saint might avoid them, but not the poet. No lover of holiness but of life, Yeats clarified his position in ' A Dialogue of Self and Soul ' (1927), where the soul summons to the continued ascent of ' the winding ancient stair ' and offers, if he will let his ' imagination scorn the earth ', to deliver him from rebirth and bring him to heaven. But Yeats's self will not have happiness on these undramatic terms, sets up its own emblems of life against the soul's emblem of darkness, and claims its right to live again and again. In 'Sailing to Byzantium', the poet had praised the life he was rejecting; here, accepting life, he reviles it:

> *My Self.* A living man is blind and drinks his drop.
> What matter if the ditches are impure?
> What matter if I live it all once more?
> Endure that toil of growing up;
> The ignominy of boyhood; the distress
> Of boyhood changing into man;
> The unfinished man and his pain
> Brought face to face with his own clumsiness;
>
> The finished man among his enemies?
> .     .     .     .     .
> I am content to live it all again
> And yet again, if it be life to pitch
> Into the frog-spawn of a blind man's ditch,
> A blind man battering blind men. . . .

This cantankerous acceptance of life is the poet's framework for several years to come; acceptance, however, did not mean passive immersion in the Heraclitean flux, for that flux though perhaps 'illusionary' was not 'capricious', and 'must reflect the soul's coherence'. We must bear this important qualification in mind, for if we ask what Yeats meant by 'life' we find as many ambiguities as in inquiring what he meant by 'heaven'. Before he was twenty he had suggested that the world might be merely a 'flaming word', and many times since he had said that life was an artifact moulded by the intense passions of man and especially of the poet. Not only was the poetic imagination the world's unacknowledged legislator, as it was for Shelley, but the world's maker. Consequently, as Yeats devotes himself to 'right mastery of natural things', we are conscious that he is likely to turn nature and life to his own uses. Thus he wrote at the end of 1926 to Mrs. Shakespear after finishing some of the poems of 'A Man

Young and Old ' : ' I think it likely that there will be yet another series upon the old man & his soul as he slowly comes to understand that the mountains are not solid, that all he sees is a mathematical line drawn between hope & memory '.   The objective world, he was quite willing to declare, had no reality apart from the observer, but he was careful not to make this position too prominent.   It remains in the background in the poems of reminiscence of ' A Man Young and Old ' (1926-27), which deal with the old theme of his frustrated love for Maud Gonne : he describes his feelings as if he were still young and mad with love, but the emotion is sharp and straightforward, not lingering and plaintive :

### HUMAN DIGNITY

Like the moon her kindness is,
If kindness I may call
What has no comprehension in't,
But is the same for all
As though my sorrow were a scene
Upon a painted wall.

So like a bit of stone I lie
Under a broken tree.
I could recover if I shrieked
My heart's agony
To passing bird, but I am dumb
From human dignity.

The hero is not really the irresolute figure, half pleased at his frustration, of a poem like ' Breasal the Fisherman ' which Yeats wrote about 1893 :

Although you hide in the ebb and flow
Of the pale tide when the moon has set,
The people of coming days will know
About the casting out of my net,
And how you have leaped times out of mind
Over the little silver cords,
And think that you were hard and unkind,
And blame you with many bitter words.

Yet in 'Human Dignity', though it is more shrewdly written, the emotion is represented rather than expressed ; we look at a picture of a man's heart rather than at the heart itself. Though Yeats would have maintained that the same could be said of any poem, it is clear that here he is not weighed down enough by ' the blood & the heavy weight of the bones ' ; the poet's mastery seems almost excessive, bordering on overmastery, which had indeed become a danger for him.

He had succeeded in fully incorporating into the scheme of reference of his system the theme of love poetry, and some of his lyrics of these years seem little more than illustrations and comments applied to passionate events. They are about life but have the detachment of a mirror. Yeats was busily exploiting some of his theories. In the dedication to *A Vision* in 1925 he had admitted that the book was not really finished, since he had said ' little of sexual love ' and ' nothing about the Beatific Vision '. The juxtaposition of the two subjects was not acci-dental, for in sexual love he had an excellent symbol for the con-flicting, interpenetrating gyres, while in ' the conflagration of the whole being ' of the sexual act he saw the antinomies resolved and the window open momentarily upon the Beatific Vision. As he wrote in a letter of May 25, 1926 : ' One feels at moments as if one could with a touch convey a vision — that the mystic vision & sexual love use the same means — opposed yet parallel existences '. On October 27 of the following year he spoke of his ' own mood between spiritual excitement, & the sexual torture & the knowledge that they are somehow inseparable ! ' He went on now to these subjects in his lyrics. In ' Chosen ' (1927) he makes an old woman say :

> If questioned on
> My utmost pleasure with a man
> By some new-married bride, I take
> That stillness for a theme
> Where his heart my heart did seem
> And both adrift on the miraculous stream
> Where—wrote a learned astrologer —
> The Zodiac is changed into a sphere.

The sphere, which contains the gyres, is reality. As might be expected, Yeats had little to tell of beatitude, the immediate apprehension of reality, beyond that aspect of it which is symbolized in sexual ecstasy, and his use of sexual imagery is entirely unlike that of a religious poet like Hopkins :

> Jesu, heart's light,
> Jesu, maid's son,
> What was the feast followed the night
> Thou hadst glory of this nun ?

With Yeats the reader suspects that the poet may prefer the symbol of beatitude to beatitude itself. He had developed amazing control over his metaphors : the interpenetrating gyres are symbolic of sexual love, but it would be equally true to say that sexual love is symbolic of the gyres ; symbols reflect one another like mirrors so that a great range of connotation is called into play, and there is no way of separating the two parts of the metaphor, ' the dancer from the dance '.

The choice of self over soul and the use of love themes implied then no renunciation of the system of the *Vision*, but an application of it to more worldly matters. Since the system was a kind of codification of his experience of life, he did not feel constrained or limited by it. He had not permitted visionary abstraction to become so great as to hide reality from his eyes. As he wrote to Sturge Moore : ' I try always to keep my philosophy within such classifications of thought as . . . to include in my definition of water a little duckweed or a few fish. I have never met that poor naked creature H2O.' He knew, however, that the first edition of *A Vision* had many defects and omissions, and set himself to prepare a second edition to correct them. To this end he read ever more deeply in philosophy, being greatly attracted to other men who had dealt with all the world or with all human history in their thought. He read widely in Bergson, ' profound McTaggart ', Kant, Whitehead, Husserl, Hegel, Croce, Berkeley, Gentile, and in the philosophy of history Spengler, Henry Adams, Flinders Petrie, Gerald Heard, Arnold Toynbee,

Vico, and many others. It is most unlikely, considering his earlier reading habits, that he would have looked into any of these had it not been for his curiosity to compare their systems with his own. 'I write verse and read Hegel', he tells Mrs. Shakespear on June 23, 1927, 'and the more I read I am but the more convinced that those invisible persons' — the communicators of *A Vision* — 'knew all.' On September 13, 1929, he writes her on the same subject : 'Four or five years reading has given me some knowledge of metaphysics & time to clear up endless errors in my understanding of the script. My conviction of the truth of it all has grown also and that makes one clear.' He writes on December 28 of the following year : 'I have a great sense of abundance — more than I have had for years. George's ghosts have educated me.' Much evidence of his reading appears in the new introduction to *A Vision* which he wrote in 1929 and 1930, and his formal testimony is emphatic :

The other day Lady Gregory said to me : 'You are a much better educated man than you were ten years ago and much more powerful in argument'. And I put *The Tower* and *The Winding Stair* into evidence to show that my poetry has gained in self-possession and power. I owe this change to an incredible experience.

In the introduction he revealed at last his wife's part in the book. The legendary trappings with which he had surrounded the first edition prevented the *Vision* from being taken seriously. Now he had greater confidence in it, so he described at some length how the automatic writing had occurred.[1] The truth was as good as any fable. Another problem which he had incompletely faced in the first edition of the book was whether it was to be considered as philosophy or mythology ; were its statements to be accepted as literal truth or as fictions ? In letters and conversation he always called it his philosophy, but in the first edition, probably out of timidity, he had labelled it a mythology.

---

[1] One dedication which he considered using for the second edition would have read as follows : 'TO MY WIFE who created this system which bores her, who made possible these pages which she will never read, and who has accepted this dedication on the condition that I write nothing but verse for a year'.

These terms no longer seemed adequate, and in a note dated 1928 he is working towards his later description of it as 'stylistic arrangements of experience comparable to the cubes in the drawing of Wyndham Lewis and to the ovoids in the sculpture of Brancusi'.

Some will ask if I believe all that this book contains, and I will not know how to answer. Does the word belief, used as they will use it, belong to our age, can I think of the world as there and I here judging it ? I will never think any thoughts but these, or some modification or extension of these ; when I write prose or verse they must be somewhere present though not it may be in the words ; they must affect my judgment of friends and of events ; but then there are many symbolisms and none exactly resembles mine.

Since he had founded several poems upon that aspect of the book which might better be called a myth, — the story of Giraldus Cambrensis, the Judwalis, and Michael Robartes, — he did not abolish the myth altogether but rewrote it so as to give it a more integral part in the volume. 'Stories of Michael Robartes and his Friends', the completed version, has the air of being merely a racy extravaganza, but is really a deliberately obscure fantasy in which the commission of an act of adultery symbolizes the beginning of a new civilization and the downfall of the old, and a bird's instinct in making a nest proves, as in Henry More, the immortality of the soul. Robartes then makes deductions from the immortality of the soul, as Yeats said, 'with an energy and a Dogmatism & a cruelty I am not capable of in my own person'. He prophesies the coming of war but is reproved by the cautious Aherne :

'Dear predatory birds, [says Robartes] prepare for war, prepare your children and all that you can reach, for how can a nation or a kindred without war become that "bright particular star" of Shakepeare, that lit the roads in boyhood ? Test art, morality, custom, thought, by Thermopylae ; make rich and poor act so to one another that they can stand together there. Love war because of its horror, that belief may be changed, civilisation renewed. We desire belief and lack it. Belief comes from shock and is not desired. When a kindred discovers through apparition and horror that the perfect cannot perish nor even the imperfect long be interrupted, who can withstand that kindred ?   Belief is renewed continually in the ordeal of death.'

Aherne said :

' Even if the next divine influx be to kindreds why should war be necessary ?   Cannot they develop their characteristics in some other way ? '  He said something more which I did not hear. . . .

While this work of clarifying, substantiating, and heightening the symbols of *A Vision* went on, Yeats's principal effort was directed towards bridging the gap between his theories and practical life.  As his Senate term came to an end in 1928 he realized that his speeches had not come from his deeper thought and never published them.  The trouble with *A Vision*, he saw, was that the only action which it demanded from readers was acceptance of its symbols, and that it gave only the most general of hints as to how to apply symbols as doctrine to life.  He began to think about conduct and to mull over possible criteria for it. Immortality might have been satisfactory, if he had accepted beatitude as the finishing point of the cycle, but in the ' Dialogue of Self and Soul ' and elsewhere in prose he explicitly accepted eternal recurrence.  The soul, therefore, could not be expected to try to attain beatitude through escaping permanently from the wheel.

Yeats might, of course, have avoided this new difficulty by simply setting himself up as the poet of eternal recurrence, as Nietzsche was its philosopher, but to do so meant a withdrawal from too many fronts of human activity in which he had an interest and a stake.  He therefore put new emphasis upon a theory which he had started to work on before marriage and had occasionally alluded to since, that the soul should strive towards the state of Unity of Being.  In the *Vision* he had left the question open as to whether such effort would have any effect if the soul were born at a phase where Unity of Being was impossible ; but now he assumed that it would be of some avail.  This Unity of Being was achieved in the past, he believed, at the time of the Renaissance.  But he needed a period in Irish history to serve as his model, and in Ireland during the fifteenth, sixteenth, and seventeenth centuries the Renaissance had not occurred.

At this juncture Yeats began to think of Ireland's eighteenth century as a Renaissance delayed by special historical conditions and as the answer to his problem. Surely Ireland's closest approach to Unity of Being occurred when it could boast of Swift, Berkeley, Burke, and Goldsmith. ' In Swift's day ', Yeats makes a character say in his play, *The Words upon the Window-Pane* (1930), ' men of intellect reached the height of their power, the greatest position they ever attained in society and the State.' Here was a model for Unity of Being, anchored in tradition, for both Ireland, which had come of age only in 1922 with the establishment of the Free State, and for himself, who had reached intellectual maturity only shortly before. Here was the answer to his question, ' What shall occupy our imagination ? ' It was no longer possible for a patriot to give his devotion to a ' personified ideal ' like Cathleen Ni Houlihan, nor for Yeats to give it to the mere mask of a man of energy and unbounded passion ; they must serve the more specific and traditional image that was offered by the eighteenth century :

. . . We can no longer permit life to be shaped by a personified ideal, we must serve with all our faculties some actual thing. Patriotism was a religion, never a philosophy. . . . I collect material [in Swift and Berkeley] for my thought and work, for some identification of my beliefs with the nation itself, I seek an image of the modern mind's discovery of itself, of its own permanent form, in that one Irish century that escaped from darkness and confusion. I would that our fifteenth, sixteenth, or even our seventeenth century had been the clear mirror, but fate decided against us.

We have seen how his life and work had converged, and how he had always tried to identify Ireland's problems with his own ; now he wanted to fuse life, work, and country into one indissoluble whole. What attracted him particularly about the eighteenth-century Irishmen was their passion and their solidity. In Swift he found a writer whose powerful emotions but gathered greater intensity by being put into literature ; Yeats was the more impressed because he always feared that his own emotions were toned down in his art, especially in his prose writings which he knew to be too graceful and charming to have Swift's effectiveness. In Berkeley he liked the ' furious young man ' who had proudly disagreed with Newton and Locke and written : ' We Irish do not think so ', and who had described ' the *summum bonum* and the reality of heaven as physical pleasure '. The later Berkeley who as Bishop of Cloyne seemed to have tempered or failed to follow out to their end the conclusions of his youth pleased Yeats less. Burke and Goldsmith were not of much interest to him, Burke being ' only tolerable in his impassioned moments ', and Goldsmith acceptable mainly because of ' his delight in the particulars of common life that shocked his contemporaries '. Yeats included all four in his image to give it mass and solidity.

The effect of discovery of that image of the eighteenth century is apparent from 1927 on. In that year he was profoundly moved by the assassination of the Irish statesman, Kevin O'Higgins. In the poem, ' Blood and the Moon ', which the incident aroused him to write, he returns to his tower and winding stair symbols, but with a difference. Now he proclaims the tower to be not only his, but also Goldsmith's, Swift's, Berkeley's, and Burke's.

> I declare this tower is my symbol ; I declare
> This winding, gyring, spiring treadmill of a stair is my ancestral
>     stair ;
> That Goldsmith and the Dean, Berkeley and Burke have travelled
>     there.

For the next few years Yeats mentioned these exemplary men constantly. In 1929 he translated Swift's epitaph, in 1930 he wrote his excellent play about Swift, *The Words upon the Window-Pane* ; in 1931 he wrote a preface to Hone and Rossi's life of Berkeley and in the same year several essays attempting, not very successfully, to define, with the eighteenth century as his example, a scheme of ' intellectual nationalism ', as he called it in a letter. More and more *tradition* competes with Unity of Being as his favourite slogan. He is greatly dependent upon the past, or rather, upon the century of the past which he had selected, to shape the future, talks much of Swift's political theory of the balance of the state between the One, the Few, and the Many, and much of Berkeley's idealism. ' Thought seems more true, emotion more deep, spoken by someone who touches my pride, who seems to claim me of his kindred, who seems to make me a part of some national mythology. . . .' Yeats sought an alliance closer than that of disciple, which Thomas Mann, thinking in the same direction, has well described :

The Ego of antiquity and its consciousness of itself was different from our own, less exclusive, less sharply defined. It was, as it were, open behind ; it received much from the past and by repeating it gave it presentness again. The Spanish scholar Ortega y Gasset puts it that the man of antiquity, before he did anything, took a step backwards, like the bullfighter who leaps back to deliver the mortal thrust. He searched the past for a pattern into which he might slip as into a diving-bell, and being thus at once disguised and protected might rush upon his present problem. Thus his life was in a sense a re-animation, an archaizing attitude. But it is just this life as reanimation that is the life as myth. Alexander walked in the footsteps of Miltiades ; the ancient biographers of Caesar were convinced, rightly or wrongly, that he took Alexander as his prototype. But such ' imitation ' meant far more than we mean by the word today. It was a mythical identification.

But while Yeats publicly espoused a kind of mythical identification of modern Ireland with eighteenth-century Ireland, he did not overly commit himself to the intellectualized image of either Swift or Berkeley. He was mindful of an even deeper conviction that, as he had written to Sturge Moore, ' all my art theories depend upon just this — rooting of mythology in the earth '. Looking back he saw that it was this rooting in the earth which had drawn him to the Irish peasantry and their stories, and which had impelled him to find much of his subject-matter in legends spoken in Ireland centuries before his family had arrived there. It is the last important aspect of his work during the years 1926 to 1932 which remains to be put in perspective. We find it epitomized in the ' Crazy Jane ' series of lyrics in which the point of view of the speaker is completely physical and anti-intellectual, and viciously anti-clerical. Rarely in the past had Yeats's poems presented the position so emphatically. He began the series while recovering from Malta fever in 1929, when his physical powers flagged to the point where he had to compensate for their insufficiency by giving the body more complete pre-eminence in his verse than he usually accorded it. Like Crazy Jane, he refused to think in respectable terms merely because he was old, and wrote to Mrs. Shakespear : ' I shall be a sinful man to the end, and think upon my death bed of all the nights I wasted in my youth '. He was uneasy, too, at the recollection that in his divorce speech in the Senate he had made the assumption ' that all lovers who ignored Priest or Registrar were immoral ', and wished to make clear that he really thought otherwise. In these poems he wanted to root deeper than conventional morality. Crazy Jane, because of her name, could speak with all the prerogatives of the Elizabethan fool without, of course, being crazy at all.

### CRAZY JANE TALKS WITH THE BISHOP

I met the Bishop on the road
And much said he and I.
' Those breasts are flat and fallen now,
Those veins must soon be dry ;
Live in a heavenly mansion,
Not in some foul sty.'

' Fair and foul are near of kin,
And fair needs foul,' I cried.
' My friends are gone, but that's a truth
Nor grave nor bed denied,
Learned in bodily lowliness,
And in the heart's pride.

' A woman can be proud and stiff
When on love intent ;
But love has pitched his mansion in
The place of excrement ;
For nothing can be sole or whole
That has not been rent.'

But Crazy Jane is not so wild as she appears, or as Yeats pretended, for, as the last two lines indicate, she shares his theories about love, and sees it as a conflict of opposites but also as an escape from them to unity, wholeness, or, to use a word which she would not have used, to beatitude. Her testimony is doubly valuable because she has never read a book. Though she prides herself on her licence, she is tightly controlled by her creator, and, when her promiscuity begins to persecute his imagination and her language to 'become unendurable', he exorcises her from his verse.

Control is victorious, but the going must be made as hard as possible, and the turbulency with which life rushes at the poet mounts as the years go on. In 'Byzantium', which he wrote in 1930, the scene is quite different from that of 'Sailing to Byzantium', which he wrote in 1926. In the earlier poem the sensual life is separated from the spiritual as Ireland from Byzantium, but in the later poem the fury and the mire of human veins, the teeming images, 'that dolphin-torn, that gong-tormented sea', flood up to the marbles of Byzantium itself, where they are at last brought under control by 'the golden smithies of the Emperor'. An unfinished poem called 'Images', on which he worked before 1926, shows him wrestling with the subject, though at that time he had planned to use Abiegnos, the Golden Dawn's sacred mountain, rather than Byzantium :

### IMAGES

I

On Abiegnos' side a multitude
Restored by drinking that miraculous wine
To human form : Day beats upon their eyes
Sounds of unfinished battle on their ears ;
One sways his head and laughs, another weeps,
Then all laugh out, discovering in laughter
That the dark valley at the mountain foot
Where wold must war on walk, abounding grass
Grow out of that foul blood, is magical ;
That they imagined it and bound themselves
Therein contented with that bitter-sweet ;

But the wind changes and the valley howls ;
One howls his answer back and one by one
They drop upon all fours, creep valley-wards.
Question that instant for these forms O heart
These chuckling & howling forms begot the sages.

Gradually the master-image of Byzantium must have assumed dominance of the scene. The completed poem has often been taken as a representation of the after-life, and Yeats wished this interpretation to be possible ; but to him, it seems safe to say, ' Byzantium ' was primarily a description of the act of making a poem. The poet, who is imprecisely identified with the Byzantine emperor,[1] takes the welter of images and masters them in an act of creation. This mastery is so astonishing to the poet himself that he calls the creation of his imagination superhuman. The image of the golden bird, ' more miracle than bird or handiwork ', may be understood to represent a poem ; the bird sings, as do Yeats's poems, either like the cocks of Hades of rebirth — the continuing cycle of reincarnating human life, or with greater glory of the eternal reality or beatitude which transcends the cycles ' and all complexities of mire or blood '. Never had he realized so completely the awesome drama of the creative act :

### BYZANTIUM

The unpurged images of day recede ;
The Emperor's drunken soldiery are abed ;
Night resonance recedes, night-walkers' song
After great cathedral gong ;
A starlit or a moonlit dome disdains
All that man is,
All mere complexities,
The fury and the mire of human veins.

[1] Yeats's amazing transmutative power can be seen by comparing this finished stanza with its first draft :

When the emperor's brawling soldiers are abed
The last be nighted victims dead or fled —
When silence falls on the cathedral gong
And the drunken harlot's song
A cloudy silence, or a silence lit
Whether by star or moon
I tread the emperor's tower
All my intricacies grown clear and sweet.

Before me floats an image, man or shade,
Shade more than man, more image than a shade ;
For Hades' bobbin bound in mummy-cloth
May unwind the winding path ;
A mouth that has no moisture and no breath
Breathless mouths may summon ;
I hail the superhuman ;
I call it death-in-life and life-in-death.

Miracle, bird or golden handiwork,
More miracle than bird or handiwork,
Planted on the star-lit golden bough,
Can like the cocks of Hades crow,
Or, by the moon embittered, scorn aloud
In glory of changeless metal
Common bird or petal
And all complexities of mire or blood.

At midnight on the Emperor's pavement flit
Flames that no faggot feeds, nor steel has lit,
Nor storm disturbs, flames begotten of flame,
Where blood-begotten spirits come
And all complexities of fury leave,
Dying into a dance,
An agony of trance,
An agony of flame that cannot singe a sleeve.

Astraddle on the dolphin's mire and blood,
Spirit after spirit !   The smithies break the flood,
The golden smithies of the Emperor !
Marbles of the dancing floor
Break bitter furies of complexity,
Those images that yet
Fresh images beget,
That dolphin-torn, that gong-tormented sea.

The distinction which Yeats made, in this great hymn to the
human imagination, between his two forms of poetry, is carried
on in the poem which may be said to bring this phase of his work
to a close, ' Vacillation '.  Here he alternates between natural and
supernatural themes as in the ' Dialogue of Self and Soul ' he had

alternated between arguments for rebirth and for escape from birth. But his final choice in ' Vacillation ' (originally entitled ' Wisdom ') is again for this world in preference to any other. ' Homer is my example and his unchristened heart.' And writing to Mrs. Shakespear on June 30, 1932, Yeats recapitulated his life in terms of this decision :

I spend my days correcting proof. I have just finished the first volume, all my lyric poetry and am greatly astonished at myself, as it is all speech rather than writing. I keep saying what man is this who in the course of two or three weeks — the improvisation suggests the time — says the same things in so many different ways. My first denunciation of old age I made in ' The Wanderings of Usheen ' (end of Part 1) before I was twenty and the same denunciation comes in the last pages of the book. The swordsman throughout repudiates the saint, but not without vacillation. Is that perhaps the sole theme — Usheen and Patrick ' So get you gone Von Hugel though with blessings on your head.'

But at the age of sixty-seven he was pushing forward to look at reality from yet another focus, and the golden smithies had not lost their power to forge dross into pure gold.

## CHAPTER XVIII

# REALITY

They have put a golden stopper into the mouth of the bottle.  Pull it,
Lord !  Let out reality.

*Upanishads* (translated by Yeats and Purohit Swami)

I pray
That I, all foliage gone,
May shoot into my joy.

YEATS, *The Herne's Egg*

DURING the last years of his life Yeats struggled to come
to even closer grips with reality.  Looking back over his
career he was conscious of much ' evasion ' and ' turning
away ', and knew how elaborate was the machinery which he had
invented, especially in his prose and in his day-to-day experience,
to prevent frontal attack.  In his moments of doubt even the
*Vision* seemed a gigantic protective mask, and like Melville's
Ahab, he sometimes wanted to break through all masks.  Frank
O'Connor has described Yeats's relations with other men as
' a circuitous and brilliant strategy performing complicated
manœuvres about non-existent armies '.  Few of the poet's friends
were aware that this proud, aggressive man, immortality in his
pocket, had evolved the strategy out of timidity.  Yeats knew it
well, however, and in 1933 admitted that, though he had overcome his shyness a little, ' I am still struggling with it and cannot
free myself from the belief that it comes from lack of courage,
that the problem is not artistic but moral '.  Although of late
years he had spoken more directly he was still unsatisfied and felt
that he had played his inner being false by dressing it in costume
and metaphor instead of expressing it directly.  Then, too, he
had submerged some of his individuality in nationalist work, in
the Abbey Theatre, in the Senate, and had more profoundly betrayed it by introspection and cautiousness.  Now he must raze

the scaffolding and reveal what he had concealed. Sometimes he was content to think that his real self was in his verse. ' My character is so little myself ', he put in a manuscript book, ' that all my life it has thwarted me. It has affected my poems, my true self, no more than the character of a dancer affects the movements of a dance.' Usually in the past he had attributed his writings to his mask, but now he suggests that the mask is his uncreative ordinary self which has so often accommodated itself to the demands of convention. At other times even his poems seemed an unsatisfactory expression of that fanatic whom he had tamed to speak an alien tongue, a conventional patter. In a letter of December 17, 1937, he writes of *On the Boiler*, the new occasional publication he is planning : ' I must lay aside the pleasant patter I have built up for years, & seek the brutality, the ill breeding, the barbarism of truth '. To do so he revealed for the first time the violence of his early quarrels with his father :

When I was in my 'teens I admired my father above all men ; from him I learnt to admire Balzac and to set certain passages in Shakespeare above all else in literature, but when I was twenty-three or twenty-four I read Ruskin's ' Unto This Last ' of which I do not remember a word, and we began to quarrel, for he was John Stuart Mill's disciple. Once he threw me against a picture with such violence that I broke the glass with the back of my head. But it was not only with my father that I quarreled, nor were economics the only theme. There was no dominant opinion I could accept. Then finding out that I (having no clear case — my opponent's case had been clarifying itself for centuries) had become both boor and bore I invented a patter, allowing myself an easy man's insincerity, and for honesty's sake a little malice, and now it seems that I can talk nothing else. But I think I have succeeded, and that none of my friends know that I am a fanatic. . . . But now I must, if I can, put away my patter, speak to the young men before the ox treads on my tongue.

Again and again he tries to tear off the polite, superficial part of himse!f,

> Leave nothing but the nothings that belong
> To this bare soul, let all men judge that can
> Whether it be an animal or a man.

He lies down ' where all the ladders start, / In the foul rag-and-bone shop of the heart '. He chooses new models ; now he is Timon, Lear, or Blake beating against the wall ' till Truth obeyed his call ' ; he is a fool, a foolish passionate man, a wild old man, a mad old man. He dreams of Swift and of Parnell, their lives raped by the stupid world. In his last prose work he imagines himself as a half-mad ship's carpenter who mounts 'on the boiler' to denounce his neighbours. He tries to return to the elemental passions as if they were the *prima materia* of the world :

> You think it horrible that lust and rage
> Should dance attendance upon my old age ;
> They were not such a plague when I was young ;
> What else have I to spur me into song ?

Lust and rage are here not the lasciviousness and irascibility of an old man's brain grown febrile, as some critics have said, but pure passions, spontaneous and complete as peasant life. To suit his subject-matter Yeats pares his style, too, down to the bone, and writes simple ballads about Cromwell, Parnell, and Roger Casement which ring far truer than the ballads about Moll Magee and Father Gilligan which he had written in his youth. It had taken him a lifetime to acquire this kind of simplicity. To help him he seeks out new friendships with people like Dorothy Wellesley, whose imagination played like his with the basic patterns of life, with F. R. Higgins, who looked on life with the eye of a ballad-maker, with Margot Ruddock, whose verse like her mind had sudden bursts of radiant illumination, with Ethel Mannin, whose naturalness he had always striven for, and with Frank O'Connor, who attracted him by his warm, laughing realism. He sought out young men to manage the Abbey Theatre, and, lest the mechanical age outrun him, he gave radio talks for the British Broadcasting Corporation.

These last years suggest the violence of some Hellenistic statue, with Yeats ' ravening, raging, and uprooting that he may come / Into the desolation of reality '. After Lady Gregory's death in May 1932 his own health went from bad to worse, until he could not climb the stairs without gasping and stopping continually for breath.  He might not have had sufficient energy for his last years of work had not a friend half jestingly mentioned to him, early in 1934, the Steinach operation for rejuvenation. Yeats was intensely excited and hopeful ; to a man who had remade himself over and over during his lifetime, rejuvenation by any means made an intense appeal.  In May 1934 a distinguished London surgeon performed the operation, and Yeats almost immediately got a great burst of energy such as he had not had for years.  His health remained very unsteady, but his attitude towards his maladies was changed.  After having written little verse since Lady Gregory's death except the rather mechanical play, *The King of the Great Clock Tower*, and the philosophical lyric, ' Mount Meru ', he broke loose after the operation with the little philosophical songs of the Hermit Ribh, which must rank among his best work, and before his death wrote four more plays, including his finest, *Purgatory*, and another book of verse.

In all these writings *reality* is the key-word ; it is the state which the poet wishes to attain and, in another sense, that which he must interpret.  He must speak, as D. H. Lawrence (whose works he was now reading with pleasure) would put it, from the solar plexus, and say finally what he had always meant to say, and perhaps even more than that, about every aspect of life. Conventional morality and all conventional attitudes were thrust aside.  Yeats's bluntness was not always well-timed ; on several occasions during these years he was abashed to find he had blamed or praised the wrong people, and had to rewrite his poems accordingly.  Sometimes, and especially in *On the Boiler*, he deliberately made his statements extravagant.  But while his sincerity had its absurd side, it did drive or enable him to think his thoughts through.

During these years he arrived at his final conclusions about politics.  He began badly in 1933 by involving himself slightly with a group of Irish fascists who wore blue shirts and at one time seemed likely to threaten the De Valera government.  Their leader was General O'Duffy, whom Yeats met not many times, as has been said, but once only. Yeats recognized from the first, as his letters prove, that O'Duffy was a demagogic, fictile man, but hoped that he might develop leaderlike qualities which he never did. Eventually O'Duffy went off with an Irish brigade to fight for Franco in the Spanish civil war. Yeats, like most of his fellow-countrymen, was by this time thoroughly disaffected, and hoped O'Duffy would not return from Spain a hero. The general, happily, did not prove a very helpful acquisition to the Falange.

Although Yeats was often seen in a blue shirt at this time, he had been wearing blue shirts since 1925 or 1926, and the reason was not political but esthetic. If he learned the habit from anyone, it was from William Morris. His brief encounter with O'Duffy must have shown that they were more at odds than in accord. What Yeats wanted was a political party which would espouse Unity of Being and turn it into ' a discipline, a way of life ', even ' a sacred drama '. In February 1934, still toying with the unofficial army, he wrote some marching songs for O'Duffy's men which included such lines as :

> What's equality ? — Muck in the yard :
> Historic Nations grow
> From above to below.

But by August of the same year he had realized his error and rewrote the poems so that nobody could sing them ; and in addition, to show that his earlier utterances had been transitory, he made another poem to embody his growing disaffection with all politics :

> What if the Church and the State
> Are the mob that howls at the door !

In 1935 Yeats still urged in conversation the despotic rule of the educated classes, but as the terror of Fascism and Nazism increased he ceased to speak in favour of any existing government. His friend Ethel Mannin, the novelist, and Ernst Toller tried on one occasion to persuade him to take a definite position against totalitarianism. They asked him to recommend Ossietsky, whom the Nazis had imprisoned, for the Nobel Peace Prize. Yeats refused, and in letters defending himself indicated his disaffection with every known governmental system :

Do not try to make a politician of me, even in Ireland I shall never I think be that again — as my sense of reality deepens, & I think it does with age, my horror at the cruelty of governments grows greater, & if I did what you want I would seem to hold one form of government more responsible than any other & that would betray my convictions. Communist, fascist, nationalist, clerical, anticlerical are all responsible according to the number of their victims. I have not been silent, I have used the only vehicle I possess — verse. If you have my poems by you look up a poem called ' The Second Coming.' It was written some sixteen or seventeen years ago & fortold what is happening. I have written of the same thing again & again since. . . . I am not callous, every nerve trembles with horror at what is happening in Europe ' the ceremony of innocence is drowned.'

He did not finally explain his political position until *On the Boiler* (written in 1938), which is chiefly a declaration that politics are irrelevant. He advocates eugenics and individualism and says that nothing else matters :

I was six years in the Irish Senate ; I am not ignorant of politics elsewhere, and on other grounds I have some right to speak. I say to those that shall rule here : If ever Ireland again seems molten wax, reverse the process of revolution. Do not try to pour Ireland into any political system. Think first how many able men the country has, how many it can hope to have in the near future, and mold your system upon those men. It does not matter how you get them, but get them. Republics, Kingdoms, Soviets, Corporate States, Parliaments, are trash, as Hugo said of something else ' not worth one blade of grass that God gives for the nest of the linnet.' These men, whether six or six thousand, are the core of Ireland, are Ireland itself.

One can imagine that, had Yeats lived on during the second World War, he would have had little to say about its issues, and would merely have repeated with more conviction a remark he made somewhat at random about the first war : ' We should not attribute a very high degree of reality to the Great War '. He would have taken the position more confidently because he thought he had come at last to ' a coherent grasp of reality ', and was now wholly preoccupied with it.

It will be remembered that *A Vision* had prophesied that after 1927 ' Men will no longer separate the idea of God from that of human genius, human productivity in all its forms '. Until late in 1931 the closest approach Yeats had discovered to his own way of thinking about reality was in Berkeley, and Berkeley did not associate God's imagination and power with man's as closely as Yeats would have wished. But in 1931 he found confirmation in an unexpected quarter. He made the acquaintance of an Indian Swami, Shri Purohit, and learned that in the wisdom literature of the East the accepted belief was that ' the individual self, eater of the fruit of action, is the universal Self, maker of past and future '. At the highest moments of consciousness the individual self, detached from action, was aware of this identity. In the efforts which the Indian holy man makes to get rid of all that prevents this knowledge Yeats found his own image of the artist who purges away the inessential to get down to the bedrock of passion. That the total meaning of the *Upanishads* was different from this did not escape him, but he imagined some reconciliation between East and West ; as he wrote to Ethel Mannin, ' I want to plunge myself into impersonal poetry, to get rid of the bitterness, irritation & hatred, my work in Ireland has brought into my soul, I want to make a last song, sweet & exultant, a sort of European *Geeta*, or rather my *Geeta* not doctrine but song '. For four years Yeats and Purohit were closely associated, until in 1936 the Swami returned to India. During their friendship Yeats wrote introductions to the Swami's autobiography, to a partial autobiography by the Swami's master, and to the Swami's translation and annotation of Patanjali's *Aphorisms of Yoga*. In 1936 poet and holy man went to Majorca to translate the *Upanishads*.

Stimulated by this friendship, Yeats seriously considered devoting his remaining years to philosophical verse ; in 1933 and 1934 he wrote a group of philosophical poems but then used his theories less directly. He was surprised and delighted, while preparing an anthology of modern verse which the Oxford University Press had asked him to make, to discover that other poets were dealing with similar themes. He read with excitement Dorothy Wellesley's ' Matrix ', where were lines like, ' The spiritual, the carnal, are one ', when he himself had written only shortly before, ' Natural and supernatural with the self-same ring are wed '. In Turner, another of the poets whom he praised extravagantly in the introduction to his anthology, he read : ' I had watched the ascension and decline of the Moon / And did not realize that it moved only in my own mind '. Yeats rejoiced to find companions on the route, and predicted that they must go even further, ' that soul must become its own betrayer, its own deliverer, the one activity, the mirror turn lamp '.

Because of this all-encompassing belief in soul, self, or imagination, words which Yeats uses interchangeably, many of his latter poems assert more peremptorily than before the virtual identity between images produced by the imagination and actual people and events. Yeats liked to tell Frank Harris's story of Ruskin's picking up a phantom cat, opening the window, and throwing the cat outside. In *A Full Moon in March*, *The Death of Cuchulain*, ' The Circus Animals' Desertion ', and elsewhere, he calls all his characters together as if to say, here is the universe which I have created and peopled and made as real as anything in the world :

> Are those things that men adore and loathe
> Their sole reality ?
> What stood in the Post Office
> With Pearse and Connolly ?
>
> .     .     .     .     .
>
> Who thought Cuchulain till it seemed
> He stood where they had stood ?
>
> Did that play of mine send out
> Certain men the English shot ?
>
> When Pearse summoned Cuchulain to his side,
> What stalked through the Post Office ?

Not only are the symbols like men, but conversely the men are like symbols or actors :

> Come gather round me, players all ;
> Come praise Nineteen-Sixteen,
> Those from the pit and gallery
> Or from the painted scene
> That fought in the Post Office
> Or round the City Hall. . . .
>
> Who was the first man shot that day ?
> The player Connolly,
> Close to the City Hall he died ;
> Carriage and voice had he ;
> He lacked those years that go with skill,
> But later might have been
> A famous, a brilliant figure
> Before the painted scene.

A man is welded to his image, a player to his role ; when we speak of the *drama* of a heroic action our language is no more figurative than when we speak of its *reality*. Yeats does not escape his own symbols, but is caught up into them also, and in the poem, ' High Talk ', he describes himself as Malachi Stilt-Jack, and insists that the stilts are part of him as much as his body is, and that, on the other hand, both are also metaphor : ' All metaphor, Malachi, stilts and all '. All that he has thought and created is part of him, as substantial as his flesh.

But even after Yeats had hammered home the power of the human imagination, one question was left. What is the relation between the human self and the universal Self of the *Upanishads*, or, to put it another way, what limitations upon man's omnipotence exist ? What is the relation, for example, between life and death, or between man and God ? Once Yeats had said that man had created death, but that was a momentary cry of defiance ; he thought a great deal more about this subject now that he was preparing the second edition of *A Vision*, and came to the conclusion that life stood in relation to death or to destiny or to God as his two gyres stood to one another. ' To me ', he wrote to Ethel Mannin, 'all things are made of the conflict of two states of consciousness, beings or persons which die each other's life live each other's death. That is true of life & death themselves.'

Rarely had he pushed his thoughts so far before. The new *Vision*, when it appeared in 1937, put a great deal of emphasis upon the Thirteenth Cycle, 'which may deliver us from the twelve cycles of time and space', a doctrine that in 1925 he had hardly touched upon. The idea of thirteen cycles seems to have come from Christ and the Twelve Apostles; and the Thirteenth Cycle, with its absurdly mechanical title, has many qualities of divinity. 'Within it live all souls that have been set free', Yeats says.

But not till the last pages of the book does the Thirteenth Cycle assume its real importance. There Yeats describes how, having fully evolved and knit together the symbol of *A Vision*, he draws himself up into the symbol, as he could well do now that it was wholly personalized as a system and systematized as an expression of personality. He declares, 'it seemed as if I should know all . . . and find everything in the symbol', and then makes a startling shift to a kind of theology :

But nothing comes — though this moment was to reward me for all my toil. Perhaps I am too old. . . . Then I understand. I have already said all that can be said. The particulars are the work of the *thirteenth sphere* or cycle which is in every man and called by every man his freedom. Doubtless, for it can do all things and knows all things, it knows what it will do with its own freedom but it has kept the secret.

Only at this point do we realize that Yeats, after building up a system over three hundred pages, in the last two pages sets up that system's anti-self. All the determinism or quasi-determinism of *A Vision* is abruptly confronted with the Thirteenth Cycle which is able to alter everything, and suddenly free will, liberty, and deity pour back into the universe. The revolt against his father's scepticism and against his own was complete at last, though it brought him to no Church. God had forced His way ineluctably into Yeats's mind :

Then my delivered soul itself shall learn
A darker knowledge and in hatred turn
From every thought of God mankind has had,
Thought is a garment and the soul's a bride
That cannot in that trash and tinsel hide :
In hating God she may creep close to God.

At stroke of midnight soul cannot endure
A bodily or mental furniture.
What can she take until her Master give !
Where can she look until He make the show !
What can she know until He bid her know !
How can she live till in her blood He live !

Looking back over Yeats's work we can see that such a God was always likely to come out of it ; the ' Eternal Darkness ' and the ' great journeyman ' were among His antecedents, but till now He had been as much as possible disregarded and His power undermined.   He is the God of unwilling belief.

Whether Yeats meant that the Thirteenth Cycle could ' do all things ' or could merely influence the ' particulars ' he does not seem to have decided.  In the passage from the *Vision* it is noticeable that he takes both positions.  Either way his theories were considerably disrupted by their enlargement.  Some of his resultant uneasiness may be observed in an essay which he wrote on Shelley, where he says that the plot in *Prometheus Unbound* was made incoherent because Shelley, in defiance of his theories, made Demogorgon terrible instead of benevolent :

Demo-gorgon made his plot incoherent, its interpretation impossible, it was thrust there by that something which again and again forced him to balance the object of desire conceived as miraculous and superhuman, with nightmare.

Yeats's God also disturbs the plot.  No doubt he was thinking of this element in his thought when, in October 1938, he wrote to Ethel Mannin that the *Vision* was his ' public philosophy ', while his ' private philosophy ' remained unpublished because he only half understood it.  Had he lived, he would probably have tried to symbolize more formally the relation between God and man.

But such systematization was not necessary for two plays which he wrote between 1936 and his death in 1939, where his new theology is introduced. The hero of *The Herne's Egg* (1936–1937), ' the strangest, wildest thing ' he had ever written, deliberately and knowingly commits sacrilege against the Great Herne by raping his priestess. The deity never appears on the stage but at the climactic moment manifests himself convincingly by thunder. As a result of the desecration the hero is doomed to die at a fool's hand, but rather than allow the prophecy to be fulfilled, and combating the supernal power to the last, he kills himself. Cuchulain, in Yeats's last play, *The Death of Cuchulain* (1938–9), recognizes that to go forth to battle will probably be fatal and suspects that his adversary is this time not an army of men but death itself ; yet, though he could avoid the combat, he goes forward flaunting his individuality against inevitability. All that is known fights with all that is unknown ; God is Himself man's opponent, and the final struggle is with Him, whether He keeps His own shape or takes that of death or destiny. As Yeats wrote in a little poem called ' The Four Ages of Man ' :

> He with body waged a fight,
> But body won ; it walks upright.
>
> Then he struggled with the heart ;
> Innocence and peace depart.
>
> Then he struggled with the mind ;
> His proud heart he left behind.
>
> Now his wars on God begin,
> At stroke of midnight God shall win.

The war on God is the ultimate heroism, and like all heroism in Yeats ends in defeat.

For the poet who had at last made room for God in his cosmogony, the stroke of midnight was fast approaching. In 1937 Yeats found breathing and walking so difficult that, though he had previously anticipated death with terror, he now told his wife that it was harder for him to live than to die. He tried to recover his

health in the south of France, but while he was staying at Cap
Martin late in the winter of 1938 he fell terribly ill. On January 21,
1939, he wrote his last poem, ' The Black Tower ', in which the
soldiers still guard the King's tower because they are sworn to do
so, though they are sure, or virtually sure, that he will never come
again. The following day he said in a letter to a friend :

> I know for certain that my time will not be long. I have put away
> everything that can be put away that I may speak what I have to speak
> & I find my expression is a part of ' study.'
>   In two or three weeks — I am now idle that I may rest after writing
> much verse — I will begin to write my most fundamental thoughts &
> the arrangement of thought which I am convinced will complete my
> studies, I am happy and I think full of an energy I had despaired of.
> It seems to me that I have found what I wanted. When I try to put
> all into a phrase I say ' Man can embody truth but he cannot know it.'
> I must embody it in the completion of my life. The abstract is not life
> and everywhere drags out its contradictions. You can refute Hegel
> but not the Saint or the Song of Sixpence.

The life of a saint was a life turned to image, and the Song of
Sixpence, too, was an image condensed out of vapours. This
letter was Yeats's final justification of his lifelong effort to cast all
his experience into symbol. Four days after writing it he suffered
a relapse, but gathered enough strength to dictate some revisions
to his wife. Then he passed into a coma and on January 28 he
was dead.

He had written his epitaph in verse for a grave at Drumcliff
churchyard near Sligo, but technicalities for the time being prevented transportation of the body to Ireland. So, as he had
himself suggested, he was carried up the long, high, winding
mountain road to the cemetery at Roquebrune for a temporary
resting-place. The procession ascending the winding path was
a last use of one of the poet's symbols.

His death was not immediately announced, so one wreath
did not arrive till after the funeral was over and everyone had
left. It was from James Joyce, a fellow-symbolist who believed
with equal intensity in natural things.

## CHAPTER XIX

# CONCLUSION

And yet, and yet,
Is this my dream, or the truth ?

YEATS, ' Men Improve with the Years '

FOR all the changes which Yeats made in his style, method, and personality, his life shows remarkable consistency and tenacity. From the boy who dreamed of controlling the world by a magician's wand to the old man who cried out, ' I make the truth ', he laboured to state with growing maturity themes which he developed in adolescence.

His physical and temperamental weaknesses as a child, his timidity as a young man, encouraged him to nourish his imagination on heroic self-projections until his dreams far exceeded reality. Then, with great courage and will, he tried to become the hero of whom he had dreamed and to instil into Ireland a heroic atmosphere. His amazing achievement was to succeed partially in both ambitions.

How amazing it was can be recognized only if we bear in mind with what dubious equipment he set out. His reading was that of most young men of the time, chiefly Shakespeare and the nineteenth-century poets. From his father he took certain ideas, or rather, certain attitudes with which to fortify himself, but they were all dangerous : a disregard of politics, an exaltation of passion, style, and personality, a sense of the dignity and necessity of the arts. These might easily have led him nowhere, as to some extent they rendered his father ineffectual. It was many years before he could grasp the point behind his father's miscellaneous remarks, that the poet's form of knowledge was different from that of priest or scientist. Dangerous to a potential poet, too, was his father's scepticism, against which he angrily revolted but by which he was deeply affected. He went into manhood without religion, ethics, or politics, but held together by a feeling of revolt against his father and his times, and a desire to make the revolt as decisive and systematic as possible.

Soon he had clothed himself in arrogant, passionate aggressiveness, but he could never feel completely sure of himself because his personal failures, especially in love, upset his confidence, and because he had acquired too much of the paternal scepticism. We can be grateful that he was not more certain, for uncertainty drove him to make an accommodation to his times and to his audience. Had he not done so, he would probably have drifted into a private world and written, like most poets in the late nineteenth and the twentieth centuries, for a small audience. But Yeats, eager to convince others so that he might have confidence in himself, plunged into the world which he condemned, now making concessions to it, now trying to change it, but always organizing opposition to things as they were and support for things as they might become. We must go back to Lamartine to find another poet participating as actively in his country's affairs, and Lamartine, unlike Yeats, kept separate his literary work and his public life.

Nationalist feeling such as that of Yeats, in which passion is almost self-justifying, might have made for demagogy, but he always drew back from such excesses. He developed the theory that ' truth is the dramatic expression of the highest man ', and would not tolerate passion unless it was noble. Passionate nationalism is a good, but not if it becomes mere impotent Anglophobia. A bad poet is a bad poet even if he is Irish, for taste too can be espoused with passion.

Just what he hoped Ireland would become is hard to say, but probably he wanted to give his country what he also lacked, a liberated, unified personality, free of uncertainty about power and principle, no longer struggling in the bonds of the past. Throughout his life he read personal problems into national ones, and national ones into personal. He poured his contempt on that self which he most feared to be, the middle self which is certain neither of this nor of that. The middle ground is his primary target during these years, whether it assumes the form of scepticism, compromise, popularity, the middle class — all, from the point of view of individuality, are weakness even if they pretend to be strength. Better to be a dreamer or a heroic man of action but not the weakling torn and irresolute between them.

Because he was torn between them Yeats deliberately magnified his sense of self-division, so that he could be alternately one part or the other and not merely a bad medley. On one side he developed his dreams, corroborating them by the support of fairy tales which, being the literature of the peasantry, were untainted by the doubt which afflicts urban life ; then by the support of Blake, then by occult research, then by direct vision, especially group vision which gave him more witnesses ; eventually he went on to psychic research, to philosophy, and to Eastern religion. All these proved to his satisfaction the power of the dream — the meaning of which he had now extended to include imagination and will — to surpass and to control reality. But it was never enough for him to prove the power without using it ; the magic wand, the sacred book, must demonstrate their efficacy in practical action and dumbfound the sceptical world. He could write with truth : ' Am I a mystic — no I am a practical man — I have seen the raising of Lazarus & the loaves & fishes & have made the usual measurements plummet, line, spirit level & have taken the temperature, but [by] pure mathematic '.

Thus Yeats can never find escape in his dreams, for they all lead more or less circuitously back to action. He tries to infuse them into Ireland as a kind of religion, first through his occult rites and Castle of the Heroes, then through the Irish theatre, which was originally intended to give plays based on occult ritual. He wishes, on a parallel level, to make his beloved, who represents for him a kind of reservoir of dreams, into an Irish Joan of Arc. But on the way to putting these notions into actuality he comes in contact with ordinary men and women, with ordinary problems, with every kind of tedious practical detail, and has to make quotidian concessions to reality. Almost in spite of himself he kept at the firing line. In addition, he becomes dissatisfied with those of his dreams which seem to fail not because failure is inevitable, but because they are invalid even as dreams. The lady whom he has dreamed into an unapproachable goddess marries a soldier. The many-coloured land of his verse fades into a region of hollow images. Perhaps he has left something out, perhaps he has made a mistake. He gives greater praise to action, he goes out to sway crowds, to win mistresses, to meet reality more directly. His dreams are not abandoned, but nobody must see them ; he must be brutal, even anti-romantic, turning for solace to less deific women, defying the mobs at the Abbey, guiding the theatre's practical affairs, purging his style of its more obvious dream-like trappings, in a word, seeming to get off his stilts. He must pit himself against the world directly and prove to it and to himself that a dreamer can beat it at its own game. Yet to him this life of action is tolerable only because it seems to him a supreme artifice.

Success in action, therefore, can never be more than ephemerally rewarding. All the time that he plays with reality he seeks confirmation of his dreams ; he haunts like a nostalgic ghost all the séances in London to try to prove that the miraculous, with which he associates the dream, is not uncommon and that all men who are willing to look with an eye unpolluted by scientific incredulity can see it. But though he often convinces himself temporarily that he has witnessed a miracle, he soon lapses into scepticism.

At last, in marriage, Yeats secures, if not entire confirmation of the supernatural, a dream so large and yet so manipulatable as to give him almost miraculous control over reality. So armed by his ' vision ' he is able to enter more completely into life than before without fear of losing his identity ; all human experience can be controlled, and he even hunts new experience over which to assert his power. But now his dream is more than a dream, it is a symbol, a ' stylistic arrangement of experience ', a representation of the flux of life which transcends the flux but is also immanent in it. He must make his dream impregnable by relating it to everything that happens, and as he finds life fits into it without too much paring and pushing he lives more and more in this stylistically arranged world, which rotates according to a geometrical design discovered in his household.

The dream is now no longer a beautiful refuge ; the symbols of *A Vision* may comfort by their coherence, but they are not beautiful and can hardly be called a refuge because they represent reality and without reality are nothing. Symbolism became Yeats's method because he could not otherwise have written ; the symbol enabled him to escape uncertainty, to partake of the advantages of both dream and reality. Drawing himself into the symbol he was protected against the sceptic with his direct arguments and the realist with his collections of disturbing facts ; he was committed to no literalist belief which he did not feel ; he was unified and liberated. To borrow a phrase of Dean Inge in another context, the symbol was ' a *modus vivendi* between scepticism and superstition '. Not only could it pin man upon a diagram but it could include God as well under the name of the Thirteenth Cycle. So labelled, God, even if He represented the uncontrollable, could be controlled. After the second edition of *A Vision* was published in 1937, Yeats wrote to Edmund Dulac : ' I do not know what my book will be to others — nothing perhaps. To me it means a last act of defence against the chaos of the world, & I hope for ten years to write out of my renewed security.'

He laboured a great deal to change his terms of reference from scepticism and superstition to knowledge and faith. He hoped to reconcile ' spiritist fact with credible philosophy '. The séance-room must be made into a scientific laboratory ; what he had learned in the back alleys of culture must be shown to be fundamentally what the greatest philosophers and religious men had always said. He never gave up hope of bringing together myth and fact into a new religion, or, as he called it, a new ' sacred drama ' of Unity of Being.

Thus Yeats, in youth, had a tower of ivory, but because he was worried at his neighbours' disapproval and uncertain, anyway, of the tower's stability, he went out into the world and brought back ordinary building materials with which he replaced every piece of ivory. At last the edifice was all brick and stone. Then, still not certain, he crowded the interior with supports which were symbols of the outside world. But to him, however rebuilt and refurnished, the tower was still the ivory one of his youth :

> . . . and yet when all is said
> It was the dream itself enchanted me :
>
> .    .    .    .    .
>
> Players and painted stage took all my love,
> And not those things that they were emblems of.

To reach this position he had made so many concessions, however, that it was impossible to know where the dream left off and reality began.

Yeats was never wholly content with what he had accomplished, and consequently his uneasy searching went on to the last. Knowing that his symbolical method had arisen in part out of timidity and evasion, he feared, even after perfecting it, that it might contain a meretricious element. Then, too, he observed in some of his friends a natural insight into reality which he could equal only through prolonged study. Console himself as he would with the belief that truth was apprehensible by symbols alone and never by direct statement, all his successes seemed at times inadequate beside his failure to achieve pure, spontaneous, child-like wisdom. When Dorothy Wellesley asked if he had a solution for the ills of the modern world, he could only reply : ' O my dear, I have no solution, none '. The answers came no more easily to him when old than when young. Hence the mood of his last poem, ' The Black Tower ', is one of heroic despair. The King would not come.

It is fair now to inquire how far this world of his arrangement was satisfactory, how far it was inclusive. Certain omissions are obvious : in Yeats's verse man is never a political animal, and almost never under economic pressure. The poet rarely indicates any pity for the poor or oppressed and despises passive suffering because it is incompatible with his vision of almighty man. His poetry is exclusively of the individual, and the individual rarely indicates social sympathies or awareness of moral laws, though he has a conscience from some unexplained source.

But when we mention these deficiencies we have missed the point. This man, who sings so loudly his praise of the individual, writes for the people. He wants his poems to be sung, spoken, and read. His later verse, especially, is written for the audience of a great orator, and a favourite device is the rhetorical question, which depends for its effect upon the orator's confidence that he has the listener's sympathy. We must not be taken in by his attacks on rhetoric, for even Cicero denounced his own art. Yeats could not speak with such force were he not sure that he speaks for all men. He berates old age, glorifies love, sensual life, and knowledge, condemns the petty and exalts the noble because he is on the side of life and ' of the Devil's Party ' more than he knows. If he puts on a mask, he informs the world and eventually justifies himself by finding that everyone has done likewise. In this he is the opposite of Whitman, who practised the utmost concealment while he pretended to be outspoken. Yeats cannot keep a secret. He is never an individualist like Blake, developing by himself and to a considerable extent for himself ; he has always an audience in mind, writes to be understood, and wants approbation. Even his dance plays, written for an aristocratic, esoteric audience, he attempts to adapt for more popular presentation. He is a great joiner and organizer, — Sean O'Casey mockingly named him ' The Great Founder ', — a gregarious man who cherishes and needs his friends, who soaks up the world which he then proceeds to dominate. He writes of his country's important events and important men, he serves in its Senate. Though he never ceases to regard himself as a rebel whom society has imprisoned, he builds his own jails, escapes from them, then builds others ; or, to put it another way, Yeats hides in the centre of the city and emblazons his name on his hiding-place and equips it with a public-address system.

If his poetry is to be understood then as not merely personal

or occult but popular, what is its content, its subject matter ?
Almost all his verse is lyrical, even his verse plays are very short,
and the brevity suggests that most of his material is moments
of great excitement. In an essay on Balzac Yeats describes the
novelist's work in terms that apply to his own : ' Will, or
passion which is but blind will, is always at crisis, or approaching crisis ; everything else seems eliminated, or is made
fantastic or violent that the will, without seeming to do so,
may exceed nature '. Yeats puts his poetic stock in those
experiences which are most passionate. His poetry is full of
miracles, for the miracle is the point at which reality and the
dream meet. The miracles with which he deals are miracles of
*possession*, sometimes sexual possession, sometimes divine or
artistic possession. There is conflagration of the whole being ;
the god descends or man rises ; matter is suddenly transmuted
into spirit or ' those holy, haughty feet descend / From emblem-
atic niches . . . / For desecration and the lover's night '. The
counter-theme is dispossession or failure to possess or be possessed, and the resultant remorse or sorrow. He is, as he called
himself in a letter, ' a short-distance runner ', and much of his
poetry is spasmic. In the early versions of ' Sailing to Byzantium',
Yeats described at some length the long voyage by which he
attained the imperial city, but as he worked on the poem the
voyage was reduced to the two lines,

> And therefore I have sailed the seas and come
> To the holy city of Byzantium,

while the main image of the poem became the enraptured prayer
for transmutation, for possession by the god ; the vision descends
and demands not belief but emotional response. In his early work
Yeats had tried to linger between spirit and sense, but he afterwards realized his mistake : ' How often had I heard men of my
time talk of the meeting of spirit and sense, yet there is no meeting
but only change upon the instant, and it is by the perception of a
change like the sudden " blacking out " of the lights of the stage,
that passion creates its most violent sensation.'

The man who emerges from his poetry is a modern man though his name be Cuchulain or Naisi. He walks a tight-rope between false choices, he is torn by an inner division and undermined by preternatural forces which he is not in a position to assess nor has sufficient power given him to dominate. If he cries out his cry of the infinite power of man it is in the teeth of the facts, not because of them. As a result, Yeats's work is full of overtones even when he appears to be shouting. Every poem is a battleground and the sounds of gunfire are heard throughout.

What saves him, though like Baudelaire he is *toujours du vertige hanté*, from making merely a case history of crisis is the tremendous organization that informs the poems and the poet ; every crisis is mastered, and every poem comes out of years of preparation. He looked the poet, and he lived the poet. He has justified and reinforced everything by autobiography, essay, and public speech, has written the history of the movements that he joined or began and the biographies of his friends to bring all into coherence ; nothing is left to chance. He keeps asking the same questions over and over until they have become profound : what is truth ? what is reality ? what is man ? His answers are symbolic, but fully in harmony one with another, for they spring from a rich, unified consciousness. During a lifetime of bitter toil Yeats constantly advanced and penetrated until he had evolved a world which has more solidity than that of any poet since Wordsworth. Few poets have found mastery of themselves and of their craft so difficult or have sought such mastery, through conflict and struggle, so unflinchingly.

# NOTES

THE numerals at the left refer to pages in this book. The two italicized words which follow the numerals are the end of the sentence or phrase which is being annotated. In the notes the following abbreviations have been used:

| | |
|---|---|
| AU | W. B. Yeats, *Autobiographies* (London, Macmillan, 1926). |
| CP | W. B. Yeats, *The Collected Poems of* (London, Macmillan, 1933). |
| DP | W. B. Yeats, *Dramatis Personae* (London, Macmillan, 1936). |
| EM | John Butler Yeats, *Early Memories* (Dundrum, Cuala Press, 1923). |
| FD | Unpublished first draft of Yeats's *Autobiographies*, written in 1916–17. |
| Hone | Joseph Hone, *W. B. Yeats, 1865–1939* (London, Macmillan, 1942). |
| JBY, *Letters* (Hone) | John Butler Yeats, *Letters to His Son W. B. Yeats and Others 1869–1922* (London, Faber and Faber, 1944). Joseph Hone, ed. |
| LP | W. B. Yeats, *Last Poems and Plays* (London, Macmillan, 1940). |
| ltr. | letter. |
| unp. | unpublished. |

Except where confusion might result, Yeats's name is omitted before works written by him. All unpublished material is in the possession of Mrs. Yeats unless otherwise specified. As the notes indicate, the Blavatsky Lodge (London), the Central Library of Belfast, the National College of Art (Dublin), and the New York Public Library have kindly made available some of the material included here.

## CHAPTER I

1 *of Shadows'*.     A name given to Yeats by A. E. (George Russell), *Some Irish Essays* (Dublin, Maunsel, 1906), 35-9.

3 *for weeks'*.     ' Introduction to the Holy Mountain ', *Essays 1931 to 1936* (Dublin, Cuala Press, 1937), 88.

3   *wicked man* '.        Desmond MacCarthy, ' W. B. Yeats ', *Sunday Times*, February 5, 1939.

*my time* ' ;        Lady Gregory, *Cuchulain of Muirthemne*, with a preface by Yeats (London, John Murray, 1902), vii.

*a stick*,        ' Those Dancing Days Are Gone ', CP, 306.

*romantic experience* '.        George Santayana, *Persons and Places* (London, Constable, 1944), 155.

*his youth* ;        Maud Gonne, ' Yeats and Ireland ', *Scattering Branches, Tributes to the Memory of W. B. Yeats* (London, Macmillan, 1940), 21.  Stephen Gwynn, ed.

6   *the world.*        Unp. notes for a London lecture on ' Contemporary Poetry ' dictated in Dublin in 1910.

*of himself* '.        *Idem.*

## CHAPTER II

7   *Parliamentary party.*        EM, 35-6.

*the dying.*        *Ibid.*, 42.

8   ' *well-mannered* '.        JBY, *Letters* (Hone), 214 ; EM, 6.

*a jockey* '.        EM, 39.

*even dancing,*        EM, 73.

*so tight.*  AU, 64.

*intellectual vice.*        EM, 15-16.

9   *not offended.*        EM, 5.

' *desperately afraid* '        JBY, *Letters* (Hone), 232.

*always speaking* '.        EM, 6-7.

*my sky* ',        EM, 10.

*its place* '.        EM, 34.

10   *my orthodoxy* '.        EM, 72-3.

*was true* '.        Unp. ltr. from J. B. Yeats to W. B. Yeats, March 26, 1919.

*artistic intuitions* '.        EM, 73.

*a barrister.*  EM, 1.

11   *of truth.*        J. B. Yeats, *An Address delivered before the Law Students' Debating Society of Dublin*, November 21, 1865 (Dublin, Joseph Dollard, 1865).

*art school.*        The date is clear from unp. ltrs. to Edward Dowden. See also J. B. Yeats, *Essays Irish and American* (Dublin, Talbot Press, and London, Fisher Unwin, 1918), 9.

*to powder* '.        Unp. ltr. from J. B. Yeats to W. B. Yeats, April 9, 1916.

*from him* '.        EM, 38-9.

12  *in reasoning'*.   EM, 2.
*in fairyland'*.   EM, 38.
*own sake*.   EM, 41.
*grey theory'*.   EM, 28.
*Rossetti woman'*.   Unp., undated essay about his art-school days by J. B. Yeats, written in New York.
*figure painting*.   J. B. Yeats, *Essays Irish and American*, 78.
*Millais's woodcuts*.   Unp. ltr. from J. B. Yeats to Edwin Ellis, August 27, 1868.

13  *the call*.   EM, 27-8.
*for passion*.   Unp. ltrs. to Edward Dowden.
*final confusion'*.   DP, 54.

14  *and applications'*.   Unp. ltr., February 23, 1910.
*father's studio'*.   Unp. ltr. to Arthur Power, June 20, 1935.
*contented negation'*.   EM, 72.
*its foundations'*.   *Essays Irish and American*, 18.

15  *common now-a-days.'*   Edward Dowden, *Fragments from Old Letters* (Second Series, London, Dent, 1914), 71 (ltr. dated January 5, 1875).
*of Goethe*.   JBY, *Letters* (Hone), 97.
*for it*.   Unp. ltr.
*J. B. Yeats*.   JBY, *Letters* (Hone), 48.

17  *for Belfast*.   EM, 48-9, 81, and *passim*.
*that counted'*.   EM, 89.
*of silence'*,   EM, 92.
*the sea-cliffs'*.   EM, 20.
*solitary man'*.   Unp. MS. on his art-school days.
*sociable-minded'*;   EM, 20.
*of opinion'*.   EM, 23.
*many opinions*.   EM, 24.
*the wind'*.   EM, 28.
*was happy'*.   EM, 37.
*own self'*.   EM, 87.

18  *nineteenth century*.   EM, 48.
*flower garden*.   EM, 82.
*vast theatre'*.   EM, 80.
*free trade*.   AU, 236.

19  *and dissolving'*.   Dowden, *Fragments from Old Letters* (Second Series), 24.
*its destiny*.   *Excerpts from Further Letters of J. B. Yeats* (Dundrum, Cuala Press, 1920), 22. Lennox Robinson, ed.
*nor religious*.   *Ibid.*, 22-3.

20  *intense movement* '.     EM, 29.

    *guerilla force* '.     Unp. papers.

    *a unity* ',     Unp. ltr. to his son, April 9, 1916.

    *the bars.*     JBY, *Letters* (Hone), 150.


CHAPTER III

22  *a merchant.*'     John Eglinton [W. K. Magee], *A Memoir of AE,
    George William Russell* (London, Macmillan, 1937), 111.

    *the heart* '.     ' The Circus Animals' Desertion ', LP, 81.

    *and Son.*     Quoted in ltr. from W. B. Yeats to his father, December
    26, 1914, in JBY, *Letters* (Hone), 203.

23  *in 1903,*     On Baile's Strand.

24  *her children.*     AU, 38.

25  *its pain.*     AU, 13.

    *so angry.*'     Unp. MS.

26  *lead me.*     Katharine Tynan, *The Middle Years* (London, Con-
    stable, 1916), 57.

    *disagreeable people* '.     AU, 38.

    *father's scepticism.*     AU, 28-31.

    *ants have?*'     Ltr. from Yeats to K. Tynan, April 20, 1888, in Tynan,
    *Middle Years,* 35.

    *must exist.*     AU, 31.

27  *to England.*     Hone, 23.

    *formal instruction.*     The date is given in an unp. ltr. from the Chair-
    man of the Godolphin School Old Boys' Association to Joseph
    Hone, in the latter's possession.

28  *to study.*     Unp. ltr. from J. B. Yeats to Dowden, 1878.

    *for himself.*     Unp. ltr. from J. B. Yeats to Dowden, July 24, 1880.

    *own wisdom.*     AU, 78.

    *by beliefs.*     AU, 80-82, and FD.

    *of Socrates.*     FD.

29  *in Hamlet.*     AU, 58, 102.

    *complete evolutionist.*     John Eglinton, ' Yeats at the High School '
    *The Erasmian,* June, 1939, 11-12 (published by the High School,
    Dublin).

    *English verse.*     F. J. Gregg, ' Going to School with the Poet Yeats ',
    *New York Herald,* December 2, 1923, 3.

    *described it,*     Unp. MS. of article for *The Listener* on ' How I
    Began '.

29  *a shell'*,    AU, 76. He gives his age as fifteen at the time of this episode in FD.

*the magician,*    AU, 57, 78.

*and women'.*    Unp. MS. of article for *The Listener* on 'How I Began'.

30  *its peace.'*    Ltr. to K. Tynan, January 31, 1899, in Tynan, *Middle Years*, 51.

*ears always.*    Unp. MS.

32  *his refusal.*    AU, 98.

*July, 1885;*    Records of Metropolitan School of Art, now in National College of Art, Dublin.

*any proficiency.*    These are now in Mrs. W. B. Yeats's possession.

*break away'.*    AU, 100-101.

33  *monkish hate'*,    AU, 101.

*interested him.*    Conversation with Eglinton.

34  *secret cruse.*    Unp. MS.

35  *and cold.*    Unp. MS.

36  *is here.*    Unp. MS.

*finding himself;*    JBY, *Letters* (Hone), 52-3.

*on Howth.*    Unp. ltr. from Laura Armstrong to Yeats ; and conversation with John Eglinton.

*own love.*    Unp. MS. See AU, 91-2, where Yeats improves upon the play in describing it.

37  *Catholic Church.*    *Mosada, A Dramatic Poem* (Dublin, Sealy, Bryers, and Walker, 1886), the poet's first published book.

*natural order,*    Dedication to *The Secret Rose* (London, Lawrence & Bullen, 1897), vii.

*that year.*    The date is given in a MS. The play was published in successive numbers of the *Dublin University Review* from April to July, 1885, and the 'Epilogue' in October, 1885.

39  *also sooth.*    *Dublin University Review*, I (October, 1885), 230-31.


CHAPTER IV

41  *all gentleness'*,    Tynan, *Twenty-five Years : Reminiscences* (London, Smith, Elder, 1913), 143.

*ana calm.*    Tynan, *Middle Years*, 47.

42  *in nationality'.*    Yeats, *If I Were Four-and-Twenty* (Dublin, Cuala Press, 1940), 1.

*father's influence.'*    AU, 109

42  *exceedingly speculative'.*     Yeats, 'A New Poet' (review of A. E.'s
    *Homeward: Songs by the Way), Bookman,* VI (August, 1894), 147-8.
    *Hermetic Society'.     Idem.*
    *as chairman.*     A notice of the meeting is given in the *Dublin Uni-
    versity Review,* I (July, 1885), 155.

43  *mouth shut.*     Unp. MS.

44  *the viceroy.'*     Yeats, 'A New Poet', *Bookman,* VI, 147-8.
    *personages, emotions.*     AU, 142.
    *literal truth'.*     AU, 111.
    *the poets'.*     Yeats, *Essays* (New York, Macmillan, 1924), 79.

45  *Speak! speak!*     Yeats, 'The Seeker', *Dublin University Review,* I
    (September, 1885), 120-23.
    *was mine.     Idem.*
    *'secret fanaticism'.*     AU, 97.

46  *years old.*     John O'Leary, *Recollections of Fenians and Fenianism*
    (London, Downey and Co., 1896), II, 25.
    *violent action.*     Conversation with Madame Maud Gonne MacBride.
    *a nation'.*     AU, 118.
    *bad verses'*,     O'Leary, *Recollections,* II, 78.

47  *for Ireland.*     O'Leary, *What Irishmen Should Know, How Irishmen
    Should Feel* (Dublin, A. & E. Cahill, [1886]).
    *to since'.*     AU, 125.

48  *Wild Olives.*     Unp. MS.
    *little circle'.*     Letter from Dowden to DeVere, August 22, 1874, in
    *Letters of Edward Dowden and His Correspondents* (London, Dent,
    1914), 68.

49  *poetry credible.*     Yeats, 'The Poetry of Sir Samuel Ferguson',
    *Dublin University Review,* II (November, 1886), 923-41.

50  *Of failure'.*     Yeats, 'The Two Titans', *Dublin University Review,*
    II (March, 1886), 265-6.

51  *abandoned art.*     He described the boredom of the art training in
    testimony before a Royal Committee of Inquiry into the Work
    Carried on by the Royal Hibernian Academy and the Metropolitan
    School of Art, Dublin.  See the Committee's *Report* (Dublin, His
    Majesty's Stationery Office, 1906), 60-61.

52  *of incidents'.*     Tynan, *Middle Years,* 51.
    *Irish original,*     See R. K. Alspach, 'Some Sources of Yeats's *The
    Wanderings of Oisin', Publications of the Modern Language Associa-
    tion,* 58 (September, 1943), 849-66.  Alspach does not suggest the
    reasons for Yeats's modifications of his sources.
    *and fell.*     Yeats, *The Wanderings of Oisin and Other Poems* (Lon-

don, Kegan Paul, Trench & Co., 1889), 2-3.

53 *the dark'.*    *Ibid.,* 22.

*physical man.*    *Wanderings of Oisin,* 23.

*but clouds.'*    Tynan, *Middle Years,* 47.

54 *an interpreter'.*    *Ibid.,* 53.

*of clouds.*    *Ibid.,* 45.

*a spectator'.*    Tynan, *Twenty-Five Years,* 247.

55 *own dropping.*    *Wanderings of Oisin,* 115.

*enamelled sea.*    *Ibid.,* 64.

*and knowledge'.*    Tynan, *Middle Years,* 39.

56 *his opponent.*    MS. of article by Frank O'Connor, in his possession.

*single mind'.*    Elizabeth A. Sharp, *William Sharp* (London, Heinemann, 1910), 335.

*really is'.*    George Henry Lewes, *Life of Goethe* (Everyman), 118.


## CHAPTER V

58 *and philosophy'*    The sub-title of *The Secret Doctrine* ; see note following.

*she announced.*    H. P. Blavatsky, *The Secret Doctrine* (3rd Point Loma Edition, Point Loma, Calif., Aryan Theosophical Press, 1926), I, 579. Her attitude towards evolution is ambiguous.

60 *is impossible'.*    Blavatsky, *ibid.,* 14.

61 *Karmic law'.*    *Ibid.,* 17.

*a string'.*    Charles Johnston, ' Esoteric Buddhism ', *Dublin University Review,* I (July, 1885), 144-5.

*in 1885.*    See note above. The main source of Johnston's article is A. P. Sinnett, *Esoteric Buddhism* (London, Trübner, 1883), 29-65.

63 *spiritual heritage.'*    Charles Johnston, ' The Theosophical Movement,' *Theosophical Quarterly* (New York), V (July, 1907), 16-26.

*lodge there'.*    Ltr. to me from P. Leslie Pielou, president of the Dublin Theosophical Society.

*Edward Dowden,*    Ernest Boyd says that Yeats's reading of *Esoteric Buddhism* in 1885 was the beginning of the Theosophical movement in Dublin. Actually Theosophical ideas were floating around Dublin at least a year before and probably earlier. George Russell, in an unpublished letter to Sean O'Faolain in the latter's possession, says that he had been reading Theosophical literature in the early 'eighties ; Charles Johnston says, in the article in the *Theosophical Quarterly* cited above, that he had read Sinnett's *The*

*Occult World* in 1884.    See Ernest Boyd, *Ireland's Literary Renaissance* (London, Grant Richards, 1923), 213-14.

63  *ever since '*.    Johnston, ' The Theosophical Movement ', *Theosophical Quarterly*, V, 16-26.

64  *Hodgson's performance '*.    *Ibid.*, 18.

*Dublin lodge.*    Announcement in *The Theosophist* (Madras, India), VII (Supplement to April, 1886, number), cxxvi.

*and refused.*    A conjecture based upon his letter to the editor of *Lucifer*, III (December 15, 1888), 339-41.

*friends' ʒeal.*    AU, 112. In FD he says he had read Hodgson's charges.

*came to London,*    Hone 69.

65  *illogical, incomprehensible '*.    FD.

*a trick.*    AU, 215.

*Hodgson's charges.*    FD.

*the world*    AU, 216-17.

*very sensitive ".'*    FD.

*greatest success '*,    *Lady Gregory's Journals, 1916–1930* (London, Putnam, 1946), 261-2. Lennox Robinson, ed.

66  *to her.*    Unp. ltr. to O'Leary, written before March 20, 1888, copy in Central Library, Belfast.

*her ' chelas '.*    Announcement of formation of Esoteric Section, *Lucifer*, III (Oct. 15, 1888), unnumbered page following 175.

*a member.*    A. E., ltr. to the editor, with her reply, *Lucifer*, III (December 15, 1888), 339-41. A. E. joined the Section, however, in December, 1890.

*fellow-men.*    Blavatsky, *The Key to Theosophy* (London, Theosophical Publishing Society, 1889), 20, 263.

*higher knowledge '*.    Reprint of *New York Times* article, ' Dr. Keightley Speaks ', *The Theosophist* (Adyar, India), X (July, 1889), 595-601.

67  *the Mystics '*.    Yeats, *A Vision* (London, Macmillan, 1938), 12.

69  *detailed account.*    Unp. MS. Yeats, because of his strange eyes, had some skill at hypnotism, and on this occasion acted as ' mesmerist '. Ltr. to K. Tynan, March, 1890. Tynan, *Middle Years*, 62.

*Modern Culture '*.    Records of Blavatsky Lodge in London.

*regretfully complied.*    AU, 225-6.

70  *a body '*,    D.E.D.I. [Yeats], ' Invoking the Irish Fairies ', *Irish Theosophist*, I (October 15, 1892), 6-7. D.E.D.I. stood for *Demon Est Deus Inversus*, the name which Yeats used in the Golden Dawn.

70  *to Yeats,*    He writes amusingly of the incident to K. Tynan. Tynan, *Twenty-Five Years,* 269.

*my poem '.*    *Wheels and Butterflies* (London, Macmillan, 1934), 102.

71  *hound. Swear !*    ' Anashuya and Vijaya ', CP, 13-14.


## CHAPTER VI

74  *your poem.'*    Vincent O'Sullivan, *Aspects of Wilde* (London, Constable, Second Edition, 1938), 223.

*of fiction.'*    Oscar Wilde, *De Profundis* (New York, Knickerbocker Press, 1909), 33. *Cf.* Max Beerbohm : ' For the era of rouge is upon us, and as only in an elaborate era can man, by the tangled accrescency of his own emotions, reach that refinement which is his highest excellence, and by making himself, so to say, independent of Nature, come nearest to God, so only in an elaborate era is woman perfect '. *Works* (London, John Lane, 1896 ; reprinted 1946), 81.

*larger scope.'*    Wilde, *De Profundis,* 32-3.

75  *formless greed '.*    *Ibid.,* 28-9 *Cf.* his remark to Gide, ' En art, voyez-vous, il n'y a pas de première personne '. André Gide, *Oscar Wilde* (Paris, Mercure de France, 1905), 46.

*a manner '.*    Joyce, *Stephen Hero* (London, Jonathan Cape, 1944), 20.

76  *he aspired.*    Eglinton, *A Memoir of AE,* 8, 27-8.

77  *double life.*    E. A. Sharp, *William Sharp,* 223.

*October, 1888,*    JBY, *Letters* (Hone), 294 (New York, Dutton, 1946 Edition only).

*of himself.'*    Eglinton, *A Memoir of AE,* 110-11.

*of mind.*    FD.

78  *the immortals.'*    Unp. ltr. from George Russell to Sean O'Faolain, in the latter's possession.

*and impudent '.*    Bernard Shaw, *Prefaces* (London, Constable, 1934), 630.

79  *was dead.*    FD.

*is fairyland ',*    Conversation with Frank O'Connor.

80  *loathe crowds. . . .'*    Tynan, *Twenty-Five Years,* 259, 265, 272.

*accept it.*    FD.

*and paper.*    Tynan, *Middle Years,* 41.

*despondent moods '.*    *Ibid.,* 42.

81  *patriotic arrogance ',*    Shaw, *Prefaces,* 638.

81  *years afterwards,*      Yeats, *Letters to the New Island* (Cambridge, Mass., Harvard University Press, 1934), xii. Horace Reynolds, ed.

*rave against.'*      Ganconagh [pseudonym], *John Sherman and Dhoya* (London, Fisher Unwin, 1891), 175.

82  *the point.*      *John Sherman and Dhoya,* 130.

*possible change'.*      *A Vision* (1938), 118-19.

*family's house.*      AU, 151-3. The date is clear from unp. ltrs.

83  *half refused.*      *The Secret Rose,* 20-21.

84  *dim hair.*      ' The Host of the Air ', CP, 64.

*named beauty.*      ' The Secret Rose ', CP, 78.

*my heart' ?*      ' The Lover Tells of the Rose in His Heart ', CP, 62.

*come away'.*      ' The Hosting of the Sidhe ', CP, 61.

85  *in bed.*      Van Wyck Brooks writes : ' [J. B.] Yeats, in preaching idleness, was consistent. He told Allston how his son " Willie ", the poet, had lain abed all day as a young man. His friends and the family remonstrated : Why should Willie lie abed when he was well in his twenties and the family so poor ?  He ought to be up and doing ; but Yeats said No. Something perhaps was brewing in Willie's mind ; and what, as it proved was brewing as he lay abed all these years ?  Willie was composing *The Wanderings of Oisin,* — there was a reward for a father's forbearance.' Brooks, *Opinions of Oliver Allston* (London, Dent, 1942), 29.

*he dies.*      ' He thinks of His Past Greatness When a Part of the Constellations of Heaven ', CP, 83.

*desolate lake.'*      ' He Hears the Cry of the Sedge ', CP, 76.

86  *a face'.*      ' Rosa Alchemica ', *The Secret Rose,* 241.

*a peasant'.*      *Ibid.,* 228.

*with terror.*      *Ibid.,* 236.

*drunkard's eye'.*      ' The Seven Sages ', CP, 278.

87  *better room.*      FD.

*clean-shaven.*      The shaving off of the beard is mentioned in a ltr. to K. Tynan. Tynan, *Middle Years,* 61.  See also his father's drawing of him, dated November, 1896, frontispiece to Vol. VII of *Collected Works in Verse and Prose* (Stratford on Avon, Shakespeare Head, 1908).

*wearing black.*      Conversation with Mrs. Yeats.

88  *soft bow.*      K. T. [Katharine Tynan], ' William Butler Yeats ', *The Sketch,* November 29, 1893, 256.

## CHAPTER VII

89   *and isolated '.*   AU, 227

91   *our immortality '*,   Sâr [Joséphin] Péladan, *L'Art idéaliste & mystique* (Paris, Chamuel, 1894), 18. This and the following translations are my own.

   *a god.'*   Adolphe Retté, *Au pays des lys noirs (Souvenirs de jeunesse et d'âge mûr)* (Paris, Pierre Téqui, 1934, 4th edition), 21.

92   *de siècle.*   Charles Morice, *La Littérature de tout à l'heure*, quoted in *Cinquantenaire de Symbolisme*, catalogue of an exhibition at the Bibliothèque Nationale (Paris, Éditions des Bibliothèques Nationales, 1936), 236.

   *into outlaws !'*   Stanislas de Guaïta, *Rosa Mystica* (Paris, Alphonse Lemerre, 1885), 3.

   *their altar.*   Jules Bois, *Les Petites Religions de Paris* (Paris, Léon Chailley, 1894 ; first published in newspapers in 1893) ; see also his *Le Monde invisible* (Paris, Flammarion, 1902), 19-20, 22, 25, 409-10.

   *Rosy Cross.*   Maurice Barrès, ' Stanislas de Guaïta (1861–1898) ', *Amori et Dolori Sacrum* (Paris, Félix Juven, 1903), 144-5 ; Charles Berlet, *Un Ami de Barrès, Stanislas de Guaïta* (Paris, Bernard Grasset, 1936), 77.

   *the sacraments.*   René-Georges Aubrun, *Péladan* (Paris, E. Sansot, 1904), 16.

93   *and Guaïta.*   Stéphane Mallarmé, ' Magie ', *National Observer*, IX (January 28, 1893), 263-4.

   *the grass.*   *Idem.*

94   *of devils.*   ' Magic,' *Essays* (1924), 48, 52-3, 60.

   *in Londinense.*   *Lucifer*, IV (June 15, 1889), 350-51.

95   *the secrets*   The most important defections were those of Aleister Crowley, who published some of the rituals, though in distorted form, in his publication, *The Equinox*, I (March, 1910), and of Israel Regardie, who published a history of the order in *My Rosicrucian Adventure* (Chicago, Aries Press, 1936), and the rituals and related material in *The Golden Dawn*, 4 vols. (Chicago, Aries Press, 1937). See also W. W. Westcott, *Data of the History of the Rosicrucians* (London, J. M. Watkins, 1916). My discussion of the Golden Dawn is based, except where otherwise indicated, on the above sources and on correspondence with Regardie, Arthur Machen, and Algernon Blackwood, and conversations with the late Aleister Crowley.

   *antiquarian research,*   A. E. Waite, *The Real History of the Rosi-*

crucians (London, Redway, 1887), 423.

95  ' external manifestations '.        Paul Chacornac, Éliphas Lévi (Paris, Chacornac Frères, 1926), 202.

of romance ',        AU, 226.

96  Jules Bois.        Frederic Lees, ' Isis Worship in Paris, Conversations with the Hierophant Rameses and the High Priestess Anari ', The Humanitarian (London), XVI (February, 1900), 82-7.

passing outside.    AU, 419.

fortieth year.    FD.

97  your garden.    Stanislas de Guaïta, Rosa Mystica, 2-3.

98  the world.        Ltr. from Yeats to O'Leary written about August, 1892, copy of which is in the Central Library, Belfast.  The letter has been published with certain omissions in ' Willie Yeats and John O'Leary ', The Irish Book Lover, XXVII (November, 1940), 248. The spelling is Yeats's.

March 24th, 1895.        Poems (London, Fisher Unwin, 1895), v-vi. In the second edition, 1899, vii-viii, this preface was toned down.

our lives '.    Unp. ltrs.

99  in tomb '.    ' Vacillation ', CP, 290.

born anew '.            ' Stream and Sun at Glendalough ', CP, 293.

to me.    Unp. Golden Dawn notebook.

100  the world'.        Aleister Crowley, The Spirit of Solitude, The Confessions of Aleister Crowley (London, Mandrake Press, 1929), 271-2.

terrestrial natures '.        A lover of Philalethes, A Short Enquiry concerning the Hermetic Art, with introduction to alchemy and notes by SSDD [Florence Farr] (London, Theosophical Publishing Society, 1894), 13.

immense wars ',    AU, 415.

the good !    Marjorie Louise Henry, Stuart Merrill (Paris, Librairie Ancienne Honoré Champion, 1927), 109.

at last ? '    Florence Farr, Bernard Shaw, and W. B. Yeats, Letters (London, Home and Van Thal, 1946), 37.  Clifford Bax. ed.

multitudinous influx '.        Wheels and Butterflies, 92.

Rose (1897) ;    Two of the stories were published separately because A. H. Bullen, the publisher, did not like them at first and refused to include them in The Secret Rose.  They made a separate little book, The Tables of the Law, The Adoration of the Magi (London, Privately Printed, 1897).

101  inviolate Rose ? '        ' The Secret Rose ', CP, 79 ; first published under the title, ' O'Sullivan Rua to the Secret Rose ', The Savoy, 5 (September, 1896), 52.

## CHAPTER VIII

103   *of it.'*   Unp. ltr. in National Library, Dublin.

104   *a tent.*   FD.

   *Gonne's tonight.*   JBY, *Letters* (Hone), 297-8. New York, Dutton, 1946. Not in London edition.

   *book greatly. . . .*   Tynan, *Middle Years*, 51.

   *many converts.*   Unp. ltr., copy in Central Library, Belfast.

105   *her youth.*   FD.

   *intellectual movement '.*   FD.

   *bugles blow.*   Unp. MS. book.

106   *fair woman '.*   FD.

   *for her. . . .'*   FD.

   *to amalgamate,*   Yeats, ' The Young Ireland League ', *United Ireland*, XI (October 3, 1891), 5. This article makes clear that the work had been under way for some time, and refutes his statement in AU, 245, that he began his active nationalist efforts after Parnell's death, which occurred on October 6.

   *her ardour.'*   Unp. ltr. in National Library, Dublin.

107   *in Dublin.*   W. P. Ryan, *The Irish Literary Revival* (London, published by the author, 1894), 53, 127.

   *the country.*   Yeats, ' The National Literary Society Libraries Scheme ', *United Ireland*, XII (September 24, 1892), 4.

   *popular personage.'*   FD. See also AU, 246.

   *of mind '*   Unp. MS. entitled *Spiritus Mundi*.

108   *was jealous.*   FD.

   *conciliate him.*   See, for example, the beginning of Yeats's lecture to the National Literary Society on ' Nationality and Literature ', where he seems to go out of his way to attack Taylor's principles. *United Ireland*, XIII (May 27, 1893), 4.

   *Pan-Celtic Society,*   Ryan, *The Irish Literary Revival*, 44-51.

   *Ireland models.*   FD.

109   *tolerant years.*   FD.

   *to disaster.*   AU, 280-82. See also Sir Charles Gavan Duffy's lecture to the Irish Literary Society in June, 1893, ' Books for the Irish People ', *The Revival of Irish Literature* (London, Fisher Unwin, 1894), 35-60. C. G. Duffy, ed. Unp. ltrs. from Edward Garnett, Unwin's reader, and O'Leary to Yeats indicate that Yeats might have secured some compromise had he been less furious.

110   *or despised.'*   FD.

   *intellectual backing.*   AU, 273. See also *The Irish Home Reading*

*Magazine*, published under the auspices of the Irish Literary Society (London, May, 1894), where Johnson is listed as one of the two editors.

110  *and Protestant.*    Unp. MS. of *Trembling of the Veil.*

   *Irish anthologies.*    *A Book of Irish Verse* (London, Methuen, 1895), xxvi-xxvii. Yeats, ed.

111  *my play.'*    FD.

   *has come " '.*    FD.

   *of it.*    FD.

   *complicated situations.*    Shaw wrote to Lady Gregory about a dispute at the Abbey Theatre over O'Casey's *The Silver Tassie* : ' But that is so like Yeats. Give him a job with which you feel sure he will play Bunthorne and he will astonish you with his unique cleverness and subtlety. Give him one that any second-rater could manage with credit and as likely as not he will make an appalling mess of it.' *Lady Gregory's Journals*, 111.

112  *stayed on.*    FD.

113  *that way '.*    FD.

   *went wild.'*    FD.

114  *the backbone.'*    FD.

115  *(loud applause).*    '98 Centennial Association of Great Britain and France, *Report of Speeches at the Inaugural Banquet Held at the Holborn Restaurant, London, on Wed., 13th April, 1898* (Dublin, Bernard Doyle, 1898), 8-10.

117  *of Ireland.*    Unp. MS.


## CHAPTER IX

118  *that sentence.'*    *If I Were Four-and-Twenty*, 1.

119  *elsewhere disappeared.*    *Fairy and Folk Tales of the Irish Peasantry* (London, Walter Scott, 1888), ix-xvi. Yeats, ed.

   *our moods '.*    Yeats, ' Regina, Regina Pigmeorum, Veni ', *The Celtic Twilight* (London, Lawrence and Bullen, 1893), 87.

120  *in Jerusalem.*    *The Works of William Blake*, I (London, Quaritch, 1893), 2-3. E. J. Ellis and Yeats, eds.

   *universal magic.*    *Ibid.*, I, 24. As already indicated, the Golden Dawn was not founded till 1888, but Yeats was not aware of this carefully guarded secret until some years after writing the passage quoted.

121  *bordered hem.*    Yeats, *The Countess Kathleen and Various Legends and Lyrics*, 135-7.

122 *with them '.* FD.

*veiled kind '.* E. A. Sharp, *William Sharp*, 282.

*the swan '.* Yeats, ' The Adoration of the Magi ', *Early Poems and Stories* (London, Macmillan, 1925), 520.

*the spear. . . .* ' The Adoration of the Magi ', *The Tables of the Law and the Adoration of the Magi* (London, Privately printed, 1897), 45-6. The passage is omitted from *Early Poems and Stories*, 522-3.

123 *Black Pig.* ' Rosa Alchemica ', *The Secret Rose*, 244-5. He later omitted the lines about the Irish divinities. See *Early Poems and Stories*, 483.

*from him.'* E. A. Sharp, *William Sharp*, 277. The date of the letter is not clear and may be early 1897.

124 *he appears.* Unp. ltr., June 2, 1896.

*this about.* *Idem.*

*new Aeon.'* Unp. ltr., probably late 1896.

*for Ireland.* AU, 313-14. He says he spent ten years trying vainly to work out a ritual and philosophy for the order, but he actually spent about six years.

125 *ancient world '.* Unp. MS. entitled *Spiritus Mundi.* See slso AU, 314-15, and F.D.

*strange places. . . .* Maud Gonne, ' Yeats and Ireland ', *Scattering Branches*, 22-3.

*the Masons,* Conversation with Maud Gonne.

*had done.* Henri Le Caron, *Twenty-Five Years in the Secret Service, The Recollections of a Spy* (London, Heinemann, 1892), 111.

*need of,* Unp. ltr. from Yeats to Lady Gregory, May 18, 1898, and AU, 314.

*become his.* FD.

126 *natural beauty.'* FD.

*of course.* Unp. ltr.

128 *as before.* Unp. notebook kept by one of the members.

*commencing grade.* Unp. ltr. from Mathers to Yeats.

*influenced him '.* Unp. MS. book.

*insuperable difficulty '.* Unp. ltr.

*their entirety '.* Unp. ltr.

129 *was vain.* AU, 314.

*without it.* Unp. MS.

131 *Miracle Play.* Programme is contained in W. A. Henderson, *The Irish National Theatre Movement*, a collection of press cuttings in the National Library of Ireland.

131   *by you.'*     Tynan, *Middle Years*, 65.
      *I propose'*.     *Ibid.*, 63.
132   *have done.*     E. A. Sharp, *William Sharp*, 280-81.
      *of devotion'*.     AU, 314.
133   *than whisper'*.     FD.
      *magical things. . . .'*     Unp. ltr., 1901.
      *the People.'*     *Beltaine, The Organ of the Irish Literary Theatre*,
         May, 1899, 22.
      *the multitude'*.     Yeats, ' John Eglinton ', *United Irishman*, November
         9, 1901.
134   *of principle.*     Yeats, A Letter, *Freeman's Journal*, November 13,
         1901.
      *visionary experiences.*     *Plays for an Irish Theatre* (London, Bullen,
         1911), 224. In a later edition, *Plays in Prose and Verse* (London,
         Macmillan, 1922), 418, he cautiously changed the word ' visionary '
         to ' dream '.
      *and sardonyx'*.     *The Shadowy Waters* (London, Hodder and
         Stoughton, 1900), 49.
135   *the world'*.     Yeats, A Letter, *United Irishman*, April 5, 1902.
      *that country. . . .'*     *The Hour Glass . . .* (London, Bullen, 1904), 4.
136   *it all'*.     *Where There Is Nothing, United Irishman*, Supplement,
         Samain, 1902. This version of the play is of special interest because,
         as the result of a quarrel with George Moore, Yeats wrote it in two
         weeks with the help of Lady Gregory and Douglas Hyde, and there-
         fore had little time to polish it.
      *into it,*     ' The Freedom of the Theatre ', *United Irishman*,
         November 1, 1902.
      *of God.'*     *Where There Is Nothing, United Irishman*, Samain, 1902.


## CHAPTER X

138   *is style'*,     DP, 143.
      *his claim.*     George Moore, *Ave* (London, Heinemann, 1911), 62-3.
139   *lay there.*     Ltr. from J. B. Yeats to W. B. Yeats, May 30, 1899, in
         JBY, *Letters* (Hone), 57.
      *possible prose.*     MS. notes for *Four Years*.
140   *a board,*     AU, 456.
      *and cadence '*.     *Letters to the New Island*, ix, and FD.
141   *my days.*     *The Countess Kathleen and Various Legends and Lyrics*,
         93-4.

141 *years later ;*    Unp. excerpt from 1908 diary.

*in everybody's.*    *Letters on Poetry from W. B. Yeats to Dorothy Wellesley* (London, O.U.P., 1940), 94-5. Dorothy Wellesley, ed.

142 *long day.*    *The Wanderings of Oisin and Other Poems*, 82.

*to mankind.*    *The Countess Kathleen and Various Legends and Lyrics*, 108-9.

143 *Rhymers' Club.*    The exact date is difficult to determine, but Albert J. Farmer, *Le Mouvement esthétique et ' décadent' en Angleterre (1873–1900)* (Paris, Librairie Ancienne Honoré Champion, 1931), 262, says the club was founded in the early months of 1891.

144 *about symbolism.*    That Yeats helped Symons with the book is made clear by some unp. ltrs. from Symons to him.

*understood Greek'.*    Yeats, ' Modern Poetry : A Broadcast, October, 1936 ', *Essays 1931 To 1936,* 7.

*but impressions '.*    AU, 206.

*the darkness.*    Yeats, ' Hopes and Fears for Irish Literature ', *United Ireland*, XII (October 15, 1892), 5.

145 *in itself',*    *Idem.*

*a cadence '.*    FD.

146 *Nov. 19th [18]94*    MS. book.

148 *a man.*    ' Village Ghosts ', *The Celtic Twilight*, 34-5.

*heavy hair.*    ' Rosa Alchemica ', *The Secret Rose*, 260.

149 *tumultuous feet.*    *The Wind Among the Reeds* (London, Elkin Matthews, 1899), 24-5.

150 *artistic development.*    ' Preface to the First Edition of *The Well of the Saints* ', in *The Cutting of an Agate* (London, Macmillan, 1919), 112.

*she preferred.*    E. A. Sharp, *William Sharp,* 271.

*early poems.'*    FD. See also AU, 456-7.

*traditional, emotional.'*    AU, 456.

*heard there.*    AU, 463-7.

151 *life itself'.*    Moore, *Ave,* 55-6.

*the few.'*    Unp. ltr. in National Library, Dublin.

153 *good resolutions.*    ' Speaking to the Psaltery ', *Essays* (1924), 23.

154 *their anonymity '.*    *Letters to the New Island*, xiii.

*the words '.*    Unp. ltr. in the possession of Dr. James Starkey.

*and precise '.*    ' Some Passages from the Letters of W. B. Yeats to A. E. ', *Dublin Magazine*, N.S. XIV (July-September, 1939), 14.

*is thrown.'*    E. A. Sharp, *William Sharp*, 335-6.

155 *hollow moon.*    CP, 91-2.

156 *in it.'*    Unp. ltr., January 16, 1903.

## CHAPTER XI

157  *my verses.*     *In the Seven Woods* (Dundrum, Dun Emer Press, July, 1903), 25.

158  *& occultism.*     Unp. ltr. in possession of Dr. James Starkey.
*July 5th, 1891*     MS. book.

159  *women members.*     Maud Gonne MacBride, *A Servant of the Queen*, 314-15.

161  *cruel one.*     MS. book.

162  *no more.'*     This account is based on FD.

163  *With lightning',*     ' Reconciliation ', CP, 104.
*blackened leaves.*     ' The Two Trees ', CP, 55.

## CHAPTER XII

165  *and sense'.*     AU, 403.
*'Many-Coloured Land',*     Russell, *Some Irish Essays*, 35-6.
*of art,*     Tynan, *Twenty-Five Years*, 262.

168  *half lately.*     Ltr. of May 14, 1903, in ' Some Passages . . . ', *Dublin Magazine*, N.S. XIV (July-September, 1939), 15.
*of craft.'*     Unp. ltr., copy in New York Public Library.

169  *her affection,*     ' Presences ', CP, 177, and FD.
*and reason'.*     ' The Cold Heaven ', CP, 142.
*active man'.*     ' Estrangement, Extracts from a Diary Kept in 1909 ', DP, 118.
*his life.*     ' The Circus Animals' Desertion ', LP, 81.

170  *and Conchubar.*     Yeats, ' Introduction ' to *The Resurrection* in *Wheels and Butterflies*, 103.
*popular man'*     *Deirdre* (London, Bullen, 1907), 5.
*of youth',*     *Ibid.*, 36.
*Helmet (1908),*     *The Golden Helmet*, in *Collected Works in Verse and Prose*, IV, 78.
*gambler's throw. . . .*     *The Green Helmet* in *Plays for an Irish Theatre*, 54.

172  *I do ?*     Unp. MS., written before August, 1910.

173  *of you —*     ' Reconciliation ', CP, 104.
*of Ulster'.*     ' The Death of Conla ', *Eriu*, I (1904), 121.
*read it'.*     *Deirdre*, 37.

174  *language rich.*     ' J. M. Synge and the Ireland of His Time ', essay

dated September 14, 1910, in *Essays* (1924), 413. *Cf.* ' Lapis Lazuli ', LP, 4.

174 *timid heart* '. ' Coole Park, 1929,' CP, 279.

175 *in me ?* ' CP, 108.

*an enemy.* Unp. MS.

*he man.* Unp. MS.

176 *from reality.*' Unp. MS.

177 *been beaten.* Unp. MS.

*perpetually renewed* '. ' The Death of Synge, Extracts from a Diary Kept in 1909 ', DP, 130.

179 *August 2, 1910.* Unp. excerpt from 1908 diary.

*of men* ', ' The Fascination of What's Difficult ', CP, 106.

181 *a clown.* Unp. excerpt from 1908 diary.

*of things. . . .* JBY, *Letters* (Hone), 97.

(note) *head abashed.* CP, 172.

182 *& truth* '. Unp. ltr.

*in enemies.*' Unp. ltr., June 13, 1906, in Joseph Hone's possession.

183 *the wind. The King's Threshold : And On Baile's Strand . . .* (London, Bullen, 1904), 70-71.

*of desire ? Ibid.*, 45.

*after death ? Deirdre*, 30.

*the cockcrow. Ibid.*, 45.

*one eye. The Shadowy Waters*, in *Collected Works*, II (1908), 186.

184 *athletic joy.* ' Some passages . . .', *Dublin Magazine*, N.S. XIV (July-September, 1939), 17-18.

185 *common passion.*' Unp. ltr., copy in New York Public Library.

*the great. . . .* ' No Second Troy ', *The Green Helmet and Other Poems* (Churchtown, Cuala Press, 1910), 4.

*awhile ago. . . .* ' The Consolation ', *ibid.*, 3.

*of mind. . . .* ' Upon a Threatened House ', *ibid.*, 9.

*Course is. . . .* ' At Galway Races ', *ibid.*, 10.

*of his. . . .* ' A Friend's Illness ', *idem.*

*his fleas ? Ibid.*, 8.

186 *road metal.* ' The Fascination of What's Difficult ', *ibid.*, 7.

*the mask.* Unp. MS.

*realistic drama.* L. A. G. Strong discusses this point in his essay, ' William Butler Yeats ', *Scattering Branches*, 220-23.

187 *faithless still. The Green Helmet and Other Poems*, 31-2.

CHAPTER XIII

189   *of style.*   *Poems, 1899–1905* (London, Bullen, 1906), xii-xiii.
      *do that. . . .'*   Unp. ltr.
      *I remake.*   This poem appears as an epigraph to *Collected Works*
      (1908), Vol. II.

190   *next another.*   Unp. excerpt from 1908 diary.
      *Golden Dawn,*   The name of the order was changed, after the ex-
      pulsion of MacGregor Mathers, to the *Stella Matutina,* but I have
      retained the earlier name for the sake of clarity.

191   *of life'.*   Farr, Shaw, and Yeats, *Letters,* 56.
      *the vineyards!*   *The Unicorn from the Stars,* in *Collected Plays*
      (London, Macmillan, 1934), 382.
      *He's dead!'*   Conversation with Ernest Walsh, who sat next to
      Moore at the play.

192   *supernal Eden.*   Unp. MS.
      *will pray.'*   Unp. excerpt from 1908 diary.

194   *groping hands.*   *Idem.*

195   *my dreams.*   CP, 114.
      *But inwardly',*   CP, 146.
      *timid sun.*   CP, 166.

196   *for days.*   AU, 128-30.

201   *blasphemous men.*   ' Ego Dominus Tuus ', CP, 183-5.
      *psychical research.*   Yeats, ' Swedenborg, Mediums, and the Deso-
      late Places ', in Lady Gregory, *Visions and Beliefs in the West of
      Ireland* (New York and London, Putnam, 1920, Second Series).

202   *me superstitious?*   *Per Amica Silentia Lunae,* in *Essays* (1924),
      485-6.

204   *is broken.*   *Passages from the Letters of J. B. Yeats* (Churchtown,
      Cuala Press, 1917), 19-20. Ezra Pound, ed.

205   *story's end,*   CP, 115.
      *thin Shade,*   ' To a Shade ', CP, 125.
      *as good.*   ' The Grey Rock ', CP, 118.
      *a bird'.*   ' The Three Hermits ', CP, 130.

206   *marvellous moon.*   CP, 140.
      *crystalline cry.*   CP, 124-5.

207   *to foot.*   CP, 142.
      *the beggar'.*   CP, 131.
      *to care'.*   CP, 129.
      *for punishment?*   CP, 142-3.

208   *Silentia Lunae.*   *Essays* (1924), 492.

208  *of Enoch,*      See, for the heaven of burning ice, 1 Enoch 14 :
5-24.


CHAPTER XIV

210  *the grave '.*      ' September 1913 ', CP, 123.
211  *(note) be correct.*      Unp. MS. book begun in 1912.
212  *my thighs.'*      ' Beggar to Beggar Cried ', CP, 130.
*dogs defile.*      CP, 146.
*his family.*      Hone, 288.
213  *' religious system ',*      Unp. ltr., June 14, probably 1915.
*mere anticlericalism.*      Unp. MS. book begun in 1912.
214  *they rose.*      *Idem.*
*withered leaves.*      Yeats, ' The Autumn of the Flesh ', in John Eglinton, W. B. Yeats, A. E., William Larminie [co-authors], *Literary
Ideals in Ireland* (London, Fisher Unwin and Dublin, *Daily Express*
Office, 1899), 72-3.
*and feeling ',*      Unp. ltr. from W. B. Yeats to J. B. Yeats, August 5,
1913.
215  *of Milton '.*      Ford Madox Ford, *Return to Yesterday* (London,
Gollancz, 1931), 370.
*so marked.*      Yeats was not the only prominent poet to be influenced
by Pound.  T. S. Eliot has described in a recent article how Pound
revised *The Waste Land,* cutting it to about half its original size.
' Ezra Pound ', *New English Weekly,* XXX (October 31, 1946),
27-8.
216  *left bare.*      *At the Hawk's Well,* in *Four Plays for Dancers* (London,
Macmillan, 1921), 4.
*most recondite.'*      Ernest Fenollosa and Ezra Pound, ' *Noh* ' *or
Accomplishment, A Study of the Classical Stage of Japan* (London,
Macmillan, 1916), 5.
*may approve.*      *Ibid.,* 5-6.
217  *14th century.*      Yeats, ' Introduction ', in Ezra Pound, *Certain Noble
Plays of Japan: From the Manuscripts of Ernest Fenollosa* (Churchtown, Cuala Press, 1916), II, V, VII.
218  *into applause.*      Yeats, *Plays and Controversies* (London, Macmillan,
1923), 212, 213, 215.
*ancient memories. . . .' ·*      Yeats, ' Introduction ', in Pound, *Certain
Noble Plays of Japan,* XIX.
219  *never comes.'*      Unp. MS.
*never happens.*      AU, 132.

219   *in order.'*     Ltr. dated August 1, 1916, copy in New York Public
      Library.
220   *its heroism.'*     *Responsibilities* (London, Macmillan, 1916), 187.
221   *is born.*     CP, 209. ' Wherever ' is misprinted as ' whatever '.
      *his opposite '.*     ' Introduction ', *The Cat and the Moon*, in *Wheels
      and Butterflies*, 138.
      *lighter tread.*     CP, 149.

## CHAPTER XV

224   *solved antinomy.'*     *A Vision* (1938), 52.
      *of life '.*     ' Some Passages . . . ', *Dublin Magazine*, N.S. XIV (July-
      September, 1939), 13.
      *into life '.*     *The Golden Book of Tagore* (Calcutta, 1931), 269.
      Ramananda Chatterjee, ed.
225   *for poetry '.*     *A Vision* (1938), 8.
226   *the writer " '.*     *Ibid.* (1925), 13-14.
228   *in contemplation. . . .'*     *Ibid.*, 69-71.
229   *once more.*     CP, 187-90.
230   *of Fate.*     *A Vision* (1925), 15.
      *everything predestined ;*     *Ibid.*, xvi.
      *nothing new ',*     *Ibid.*, xi.
231   *first parents '.*     *Ibid.*, 130-31.
232   *magical beatitude.*     Yeats writes to Dorothy Wellesley : ' . . . .
      when I was a young man I was accustomed to a Kabbalistic cere-
      mony where there were two pillars, one symbolic of water and one
      of fire. The fire mark is △, the water mark is ▽, these are com-
      bined to make Solomon's seal ⚕. The water is sensation, peace,
      night, silence, indolence, the fire is passion, tension, day, music,
      energy.' *Letters on Poetry from W. B. Yeats to Dorothy Wellesley*,
      95.
      (note 1) *inevitable murder '.*     Unp. ltr.
      (note 2) *contains them.*     *A Vision* (1938), 73.
234   *That loveliness?*     *Four Plays for Dancers*, 28.
      *sweeter ignorance.*     CP, 165.
235   *the top.*     CP, 156.
      *never find.*     CP, 187.
236   *are gone '.*     ' Nineteen Hundred and Nineteen ', CP, 239.
      *be born?*     CP, 215.
239   *twenty-eight phases.*     He justified this explicitly : ' Every phase is

in itself a wheel ; the individual soul is awakened by a violent
oscillation . . . until it sinks in on that Whole where the contraries
are united, the antinomies resolved '. *A Vision* (1938), 89. Early
drafts of the phasal system were even closer to autobiography than
the completed form.

239   *its forms '.*   *Wheels and Butterflies,* 103.

      *into philosophy '*,   ' Nineteen Hundred and Nineteen ', CP, 240.

240   *are wound.*   ' All Souls' Night ', CP, 266.

      *crowds, propaganda.'*   *A Vision* (1925), 75, 77.

241   *cultivated man.*   *If I Were Four-and-Twenty,* 1.

      *tragic minority '.*   AU, 361-2.

242   *rootless people.'*   Unp. ltr., December 30, 1920.

      *and antiquity '* ;   Unp. ltr.

      *and symbol.'*   Unp. ltr.

      *symbolic rose '.*   ' Meditations in Time of Civil War ', CP, 232.


# CHAPTER XVI

245   *him again.'*   Unp. ltr. to Mrs. Shakespear, October 9, 1922.

      *of Being.*   *If I Were Four-and-Twenty, passim.* The essay was
written in 1919.

      *practical life '.*   Unp. ltr.

      *& think '.*   Unp. ltr.

246   *her drop ?*   CP, 248.

      *with envy.*   ' The Road at My Door ' (1922), CP, 235-6.

      *our lineaments.*   ' The Gift of Harun Al-Rashid ' (1923), CP, 433.

      *growing boy.*   ' I see Phantoms of Hatred and of the Heart's Full-
ness and of the Coming Emptiness ' (1922-3), CP, 238.

247   *and cruelty.'*   Unp. ltr., March 22, 1923.

      *with it '.*   Unp. ltr. to Mrs. Shakespear, December 18, 1922.

      *their disposal,*   *A Vision* (1938), 26-7.

248   *to come '.*   Unp. ltr. to Mrs. Shakespear, April 9, 1921.

      *so abbreviated.'*   Unp. ltr. to Mrs. Shakespear.

249   *for guidance.*   Unp. MS. Hone prints part of the speech with slight
variations, 389-90.

      *new drama '.*   *A Vision* (1925), xii (dated February, 1925).

      *and heavy.*   *The Bounty of Sweden,* in DP, 168. First published in
1925.

250   *the soul.'*   Unp. ltr. to Mrs. Shakespear, June 21, 1924.

251  *the stars.*     This editorial is signed H. Stuart and Cecil Salkeld, but was written by Yeats, according to Mrs. Stuart.  The style makes the authorship quite clear.  *To-morrow*, I (August, 1924), 4.

252  *its forms.*     *A Vision* (1925), 214-15.

   *deeply rooted'.*     Unp. MS.

253  *be transformed.*     Seanad Eirann, *Parliamentary Debates*, V (June 11, 1925), 443.

   *to refuse. . . .*     'The Tower', CP, 228-9.

   *statesmen right',*     'On Being Asked for a War Poem', CP, 178.

254  *Translunar Paradise.*     CP, 228-9.

   *the impossible. . . .*     CP, 224.

255  *deepening shades.*     CP, 230-31.

256  *has come',*     Unp. ltr. to Mrs. Shakespear, September 24, 1926.

   *the dance?*     CP, 251.

257  *to come.*     CP, 223-4.

258  *a man.*     *A Vision* (1938), 277.

   *all rest'.*     *Essays* (1924), 524.

259  *child-like soul.*     *Irish Times*, February 11, 1908.

   *wide open.*     Unp. diary.

260  *very self'.*     *A Vision* (1925), xiii.


## CHAPTER XVII

261  *the lungs,*     Unp. ltr. to Mrs. Shakespear, November 29, 1927.

   *all impersonal'.*     Unp. ltr. to Mrs. Shakespear, March 2, 1929.

262  *blind men. . . .*     CP, 272.

   *soul's coherence'.*     *Wheels and Butterflies*, 107.

   *natural things',*     'Demon and Beast', CP, 214.

263  *& memory'.*     Unp. ltr., December 7, 1926.

   *human dignity.*     CP, 257.

   *bitter words.*     *The Wind Among the Reeds* (1899), 10 ; the poem appears under the title of 'The Fish' in CP, 64-5.

264  *Beatific Vision'.*     *A Vision* (1925), xii.

   *parallel existences'.*     Unp. ltr. to Mrs. Shakespear.

   *somehow inseparable!'*     Unp. ltr. to Mrs. Shakespear.

   *a sphere.*     CP, 313.

265  *this nun?*     Gerard Manley Hopkins, 'The Wreck of the Deutschland', *Poems* (London, O.U.P., 1930), 21.  Robert Bridges, ed.

   *creature* $H_2O.$'     Unp. ltr. to Sturge Moore, written probably in 1927 or 1928, in Mrs. Moore's possession.

265  ' *profound McTaggart* ',          ' A Bronze Head ', LP, 67.
266  ' *knew all*.'        Unp. ltr.
     *one clear*.'        Unp. ltr.
     *educated me*.'        Unp. ltr.
     *incredible experience*.     *A Vision* (1938), 8.
     *had occurred*.     *Ibid*., 8-25.
     *a mythology*.     *A Vision* (1925), 252.
267  *of Brancusi* '.     *A Vision* (1938), 25.
     *resembles mine*.     *A Packet for Ezra Pound* (Dublin, Cuala Press,
        1929), 32-3. *Cf. A Vision* (1938), 24-5.
     *own person* '.     Unp. ltr. to Mrs. Shakespear, September 13, 1929.
268  *not hear*. . . .     *A Vision* (1938), 52-3.
     *and elsewhere*.     As at the end of his dedication to the first edition :
     '. . . I murmured, as I have countless times, " I have been part of
     it always and there is maybe no escape, forgetting and returning life
     after life like an insect in the roots of the grass." But murmured it
     without terror, in exultation almost.' *A Vision* (1925), xiii.
269  *the State*.'     *Wheels and Butterflies*, 8-9.
     *our imagination* ? '     *Ibid*., 6.
     *against us*.     *Ibid*., 7.
270  *think so* ',     Yeats, ' Introduction ', in J. M. Hone and M. M. Rossi,
     *Bishop Berkeley* (London, Faber, 1931), xv.  He describes the
     impact of Swift and Berkeley upon him a little further on : '. . . I
     understand now, what I once but vaguely guessed, that these two
     images, standing and sounding together, Swift and Berkeley, con-
     cern all those who feel a responsibility for the thought of modern
     Ireland that can take away their sleep ', xvi.
     *physical pleasure*.'     *Ibid*., xxviii.
     *impassioned moments* ',     Hone, 416 *n*.
     *his contemporaries* '.     ' Introduction ' to Hone and Rossi, *Bishop
     Berkeley*, xx.
     *travelled there*.     CP, 273-4.
     *a letter*.     Unp. ltr. to Mrs. Shakespear, December 4, 1930.
271  *national mythology*. . . .'     *Wheels and Butterflies*, 8.
     *mythical identification*. . . .     Thomas Mann, *Freud, Goethe, Wag-
     ner* (New York, Knopf, 1942), 34-5.
     *the earth* '.     Hone, 439.
272  *my youth* '.     Unp. ltr., January 3, 1932.
     *were immoral* ',     ' Introduction ' to Hone and Rossi, *Bishop
     Berkeley*, xix.
     *been rent*.'     CP, 298.

273   *his verse.*       ' I want to exorcise that slut Crazy Jane whose language
      has become unendurable.' Ltr. from Yeats to his wife quoted in
      Hone, 424-5.

275   *gong-tormented sea.*       CP, 285-6.

276   *your head.'*   Unp. ltr.


CHAPTER XVIII

277   *non-existent armies'.*       MS. of article by Frank O'Connor, in his
      possession.

      *but moral'.*       *Letters to the New Island*, xii-xiii.

278   *a dance.'*   Hone, 414.

      *of truth'.*   Unp. ltr. to Ethel Mannin. This and other letters to
      Miss Mannin quoted in this chapter are in her possession.

      *my tongue.*       *On the Boiler* (Dublin, Cuala Press, 1941), 14-15.

      *a man.*       ' Parnell's Funeral ', *A Full Moon in March* (London,
      Macmillan, 1935), 45.

279   *the heart'.*       ' The Circus Animals' Desertion ', LP. 81.

      *his call'* ;       ' An Acre of Grass ', LP, 17.

      *passionate man,*       *A Full Moon in March*, 59.

      *wild old man,*       ' The Wild Old Wicked Man ', LP. 32.

      *mad old man.*       ' Why Should Not Old Men Be Mad ? ' LP, 76.

      *into song?*       ' The Spur ', LP, 37.

      *of reality.'*   ' Meru ', *A Full Moon in March*, 70.

281   ' *sacred drama* '.       *The King of the Great Clock Tower, Commentaries
      and Poems* (Dublin, Cuala Press, 1934), 37.

      *to below.*       ' Three Songs to the Same Tune ', *Spectator*, 152
      (February 23, 1934), 276.

      *the door !*       *A Full Moon in March*, 60.

282   *Peace Prize.*       Ethel Mannin, *Privileged Spectator* (London, Hutch-
      inson, 1939), 80-84.

      *is drowned'.*   Unp. ltr., April 7, 1936.

      *Ireland itself.*       *On the Boiler*, 13.

      *Great War* '.       Unp. note among MSS. of first edition of *A Vision*.

283   *of reality* ',       Unp. ltr. to Mrs. Shakespear, February 21, 1933.

      *and future* '.       Shree Purohit Swami and Yeats, *The Ten Principal
      Upanishads* (London, Faber, 1937), 34.

      *but song* '.       Unp. ltr. to Ethel Mannin, June 24, 1935.

284   *are wed* '.       ' Ribh Denounces Patrick ', *A Full Moon in March*,
      63.

284  *turn lamp*'.     Yeats, ' Introduction ', *Oxford Book of Modern Verse*, xxxiii.

  *had stood?*     *The Death of Cuchulain*, LP, 125-6.

  *English shot?*     ' The Man and the Echo ', LP, 83.

  *Post Office?*     ' The Statues ', LP, 57.

285  *painted scene.*     ' Three Songs to the One Burden ', LP, 54.

286  *death themselves.*'     Unp. ltr., October 20, 1938.

  *and space*',     *A Vision* (1938), 210.

  *Yeats says.*     *Idem.*

  *the secret.*     *A Vision* (1938), 301-2.

287  *He live!*     *A Full Moon in March*, 65-6.

  *unwilling belief.*     In one of his last essays, Yeats makes the significant remark: ' I think profound philosophy must come from terror. An abyss opens under our feet ; inherited convictions, the presuppositions of our thoughts, those Fathers of the Church Lionel Johnson expounded, drop into the abyss. Whether we will or no we must ask the ancient questions : Is there reality anywhere ? Is there a God ? Is there a Soul ? ' ' Modern Poetry: A Broadcast ', *Essays 1931 to 1936*, 21. *Cf. A Vision* (1938), 301.

  *with nightmare.*     ' Prometheus Unbound ', *Essays 1931 to 1936*, 57.

  *understood it.*     Unp. ltr., October 9, 1938.

288  *wildest thing*'     Unp. ltr. to Ethel Mannin, December 19, 1935.

  *shall win.*     *A Full Moon in March*, 68-9.

289  *of Sixpence.*     Ltr. to Lady Elizabeth Pelham, in Hone, 476. Corrected by reference to her copy.

  *natural things.*     Allan Wade, who came to Roquebrune shortly after the funeral, has supplied me with this information.


## CHAPTER XIX

290  *the truth*',     *The Death of Cuchulain*, LP, 117.

292  *pure mathematic*'.     Unp. ltr. to Ethel Mannin, December 23, 1938.

293  *his stilts.*     ' Then in 1900 everybody got down off his stilts ', Yeats wrote in the *Oxford Book of Modern Verse*, xi. The date in his case was 1903.

294  *and superstition*'.     W. R. Inge, ' Roman Catholic Modernism ', *Outspoken Essays* (London, Longmans, 1920), 170.

  *renewed security.*'     Unp. ltr., written in 1937, in the possession of Edmund Dulac.

294  *credible philosophy* '.    Unp. ltr. to Mrs. Shakespear, March 4, 1926.

295  *emblems of.*    ' The Circus Animals' Desertion ', LP, 81.

 *solution, none* '.    *Letters on Poetry from W. B. Yeats to Dorothy Wellesley*, 196.

296  *passive suffering*    ' . . . passive suffering is not a theme for poetry '. Yeats, ' Introduction,' *Oxford Book of Modern Verse*, xxxiv.

 *Great Founder* ',    The number of organizations in which Yeats was active, and most of which he organized, is very large.  The following is an incomplete list : Contemporary Club, Dublin Hermetic Society, Blavatsky Lodge, Young Ireland Society, Golden Dawn, Irish Literary Society, Rhymers' Club, National Literary Society, Irish Mystical Order, Stella Matutina (an offshoot of the Golden Dawn), Abbey Theatre, Free State Senate, To-Morrow, Irish Academy.

297  *exceed nature* '.    ' Louis Lambert ', *Essays 1931 to 1936*, 70.

 *lover's night* '.    *A Full Moon in March*, 21.

 *short-distance runner* ',    Unp. ltr. to Lady Gregory, October 19, 1921.

 *violent sensation.*'    AU, 403.

# INDEX

## THE END

# READ MORE IN PENGUIN

In every corner of the world, on every subject under the sun, Penguin represents quality and variety – the very best in publishing today.

For complete information about books available from Penguin – including Puffins, Penguin Classics and Arkana – and how to order them, write to us at the appropriate address below. Please note that for copyright reasons the selection of books varies from country to country.

**In the United Kingdom**: Please write to *Dept. EP, Penguin Books Ltd, Bath Road, Harmondsworth, West Drayton, Middlesex UB7 0DA*

**In the United States**: Please write to *Consumer Sales, Penguin USA, P.O. Box 999, Dept. 17109, Bergenfield, New Jersey 07621-0120.* VISA and MasterCard holders call 1-800-253-6476 to order Penguin titles

**In Canada**: Please write to *Penguin Books Canada Ltd, 10 Alcorn Avenue, Suite 300, Toronto, Ontario M4V 3B2*

**In Australia**: Please write to *Penguin Books Australia Ltd, P.O. Box 257, Ringwood, Victoria 3134*

**In New Zealand**: Please write to *Penguin Books (NZ) Ltd, Private Bag 102902, North Shore Mail Centre, Auckland 10*

**In India**: Please write to *Penguin Books India Pvt Ltd, 706 Eros Apartments, 56 Nehru Place, New Delhi 110 019*

**In the Netherlands**: Please write to *Penguin Books Netherlands bv, Postbus 3507, NL-1001 AH Amsterdam*

**In Germany**: Please write to *Penguin Books Deutschland GmbH, Metzlerstrasse 26, 60594 Frankfurt am Main*

**In Spain**: Please write to *Penguin Books S. A., Bravo Murillo 19, 1° B, 28015 Madrid*

**In Italy**: Please write to *Penguin Italia s.r.l., Via Felice Casati 20, I–20124 Milano*

**In France**: Please write to *Penguin France S. A., 17 rue Lejeune, F–31000 Toulouse*

**In Japan**: Please write to *Penguin Books Japan, Ishikiribashi Building, 2–5–4, Suido, Bunkyo-ku, Tokyo 112*

**In South Africa**: Please write to *Longman Penguin Southern Africa (Pty) Ltd, Private Bag X08, Bertsham 2013*

# BY THE SAME AUTHOR

**Oscar Wilde**

'Wilde had to live his life twice over, first in slow motion, then at top speed. During the first period he was a scapegrace, during the second a scapegoat' – Richard Ellmann

'Lovable, pitiful, brilliant and self-destructive . . . Oscar Wilde lived his life as though planning to be the ideal subject for a biographer . . . Richard Ellmann pays him the tribute of a near-perfect biography. The witty subject has found a witty biographer who is also distinguished for his erudition and humanity' – Claire Tomlin in the *Independent*

'Exquisite critical sense, wide and deep learning, and profound humanity . . . a great subject and a great book' – Anthony Burgess in the *Observer*

'His account, completed in the shadow of incurable illness, is unfailingly generous. He stresses Wilde's kindness, his innocence, and the cynicism with which friends cut him at his fall . . . The whole book is a masterpiece of understanding' – John Carey in the *Sunday Times*

'Pellucid in prose, organization and clarity' – Andrew Lumsden in the *New Statesman*

'Richard Ellmann obviously adores Wilde and such a love is the foundation of the best biography . . . Packed with nineties life as it is this enthralling biography is also full of surprises' – John Bayley in the *Guardian*